CONTRACTUAL OBLIGATIONS
IN GHANA AND NIGERIA

CONTRACTUAL OBLIGATIONS IN GHANA AND NIGERIA

U. U. Uche, LL.M., PH.D. (LONDON)
Of Gray's Inn,

Barrister-at-Law, Lecturer in African Law,
School of Oriental and African Studies,
University of London

Routledge
Taylor & Francis Group

LONDON AND NEW YORK

First published in 1971 by

FRANK CASS AND COMPANY LIMITED

Published 2013 by Routledge
2 Park Square, Milton Park, Abingdon, Oxon OX14 4RN
711 Third Avenue, New York, NY 10017 USA

Routledge is an imprint of the Taylor & Francis Group, an informa business

First issued in paperback 2016

ISBN13: 978-1-138-97177-6 (pbk)
ISBN13: 978-0-7146-5215-3 (hbk)

CONTENTS

ABBREVIATIONS

All	All England Law Reports
All N.L.R.	All Nigeria Law Reports
A.L.J.	Australian Law Journal
A.L.R.	Australian Law Reports
B.Y.B.I.L.	British Year Book of International Law
Cam. L.J.	Cambridge Law Journal
Can. Bar. Rev.	Canadian Bar Review
Cmnd.	Command Papers
C.L.R.	Commonwealth Law Reports (Australia)
C.C.	Current Cases (Ghana)
C.L.J.	Current Law Journal
Div. Ct.	Divisional Court Reports (Gold Coast)
Enc. Soc. Sci.	Encyclopaedia of Social Sciences
E.R.	English Reports
E.R.N.L.R.	Eastern Region of Nigeria Law Reports
F.S.C.	Federal Supreme Court Reports (Nigeria)
F. Ct.	Full Court Reports (Gold Coast)
G.L.R.	Ghana Law Reports
Harv. L. Rev.	Harvard Law Review
I.C.L.Q.	International and Comparative Law Quarterly
I.R.	Irish Reports
J.A.A.	Journal of African Administration
J.A.L.	Journal of African Law
J.A. Comp. Leg.	Journal of Comparative Legislation
J. of Soc. of Pub. Teach. Law	Journal of the Society of Public Teachers of Law
L.L.R.	Lagos Law Reports
Law & Contemp. Prob.	Law and Contemporary Problems
L.Q.R.	Law Quarterly Review
L.J.Q.B.	Law Journal Queen's Bench
L.I.	Legislative Instrument
Minn. L.R.	Minnesota Law Review
M.L.R.	Modern Law Review
N.Y. Uni. L.R.	New York University Law Review
N.Z.L.R.	New Zealand Law Reports
Nig. B.J.	Nigeria Bar Journal
Nig. L.J.	Nigeria Law Journal

N.M.L.R.	Nigeria Monthly Law Reports
N.R.N.L.R.	Northern Region of Nigeria Law Reports
N.N.L.R.	Northern Nigeria Law Reports
O.R.	Ontario Reports (Canada)
P.C.	Privy Council
Ren.	Renner's Reports
Sar. F.C.L.	Sarbah's Fanti Customary Law
Sar. F.L.R.	Sarbah's Fanti Law Reports
S.L.T.	Scottish Law Times
T.L.R.	Times Law Reports
Tul, L.R.	Tulane Law Review
U.C.G.	University College of Ghana
Un. of Gh. L.J.	University of Ghana Law Journal
W.A.C.A.	West African Court of Appeal Reports
W.A.L.R.	West African Law Reports
W.L.R.	Weekly Law Reports
W.N.L.R.	Western Nigeria Law Reports
W.R.N.L.R.	Western Region of Nigeria Law Reports
Y.L.T.	Yale Law Journal

INDEX OF CASES

INDEX OF LEGISLATION

MISCELLANEOUS

PREFACE

This study which is part of a thesis that I submitted to the University of London for the award of the degree of doctor of philosophy in laws, is a comparative investigation of contractual obligations in Ghana and Nigeria.

It has often been suggested that the law of civil responsibility in West Africa is the same as the current English law position on the subject. This book sets out to examine the basis of this assumption, an exercise which has never before been attempted by any previous writer in West African law. The study has been divided into five major parts.

In the first part, the meaning, scope and content of the title are fully discussed. The case for a new approach to the classification of obligations in Ghana and Nigeria is stated and argued. The law of obligations is substantially made up of case law. Chapters two and three of this part are therefore devoted to an examination of what cases bind which courts in both Ghana and Nigeria.

Parts two and three are a two-tier study of contractual obligations the former made up of two-party situations and the latter of more than two parties. In part four all the agreements that contain any vitiating element are examined under the heading of defective agreements. Part five is a functional study of contractual obligations. Here in three chapters the role of the courts and the State in the enforcement of agreements, and the effectiveness of remedies for the breach of agreements are examined.

It remains to add the necessary acknowledgements. As has been mentioned earlier, this work is part of a thesis submitted to the University of London for the award of a Ph.D degree in law. That thesis in turn was the product of two field studies which I undertook, first in 1961 into customary court records in the former Eastern Region of Nigeria and later in 1965, into Superior Court records in Ghana and Nigeria.

Predictably, several persons have in different ways contributed to make the burden of producing this book less onerous than it would otherwise have been. If all the relevant and deserving names are not specifically mentioned here, I would like to assure all those involved that this omission does not detract from my profound gratitude to them for their very many kindnesses.

My special gratitude goes to the former Eastern Nigeria Ministry of Justice who in 1961 provided me with a generous grant for my first field study. The same goes for the Nigerian Federal Government who not only offered me a postgraduate Scholarship which made my thesis possible, but also sponsored my field studies in Ghana and Nigeria as part of the award.

My profound gratitude also goes to Professor A. N. Allott, Professor of African Law in the University of London, who supervised this work as a thesis for the Ph.D degree and made several useful suggestions in its production as a book. No one who has not worked with Tony Allott can fully appreciate and none who has can sincerely deny his depth of knowledge in this area of the law and his transparent willingness to share this knowledge with his students and colleagues. I have had the unique privilege of having belonged at different times to both categories of beneficiaries. At those times when my spirits were low and my initiative and sense of direction rather dazed, he was to me not only a mentor of inexhaustible inventiveness and industry but a friend of inexhaustible kindness. Needless to add that he does not share with me any failings of this work of which there might well be several.

Finally my thanks go to my colleagues of the S.O.A.S. department of law for their very many useful suggestions, to Mrs. Vera Williams who had the unenviable task of typing the manuscripts, and to the staff of the Institute of Advanced Legal Studies for their kind co-operation with me in the preparation of the book at its different stages. The law stated here is the law as it stood on 1st June, 1968. References in the work to Regions in Nigeria should read " states ". This is of course one of the issues decided by the Nigerian Civil War.

S.O.A.S., London, 1970.   U. U. Uche

PART I

CHAPTER 1

INTRODUCTION

Why obligations

The word " obligation " is an exotic term in Anglo-American jurisprudence. As a special branch of the law, it occupies a prominent place in the Civil law systems. Its introduction into an investigation of legal systems substantially based on English law, as those in Ghana and Nigeria are, calls for some explanation if it is not to be lightly dismissed as a red herring. This explanation is one object of this introduction.

Meaning of obligation

The Latin verb " obligare " (meaning " to bind ") is a comparatively old one.[1] In Classical and post-classical Roman legal language, it occurs in two connections, namely—obligare rem—to bind a thing[2]; and obligare personam—to impose a duty upon a person.

In contrast to the verb, the noun obligatio, appeared much later. This is, of course, attributable to the reluctance of the Latin language to admit nouns where a verb could have served the same purpose.[3]

Obligatio was not defined by the classical lawyers but it was used, like obligare, in connection with things and persons. Its meaning in that context was " a legal bond between two persons which implied a duty of one towards the other, recognised by ius civile and enforceable by actio in personam "[4]. Its use in this way in the Classical Roman law period was restricted to the ius civile (c.f. ius honorarium) and only arose where a duty was enforceable in personam.

It was not until the post-classical Roman law period that obligatio fused the dual conceptions of ius civile and ius honorarium. Contemporary Roman law definition of the term is that attempted by Lewin and Short as " an engaging or pledging; an obligation, an obligatory relation between two persons one of whom has a right and the other a duty, e.g. the right of a creditor and the duty of a debtor."[5]

As a special branch of the law, obligation attained a high degree

3

of sophistication in Roman law. Justinian, following Gaius, had attempted a classification under four heads, namely:

    (a) ex contractu,
    (b) ex quasi-contractu,
    (c) ex delicto, and
    (d) ex quasi-delicto.

This arrangement has had considerable influence on European systems of law as Otto Gierke admitted in these words:

> "The victory of Roman law was more complete in the domain of the law of obligations than in any other. Undoubtedly, this law was the greatest and most perfect creation of the Roman legal genius, applicable to a world-wide commerce and trade and logically developed down to the finest issues, which under Germanic law had hardly been raised. Besides, it had a universal character and was not as closely connected with the special conditions of Roman law. Thus it ascended the throne and has maintained its sovereign power down to the present."[6]

Classification in English law

In spite of the above merits of a law of obligations, one is still up against the taunt that there is no such thing as a law of obligations as a separate branch of study in Anglo-American legal classification. Earl Jowitt's definition of obligation in his Dictionary of English law[7] as "the relation between two persons, one of whom can take judicial proceedings, or other legal steps to compel the other to do or abstain from doing a certain act," would tend to lend support to this view. Consistently with the learned author's definition, obligations would span the whole gamut of English municipal law, encompassing among other things, trust, matrimonial causes, admiralty law, landlord and tenant, and even the law of succession, not to mention contract, tort and allied subjects. Obligations in the above sense, worthy as it is as a life-time pursuit with a view to imitating Blackstone and Kent in English and American laws respectively, is hardly a subject that could be usefully discussed in a single volume even if the author was qualified to undertake it.

Now, this attitude of English law towards obligations is attributable to history. The early common law did not concern itself with the classification of rights that could be enforced against a person. In his description of medieval English jurisprudence, Maitland[8] aptly pointed out that

> "Legal remedies, legal procedure, these are the all-important topics for the student. These being mastered, a knowledge of

substantive law will come of itself. Not the nature of rights but the nature of writs must be his theme. . . . so thought our fore-fathers."

But the forms of action were abolished in 1852 by the Common Law Procedure Act of that year, and English law was faced with the necessity of classifying substantive rights. Unfortunately, it has not quite succeeded in shaking off the procedural inhibitions of the forms of action. Thus, for a century English law has been stuck with an attempt to classify civil responsibility into contract and tort.[9]

Critique of the English classification

The classification of civil liability into contract and tort has been found both inadequate and productive of unjust results. There are several factual situations in which a plaintiff can neither sue in contract nor in tort, but where the law ought not to allow the defendant to retain a benefit obtained at the expense of the plaintiff. If A intended to pay a grocer B for items bought from his stores, but paid grocer C in error, there is neither a contract between A and C, in any ordinary sense of the term, nor has a tort been committed by any of them. It is not enough to imply a contract to repay A, since C did not request the payment from A in the first instance. Also if I left my suit-case in the boot of X's car with his consent, but the car was towed away by the police for some reason, and I had to pay £2 to redeem the car (in order to recover my suit-case), there has been no contract between A and me for the refund of the £2, nor can any tort be proved on the above facts. Yet the law ought to take care of situations such as these and several others.

It might be asked, what about quasi-contract, does it not cater for the residual group of heads of liability to which reference is made above? The answer to this is a predictable negative and for two reasons. Firstly, nobody quite knows what quasi-contract is. A typical definition of the term by Sir Percy Winfield, that it " signifies liability not exclusively referable to any other head of the law, imposed upon a particular person to pay money to another particular person on the ground of unjust benefit,"[10] leaves an enquirer more confused than before. Quite apart from the curious attempt at defining a term by excluding every other term, one has still the secondary duty of finding out what " other head " of the law means, as used in the learned author's context.

It is unpersuasive to enumerate specific heads of claim, such as " money had and received to the plaintiff's use ", claims on

quantum meruit and quantum valebant; all of which are said to
come under quasi-contractual liability. Quite apart from the fact
that all these are money claims (c.f. property claims), it has not
been easy to delimit the scope and content of quasi-contract on
this basis, and this leads us to the second reason.

The controversy over the juristic basis of quasi-contractual liability is another cause of its ineffectiveness as a third head of civil
liability even for monetary claims. Maitland's gibe about the forms
of action ruling the courts from the grave is most true in this branch
of the law. This is of course the whole question of whether quasi-
contractual liability is based on a contract implied by law, or on a
concept of unjust enrichment. A good deal of the argument has
centred on Lord Mansfield's attempt in 1760 in the case of *Moses*
v. *Macfarlan*,[11] at a statement of a general principle based on the
idea of unjust enrichment.

The facts were that Moses had received from Jacob four promissory notes of 30/- each. He endorsed these to Macfarlan who, by a
written agreement, contracted that he would not hold Moses liable
on the indorsement. Subsequently, however, Macfarlan sued Moses
on the notes in a court of conscience which refused to recognise
Macfarlan's written agreement not to sue Moses, and therefore,
decided in favour of Macfarlan. Moses then brought this action in
the King's Bench for money had and received to his use. In
deciding in favour of the plaintiff Lord Mansfield had had this to
say about the basis of this type of action:[12]

> "This kind of equitable action, to recover back money which
> ought not in justice to be kept, is very beneficial, and therefore
> much encouraged. It lies only for money which, *ex aequo et bono*,
> the defendant ought to refund; it does not lie for money paid by
> the plaintiff, which is claimed of him as payable in point of
> honour and honesty, although it could not have been recovered
> from him by any course of law; as in payment of a debt barred
> by the statute of limitations, or contracted during infancy, or to
> the extent of principal and legal interest on an usurious contract,
> or, for money fairly lost at play; because in all these cases, the
> defendant may retain it with a safe conscience, though by positive
> law he was barred from recovering.
>
> But it lies for money paid by mistake; or upon a consideration
> which happens to fail; or for money got through imposition
> (express or implied); or extortion; or oppression; or an undue
> advantage taken of the plaintiff's situation, contrary to laws made
> for the protection of persons under those circumstances. In one
> word, the gist of this kind of action is, that the defendant, upon
> the circumstances of the case, is obliged by the ties of natural
> justice and equity to refund the money."

Now, like many general theories, this statement of the position by Lord Mansfield needed, and did in fact receive various modifications in theory and was subjected to severe restrictions in application. It is remarkable that although the learned judge did not say that the law would imply a promise (he in fact said that the law will imply an obligation, which is not synonymous with promise), critics have concentrated on those instances where the law cannot imply a promise, in order to discredit his basis for a general principle. Infants' contracts and *ultra vires* agreements, have been freely cited as cases in which the law cannot de facto imply promises which, if made *de jure* it would inexorably avoid.[13] Again, the idea of *aequum et bonum* on which Lord Mansfield's generalisation was based, was not a popular concept in nineteenth century legal or political thinking. It is not surprising therefore, that it has been variously stigmatised as " well-meaning sloppiness of thought,"[14] and " vague jurisprudence which is sometimes attractively styled justice as between man and man."[15]

Unjust enrichment or unjust benefit as the basis of quasi-contractual actions was said to have been finally rejected in the House of Lords decision of *Sinclair* v. *Brougham*[16] decided in 1914. Here the House of Lords refused to allow the action for money had and received, to depositors of money with a Building Society which was carrying on an *ultra vires* banking business with the deposits. The House, however, allowed a quasi-proprietary remedy in favour of the depositors. The basis for the refusal of the action for money had and received in this case was summarised in the famous dictum of Lord Summer in these words:

> " The law cannot de jure impute promises to repay, whether for money had and received or otherwise, which, if made de facto, it would inexorably avoid."[17]

In other words, the ultra vires doctrine precludes the implication of any agreement to refund the amount lent by the depositors.

There have been doubts as to whether or not their Lordships of the House of Lords have said the last word on the juridical basis of quasi-contractual actions in English law. Lord Wright[18] has pointed out that the statement of the position in *Sinclair* v. *Brougham*[19] was obiter, and could not therefore be said to have put the authority of the House on the implied contract theory of quasi-contractual actions. Lord Atkin[20] has said that it is not altogether certain whether the law Lords locked the door when they decided the point as it arose in *Sinclair* v. *Brougham*, while Winfield[21] has contended that " even if they did lock the door for purposes of that case, they left the key hanging on a nail so that if anyone now wishes to enter he can still do so." Winfield relied on the quasi-contractual nature of actions to enforce foreign judgments in English courts, on cases of waiver of tort and cases of recovery of money paid as a result of ineffective transactions. He concluded that the rationale of the cases on these heads was the theory of the recovery of unjust benefit and not contracts implied by law. In a judgment Cotton L. J. in an earlier case[22] had however, pointed out the vital distinction between the law implying a promise to repay, and imposing an obligation to refund in these terms:

> "Now the term 'implied contract' is a most unfortunate expression, because there cannot be a contract by a lunatic. But whenever necessaries are supplied to a person who by reason of disability cannot himself contract, the law implies an obligation on the part of such person to pay for such necessaries out of his own property. It is asked, can there be an implied contract by a person who cannot himself contract in express terms? The answer is that what the law implies on the part of such a person is an obligation, which has been improperly termed a contract, to repay money spent in supplying necessaries. I think that the expression 'implied contract' is erroneous and very unfortunate."[23]

Unfortunately, this timely warning by the learned judge received scant judicial support. Mention has already been made of the dicta of their Lordships of the House of Lords in this connection. It is interesting to note that two years after the decision of *Re Rhodes*[26] the French Courts laid the foundation of the *actio de in rem verso*, an action by which a plaintiff could recover any unjust benefits which the defendant had obtained to the plaintiff's detriment. The point to emphasise here is the fact that the judicial and doctrinal ambivalence in English law as to the juridical basis of obligations imposed by law, has had at least two far-reaching adverse consequences. Firstly, the "implied contract" theory has been used to deny the plaintiff any remedy in situations where in the opinion of the court a promise cannot be implied in law. Thus where an infant had fraudulently misrepresented his age in order to get a loan from the plaintiff, it was held that a promise to repay could not be implied,[24] since such a promise would be in conflict with the provisions of the Infants Relief Act, 1874. Again, in a case where the defendant who was an infant businessman, had received £35 from the plaintiff but did not deliver the goods ordered, the court, also on the basis of the 1874 enactment on Infants, refused to allow the plaintiff to recover.[25] It is curious that the Infants Relief Act, 1874, which was primarily intended to protect infants against indiscreet adults, should be used as a shield to cover infantile fraud.

This is a sad commentary on the implied contract theory, and stresses the urgency of a general law of restitution based on the theory of unjust enrichment.[26]

Secondly, the implied contract theory has been a major set-back in any attempt by English law to evolve a general law of restitution as has been done in the United States. The principle of the restoration of unjust benefit is present in many branches of English law, but its development has been impaired by the strict requirements of the different branches. Maritime salvage and general average have developed within the confines of maritime law. The constructive trust has been treated as an aspect of the law of trust, with its strict requirements of a fiduciary relationship as a condition for the granting of any remedies. Waters has convincingly demonstrated the seriousness of this latter limitation on a general law of restitution, and has opted for the American solution on the matter.[26] Subrogation and quasi-subrogation have been treated as facets of the law of insurance or as equitable remedies. Limited legislative recognition of the principle of unjust enrichment as a basis for restitution is found in the Partnership Act, 1890, the Law Reform (Married Women and Tortfeasors) Acts, 1935 and the Law Reform (Frustrated Contracts) Act, 1943. It need hardly be pointed out that the above situation is indeed chaotic and that the factors which helped to mould the law of tort out of a similar collection of remedies[27] are present in English law. In fact it could be argued and has been, that the recognition of an effective tertium quid in civil liability in English law has become urgent.

This recognition has been ably canvassed in two recently published works,[28] and has been partially accepted by the English Law Commission, established under the Law Commission Act (England), 1965.[29] It must, however be pointed out that the pathology of civil liability in English law is outside the immediate scope of this work. Our main concern is with the state of the law in Ghana and Nigeria, and to this we shall now return.

CLASSIFICATION IN GHANA AND NIGERIA: THE CASE FOR A NEW APPROACH

From our examination of the classification of civil responsibility in English law between contract and tort, it is clear that this division is unsuitable even in English law and that steps are already being taken to improve on the system. What is not so clear is why in Ghana and Nigeria, civil liability should adopt the same mode of classification that is already being discredited in England. Yet this is what the learned authors of *Nigerian Cases and Statutes on Contract and Tort*,[30] have done. More will be said about this work later. Here it must be stated that the division of civil liability into contract, tort and a doubtful third (quasi-contract), is confusing in theory and clumsy in practical application. This is made more so by the statutory recognition in Ghana and Nigeria of laws other than the imported law. The categories of the latter set of laws are not exhausted by the English classification into contract and tort. A new mode of classification is therefore called for.

It has to be admitted that the English law of civil responsibility was introduced into Ghana and Nigeria.[31] But this does not presume that its development need follow the nominal compartments as existed in English law on the dates of reception.[32] If it becomes necessary (and this necessity has been sufficiently demonstrated), to change or modify the system of classification to suit local conditions or to meet the requirements of justice, this will not be the end of a thousand years of history, as could easily be said in the case of any change in the English system. American law, also based on the English common law,[33] has evolved the concept of Restitution as a separate and independent head of civil remedy, similar to the continental concept of unjust enrichment. Recent academic opinion in England, tends to favour the American classification.

Secondly, the State of California in the United States, adopted a Civil Code in 1872, with a classification and terminology that differed from the traditional common law system.[34] The aim of the Code was said to be, " to restate in systematic and accessible form, the common law as it had been modified to suit American conditions; to settle questions upon which disputes had arisen, and to introduce such reforms as might seem necessary to make the legal system harmonious and free from anachronism."[35]

A re-appraisal of the position fifty years afterwards, revealed a remarkable harmony in the State's judicial system.[36]

Thirdly, the State of Senegal, an ex-French West African colony, has embarked upon a project of reforming her private law. On this experiment, a learned author has had this to say in a recent article:[37]

" The importance of the reform derives rather from the light that they may shed upon the problems of adapting a European legal system to a developing country. The need for some re-shaping of French private law for continued use in the newly independent States of francophone Africa is two-fold. First, since the Napoleonic Codes date from another century, they have become less suitable simply by the passage of time. Secondly, because the Napolenic Codes were designed for European social institutions and economic conditions, they are less suitable to those of a distant and developing land. These two factors of time and space lie at the roots of most of the reform in Senegal."

It may be added that what the learned author has said about " time and space " is to some extent true of the common law and its application in Ghana and Nigeria. In fact the *Senegalese Code of Civil and Commercial Obligations,* has modified several aspects of the received French law. A particular instance is the abolition by the code of the notion of tort and contract, treating both bases of liability together.

Another unique feature of the reform in Senegal is the acceptance of French law as the basis of Senegalese jurisprudence, with modifications taken from the laws of Morocco, Italy and Switzerland.

Finally, brief mention will be made of the case of Ethiopia, where a Civil Code primarily based on the French system, but with obvious modifications,[38] was adopted in 1960.[39] It must be observed, however, that the common law is too firmly rooted in the jurisprudence of Ghana and Nigeria, for any useful guidance to be had from the Ethiopian experiment.

Yet the futility of striving to justify the use of terms has often been stressed. Lawyers move within definitions and terms of their own creation. A vital consideration is how conducive to harmonious analytical treatment any chosen term is.

In our comparative investigation of civil responsibility in Ghana and Nigeria, therefore, we have postulated a general theory of civil responsibility, which we call obligations. This we have defined to mean " a legally enforceable relationship created either by the act of the parties or imposed by law ". The use of obligations in this way has, however, been criticised by Roscoe Pound in his *Introduction to the Philosophy of Law.*[40] He argues that the relationship imported by the Roman law sense of the term is not a significant factor extending obligations to the " capacity or claim to exact, and the duty to answer to the exaction." He would prefer the use of the term " liability " for this purpose.

Our quick retort would, of course, be that we are not using the term here in its Roman law sense. But even if we were, the fact that some obligations are not enforceable against persons, is only valid as an exception to a general rule of its enforceability. The category of imperfect obligations (i.e. obligations which cannot be enforced), have no common universal content. They vary according to any given legal system. Further, Pound's use of the word " liability," in this context presupposes the qualifying adjective

" civil," to distinguish it from criminal liability. Civil liability could then be used interchangeably with obligations. It is submitted, however, that " obligations " has the added advantage of avoiding the confusion which could arise from the use of " civil liability " in Ghana and Nigerian legislation to refer to tort liability.[41]

Finally, Sir Frederick Pollock[42] has entitled his work on the law of torts, " *A treatise on the principles of obligations arising from civil wrongs,*" and throughout the book's fifteen editions, no one has objected to this mode of treatment.

Classification in Customary Laws

The celebrated controversy as to the claim of customary law to be included in the definition of " law properly so called," is outside the scope of this work.[43] It is enough to repeat what Julius Stone has said in this connection, that it is very difficult to justify any theory or definition of law that would exclude even " institutionalised social control in less developed societies, whose function and effectiveness are scarcely distinguishable from those of law in modern societies."[44] The futile and academic nature of the anxiety to prove that customary law is law, is underlined by the actual practice of British colonial policy, which steered clear of the Austinian imperative theory of law, by laying down machinery for the recognition and enforcement of customary laws.[45] On the other hand, the conceptual query as to whether customary law admits of any classification at all, cannot lightly be passed over in the same way. Two facets of this query have been recognised, namely:

(i) Is there any division into civil and criminal liability in customary laws; and

(ii) If the answer to (i) is positive, are there any other recognised sub-classifications in civil liability?

It is, however, with the second facet that we are primarily concerned here.

It must be admitted that until rather recently, all discussion on this subject had been conducted at a very high level of abstraction, based on generalisations about the basic qualities of " primitive law." Sir Henry Maine,[46] Radcliffe-Brown,[47], Seagle,[48] Driberg,[49] and lately, Elias,[50] are but a few of the participants in this exercise. Fortunately, contemporary conclusions on the existence or otherwise of the categories of contract, tort and unjust enrichment, have proceeded on the basis of the actual practices of some of the individual systems.[51] We shall first look at Paul Bohannan's monograph on the Tiv of Northern Nigeria. He states that the "cardinal error of ethnographic and social analysis . . . is raising folk systems like 'the law,' designed for social action in one's own system, to the status of an analytical system, and then trying to organise the raw social data from other societies into its categories."[52] In an attempt to avoid this error, he explains that the Tiv word *injô*, translated as "debt," covers a wider range of phenomena and social relations than the English word "debt" usually does. One is in debt if one borrowed but did not repay; if he herds stock for his kinsman; if his animals damage his neighbour's crops; if he marries a woman from another group without return, and if one assaults another. Liability arising from witchcraft is referred to in Tiv law as "flesh-debts."[53] In addition to these, personal relationships in Tivland are expressed in terms of debt. Bohannan concludes that

> "rather than fit Tiv cases into European categories like tort, contract, property rights, etc., thus hiding the most important thing about them, I have organised the cases in such a way as to illustrate the Tiv notion of debt or *injô*, while allowing us to make finer distinctions outlined. . . . Though we found it possible to say that Tiv have actions which resemble tort, contract, or the like. . . . . were we to do merely that, we should miss the organising concept which contains several English categories. This categorising concept is debt. Many torts have debt aspects; most contracts have debt aspects. Tiv classify on the notion of debt, as it were, not on the notion of tort or contract."

He adds that the same general type of material can be classified in several ways, but that the one that interests the social anthropologist is the folk-classification of concepts.[54] Bohannan's insistence on a detailed study of the folk-classification of concepts, is understandable. It may be added that the folk-classification is equally of interest to the lawyer. But surely in the cases collected by the learned author, there are several contractual situations,[55] many cases of delictual liability[56] and other cases where the mbatarev imposed liability because of the strength of the plaintiff's case irrespective of contract or tort.[57] Even if his term "debt" is accepted as the general basis of these categories of liability, it could only serve as a genus of which the other sub-heads are species. This argument is given greater force by the fact that the Tiv word *injô* has been said to mean "liability" or "debt." This information was given to the present writer by some Tiv colleagues.[58]

Secondly, even if the Tiv concept of debt is very different from its English law counterpart, there is no doubt that its function in Tiv law is similar to the function civil liability plays in English law. This functional approach to the subject, it must be observed, received scant treatment in Bohannan's scheme. It is submitted however, that the value of any folk-classification of concepts is better appreciated on a basis of functional comparison with other systems. Whether the name is debt or civil liability the important consideration is that each covers situations in which a relevant system recognises, and in varying degrees, enforces rights. The "debt" mode of classifying heads of civil liability was adopted in respect of cases in the Ghana local courts in 1963.[59] It is obvious from this attempt, that "debt" was treated as a genus of which contract, tort and restitution were species.[60]

Apart from the actual instances of contracts, delicts and a third category of civil liability, a linguistic study of the subject in at least three of the indigenous systems in West Africa points very clearly to the conclusion that classification into contract, tort, etc, is recognised. Among the Yoruba there is a general theory of contract, represented by the word *ipihun*, or *adehun*, each of which means an agreement or promise to perform. The verb "to agree" or "to promise" is represented by the words *ke-kuru* or *dinku*.

Among the Ashantis (in Ghana), there does not appear to be any general theory of agreements; specific types of agreement are recognised. *Bopaa* means to hire labour, or a "labour agreement," while *abusa* and *abunum*, are varieties of land agreements. Also among the Ibos, the word "agreement" or "covenant" is represented by the indigenous word *mgbugba*; while debt is represented by *ugwo*.[61]

Classification in Islamic Law[62]

Writers on Muhammedan jurisprudence divide law broadly into the religious and the secular. The former category of laws relates to matters appertaining to the next world, namely acts of worship. Secular laws are those dealing with matters of this world. This second category of laws are also sub-divided into public and private. Public rights are the rights of God while private rights reside in individuals. Since public rights exist for the benefit of the community, they are exercised by the State in the form of criminal or revenue laws. The law of obligations belongs to private rights.

The Muhammedan jurists do not, however, recognise "law of things" as forming a separate and independent juristic division. Laws, according to them, are concerned with the acts of men through the juridical medium of rights and obligations. Often such acts have reference to physical objects, but not always. The law does not deal with such objects except as "property," i.e. things over which men exercise acts of possession and enjoyment.[63]

Nevertheless, the categories of contract, tort and unjust enrichment have been treated by a recent author on Islamic law under the heading of obligations.[64] After a general discussion on the concept of the law of obligations in Islamic law, Schacht proceeded in Chapter 21 of his very informative work, to treat specific obligations. This latter head included instances of specific contracts like the *suftaja*, the *hawala* and what he called aleatory transactions.[65]

On the juristic basis of obligations created by agreement in Islamic law, Anderson and Coulson in the article to which reference has been made above, came to the conclusion, after a penetrating survey of the authorities, that the category of contract is recognised in Islamic legal theory. From the Koran, the following are but a few of their available documentary data:

1. "'Oh ye who believe, observe your covenants' (or 'be faithful to your engagements').[66] Here the leading commentators are agreed that the words apply to all contracts and covenants concluded between man and man, in addition to spiritual covenants between man and God."[67]
2. "Be faithful in the covenant of God when you have covenanted, and break not your oaths after you have ratified them: for you have made God your surety. Verily, God knows what you do. And be not like unto her who unravels to thin filaments the thread which she hath strongly spun, taking your oaths between you with perfidy, because one party is more numerous than the others."

Apart from the Koran, there are also passages from the practice of the prophet which indicate quite clearly that agreements were recognised in Islamic law. The following is a typical example of this:

"Moslems are bound by their stipulations except a stipulation which makes lawful what is unlawful, or makes unlawful what is lawful."[68]

Ibn Taymiya, a leading Islamic legal scholar has also been quoted as saying:

"God has commanded that contracts be fulfilled, and this is of general application. He has thus commanded us to fulfil the covenant of God and covenants in general, and has included in this the contracts a man takes upon himself. This is proved by the Qur'anic verse: 'They had previous covenanted with God that they would not turn their backs and of the covenant of God equity will be made.' This indicates that in the covenant of God is included the contracts a man takes upon himself, even though God has not expressly commanded this particular covenant before, as in the case of an oath or sale, but merely commanded that it be fulfilled."[69]

It is obvious from these authorities that Islamic law recognises and observes a general category of obligations, of which contract, tort and unjust enrichment are parts.

Why Ghana[70] and Nigeria

The choice of Ghana and Nigeria might at first sight appear questionable. The reason for this joint treatment is fourfold. Firstly there is the fact of common descent in the imported laws of the two territories.

The former colony of the Gold Coast and the Lagos Colony were jointly administered between the years 1874 and 1886. Thus the Supreme Court Ordinance, 1876 which introduced English law into the Gold Coast, was also the reception statute for the Lagos colony. The law in force in both colonies was the common law of England as was in force on 24th July, 1874; together with statutes of general application and doctrines of equity. Also, both the Gold Coast and Nigeria were served by the former West African Court of Appeal (which was also a Court of Appeal for the Gambia and Sierra Leone). The judges of the Full Courts of Nigeria were ex-officio members of the Gold Coast Full Court, and vice versa. These administrative and judicial links were factors that tended to unite the two countries and made for a uniform development of their laws. Instances of such similarity are easily found in their enacted laws. The Moneylenders Ordinance of the Gold Coast was in similar terms to the corresponding Nigerian enactment on the subject. This was equally true of the Illiterates Protection Ordinances, the Pawnbrokers Ordinances, the Auction-eers Ordinances and the Bills of Exchange Ordinances.

The case law also developed along similar lines because of both the West African Court of Appeal and the Judicial Committee of the Privy Council, which latter Board was the last court of appeal for the two countries.

The second reason for the joint treatment is the existence and recognition in both countries of laws other than the imported law. This is, of course, the whole question of the recognition and enforcement of customary and other personal laws. Mention has already been made of the Supreme Court Ordinance, 1876, which introduced the main body of English law into the two territories (the reception date for Nigeria was later shifted to 1st January, 1900). It must be mentioned here that the same ordinance under its section 19 also empowered the courts to observe and enforce the observance of customary laws under certain conditions. No doubt, the details of the rules of customary laws in the different societies that made up the two countries, varied. But these variations in details did not distort the similarity of the structure of the two judicial systems. In addition to this structural similarity, certain rules of customary law, through the agency of the courts, came to be recognised as generally applicable to the two countries. The rule in the *Amodu Tijani*[71] case was an example of this.

Thirdly, apart from the two above instances of similarity, there is also the interesting question of the varying fortunes of the imported law in the two territories. This has been almost entirely due to legislative action. Since Independence, Ghana has modified different aspects of the received law. Company law, Sale of Goods, Bills of Exchange, Contract law generally, Gaming and Lotteries, the law of Insolvency, and Civil liability are but a few of these instances of modifying the imported law. On the other hand, in Nigeria, apart from the Western Region (which for this purpose includes the Mid-Western Region), and to a rather limited extent, Lagos (Federal territory), the search for the applicable law still involves researching into old and in many cases, long repealed English statutes, and to some extent, English case law. A joint and comparative treatment of the positions in Ghana and the different jurisdictions in Nigeria will necessarily spotlight these instances of divergence.

Finally, the value of this type of treatment both as an opportunity for re-stating the applicable imputed laws and for noting any recognised rules of indigenous laws, can hardly be over-emphasised.[72]

CONTRACTUAL OBLIGATIONS IN GHANA AND NIGERIA; A GENERAL EXPLANATION

In the preceding section we laid down a basic structural mould for the investigation of this topic. In this section we are concerned with the scope and content of the title and our method of approach.

Scope and content of the title

The definition of obligations as a legally enforceable relationship created by the act of the parties or imposed by the law, has already been noted. The former category of obligations could be created by the agreement of the parties to a relationship or arise out of delict. This work is, however, concerned with obligations that are created by the agreement of the parties. Fascinating as it is for us to discuss the other facets of obligations, it is felt that the latter subject cannot usefully be included here without sacrificing necessary detail for brevity. This does not derogate one bit from the case which has already been made out, that there are three constituent elements in civil responsibility, i.e. that agreement, delict and restitution are all species of the same genus—obligations. It rather emphasises the importance of a detailed examination of each of these heads of liability. It is very strongly felt that a general treatment of the three heads together will still leave the vital need for a detailed treatment of each of them. For our purpose here, therefore, obligations created by the acts of the parties will be co-extensive with obligations created by agreement. The other head of liability will still be that of obligations imposed by law.

Having said this, the case for this kind of study has got to be stated and argued. Two factors would apparently tend to militate against a separate treatment of any facet of civil responsibility in Ghana and Nigeria, or, for that matter, any other jurisdiction that has received English law. One of such factors is the feeling that Ghana or Nigerian law on a subject like, say contract, is the same as English law. All one has to do in order to ascertain the Ghana or Nigerian position on the subject, is to refer to the handy and available English legal literature on the subject. It must be admitted that this would be a good thing if two basic conditions were satisfied, namely, if the imported law in the two countries were the current English law on the subject; and, secondly, if the said current English law, even if it were applicable, were in a satisfactory state. Unfortunately, however, neither of the two basic requirements is present in the case of Ghana and Nigeria. The law received into Ghana was the law in force in England on 24th July, 1874, and for Nigeria, the reception date was 1st January, 1900. It needs hardly be argued that English law has changed considerably since 1874 and 1900 respectively, and that these changes in English law have not all been adopted in either Ghana or Nigeria. Further, the received laws were made applicable so far as local circumstances allowed, and in some cases subject to customary and Islamic law rules. Surely such instances of modification, as are shown in this study, cannot be said to represent the 1874 or 1900 state of English law on any matter. In any case, even if it could be said to be the same as the then English law position, that will represent one viewpoint about the impact of indigenous laws on the common law. It is the intention of the present writer to state and argue all the available points of view, after examining all the documentary and other extant data. This need for an examination of all the available evidence, judicial, statutory and academic, enhances the unique place of a study such as this, in the overall legal system of each of Ghana and Nigeria.

The second factor, particularly in the case of Nigeria, is the recent publication by two learned authors of *Nigerian cases and statutes on contract and tort*.[73] This is, of course, the first more or less comprehensive digest on this aspect of the law in any Anglophonic West African territory.[74] Undoubtedly it is the product of the painstaking efforts of the learned authors, intended, as it was said to be, to fill a gap in this sector of Nigerian law. It is respectfully submitted, however, that the limitations of this work enhance, rather than diminish the need for and the value of this work, even if the book had covered identical ground in Ghana law. A close study of the work will reveal the following short-comings:

Firstly, the case for a new approach to the classification of civil responsibility in Nigeria and Ghana has already been convincingly made out in the preceding section. It must be added here that the learned authors, by adopting the English law classification without comment, are perpetuating a system which, even in English law, is undergoing thorough revision and modification.

Secondly, a digest on this or any aspect of Nigerian law as in any other African country cannot be complete without adverting sufficiently or at all, to the customary and Islamic law facets of the subject. The authors' preoccupation with and emphasis on the decisions of the superior courts, has left the question of the place of customary obligations still to be argued.

Thirdly, the learned authors did not show any interest or concern in the all-important question of the freedom or otherwise of the parties to a transaction to choose their own law. This is, of course, the whole question of the internal conflict of laws. Any digest on any aspect of civil liability in Nigeria or for that matter, Ghana, that overlooks this facet of the subject is necessarily incomplete.

Fourthly, there is no discussion at all on the authority of English decisions in Nigerian Courts. One is not at all persuaded by the authors' casual mention in their introduction, that there is a case for the view that English decisions have binding authority in Nigerian Courts. No indication is given of which English decisions are binding on which Nigerian Courts. In a digest on the law of contract and tort, which law is largely dependent on judicial precedent, a clear statement of which decisions are binding on which Courts is of paramount importance. An authors' omission of such a clear statement can be very frustrating to the student.

Fifthly, the learned authors made generous use of the process of filling the so-called gaps in Nigerian law. Ghanaian[75] and Australian[76] decisions were freely cited as authoritative in the Nigerian Courts. It is submitted that there ought to have been a qualifying statement to the effect that non-Nigerian authorities[77] are only persuasive but not binding on the Nigerian Courts.

Sixthly, the authors merely narrated the facts of the decided cases and presented the courts' decisions in such cases without any comments on the value of the legal principles laid down in any of them. It would obviously have been more helpful to the law student (for whom the work is said to be primarily intended) if, instead of " purple " passages from the decisions of the judges, a more complete picture of the judges' reasoning was included in the reported cases. This aspect of the reports as presented in the work under review, is sadly inadequate.

Finally, mention must be made of some cases, the basis of whose decision has been altered by subsequent legislation. In *Solanke* v. *Abed & Ogunlowo*,[78] the defendant in an action for trespass to land, could not successfully plead an illegality caused by his own failure to comply with Section 11 of the Nigerian Land and Native Rights Ordinance.[79] One of the reasons for this conclusion was that section 11 did not impose any penalty for non-compliance. But the Northern Nigeria Land Tenure Law,[80] which repealed and re-enacted the former Ordinance (so far as it applies to Northern Nigeria), does under Section 6 (f) impose such a penalty. One would have thought that the effect of this change in the law could have been mentioned by the learned authors in assessing the authority of the *Solanke* decision.[81]

It may be added, but without emphasis, that although a case-book is not the appropriate place to draw any conclusions on the functional aspects of the subject treated, yet if, as his Lordship the Chief Justice of the Nigerian Supreme Court, suggested in his introduction to the work under discussion, the case-law method of the American law schools is to be usefully deployed, then the role of contract and tort in Nigerian law should have been assessed in the light of the decided cases. This the learned authors have not done.

The above limitations notwithstanding, it must be re-stated that the learned authors have made some useful contribution to the study of this facet of Nigerian law.

Method of approach

Comparative law, it has often been said, is not a topic but a method of study. In this sub-section we shall be attempting answers to the questions:

(i) What is to be compared with what?; and

(ii) What factors determine the emphasis to be left on what features of the analysis?

(i) What is to be compared with what?

It is common knowledge that in the two territories with which the title is primarily concerned, i.e. Ghana and Nigeria, customary and Islamic laws exist side by side with the imported law. It is also true that the general laws of both Ghana and Nigeria stem from English law. There have, of course, been many variations from the parent stock (i.e. from English law) in both cases, and also several variations *inter se*. At least three varieties of law emerge from the nature of the topic, namely, the customary laws of Ghana and Nigeria, the general laws of Ghana and Nigeria, and finally, English law, the common parent of the two general laws. A comparative study of the law of obligations in Ghana and Nigeria necessarily involves an examination of all these, although there will be varied emphasis in detail. The issue of emphasis leads us to the next question, namely,

(ii) What factors determine the emphasis to be left on what features of the analysis?

Professor Lawson has aptly said in his Cooley lectures at Michigan University in 1953, that one of the virtues of legal comparison (which it shares with legal history) is that it allows a scholar to place himself outside the labyrinth of minutiae in which legal thinking so easily loses its way and to see the great contours of the law, and its dominant characteristics.[82] In his famous work,[83] however, what one sees is clear evidence of the fact that the " eye of one who can see the wood need not be blind to the tree or even to its smallest twigs and leaves."[84] One view of a synthesis of this apparent paradox is that selective emphasis is vital to any comparative analytical exercise. The factors that determine the emphasis do predictably vary from subject to subject. The law of obligations as defined above is one branch of the law in which the relationship between the different varieties of the law—imported, customary and Islamic, are yet to be worked out. The impact of illiteracy on the notion of agreement,[85] particularly in exception clauses in standard-form contracts and the immunity of family head from account in certain jurisdictions on the notion of agency and fiduciary relationships, do require, and have been accorded some emphasis in the work. Also the reconciling of the Islamic law prohibition against aleatory transactions to the notion of hire-purchase agreements and moneylending transactions are other instances of customary/Islamic law and imported law cleavage. Any treatment of the law of obligations in Ghana and Nigeria that does not advert sufficiently or at all to these aspects of the subject, is so much the poorer for it.

Apart from the cleavage between the customary and the imported laws, there is also the divergence of the imported laws in Ghana and Nigeria from the current position in English law. Reference has already been made to this divergence in the preceding section. Here it must be stated that such differences are due to any one or both of the following two factors, namely, changes in the law in England; and/or modifications or changes in the imported law. A quick example of the former situation is the English law relating to resale price maintenance. While this is regulated in England by Statute,[86] it has been abolished in Ghana by the Contracts Act, 1960.[87] An example of the latter feature is found in the Ghana modification of the doctrine of consideration, third-party rights in agreements, and the treatment of fundamental obligation in the Ghana Sale of Goods Act, 1962.[88] Situations such as these do deserve, and have, in fact, been given emphasis in this study.

Also, there are differences in the rates of growth of the received law, between Ghana on the one hand, and the various jurisdictions in Nigeria. In the field of sale of goods, for instance, the English Sale of Goods Act, 1893, is not a Statute of general application in Ghana, being a post-1874 English enactment, not specifically said to apply to Ghana. The local enactment on the subject (the Ghana Sale of Goods Act, 1962) has repealed sections 4 and 17 of the Statute of Frauds (England); i.e. the provisions relating to contracts in writing. The Ghana enactment retains writing for contracts of guarantee and land agreements, with saving made for transactions governed by customary law. This is also the position in Nigeria (Lagos), and to a certain extent, in the Western and Mid-Western Regions. But in the Eastern and Northern Regions of Nigeria, the Sale of Goods Act, 1893 (England) still applies without modification. It is quite possible, therefore, and this has been argued somewhere else, that an agreement may be valid and enforceable if made in Accra, Lagos, Ibadan or Benin, but unenforceable if made at Enugu or Kaduna in the Eastern and Northern Regions (Nigeria) respectively.

There is also the Ghana Lotteries and Gaming Act, 1960, which governs gaming and wagering agreements, but which has no counterpart in any of the jurisdictions in Nigeria.

Instances such as these have been treated with some emphasis in this book.

Apart from these instances of cleavage between the different varieties of law, we have adopted an entirely new mode of presentation for the discussion of obligations created by agreement. For this purpose agreements are divided into two groups, namely, "valid agreements" and "defective agreements." The former category have been sub-divided into (i) agreements involving two parties; and (ii) agreements involving more than two parties. The merits of this treatment have been discussed in another place. Further, the vital question of a functional study of agreements (including interpretation of agreements and their enforcement) has also been fully investigated. The menace of exception clauses and standard-form contracts has been fully investigated, and there is a special plea for a change of judicial and legislative attitudes to suit modern conditions. These facets of the subject have received scant attention in the conventional treatment.

Finally, our treatment of the subject has been on the basis of an integrated law of obligations, clearly recognising the freedom of the parties to choose a "proper law" to govern their transaction. This approach to the topic has been canvassed by recent academic opinion of which the following are but a few.

(i) "The clock cannot be put back. It is impossible to restore the 'tribal' legal systems of the pre-colonial past. The communities which evolved these systems have radically altered or, in some cases, vanished. They are no longer closed and autonomous communities; their economic basis has altered; the social organisation of which the legal order was the expression is daily crumbling away. African countries are now part of the modern industrialising world; and their legal systems must recognise this fact."—A. N. Allott.[89]

(ii) "The task of the court is to divert the gradual convergence of native and European notions of civil law, to fuse them where fusion does not damage the feelings of those concerned, to adapt old customs to modern life, and to interpret one legal system to the other with insight, sympathy and dignity."[90]

(iii) "If we look at Commonwealth countries in Africa as a whole, it is clear that, today, Islamic law represents a very minor problem outside the sphere of family relationships and succession —or, in East Africa, the law of waqf (i.e. pious foundations). In the law of contract there can be scant objection to its application, probably to an ever decreasing extent, as the law under which a particular contract was concluded. In the field of tort there is little difficulty in reconciling Islamic concepts with English principles, and the Islamic law of tort is in fact seldom cited as such today."—J. N. D. Anderson.[91]

The above views were shared by the London Conference on the Future of Law in Africa in 1960;[92] by H. F. Morris and J. S. Read in their recent work on Uganda law,[93] and by B. O. Nwabueze[94] in a paper submitted to the Ife Conference on the integration of laws in African countries.

It has not been considered necessary, therefore, to devote any special parts of the study to a discussion of customary and Islamic obligations. These have been sub-joined to each relevant section of the investigation.

NOTES

All cases referred to in this book, both African and non-African, have been placed in round brackets.

1. See F. Schulz, Classical Roman Law (Oxford, 1951), pp. 445 et seq. We find obligare used as early as Plauto's Comedies, Bacch. 748—cited by Schulz.
2. e.g. to give it as a mortgage, pignus or hypothec.
3. Other examples can be seen in the verb contrahere, which was in use long before its noun, contractus; this is equally true of adstringere used by the classical lawyers, while the noun adstrinctio, came much later.
4. F. Schulz, op. cit. p. 456.
5. Lewin & Short, A Latin Dictionary, p. 1236.
6. Cited by Schulz, op. cit. p. 462.
7. (1959) p. 1256.
8. " The history of the register of writs " (1889), in Select Essays in Anglo-American legal history, (1908).
9. For the doubtful third head of liability in English law, i.e. quasi-contract, see infra.
10. Province of the law of tort, (1930), p. 119.
11. (1760) 2 Burr. 1005 at p. 1012.
12. (1760) 2 Burr 1005 at p. 1012.
13. Per Lord Haldane in Sinclair v. Brougham (1914) A. C. 398; see also Leslie v. Sheill (1914) 3 K.B. 607.
14. Per Scurton L.J. in Holt v. Markman (1923) 1 K.B. 504 at p. 513.
15. " Whatever may have been the case 146 years ago, we are not now free in the twentieth century to administer that vague jurisprudence which is sometimes attractively styled ' justice between man and man ' " —per Hamilton L.J. in Baylis v. Bishop of London (1913) 1 Ch. 127 at p. 140.
16. (1914) A.C. 398.
17. Op. cit. at p. 452. Cf. Lord Dunedin in the same case who was prepared to admit the existence of a " supereminent equity " in cases of unjust enrichment.

18. *Brook's Wharf and Bull Warf. Ltd.* v. *Goodman Bros.* (1937) 1 K.B. 534.
19. Supra.
20. *Banque Belge* v. *Hambrouck* (1921) 1 K.B. at p. 335. See also the learned Judge's dictum in *United Australia Ltd.* v. *Barclays Bank Ltd.* (1941) A.C. 1 at pp. 28-29. " These fantastic resemblances of contracts invented in order to meet the requirements of the law as to forms of action which have now disappeared, should not be allowed to disturb actual rights. When these ghosts of the past stand in the path of justice clanking their medieval chains, the proper course for the judge is to pass them undeterred."
21. *Province of the Law of Tort* p. 137. See also Lord Denning in *Kiriri Cotton Co.* v. *Dewani* (1960) A.C. 192 at p. 204 and Greer, L.J. in *Craven-Ellis* v. *Canons Ltd.* (1936) 2 K.B. 403 at p. 412.
22. (1890) 44 Ch. D.94.
23. Op. Cit. p. 105.
24. *Leslie* v. *Sheill* (1914) 3 K.B. 607.
25. *Cowern* v. *Nield* (1912) 2 K.B. 419. Goff and Jones have argued in their recent work, *The Law of Restitution*, (1966), that these two cases could be reconciled to a general theory of restitution on the basis that any such theory must have its limits and that the case of infants contracts can be said to be one of such limits. It is submitted however, that, to pass as an exception to a rule such an exception should not be negation of the rule. The two cases above are difficult to reconcile to any notions of justice and fair dealing.
26. D. W. M. Waters, *The Constructive Trust: The case for a new approach in English Law.* (1964) passim.
27. " We are inclined to think that torts is not a proper subject for a law book," per O. W. Holmes Jnr. (1871) 5 American L.R. pp. 340-341, reviewing an abridged edition of *Addison's Torts.* Three years later, Holmes came " to recognise there were satisfactory reasons, both historical and analytical, for including the subject in the corpus juris." Mark De Wolfe Howe, *Mr. Justice Holmes, The Proving Years, 1870-1882*, pp. 65, 184. Cited by Goff and Jones, op. cit. p. 5.
28. D. W. M. Waters, *The Constructive Trust*, (London, 1964). R. Goff & G. H. Jones, *The Law of Restitution*, (London, 1966).
29. In their *First Programme*, the Commission has the following: ". . . . an examination of the law of contract, quasi-contract, and such other topics as may appear in the course of the examination to be inseparably connected with them, with a view to their codification. In this examination it will be necessary to take into account the results of the examination recommended under headings II (Exemption by contract from common law liabilities), and III (consideration, third party rights etc.), and pay special attention to the recommendations on innocent misrepresentation made by the Law Reform Committee in its Tenth Report (1962, Cmnd. 1782), to its pending report on the transfer of chattels, and to those topics on which the law may be considered to be unsatisfactory, such as mistake, unjust enrichment and the restitution of money, and (so far as relevant), other property."—See p. 6 of the *Programme.*
30. McNeil & R. Rains, (London, Sweet & Maxwell, 1966).
31. The reception of English law will be examined in the subsequent part.
32. 24th July, 1874 for Ghana; and 1st January, 1900 for Nigeria.

E

33. With the minor exception of the State of Louisiana which has civil law background.
34. e.g. Trust and bailment were both classified under contract; the distinction between law and equity was abolished.
35. See (1921-22) California L.R. 185. It is remarkable that while Justice Stephen J. Field described the Code rules as " perfect in their analysis, admirable in their arrangement, and furnishing a complete code of laws," Sir Frederick Pollock condemned them as " about the worst piece of codification ever produced." The explanation for this conflict lies, of course, in the divergent attitudes of the authors, to codification.
36. See M. E. Harrison, " The first half-century of the California Civil Code " (1921-2) 10 California L.R. 185.
37. E. A. Farnsworth, " Law Reform in a developing country: A new Code of obligations for Senegal " (1964) 8 J.A.L. 6.
38. The French law distinction between civil and administrative contracts, for instance, was not observed in the Code.
39. See René David, " A Civil Code for Ethiopia " (1962-3) 37, Tulane L. Rev. 187.
40. Yale University Press, 1961, p. 73.
41. See the Ghana Civil Liability Act, 1963 (Act 176); and the Nigerian (Federal) Civil Liability (Miscellaneous Provisions) Act, 1961.
42. Pollock on Torts, (15th ed. P.A. London, 1950).
43. The wealth of literature in this facet of legal theory is out of all proportion to its material value in the analysis of the actual practice of individual systems. See for example: The Austinian theory of law (ed. Jethro Brown, 1926), pp. 27-28; Lord Bryce, Studies in history and Jurisprudence, (1901) Vol. 11, pp. 44 and 249; Sir Frederick Pollock, First Book of jurisprudence, (6th ed. 1929), p. 24.
44. Province and Function of Law (1950) p. 715.
45. For a further discussion of this topic, see infra.
46. Sir Henry Maine, Ancient Law, (10th ed.), J. Murray, (1909).
47. Radcliffe-Brown, " Primitive Law ", in Structure and Function in Primitive Society, (London, Cohen & West, 1952), reprinted from the Encyclopaedia of the Social Sciences, 1933, ix pp. 202-6; see also Hoebel " Three Studies in African Law " op. cit. pp. 423-4.
48. W. Seagle, The quest for law, (New York: Knopf, 1941) p. 34.
49. J. H. Driberg, " The African conception of law," (1934) Journal of Comp. Leg., 230.
50. T. O. Elias, The Nature of African Customary Law, (Manchester U. Press, 1956).
51. See M. Gluckman, The judicial process among the Barotse, (Manchester U. Press, 1955); I. Schapera, A handbook of Tswana law and custom, (London, O.U.P., 1955 reprinted by Frank Cass in 1970); also " Contracts in Tswana Law," (1966, Int. African Institute).
52. P. Bohannan, Justice and Judgment among the Tiv, (Int. African Inst., O.U.P., 1957), p. 61.
53. op. cit., pp. 69 et seq.
54. at p. 212. See also M. Gluckman, African Jurisprudence. Reprinted from " The Advancement of Science," No. 74, November, 1961, where the learned author joined issue with Bohannan.
55. See Market Jir Nos. 2 and 3 at pp. 154-155.
56. See Market Nos. 4 and 5, pp. 155-156.
57. See Criminal jir disputes Nos. 63 and 72 at pp. 129 and 145.
58. During field studies in 1965 and from some Tiv students in London.

59. Ghana: Local Court returns, 1963, Ministry of Justice, Accra.

Region	Debt cases	Other heads of liability
Central Region	8090	9 maintenance, 11 land.
Western Region	11407	4 succession, 574 defamation.
Ashanti Region	4884	12 succession, 467 defamation.
Volta Region	2593	480 land, 2 succession.
Buong Ahafo	275	1 succession.
Northern	870	159 matrimonial causes.
Upper	586	336 matrimonial causes.

Under debt were included such heads of liability as detinue, petty debts, and service agreements; defamation cases, curiously enough, were given a separate head.

60. *Ibo Village Affairs* (1947). See also J. S. Read and H. Morris, *Uganda: the development of its laws and constitution*, (London, 1966), p. 308 on customary contracts in Uganda.

61. Similar linguistic evidence is available for the proof of the existence of wrongs and other heads of civil liability. See Rattray, *Ashanti law and Constitution*, pp. 285 et seq. On the linguistic approach generally, see A. N. Allott, *Law and Language*, (1965).

62. See Abdur Rahim, *Muhammedan jurisprudence*, (1903), pp. 50 et seq.; F. H. Ruxton, *Maliki Law*, (London, 1916) passim; see especially J. N. D. Anderson "The Moslem ruler and contractual obligations" (1958) 33 New York Uni. L. Rev. 917; and also, J. N. D. Anderson, "The Future of Islamic law in British commonwealth Territories" (1962) 27, Law & Contemp. Prob. 617; J. Schacht, Introduction to Islamic Law (Oxford, 1964) p. 144; L. Milliot, *Droit Musulman*, SS 641 et seq.

63. Abdur Rahim, op. cit., p. 50.

64. Schacht, op. cit., p. 144.

65. op. cit., p. 154.

66. Sura, V.1. cited by the learned authors at p. 923 of the article.

67. See Anderson and Coulson, op. cit., p. 923.

68. Bukhari, Sahih, 111, 187 (Qastallani, Bulaq, 1879) cited by Anderson & Coulson, op. cit., p. 925.

69. Majmu'at Fatawa, 111, 329 (Cairo 1908-1911).

70. Until midnight on March 5, 1957, the territory now called Ghana, was the British colony of the Gold Coast. The name Ghana is taken from an old African empire of the same name. Ghana had been one of the three great African empires of Gana, Melle and Songhay. The adoption of the name for the Gold Coast was first suggested by the late Dr. J. B. Danquah. But it was Dr. Nkrumah, the then Prime Minister of Ghana, who on August 3, 1956, in a motion in the then Gold Coast National Assembly, requested Her Majesty's Government in the United Kingdom, for the independence of the territory under the name of "Ghana." Thus, from the 6th March, 1957, Gold Coast became the Sovereign State of Ghana. The new name was said to have obvious advantages. Apart from its being a much more convenient name than Gold Coast (which latter name was considered too clumsy and involved); it served as a necessary emotional break with the colonial past. It was also intended to serve as a reminder to Africans of the glories of the former empire of Ghana.

At the early stages of our enquiry, "Ghana" and the "Gold Coast" will be used interchangeably, since all the pre-independence legislation came under the latter name. All post-independence references will, however, be made under the name " Ghana."

71. (1915) 3 N.L.R. 21.
72. See A. N. Allott & E. Cotran, " Restatement of laws in Africa," where the learned authors made out a convincing case for restatement both in the imported laws in Africa and in the indigenous rules of law.
73. J. L. McNeil & R. Rains, (London, Sweet & Maxwell, 1966).
74. For general discussions on civil liability in Ghana and Nigeria, see T. O. Elias, *Nigerian Legal System,* (London 1961); W. C. E. Daniels, *Common law in West Africa,* (London, 1964).
75. At p. 41 the learned authors cited the Ghana case of *Hamilton* v. *Mensah* (1937) 3 W.A.C.A. 224 as authority for the application in Nigeria of the Statute of Frauds, 1677. Also at p. 82 *Thomas Hutton-Mills* v. *Nkansah* (1940) 6 W.A.C.A. 32, another Ghana case, was cited as a Nigerian authority on " implied terms " in contract.
76. At p. 420 the New South Wales appeal of *Overseas Tankship Ltd.* v. *Morts Dock & Engineering Co. Ltd.* (1961) A.C. 388 was cited as a Nigerian authority on measure of damages in tort.
77. (1962) N.R.N.L.R. 92 at p. 59 of the authors' work.
78. (1962) N.R.N.L.R. 92 at p. 59 of the authors' work.
79. Cap. 105, Laws of Nigeria (1948).
80. Cap. 59, Laws of Northern Nigeria, (1963 Consolidation).
81. This is specially desirable in view of the fact that the latter statute was not included in the learned authors' digest of statutes subjoined to the cases.
Although this statement refers to two mature and relatively independent legal systems, it is submitted that it is equally true of any comparative study at all.
82. F. H. Lawson, *A common lawyer looks at the Civil Law,* 1953.
83. F. H. Lawson, *Negligence in the Civil Law,* (Oxford, 1950).
84. O. Kahn Freund, *Comparative law as an academic subject,* (Oxford, 1965).
85. This was in issue in the Ghana case of *Reindorf* v. *Akua,* (1926-29) F.Ct.152, where the Full Court held that the question of an illiterate understanding the terms of a written agreement is one of fact.
86. See the Resale Prices Act, 1964 (England).
87. S.5(2)(b) of the Ghana Contracts Act, 1960.
88. S.5(2)(a) of the Ghana Contracts Act, 1960.
89. Cited by E. Cotran in " The law of Civil wrongs and obligations in Commonwealth African Countries," 1966, p. 12.
90. Cited in *The future of law in Africa* (ed. A. N. Allott, 1960), p. 13.
91. " The Future of Islamic law in British Commonwealth Territories " (1962) 27 law & Contemp. Problems, 617.
92. pp. 39-41 of the Report of the proceedings.
93. *Uganda, The development of its laws and constitutions,* (London, Stevens & Sons), p. 308.
94. " Integration of the law of contracts " (1964).

CHAPTER 2

PRECEDENT AND THE AUTHORITY OF ENGLISH DECISIONS

In this chapter we shall firstly be examining in some detail the authority of English decisions in the Ghanaian and Nigerian Courts, and in chapter 3, the binding nature of judicial precedent in the two countries. We shall also be examining whether the received common law was the common law of England as at a particular date or whether common law is by its nature dateless. It is important to investigate the authority of English decisions in the West African Courts. Such an exercise will reveal the merits or otherwise of the common practice of " filling gaps " in the law, to which many an author has resorted with a view to presenting a so-called complete picture of the law of any particular territory. The importance of an examination of the practice of the Nigerian and Ghanaian Courts with regard to judicial precedent cannot be over-emphasised. Almost the whole corpus of the law of obligations is case law. In order to know what that law is, it is vital to ascertain the value that the courts will attach to their previous decisions.

The authority of English decisions in the Ghanaian and Nigerian Courts.[1]

The title of this chapter might appear irrelevant at first sight, at least in respect of one of the countries, i.e. Ghana. What is the value of a disquisition on the authority of English decisions in a country where by statute the Courts are empowered to refer to the decisions of courts in any other parts of the world in deciding any matter before them,[2] and the Supreme Court is not bound by the previous decisions of any other court?[3] Apparently, the legislative authorities have purported to present a clean judicial sheet for the courts to write in fresh decisions, and any long discourse on whether or not the Ghanaian Courts are nevertheless bound by English decisions is therefore a boring irrelevance! But the position is much more complicated than this. The attempt to jettison English authority and concepts, baby-and-bathwater, has been far from complete. Firstly, Article 40 (d) of the Republican Constitution which has been saved by paragraph 3 of the National Liberation Council Proclamation of 24th February, 1966 still retains "enactments in force immediately before coming into operation of the constitution," as one of the major sources of Ghana law. Also Article 40 (e) of the same constitution provides that the common law is part of the law of Ghana, howbeit, with a local definition.[4]

Secondly, paragraph 93 (2) of the Courts Decree, 1966[5] which repeals and substantially re-enacts Section 154 (2)[6] of the Courts Act, 1960, provides as follows:

> "the provisions relating to Admiralty jurisdiction, infants, persons of unsound mind, probate and matrimonial causes, and statutes of general application which were in force in England on 24th July, 1874 and applicable to Ghana immediately before the commencement of this decree, shall continue to apply on and after such commencement until such provisions are modified, amended or revoked under this decree."

Thirdly, there have been doubts[7] as to the intentions of the legislature in enacting the new provisions. This uncertainty makes " the authority of English decisions " in Ghana Courts still a live issue.

Finally the practice of the courts in Ghana since the promulgation of the Republican Constitution (now substantially repealed) and the attendant mass of subsequent legislation, has not revealed any noticeable deviation from the hitherto understandable dependance on English authority in pre-1960 days. A re-appraisal of the position is therefore called for.

In Nigeria the position is different. Here the change-over to a Republican form of constitution involved[8] only the ministerial detail of changing names.[9] There have not been any remarkable changes in the reception provisions, except perhaps in the Western Region, which changes are not important for our purpose here. In Nigeria, therefore, as in Ghana, there is a pressing need to investigate the authority of English decisions in the Courts. We shall examine the subject in the following three stages, namely:

(a) decisions at common law;

(b) decisions made under pre-1900 (or in the case of Ghana, pre-1874) English Statutes, and

(c) decisions under statutes in pari materia.

First we shall look at the structure of the courts. We are not here concerned with the autopsy of the defunct West African Court of Appeal or any other regional courts of appeal. It is enough to mention that their functions have now been taken over by the penultimate courts of appeal in the respective territories. Also, in both Ghana and Nigeria, appeals to the Judicial Committee of the

Privy Council have been abolished by the respective Republican Constitutions, and the functions of the Privy Council as far as appeals go, devolve on the Supreme Courts of the Republics.[10]

Before the abolition of the West African Court of Appeal and the abrogation of appeals to the Judicial Committee, the orthodox equation of the court structures in Ghana and Nigeria on the one hand, and England on the other, was that the territorial Supreme Courts or the Full Courts were equivalent to the English High Court; the West African Court of Appeal, to the English Court of Appeal (and the then Court of Criminal Appeal), and the Privy Council on the one hand, to the House of Lords on the other, in a kind of co-ordinate friendly neutrality, at the apex of the two respective systems.[11] But this striking of an equivalence between English and African Courts was based on the colonial system. With the coming of independence the whole question will be looked at afresh. This aspect of the subject will be examined in the next following section. We shall now go back to the question of whether the received common law is dateless.

Was the received common law the common law of England at a particular date? :

As has been mentioned earlier, the question of the dating or otherwise of the imported common law, will be investigated in the context of the authority of English decisions on the common law before and after the reception dates. Since there has been considerable controversy in attempts to tackle this problem, it will be worth our while to try and disentangle the strands and to call for a truce in what could rightly be described as a battle of words. The standard-form provision has often been as follows :

> " the common law, the doctrines of equity and statutes of general application which were in force in England on the 24th day of July, 1874, (for Ghana) shall be in force within the jurisdiction of the Courts."

In some territories there are no commas separating the " common law," " doctrines of equity," on the one hand and statutes of general application on the other,[12] and in other jurisdictions the words " together with " are used instead of " and " in separating the statutes of general application from the rest of the provisions.[13] Still in other territories the three items are given separate subsections.[14]

The controversy has been on whether the limiting date only refers to the Statutes of general application or whether it also extend to the received common law. In other words whether in deciding on the content of any common law rule the courts will look for such rules only in pre-1900 (in the case of Nigeria) decisions. Now let us look at the authorities.

In August, 1895, Lord Herschell, the President of the Society,* in a letter to Mr. Chamberlain, the then Colonial Secretary, enclosed a series of questions by means of which it was sought to obtain information respecting, among other things, the common and statute law of the several colonies. The questions were transmitted by Mr. Chamberlain to the respective colonial Governments and the official reply from Ghana (then Gold Coast) is very instructive. This reply was prepared by Sir William Brandford Griffith, then Chief Justice of the territory, and it goes:

> " The common law in the Colony is that which was common law in England on July 24, 1874 (14 $\frac{4}{18}$). This enactment is modified by SS 7, 12, 13 of the Criminal Code ($\frac{12}{63}$), with respect to Acts which are offences under that Code."[15]

It can hardly be disputed then that the above statement of the position represents the Official attitude towards the provision. Coming as it does from the Chief Justice of the Territory and one of the greatest judges of his time, the statement should, and has till recently, been regarded as the authoritative interpretation of the law on the subject. This is the more so since the Ordinance that the learned Chief Justice was construing to the Colonial Secretary applied both in Ghana and Nigeria.

Against this however is the view of the learned editors of the Gold Coast Assize,[16] a legal journal, who in construing the same section of the Ordinance had this to say.[17] " From the very punctuation it would appear that the words 'which were in force' etc., apply simply to the statutes of general application."

Thus the editor argues that the reception date does not refer to the common law and equity. But he could only come to this conclusion on the basis of the punctuation of the provision. We have already demonstrated convincingly that Ghana (then Gold Coast) adopted English practice and procedure which includes rules of interpretation of statutes. It is remarkable that the learned editors left so much weight on punctuation when it had repeatedly been decided that punctuation is not part of a statute and should not be resorted to as aid to its construction.[18] Admittedly, new provisions[19] have now been made in Ghana and Nigeria (Federation and Lagos) about the significance of punctuation marks in the construction of statutes. But these provisions are new and it can rightly be argued that it is the state of the law before their enactment that prompted the change. We shall however proceed with our examination of the authorities.

In *Solomon* v. *African Steamship Co.*,[20] Petrides J. had this to say:

> " I am satisfied that the Statutes of limitation, which are applicable to the present cause of action, were statutes of general application which were in force in England on the 1st January, 1900, and that they, in common with other Statutes of general application which were in force on that date, are, together with the common law and the doctrines of equity which were in force in England on the same date,[21] in force within the jurisdiction . . . . of this court by reason of section fourteen of the Supreme Court Ordinance, subject to the terms of any existing Ordinance."

This view of the provision has been criticised by a learned author.[22] We shall be going into the points of his objection presently.

Another of our eminent witnesses who support what could rightly be described as the orthodox view is Allott.[23] The details of his views need not detain us here. What must, however, be made here is the point that some sections of the reception enactment empower the courts to apply English law for the time being in force, in certain matters.[24] If the legislature had intended a timeless provision in respect of English common law they could have said this in so many words. This view has of course been strengthened by the new provisions in Western Nigeria,[25] Northern Nigeria,[26] and Ghana.[27] It is interesting to note that Park has argued that the new provisions support the contention that the limiting date referred only to the Statutes of general application. As has been pointed out by another author, we have got to draw a line between what " is " and what " ought to be " the law. An ideal reception provision should introduce English common law for the time being in force in England subject to adaptation to local circumstances. It is submitted that the new provisions in Ghana and some jurisdictions in Nigeria were aimed at achieving this ideal. How far they have in fact done so is another matter. But it is quite a different stand to take from stating categorically that that had always been the position even before the new provisions were enacted.

In a recent lecture[28] a leading judge from Ghana has also supported the orthodox view of the old provisions. He had this to say:

> " Now the Courts Ordinance passed by each of the Legislatures of Gambia, Sierra Leone, Ghana and Nigeria, made it clear that

only so much of the English law as was suitable to the circumstances of the territory was applicable, and since each legislature was empowered as from the date of its establishment to make laws for the good government of its territory, the English law applicable was further limited to such of it as was in existence at the date of the constitution of the particular legislature."[29]

From the above passage it is clear that the learned judge supports the view that the limiting date refers to the statutes of general application as well as the English common law. This position is consistent with the interpretation of the provisions in several jurisdictions in the United States.[30] Here the view is that where a State Constitution provides that "the common law of England shall remain in force," it is usually construed as referring to the common law of England as it stood at the time of the adoption of such constitution.[31] To the same effect is the practice described by Dean Griswold in his Hamlyn Lectures[32] entitled "*Law and Lawyers in the United States.*" Between the years 1779 and 1810 the legislatures of the States of New Jersey, Pennsylvania and Kentucky passed laws making it an offence for a lawyer to cite in Court an English decision which appeared after 1st July, 1776.

This, then, is the state of the authorities as far as the argument that the date of reception governs the common law and equity as well as statute, goes.

There are, however, others who have ably argued that the date of reception governs only the Statutes of general application. Said Roscoe Pound:[33]

" The English materials as the colonies received them, were for the most part set forth authoritatively in the writings of Sir Edward Coke, Attorney General under Elizabeth and Chief Justice under James I. Yet the common law of England, in the sense of the traditional body of legal precepts administered in the King's Courts of law continued to develop throughout the seventeenth century and in the eighteenth century. Also the common law as a system had an important development in England in the nineteenth century, *if the statutes limit American Courts to the English legal precepts as they stood in* 1601 *the traditional element of the law would have to stand still in America in its early seventeenth century form, while going forward in England.*[34] Thus the courts would be grievously hampered in dealing with many subjects where in default of legislation, resort must be had to the common law. Hence, although some courts insist that in the absence of statutory rules they must apply English decisions as they stood in the first year of James I, the tendency of American decisions is to hold that the doctrine and statutes refer primarily to the common law as a system. On this ground courts consider

that they may refer to recent English decisions, as against the
seventeenth century authorities, if the former are better expres-
sions of the principles of the common law system."

It is submitted with respect that the learned author's fears about
the consequences of accepting the reception date to refer to the
common law, are unsound in principle and falsified by experience.
If the common law as received is the common law of England in
the seventeenth century, its application and development in
America is subject to local circumstances. The suggestion that the
law in America will consequently stand still is a grotesque under-
statement. American judges have always been quick in discarding
an English doctrine if in their opinion it was " un-American." A
judge in Pennsylvania has been said to speak with the " romantic
fervour of a patriot " when he refused to enforce the rule of English
law which permitted a husband to disinherit his wife if she should
remarry. Said Judge Lewis:

> " the principle of reproduction . . . . is the blessing which
> tempered with mercy the justice of expulsion from paradise. From
> the lord of the forest to the monster of the deep—from the elastic
> embrace of the mountain Kalmia to the descending fructification
> of the lily of the plain, all nature bows submissively to this
> primeval law. Even the flowers which perfume the air with their
> fragrance, and decorate the forests and fields with their hues, are
> but curtains to the nuptial bed. *The principles of mortality—the
> law of nature and the law of God — — — — unite in condemning
> as void*[35] the condition attempted to be imposed by this testator
> upon his widow."[36]

The importance of this remarkable piece of legal rhetoric is to
emphasise the fact that irrespective of the date of reception the
common law is adaptable to local conditions and circumstances.
When the Texas judges were called upon to interpret the State's
reception statute providing that the common law of England should
be the rule of decision, they announced that it meant that the
common law of England as " declared by the courts of the different
States of the United States " should govern the controversies of
Texans.[37] Thus the fact that the common law as received was the
common law in force in England at a particular date forms the
basis of a new legal system. The new common law then becomes a
naturalised citizen whose growth, change and development are
determined by local circumstances and conditions. This was the
case in the United States and the older Commonwealth countries.
It is submitted that it is equally the case in Ghana and the
Nigerian jurisdiction.[38] Park's strictures on the orthodox view are

partly based on the Privy Council appeal from Nigeria of *United Africa Co. Ltd.* v. *Saka Owade*[39] in which their Lordships were said to have followed the House of Lords decision in *Lloyd* v. *Grace, Smith & Co.*,[40] a post-1900 English authority on vicarious liability. One cannot rebut Park's contention, however, without stating the facts of the case in greater detail.

In *United Africa Company Ltd.* v. *Saka Owade*[41] the respondent was a lorry-owner and a transport contractor. He had introduced two of his servants to the appellants adding that any goods for carriage up country (Northern Nigeria) meant for him could be delivered to the said servants. Accordingly the appellants delivered goods worth £4,732 : 13 : 4d. to the servants for the appellants' branches up country. The servants stole these goods, were convicted of the theft and the company sued the respondent among other things in conversion for the total sum being the value of the goods converted. At first instance it was held, following the House of Lords decision in *Lloyd* v. *Grace, Smith & Co.*[42] that the respondent was liable. On appeal to the West African Court of Appeal, the appeal court reversed this finding and held that the respondent was not liable since it had not been proved that he was a common carrier. The appellants appealed to the Judicial Committee of the Privy Council. Here the learned counsel for the respondent ably argued that the facts of the case were on all fours with those in *Cheshire* v. *Bailey*[43] where it was held that the theft by a servant of a bailee does not arise in the course of the servant's employment. It is worth noting that the Cheshire case is also a post-1900 decision. On this submission by the learned counsel their Lordships had this to say :

> " Their Lordships do not find it necessary to decide whether that case is distinguishable on the facts from *Lloyd* v. *Grace, Smith & Co.*,[44] or has been overruled by the decision in *Lloyd* v. *Grace Smith & Co.*"

It was however held that the respondent was liable on the ground that he was liable for the theft of his servants committed in the course of their employment. The relevance of this voyage of discovery into the facts of the *Owade* case is threefold. Firstly, it is to stress the fact that Park's submission that the Privy Council had to choose between a pre-1900 and a post-1900 English common law rule, is not borne out by the facts. *Cheshire* v. *Bailey*[45] on which the old rule was supposed to have been based was decided in 1905, thus itself also a post-1900 decision of English Courts. Secondly, their Lordships of the Privy Council did not have the choice attributed to them by the learned author. The dictum of

Lord Oaksey who read the judgment of the Board bears out this submission.

Finally, even if the Privy Council were persuaded by the House of Lords decision in the *Grace* case (Park did not suggest that they were bound), the Board as the final court of appeal in the then judicial hierarchy of the territory (i.e. Nigeria) could and did guide the growth and development of the received common law.[46] This it had done in the *Owade* case. How that decision could be said to have advanced the argument for a dateless common law one bit, is fanciful in the extreme. It is submitted that the date of reception governs both the common law and the statutes of general application.[47]

Decisions at common law

A judicial decision in England is based either on a statutory provision or on a common law rule. We shall be examining here the authority of the decisions of English courts where such decisions are based on a common law rule. We must, however, hasten to explain some of our terms. When we say that English decisions are authoritative in, say, Nigerian courts, what exactly do we mean? In the following investigation authoritative will mean " binding ". It is important to have this clear picture in our minds because many authors whose minds have adverted to this problem do not appear to have given sufficient consideration to the distinction between persuasive and binding authority.[48]

It is particularly desirable to draw this line in an investigation of the law of obligation since almost the whole corpus of this law is case law. Another necessary distinction that must be made is that between the authority of pre-1900 (in the case of Nigeria) English cases on the common law and the post-1900 cases. The fact that pre-1900 decisions of the superior courts in England are part of the common law and equity, cannot be overemphasised. Now it is this common law and equity that was received in Nigeria on 1st January, 1900, and, it is submitted, these decisions are binding on the Nigerian courts irrespective of which English courts decided any particular case whose ratio is under consideration.[49] It is further submitted that this statement of the position is separate and distinct from any consideration of judicial precedent. But the statement is subject to certain exceptions. Firstly, the last court of Appeal in each territory could and does guide the growth and development of the received common law and equity. Reference has already been made to the Privy Council decision in *U.A.C.* v. *Saka Owade*.[50] It is submitted that the ultimate courts of appeal in Ghana and Nigeria respectively have this power of moulding and shaping the common law and equity. If any pre-1900 decision is deemed un-Nigerian the Nigerian Supreme Court are not bound to follow it. But a pre-1900 decision of the House of Lords is binding on the Nigerian Supreme Court.[51] Such a rule if it occasions hardship could of course be remedied by legislative action.

The *Fatal Accidents Act,* 1961,[52] the *Law Reform (Torts) Act,* 1961,[53] and the *Law Reform (Contracts) Act,* 1961,[54] are instances of the Federal Government of Nigeria anticipating a call for help from the Nigerian Supreme Court in these fields. Our remark about the creative power of the courts finds authoritative support from the speech of Sir Adetokunbo Ademola, Chief Justice of the Federal Republic of Nigeria, to the Nigerian Bar Association.[55] He said among other things that

> " The common law of England, as all know, does not necessarily fit in with every one of our problems in Nigeria; they have their technicalities; their unsuitability in some cases is well known to you and need not be emphasised. It is evident that to understand our own country and law, more researches are necessary."

To the same effect are the dicta of Denning L. J. (as he then was) in the case of *Nyali, Ltd.* v. *Attorney-General*[56] at the court of Appeal. The learned judge was construing a sub-section of the Kenya Protectorate Order in Council 1902[57] which laid down a proviso as follows:

> " . . . . Provided always that the said common law, doctrines of equity and statutes of general application shall be in force in the protectorate so far only as the circumstances of the protectorate and its inhabitants . . . . permit and subject to such qualifications as local circumstances render necessary."

The learned Lord Justice had this to say on the proviso:

> " It is a recognition that the common law (of England) cannot be applied in a foreign land without considerable qualifications. Just as with an English oak, so with the common law. You cannot transplant it to the African continent and expect it to retain the tough character which it has in England. It will flourish indeed but it needs careful tending. So with the common law. It has many principles of manifest justice and good sense which can be applied with advantage to people of every race and colour all the world over; but it has also many refinements and technicalities which are not suited to other folk. These off-shoots must be cut away. In these far-off lands the people must have a law which they understand and which they will respect with considerable quali-fications. The task of making these qualifications is entrusted to

the judges of these lands. It is a great one, I trust that they will not fail therein."[58]

Consequently the learned judge modified the English common law concepts of tolls-thorough and tolls-traverse to suit Kenyan circumstances.

It has further been suggested by a learned author[59] that a House of Lords decision may not be binding on a Commonwealth court if the House of Lords were constrained to decide in a particular way by the binding nature of judicial precedent. Since Daniels had already adopted the attitude of regarding the received common law and equity as dateless he did not go further to indicate whether it was pre-reception date or post-reception date decisions of the House of Lords that would not be binding. If his reference is to the former, it is submitted that it is not supported by the authority of Ghanaian and Nigerian courts.[60] These courts regard themselves as bound by the decisions of pre-reception decisions of the Superior English Courts. Daniels' suggestion is also directly contrary to the Privy Council decision of *Robins* v. *National Trust Co. Ltd.*[61] If, however, his suggestion refers to post-reception date decisions of English Courts, it is submitted that it is not only the decisions of the House of Lords but those of any other English Courts that are only of persuasive authority in Ghanaian and Nigerian Courts. As has been repeatedly asserted, the reception of English law into Ghana and Nigeria marked the beginning of a new system. There could be no question of Nigerian or Ghanaian Courts being bound by the post-reception decisions of English courts.

The second exception to our general principle of Nigerian courts being bound by pre-reception date English decisions is the fact that certain cases are governed by customary law rules. In such cases therefore, the principles of customary law may be preferred to the rules of English Common Law. *Chike Ogo* v. *Adiba Ogo*[62] was a Nigerian case of customary defamation. Said Mbanefo C.J.

" In arguing the appeal, appellant's counsel has referred me to a number of English authorities and text-books on what a plaintiff must prove before he could succeed in a case of slander. The essence of an action for defamation is publication and in the case of spoken words, the exact words or something as close to them as possible must be proved by evidence. Is such strict proof necessary in a case of slander in the customary court? It has not been suggested that slander as a cause of action is not known in the customary courts. Any words spoken of a person which exposes him to hatred, ridicule and contempt would appear in customary law to be actionable. . . . . . ."[63]

Concluding, the learned Chief Justice held inter alia that there was no need for proof of special damage in customary slander actions and secondly that the strict proof necessary under English law was not necessary under customary law procedure.

Customary law has also operated to reduce damages for a breach of promise of marriage action[64] to nominal damages. Said Waddington, Asst. J.:

> " I am little disposed to assess damages at a high figure; it is impossible to ignore the fact that in the customs of plaintiff's people, the customs into which she and defendant were born, there is no conception in the least comparable to that of damages for breach of a promise of marriage."[65]

A third exception to our general rule, is that English public policy decisions do not have the same binding force on the Nigerian courts or for that matter on the courts of Ghana, as decisions based on rules of law. If the primary function of law is the " adjustment of conflicting interests,"[66] then it must have a direct bearing on the state of civilisation of the society in which it is applied. As was aptly pointed out by Lord Watson in *Nordenfelt* v. *Maxim Nordenfelt Guns and Ammunition Co.*:[67]

> " A series of decisions based upon grounds of public policy, how-ever eminent the judges by whom they were delivered, cannot possess the same binding authority as decisions which deal and promulgate principles which are purely legal."[68]

This statement of Lord Watson has not, however, received unqualified support both of judicial and academic opinion. As to this we shall be saying more in a subsequent chapter.[69] It is, how-ever, in the domain of personal law in Ghana and Nigeria that Lord Watson's dictum comes to its own. The old and familiar theories of polygamous marriages as enunciated in *Warrender* v. *Warrender*[70] and rephrased in *Hyde* v. *Hyde*[71] have been submerged in a deluge of recent judicial and academic authority.[72] The same is true of succession.[73] In *Dawodu and others* v. *Danmole and others*,[74] already referred to, their Lordships of the Privy Council observed that public policy in a country where polygamy was generally accepted should not easily be equated to that of a society governed by the principles of monogamy.

Post-Reception date decisions at Common Law

We shall now examine the authority of post-reception date deci-sions of English Courts in Ghana and Nigeria. Two theories have often been propounded the import of which is that post-reception date decisions are as authoritative as those before the date of reception.

One of such theories and the least with anything to commend it is the declaratory theory of the common law. This theory, originally propounded by Blackstone, has been worn so thin as to have become a transparent fiction. In the South West African case of *R. v. Goseb*[75] Classen, J.P. had this to say in support of the theory:

> "It is further true that a decision interpreting the common law has retrospective effect as if the common law had always been in conformity with the later decision."

It was held in this case that a post-reception decision by the Appellate Division of South Africa must be read as if it were already operative at the date of reception. But as has been rightly observed by Allott[76] this may well be the position in South-West Africa since there is a common ultimate Court of Appeal serving the receiving country and the country whose legal system is received. But this cannot be true of Ghana and Nigeria on the one hand and England on the other. The House of Lords, the final Court of Appeal in England in most matters, has no jurisdiction to hear appeals from Ghana and Nigeria.[77]

The other theory is that comity requires that Commonwealth Courts should hold identical views on the growth and development of the Common Law. Thus if the House of Lords comes to any conclusion about the principle of the common law, that is the law for the other Commonwealth Courts.[78] It is, however, submitted that the one thing that comity cannot and should not import is the idea that the decision of one Commonwealth Court is binding on the courts of another country. In *Corbett* v. *Social Security Commission*[79] the New Zealand Court of Appeal refused to hold itself bound by the decision of the House of Lords in *Duncan* v. *Cammell Laird*.[80] Also in the Australian case of *Parker* v. *The Queen*,[81] the High Court of Australia refused to follow the decision of the House of Lords in *D.P.P.* v. *Smith*.[82] In his judgment in the Australian case Dixon, C.J. said:

> "In *Stapleton* v. *The Queen*,[83] we said: 'The introduction of the maxim or statement that a man is presumed to intend the reasonable consequences of his act is seldom helpful and always dangerous.' That was some years before the decision in *D.P.P.* v. *Smith*[84] which seems only too unfortunately to confirm the observation. I say 'too unfortunately' for I think it forces a critical situation in our relation to the judicial authority as precedents of decisions in England. Hitherto *I had thought that we*

ought to follow decisions of the House of Lords at the expense of our own opinions and cases decided here, but having carefully studied Smith's case I think that we cannot adhere to that view or policy.[85] There are propositions laid down in the judgment which I believe to be misconceived and wrong. They are fundamental and they are propositions which I could never bring myself to accept . . . . I think *Smith's case* should not be used as authority in Australia at all. . . ."[86]

It is submitted that the attitudes of the New Zealand Court of Appeal and the Australian High Court in the cases cited above should be adopted in the Nigerian Courts with regard to post-reception decisions of the House of Lords. In this connection Allott's summary of the position is very apt indeed. He said that:

" Decisions of English Courts on the principle of common law or doctrines of equity given after the date when a territory received its English law are not of binding authority in the Courts of the territory; though they are entitled to the highest respect if the English law has not been subsequently statutorily modified."[87]

It remains to add that the above summary of the position represents a more realistic definition of comity than a suggestion that the courts of Nigeria or Ghana for that matter are bound by post-reception decisions of English Courts.[88]

Decisions under Statute

In examining the authority of English decisions based on the interpretation of Statutes one has got to look at three different categories of Statutes. Firstly we have the pre-reception-date statutes or statutes of general application as they are more often called. Secondly there are such Statutes of the United Kingdom Parliament as are still part of the laws of Ghana and Nigeria even although they are post-reception date Statutes. Finally there are English Statutes that have been re-enacted in Ghana and Nigeria as part of their respective territorial laws—these are popularly called Statutes in pari materia. The important question is, what is the authority of English decisions based on the interpretation of these statutes? We shall begin with decisions made under the Statutes of general application.

Decisions made under Statutes of general application

The theory has often been put forward that when a colonial (or a Commonwealth) legislature decided to adopt the pre-reception English statutes, it also adopted the interpretation placed on the provisions of these Statutes by the English courts.[89] Consistently with this theory, therefore, English decisions made before the date of reception are binding on the Nigerian and Ghanaian courts. But much will depend on the stature of the English Court which made the decision, and also the stature of the Nigerian[90] court that is called upon to adopt the interpretation. Thus a decision of an English High Court will not be binding on the Nigerian Supreme Court, although it will have persuasive authority. But the decision of the English Court of Appeal or the House of Lords will be binding on all the courts in Nigeria, saving for the liberty of the highest court of the land to adapt the law to suit local conditions.

It must be added but without any emphasis that the courts in Nigeria have regarded themselves as bound by the decisions of English courts. But the courts have also been quick to recognise the significance of the limitation on the application of imperial statutes. Section 45 (2) of the Interpretation Act of Nigeria provides that:

> " Such imperial laws shall be in force so far only as the limits of the local jurisdiction and local circumstances shall permit and subject to any Federal law."[91]

Thus in *Lawal* v. *Younan*[92] the Nigerian Federal Supreme Court held that under the Fatal Accidents Acts, 1846-1864, children not born in lawful wedlock under the Marriage Ordinance or who are not the issue of a marriage under Native Law and Custom, are, if acknowledged as children by the putative fathers, legitimate in Nigeria for the purposes of the Acts. In *Bamgbose* v. *Daniel*,[93] it was held by the West African Court of Appeal and affirmed by the Privy Council that " child " under the English statute of distributions included any child legitimate under the law of his domicile. Thus the children of polygamous unions ranked equally with any child of a marriage under the Marriage Ordinance. This was also the decision in the Ghana case of *Coleman* v. *Shang*.[94] In each of the above cited decisions the courts in Nigeria did not hold themselves bound by the interpretation placed on such words as " child " and " legitimate " by the English Courts.

Of the decisions based on such statutes as were expressly said to apply to Ghana and Nigeria, one thing is very clear. It is that the argument, based on " imperial legislation being designed to form a coherent system of law prevailing in the British possessions " has lost much of its force. Neither Ghana nor Nigeria now form part of Her Majesty's Dominions and each of these territories has got her own Nationality and Citizenship Laws.[95] The Territorial Waters Jurisdiction Act, 1878 ceased to apply to both territories on the attainment of Independence.[96] Since most of these enactments were operative in the colonies as a necessary consequence of Britain's responsibility for them in international law, it is most unlikely that the Courts of Nigeria will consider themselves bound by the interpretation placed on these Statutes by English Courts. It is submitted that such decisions will only be of persuasive authority in the Nigerian Courts.

Statutes in pari materia

We shall finally be looking at decisions based on the interpretation of English Statutes which have in part or wholly been materially re-enacted in Ghana and Nigeria. Examples of such statutes are legion. We shall, however, mention only the following for our particular purpose. The Nigerian Bills of Exchange Act[97] and Bills of Sale Act[98] are carbon copies of the English Bills of Exchange Act, 1882[99] and the Bills of Sale Act, 1878 (as amended in 1882).[100] The Nigerian Companies Act[101] is a material re-enactment of the English Companies Act of 1929. The Civil Liability (Miscellaneous Provisions) Act, 1961[102] is a mixed bag of provisions copied from the English Law Reform (Miscellaneous Provisions) Act, 1934; Married women and Tort-feasors Act, 1935, and the Law Reform (Contributory Negligence) Act, 1945. The Law Reform (Contracts) Act, 1961[103] is to the same effect, a combination of provisions from the English Law Reform (Frustrated Contracts) Act, 1943; the Statute of Frauds, 1677 and the Sale of Goods Act, 1893. In 1959 the Western Nigeria legislature adopted the English Law of Property legislation of 1925.[104] The above practice is equally true of Ghana.[105] The question which often recurs is the extent to which the Nigerian Courts are bound by the interpretation of these provisions in English Courts.

The oft-cited authority in this connection is the observation of their Lordships of the Privy Council in the New South Wales appeal of *Trimble* v. *Hill*.[106] The Board was faced with the interpretation of an enactment[107] of the English Act on wagering Contracts and had this to say:[108]

> " Their Lordships think that the Court in the Colony might well have taken this decision[109] as an authoritative construction of the statute. It is the judgment of the Court of Appeal, by which all the courts in England are bound, until a contrary determination has been arrived at by the House of Lords. Their Lordships think that in colonies where a like enactment has been passed by the Legislature, the Colonial Courts should also govern themselves by it."[110]

It is tempting to give unreserved approval to this line of reasoning by their Lordships. After all, the Commonwealth Courts ought to benefit from the experience of the English Courts who have construed the provisions and it could be inferred that the copying legislature also intended to adopt the interpretation placed on those provisions in judicial decisions, more so if the decisions were made before the Commonwealth legislature passed the Act. But one of the cardinal features of this theory is that the legislature is consistent in its use of language. The first objection is, of course, that in this case different legislatures are involved. Another objection is that this practice of following the construction placed on enactments by English Courts could easily be overdone. It is not very helpful to argue that a statute enacted by one legislature is in *pari materia* with an Act of a different legislative body. In fact their Lordships of the Privy Council recognised in *Grand Trunk Railway* v. *Washington*,[111] an appeal from Canada, that

> " As these are enactments emanating from a different legislative body from that which passed the Statute to be interpreted and cannot be said to be in pari materia with that, their Lordships are unable to see that they ought to have any influence upon the question to be decided arising exclusively upon the Dominion Act, and relating only to Dominion Railways."[112]

To the same effect is the Ceylon appeal of *Chettiar* v. *Mahamtee*,[113] where their Lordships also pointed out the danger of importing the decisions of English Courts in interpreting local enactments on similar terms as the corresponding English Acts. In *Karam* v. *Commissioner of Income Tax*,[114] it was held by the West African Court of Appeal that it would be unsafe for the Ghana Courts to rely on English authority in tax cases. It is respectfully submitted that there can be no question of the Nigerian Courts being bound by decisions of English Courts on statutes which are in similar terms to local ones. At best, these decisions should be of persuasive authority and the degree of their persuasiveness should be determined by the position in the judicial hierarchy of the English Court that made the decision.[115]

The Privy Council

The position of the Privy Council in England is a very peculiar one. Although it is an English institution, yet it is not, except in prize, Ecclesiastical and Admiralty cases considered as part of the English judicial system.[116] Its decisions, except perhaps on the above matters, are not binding on the English Court of Appeal,[117] or even on an English Divisional Court.[118] They are obviously not binding on the House of Lords.[119] But the observation in the *City of Chester* (1884) L.R.9 P.D.182 that " In mercantile or admiralty law, where the same principles are followed in the colonies as in this country (England), it is highly undesirable that there should be any conflict between the decisions of the Judicial Committee and those of the High Court or Courts of Appeal in this country,"[120] seems to leave us with the impression that in these matters the High Courts and the Courts of Appeal are bound by the decisions of the Privy Council.

The Board was also till lately the last Court of Appeal for Ghana and Nigeria. It is still the final Court of Appeal for the colonies and some of the Dominions. Thus we had a curious situation whereby the Council was both a Ghanaian and a Nigerian Court as well as an English Court.

The significance of the Board is twofold for our purpose here. Firstly, what is the authority of its previous decisions in Ghanaian and Nigerian Courts? Secondly, what was or still is its practice with regard to the binding nature of judicial precedent, which practice the Supreme Courts of Ghana and Nigeria as the Board's successors may have inherited?

The Authority of Privy Council Decisions

Here a distinction must be made between decisions of the Board arising out of appeals from a particular territory on the one hand, and appeals from other territories on the other. It is necessary to make this vital distinction because of the growing habit of certain writers and judges to cite decisions of the Council arising from appeals from other Commonwealth courts as binding authority in the Nigerian Courts.[121] It is submitted with respect that only the first category of the Board's decisions are binding on the Nigerian Courts. This must be so for the simple reason that it is only when hearing an appeal from Nigeria that the Privy Council was sitting as a Nigerian Court. It is further respectfully submitted that the observation of the Supreme Court of Nigeria in *Thomas* v. *Ademol II and Others*,[122] that

> " Colonial courts must give precedence to the decisions of the Privy Council before those of any other tribunal ",

lays down too wide a principle and was unnecessary for the decision of the case.[123] In fact a contrary view is by inference supported by the Authority of the Board itself in the Zanzibar appeal of *Fatuma Binti Mohammed Bin Salim Bakhshuwen* v. *Mohammed Bin Bakhshuwen*.[124] In that case their Lordships warned against the assumption that its judgments in a series of cases from India on points of Mohammedan Law were confined to that law as applied in India. It was stressed that on a question of Mohammedan Law, which was alleged to be the same in East Africa as in India, the judgments of the Privy Council in appeals from India must be taken as binding on the East African Court of Appeal. Thus where there is no such similarity the Board's decisions will not be binding on the courts of another territory. This view is further strengthened by the case of *Negro* v. *Pietro's Bread Co. Ltd.*,[125] where the Ontario Court of Appeal declined to follow the Privy Council decision in *Victoria Railway Comm.* v. *Coultas*.[126] Their reason was that since the latter case was a New Zealand appeal it was not binding on the Canadian Courts. An analogy can be drawn to the practice of the Scottish Courts who feel that they are not bound by the decisions[127] of the House of Lords on appeals other than those from Scottish Courts. Thus it was held in *Glasgow Corporation* v. *Central Land Board*[128] that a decision of an English appeal does not override a different, pre-existing rule of Scots law. Thus the House of Lords decision in *Duncan* v. *Cammel, Laird & Co.*[129] which laid down the rule concerning the Court's discretion as to privileged documents, was said not to apply to Scotland. The position is, of course, different where English law and Scottish law are the same on a particular subject. It is submitted that this attitude is the correct one and should be adopted by the Nigerian Courts in relation to Privy Council decisions on appeals from other than Nigerian courts.[130]

NOTES

1. See T. O. Elias, "Colonial Courts and the doctrine of judicial precedent" (1955) 18 M.L.R. 356; A. N. Allott, "The authority of English decisions in colonial courts" (1957) 1 J.A.L. 23; *Essays*, 6. 28; A. J. Kerr, "The reception and codification of systems of law in Southern Africa" (1958) 2 J.A.L. 82; Sir Kenneth Roberts-Wray, "The adaptation of imported law in Africa" (1960) 4 J.A.L. 66; F. A. Ajayi, "English law and Customary law in Western Nigeria" (1960) 4 J.A.L. 98; N. A. Ollennu, "The influence of English law on West Africa" (1961) 5 J.A.L. 21; See also Sir Kenneth Roberts-Wray, *Commonwealth & Colonial law*, (London, Stevens, 1966); Allott, "Judicial Precedent in Africa Revisited" (1968) J.A.L., p. 1.
2. S. 17 (4) of the Interpretation Act, 1960 (C.A.4.).
3. For the current provision on the subject, see Paragraph 2 (3) of the Courts Decree, 1966.
4. S. 17 of the Interpretation Act, 1960 (C.A.4.).
5. N.L.C.D. No. 84.
6. C.A.9.

7. See N. A. Ollennu, Speech to Sarbah Society, Sept. 1962 (Unpublished); S. K. B. Asante, " Stare decisis in the Supreme Court of Ghana " (1964), University of Gh.L.J. 52; W. C. E. Daniels, *Common law in West Africa* (1964), pp. 182 et seq.

8. There is no Nigerian equivalent of the Ghana Courts Act that is effective all over the country. There are Regional High Court laws and a High Court of Lagos Act.

9. Although certain parts of the Nigerian Constitution were suspended at midnight on Sunday, 16th January, the reception provisions have not been in any way affected.

10. S. 120 of the Nigerian Republican Constitution (1963); and S. 42 (1) of the Ghana Republican Constitution, 1960.

11. See Allott, *Essays*, p. 28.

12. S. 45, Interpretation Act, Cap. 89 Laws of Nigeria (1958).

13. Interpretation Act, Cap. 89 Laws of Nigeria (1958).

14. Northern Nigeria High Court Law, Cap. 49 S. 28 Laws of Northern Nigeria (1963) Revision. In Western Nigeria there is no reference to any dates in the section receiving English common law. It has been argued by Professor Allott that one of the possible meanings of the provision is that current English law as modified by Western Nigerian Courts will be applied.

15. (1896-7) 1, J. of Comp. Leg., p. 146, i.e. the Society for the study of comparative legislation.

16. (1884) Vol. 2. No. 5 Cited by Daniels in his book, *Common Law in West Africa*, p. 123.

17. Op. cit., p. 3.

18. Odgers, *The Construction of deeds and statutes, (4th ed.)*, p. 220.

19. Ghana Interpretation Act, 1960, C.A.4; Nigeria (Federation and Lagos) Interpretation Act, 1964.

20. (1928) 9, N.L.R. 99 at p. 100.

21. My emphasis.

22. Park, *Sources of Nigerian law*, p. 21.

23. Allott, " The Authority of English decisions in Colonial Courts " (1957) 1, J.A.L. 23; *Essays*, p. 28; " The common law of Nigeria " (1965) I.C.L.Q. Supplement, p. 31. See Allott, " The Nigerian common law " (1964) I.C.L.Q. Supplement; " Judicial Precedent in Africa Revisited " (1968) J.A.L. 1.

24. Probate, Divorce and Matrimonial Causes.

25. Western Nigeria, Law of England (Application) Law.

26. Northern Nigeria High Court Law, Cap. 49, S. 28.

27. Ghana, Interpretation Act, (1960) S. 17 C.A.4. Cf. the position in Liberia where Article VI of the Constitution for the Government of the African Colony at Liberia, 1825, stated that the common law, as in force in the U.S. shall apply in Liberia. Here the reception of the common law is dateless. See R. H. Culp, " Sources of Liberian Law " (1966) 2 Liberia L.J. 130.

28. N. A. Ollennu, " The Influence of English law on West Africa." Text of a lecture delivered at the University of Hull, 13th October, 1960. (1961) 5 J.A.L. 21.

29. Ibid at p. 24.

30. Cf. Roscoe Pound in " Common Law " (1931), 4 Enc. Soc. Sci. 53.

31. 15 Corpus Juris Secundum, " Common law ", p. 617 (1939 Edn.). Cited by Dr. Daniels, *Common Law in West Africa*, p. 122.

32. See Sir Lionel Brett, "Stare decisis in Nigeria—Some Random thoughts" (1965) 6 N.B.J. 74.
33. Common Law (1931) 4 Enc. Soc. Sci. 53.
34. My emphasis.
35. My emphasis.
36. Cited by Professor Mark Dewolfe Howe, *The Migration of the Common Law* (ed. A. L. Goodhart, 1960), p. 13.
37. See Howe op. cit., p. 14.
38. Cf. Sir Kenneth Roberts-Wray, "The adaptation of imported law in Africa" (1960) 4 J.A.L. 66; Kerr, "The reception and codification of systems of law in Southern Africa"; Daniels, *Common Law in West Africa*, p. 122.
39. (1955) A.C. 130.
40. (1912) A.C. 716.
41. Supra.
42. (1912) A.C. 716.
43. (1905) 1 K.B. 237.
44. (1955) A.C. 130 at p. 144.
45. (1905) 1 K.B. 237.
46. See the Tanganyika case of *Dabholkar V.R.* (1948) A.C. 221 P.C. and the Hong Kong appeal of *Civil Air Transport* v. *Central Air Transport* (1953) A.C. 70 in which the Privy Council applied post-reception date common law principles.
47. Mention has already been made of the recent provisions in Ghana and some jurisdictions in Nigeria.
48. Elias in his article, "Colonial courts and the doctrine of judicial precedent," uses the neutral word "apply" in referring to the authority of the decision of English courts in the colonial courts. Also per Mr. Justice Ollennu at p. 39 of his article supra, "The courts of the Commonwealth countries of West Africa have hitherto been guided and bound by decisions of superior courts in England."
49. Cf. Kerr, "The Reception and codification of systems of law in Southern Africa" (1958) 2 J.A.L. 82. "When there is a decision, given before reception, in a court in the country from which the system of law has been received and when that court is superior in rank to the court called upon to decide a matter in the receiving country, the difference in rank is a factor requiring consideration," at p. 85. It is submitted that this statement cannot be true of the ultimate courts of appeal in Ghana and Nigeria for the simple reason that no other court can be of a superior rank to the territorial final appeal courts. The case for Ghana is further strengthened by a statutory provision, *The Interpretation Act, Section 17.* See also *Amissah* v. *Amissah*, Div. Ct. (1926-9) (Ghana) where Yates, J. regarded himself bound by *Stoate* v. *Stoate* (1861) 3 L.T. 757.
50. (1955) A.C. 130, P.C.
51. *Robins* v. *National Trust Co. Ltd.* (1927) A.C. 515.
52. No. 34 of 1961.
53. No. 63 of 1961.
54. No. 64 of 1961.
55. (1959) 2, N.B.J. 29.
56. (1955) 1 All E.R. 646 at p. 653. See also (1956) 1 Q.B. 1 99 Sot. Jo. 218; affirmed (1956) 2 All E.R. 689 by H.L.; (1957) A.C. 253; 100 Sol. Jo. 489; 3rd Dig. Supp.

57. Art. 15 No. 661 of 1902 is amended by the 1911 Order (S. R & O. 1911 No. 243).
58. See also Allott, *Essays*, p. 25; Park, *Sources of Nigerian Law*, p. 38; Daniels, *Common Law*, p. 188.
59. Daniels, *Common Law*, pp. 188 et seq.
60. On Ghana, see *Amissah* v. *Amissah*, Div. Court Rep. (1926-9) where Yates, J. regarded himself as bound by the English decision in *Stoate* v. *Stoate* (1861) 3 L.T. 757, a case relating to the time of the discharge of an order for payment of alimony; *Hage* v. *Oda Sawmills Ltd.*, per Ollennu, J: H.Ct. Suit No. 35/1958, Unreported (contract damages); *Allotey* v. *Ghana Aluminum Products Ltd.*; Mills-Odoi, J.; H.Ct. Suit No. 14/60, unreported (admissibility of oral evidence to vary a written contract).
   On Nigeria, see *MacIver and Co. Ltd.* v. *C.F.A.O.* (1917) 3, N.L.R. 16; *Lawson* v. *Siffre and Mati*, Coker (1932) 11, N.L.R. 138; *Onuchugu* v. *Christiana Williams* (1935) 12, N.L.R. 19; *Bada* v. *The Premier Thrift Society* (1936) 13, N.L.R. 47.
61. (1927) A.C. 515 P.C. See particularly Lord Dunedin's statement of the position at p. 519.
62. (1964) N.M.L.R. (Dec.) 117.
63. Op. cit., p. 118.
64. *Ugboma* v. *Morah* (1940) 15, N.L.R. 78.
65. Op. cit. at p. 82. See also *Labinjoh* v. *Abake* (1924) 5, N.L.R. 33, where it was held by Combe, C.J. that if there is a native custom whereby an unmarried girl living with her parent or guardian will not be held liable for the price of goods supplied to her for trading purposes without her parent's consent, the court (at a retrial) should consider whether such custom should not be applied instead of English law. Here, of course, the English law referred to was the *Infants Relief Act, 1874.*
66. J. Stone, *Province and Function of Law*, p. 495.
67. (1894) A.C. 535. See also *Fender* v. *St. John Mildmay* (1938) A.C. 1, 23.
68. At p. 553.
69. pp. 240 et seq., infra.
70. (1835) 2 C.L. and Fin. 433.
71. (1866) L.R. 1 P. and D. 130.
72. *Bamgbose* v. *Daniel* (1954) 3 All E.R. 263 P.C. (1955) A.C. 107; *Ohochuku* v. *Ohochuku* (1960) 1 All E.R. 253 (1960) 1 W.L.R. 183; *Coleman* v. *Shang* (1959) G.L.R. 390, on appeal (1961) A.C. 481 P.C. It must be added that *Hyde* v. *Hyde* is not yet overruled.
73. *Dowodu* v. *Dunmole* (1962) 1 W.L.R. 1053; *Tairro* v. *Lawani L. Anor* (1961) 1 All N.L.R. 703. Cf. *Cole* v. *Cole* (1898) 1 N.L.R. 15.
74. (1962) 1 W.L.R. 1053.
75. (1956) (2) 5 A. 696 (S.W.A.). Cited by A. J. Kerr in the " Reception and Codification of Systems of Law in Southern Africa " (1958) 2 J.A.L. 82.
76. *Essays*, p. 33.
77. Although in many cases the same panel of judges may serve the House of Lords as the Privy Council.
78. Brett, *Stare Decisis in Nigeria*, p. 74 (1965) 6 N.B.J. 74.
79. (1962) N.Z. L.R. 878.
80. (1942) A.C. 624.
81. (1963) A.L.R. 524; (1964) 38 A.L.J. 285; (1964) 3 W.L.R. 70.

82. (1961) A.C. 2.
83. (1952) 66 C.L.R. 358 at p. 365.
84. Supra.
85. My emphasis.
86. Op. cit. p. 537. See also A. L. Goodhart (1963) 79, L.Q.R., 313.
87. *Essays*, p. 33.
88. The above discussion on the authority of English decisions under common law and equity has been inevitably confined to non-criminal and non-constitutional law decisions. Fascinating as it is to investigate the impact of English decisions on the criminal laws of Ghana and Nigeria, and the place of constitutional conventions in the constitutional laws of the two countries, these are only remotely germane to our subject of enquiry. The above discussion has therefore been restricted to civil obligations. As neither Ghana nor Nigeria has codified their laws of contract and tort we have not found it necessary to discuss the effect of codification on the authority of English decisions.
89. Allott, *Essays*, p. 40.
90. Since the same argument holds good for Nigeria as for Ghana as far as the statutes go, reference to Nigerian courts in the sub-head will be deemed to include reference to the Ghana Courts.
91. Cap. 89, Laws of the Federation of Nigeria and Lagos. See also S. 154 of the Ghana Courts Act, C.A. 9: " Provided that the said statutes shall be subject to such modification as may be requisite to enable them to be conveniently applied in Ghana."
92. (1961) 1 All N.L.R. 245.
93. (1954) 3 All E.R. 264; (1955) A.C. 107.
94. (1959) G.L.R. 390, affirmed (1961) A.C. 481. See also the recent Nigerian case of *Obadara & ors.* v. *The President*, Ibadan West District Council Grade " B" Customary Ct. (1965) N.M.L.R. 39.
95. Such statutes were generally said to apply in all Her Majesty's Dominions. Ghana became a Republic on 1st July, 1960 and Nigeria adopted a Republican Constitution on 1st October, 1963.
96. See Ghana Independence Act, 1957, 5 & 6 Eliz. 2.
97. Cap. 21, Laws of Nigeria (1958) Revision.
98. Cap. 22.
99. Ch. 61 (1882 statutes).
100. Ch. 43 (1882 statutes).
101. Cap. 37 (1958) Revision.
102. No. 33 of 1961.
103. No. 64 of 1961.
104. See Property and Conveyancing Law, Cap. 100, Laws of Western Nigeria.
105. On Ghana see Bill of Exchange Act, 1961 (Act 55); Administration of Estates Act, 1961 (Act 63); Sale of Goods Act, 1962 (Act 137); Workmen's Compensation Act, 1963 (Act 174); Civil Liability Act, 1963 (Act 176) and Merchant Shipping Act, 1963 (Act 183). These are material re-enactments (in some cases, better drafting) of the Corresponding English Statutes.
106. (1879) 5 App. Cas. 342.
107. The Colonial Act 14 Vict. No. 9, S. 8. In the same terms as 8 & 9 Vict. C. 109, S. 8.
108. Per Sir Montague E. Smith who read the judgment of the Board, at p. 344.

109. *Diggle* v. *Higgs*, 2 Ex. D. 422. See also *Catterall* v. *Sweetman* (1845) 9 Jur. 951.
110. This decision was followed in *Hunt* v. *Fripp* (1898) 1 Ch. 675.
111. (1899) A.C. 275.
112. Op. cit. at p. 286.
113. (1950) A.C. 481; but cf. the West African Court of Appeal decision in *Motayo* v. *Commissioner of Police* (1950) 13, W.A.C.A. 114.
114. (1948) 12, W.A.C.A. 331.
115. See further, Allott, *Essays*, p. 43; *Staines* v. *Victor La Rosa* (1933) 1 W.L.R. 474. In the recent Kenya Appeal to the Privy Council of *National and Grindlays Bank* v. *Dharamshi & ors* (1966) 2 All E.R. 626, New Zealand cases based on a statute materially similar to the Kenya chattels Transfer Ordinance, 1930, were referred to and approved of as a guide to Kenya courts in construing the Kenya enactment provisions.
116. It also has appellate jurisdiction in determinations of the Disciplinary Committee of the General Medical Council (by the Medical Act, 1950); and also certain default powers under the Profession Supplementary to Medicine Act, 1960.
117. In *Fanton* v. *Denville* (1932) 2 K.B. 309, Greer, L.J. refused to follow the Privy Council's decision in *Toronto Power Company* v. *Paskwan* (1915) A.C. 734, describing the latter decision as inconsistent with the whole trend of the English decisions. Also in *Re Hastings* No. 3 (1959) 1 All E.R. 698, the Court of Appeal refused to follow the Privy Council decision in the Nigerian appeal of *Eleko* v. *Government of Nigeria* (1928) A.C. 459.
118. In *Port Line Ltd.* v. *Ren Line Steamers Ltd.* (1958) 2 Q.B. 146, Diplock, J. declined to follow the Privy Council decision in *Lord Strathcona Steamship Co. Ltd.* v. *Dominion Coal Co. Ltd.* (1926) A.C. 108. See also *Venn* v. *Tedesco* (1926) 2 K.B. 227, *Lynn* v. *Ramber* (1930) 2 K.B. 72; *Dulieu* v. *White* (1901) 2 K.B. 669. Cf. *Smith* v. *Leach Brain & Co.* (1962) 2 Q.B. 405, where Lord Parker, C.J. preferred the Privy Council decision in the *Wagon Mound* (1961) A.C. 388 to the Court of Appeal decision in *Re Polemis* (1921) 3 K.B. 560.
119. *Absalom* v. *Talbot* (1944) A.C. 204; *Bristow* v. *Dickenson* (1946) K.B. 321; *Duncan* v. *Cammel Laird & Co.* (1942) A.C. 624.
120. Op. cit at p. 207.
121. See McNeil and Rains, *Nigerian Cases and Statutes on Contract and Tort* (1965) passim.
122. (1945) 18, N.L.R. 12. See also *Onogen* v. *Leventis* (1959) G.L.R. 105, cf. *Goodwin* v. *Crowther* (1934) W.A.C.A. 109.
123. See also the New Zealand case of *Stevenson* v. *Basham & Another* (1922) N.Z.L.R. 225, where a similar attitude was adopted by the New Zealand High Court.
124. (1952) A.C. 1, cf. J. N. D. Anderson who feels that the laws are different, *Islamic Law in Africa*, pp. 96-7, 340-2.
125. (1933) O.R. 112.
126. (1887) 13 App. Cas. 22.
127. Except perhaps pronouncements of " general jurisprudence." But cf. Prof. Walker, " Some Characteristics of Scots Law " 18 M.L.R. 321.
128. (1955) S.L.T. 155; and (1956) S.L.T. 41.
129. (1942) A.C. 624.
130. As to the position in Ghana, see the discussion on judicial precedent in the Ghana Court of Appeal, infra.

CHAPTER 3

JUDICIAL PRECEDENT IN GHANA AND NIGERIA

The pros and cons of the binding nature of judicial precedent in English law need not detain us here, nor are we concerned with a comparative study of the Anglo-American and Continental practices on the subject. It is enough to say that any workable system of binding judicial precedent depends for its success on three primary pre-requisites. These are: an easily ascertainable hierarchical system of courts; an efficient and fairly reliable system of law-reporting, and an independent Bar, i.e. of legal practitioners. In England, since the nineteenth century, these three conditions appear to be present. This is exemplified in the often cited dictum of Park, J.; in *Mirehouse* v. *Rennell*,[1] that

> " Our common law system consists in the applying to new combinations of circumstances those rules of law which we derive from legal principles and judicial precedents; and for the sake of attaining uniformity, consistency and certainty, we must apply these rules, where they are not plainly unreasonable and inconvenient, to all cases which arise; and we are not at liberty to reject them, and to abandon all analogy to them, in those to which they have not yet been judicially applied, because we think that the rules are not as convenient and reasonable as we ourselves could have devised. It appears to me to be of great importance to keep this principle of decision steadily in view, not merely for the determination of the particular cause, but for the interests of law as a science."

This dictum is, of course, an elaboration of Blackstone's statement that " it is an established rule to abide by former precedents except when they are contrary to reason."[2] There have been a number of decisions in English Courts since 1883, laying down that the Divisional Courts are bound by their previous decisions;[3] that the Court of Appeal is bound by its previous decisions,[4] and that the House of Lords is also bound by its previous decisions.[5]

Judicial precedent in the Privy Council:

Although the Privy Council is no longer part of the court structure of either Ghana or Nigeria, yet its practice with regard to judicial precedent is still of considerable interest in the two countries for two reasons. Firstly, the attitude of the Judicial Committee towards its previous decisions, particularly when such previous decisions come from a jurisdiction different from that of a case in point, will determine, to some extent, the attitude of the final courts of appeal in Ghana and Nigeria towards such cases. Secondly, since the Privy Council was, till recently, the last court of appeal for the two countries, their practice in precedent matters might serve as a guide to the present penultimate courts of appeal in both Ghana and Nigeria, particularly in the latter territory where there are no statutory provisions regulating judicial precedent.

There appears to be an apparent conflict in the authorities as to whether or not the Privy Council is bound to follow its previous decisions. In *Gideon Nkambule* v. *R*,[6] a Swaziland appeal, the Board declined to follow their previous decision[7] on the construction of section 231 of the Swaziland Criminal Procedure and Evidence Proclamation, 1938 (as amended by Proclamation No. 14 of 1944), and adopted the attitude of the former English court of Criminal Appeal. This was stated by Lord Parker in *R.* v. *Taylor*,[8] to be that a Full Court would, when the liberty of the subject was involved, not feel absolutely bound by a previous decision, which in its opinion was wrong.

But in *Attorney-General for Ontario* v. *Canada Temperance Federation*,[9] the Board felt bound by its decision in *Russell* v. *Reg*,[10] on the ground that the latter decision established a principle which was deeply embedded in the constitutional law of Canada. This former case has been widely relied on by writers as laying down the principle that the Board is bound by its previous decisions in constitutional law cases. But the dictum of Viscount Simon who read the judgment of the Board, that

> " Their Lordships do not doubt that in tending humble advice to His Majesty they are not absolutely bound by previous decisions of the Board, as is the House of Lords by its own judgments,"[11]

cannot be said to lend support to any rigid theory of binding judicial precedent. On the contrary, in the case of *Mercantile Bank of India* v. *Central Bank of India*,[12] the Board refused to follow its own previous decision in *Commonwealth Trust* v. *Allotey*,[13] a Ghana appeal. An attempt to reconcile the decisions in these cases can be attempted along the following lines. The Privy Council is in principle bound by its previous decisions. The fact that the appeals arise from different jurisdictions does not affect this principle. But the Board may refuse to follow a previous decision, (1) on the principle in *R. v. Taylor* as mentioned above; and/or (2) if the older decision is, in the opinion of the Board, no longer good law, having regard to all the circumstances.[14]

Judicial precedent in Ghana:[15]

As has already been shown in another sub-section, the essential requirements of any workable system of binding judicial precedent are a unified hierarchical arrangement of courts, a reliable and regular system of law-reporting, and an independent Bar (which includes the Bench). As far as the first requirement goes, the Courts Act, 1960, established in Ghana, a kind of judicial pyramid with the Local Courts at the base and the Supreme Court at the apex. The present position, however, is that contained in the recent Courts Decree of the National Liberation Council. This decree establishes a Supreme Court of Judicature, consisting of the Court of Appeal and the High Courts (these constitute the Superior Courts of Ghana), and the Circuit and District Courts.[16] The Local Courts which were established under Section 92 of the Courts Act, 1960, have been abolished and it appears[17] that their jurisdiction has been transferred to the District Courts.

Appeals from District Courts in civil and criminal matters lie to the High Court.[18] Above the District Courts are the Circuit Courts,[19] which could be described as a strange hybrid of the English Quarter Sessions, the County Courts, and a bit of the English High Court jurisdiction in civil matters where the amount involved does not exceed C 4,800 (i.e. £2,000). Then there is the High Court[20] whose jurisdiction and powers are similar to those of a Divisional Court in England, and to which appeals lie in criminal matters from the District Courts, and in civil matters from the Circuit Courts. The Court of appeal is at the apex of the judicial system.[21]

The second requirement is law-reporting. It is, of course, essential that a judgment which is being cited and relied upon as an authority should be available to both the Bench and the profession. Unfortunately, the history of law reporting in Ghana as in other parts of West Africa has not been at all encouraging. This of course explains, though it does not justify, the all too ready reliance on the handy reports of English Courts. The first reports in Ghana, those of John Mensah Sarbah, appeared in 1896, twenty years after the enactment of the first Supreme Court Ordinance in 1876. Even these were essentially on Fanti Customary Law. The Fanti Law Reports followed in 1906 edited also by Sarbah. Between 1907 and 1919, law reporting was in its doldrums. There were, however, sporadic attempts by both the Bench and the Bar as evidenced in the two volumes of *Renner's Reports* and those of Earnshaw in 1910. In 1920 there was instituted a kind of official reports of the Divisional and Full Courts which slowly ground to a halt in 1937. The establishment of the West African Courts of Appeal started a new series, usually called the W.A.C.A. reports. These, like its predecessors, were most irregular. Ten years elapsed between the publication of 11 W.A.C.A. in 1946 and the publication in 1956 of 12, 13 and 14 W.A.C.A! Volume 15 appeared in 1957.

The years 1956 and 1957 saw a new series called the West African Law Reports which ceased to exist after the publication of the first three volumes. Since 1959 there have been the Ghana Law Reports organised by the General Legal Council which was established by the Legal Practitioners' Act, 1958. But in spite of its ambitious take-off (three volumes were published in 1959) it is still six years behind the cases in the courts. But the reports of the decisions of English Courts are always available and are freely cited. We discussed their authority in another place.

It remains to add that on the third requirement, the Bench and Bar in Ghana are as independent as they could be in spite of heavy knocks from the executive in 1963.

We shall proceed to examining which decisions bind which courts in Ghana. It needs hardly be argued that Ghana inherited the common law tradition of judicial precedent as laid down in *Blackstone's Commentaries*[22] and by Parke, J. in *Mirehouse* v. *Rennell*[23] to which reference has already been made. The common practice has always been that courts which are lower in the judicial hierarchy consider themselves bound by the decisions of courts higher in the judicial pyramid. Thus, the District and Circuit Courts will consider themselves bound by the decisions of the Supreme Court. It appears, however, that the opinions of a Superior Customary Court on a question of customary law will be accorded high persuasive force in the Supreme Court, as shown in this pointed dictum of the Ghana Court of Appeal (as it then was) in *Anane* v. *Mensah*,[24] that

> " Native Customary law is peculiarly within the knowledge of the Native Courts, and the opinion of a superior native court on native custom must be preferred to the opinion of an inferior native court, unless it is either contrary to a decision of the Supreme Court or the Privy Council on the point."

The handicap in this regard is that cases decided in the Customary Courts, except those that go on appeal to the Superior Courts are not reported. This is equally true of the District Courts. The decision of one circuit judge will not be binding on another circuit judge although the latter will be reluctant to depart from the principle laid down in such previous decisions.

The High Court

The position in the High Court is a bit more complex. Under paragraph 2 (3) of the Courts Decree, 1966, the High Court is bound to follow the previous decisions of the Court of Appeal, although it is not bound by the decisions of any other court on questions of law. The provision is, however, silent on the question as to whether or not the High Court of Ghana is bound by its own previous decisions. This question has also been posed by the learned editors of the *Ghana Current Cases*, under the heading of " Stare decisis, what binds whom? " Now, section 89 (3) of the Courts Act, 1960, which Act repealed the former Courts Ordinances,[25] made savings for pre-1960 practice and procedure.[26] Although paragraph 86 of the Courts Decree, 1966[27] empowers the Rules Committee established under that paragraph to make rules regulating practice and procedure, the position is still the same as it was under the Courts Act, 1960, which was repealed by the Courts Decree, since no such rules have been made. It could therefore be argued that the practice and procedure of the English High Court of Justice still covers the position in Ghana. This position was re-stated in *Osborn* v. *Rowlett*,[28] that " while a High Court judge will always follow a decision of another judge of co-ordinate jurisdiction, he is not bound by it and if, after careful considera- tion, he comes to the conclusion that he does not agree with it, it would be his duty to depart from it." It is submitted that the High Court in Ghana is not absolutely bound by its previous decisions made in the exercise of its original jurisdiction. On the other hand, decisions made in the exercise of its appellate jurisdiction, i.e. on appeals from the District and Circuit Courts, should be binding unless such decisions were made in ignorance of a Statutory pro- vision, a decision of the Ghana Supreme Court or any of its prede- cessors in functions, or inconsistent with an earlier decision of the High Court which was binding. It appears that the principle enunciated by Brown C. J. in the Northern Nigerian case of *Olowayin* v. *Attorney-General*,[29] that the High Court is bound by its previous decision given in the exercise of its appellate jurisdic- tion, is equally applicable in Ghana. This is because Section 35 of the Northern Nigeria High Court law is in the same terms as Sections 15 and 84 of the Ghana Supreme Court Ordinance (Cap. 4 of 1951). It has already been shown that those provisions of the Supreme Court Ordinance were retained under Section 89 (3) of the

G

Courts Act, 1960, and that the later provisions are still in force, although they could be altered under paragraph 86 of the Courts Decree, 1966.

Precedent in the Court of Appeal

Paragraph 2 (3) of the Courts Decree, 1966, provides as follows:

> "The Court of Appeal shall be bound in principle to follow its own previous decisions on questions of law and the High Court shall be bound to follow the previous decisions of the Court of Appeal, but neither Court shall be otherwise bound to follow the previous decisions of any Court on questions of law."

This provision which is a re-enactment of Article 42 (2) of the Ghana Republican Constitution, has been the subject of some controversy recently. The sitting targets of this powder and shot have been (1) the meaning and significance of the words " in principle " for purposes of coercive judicial precedent; and (2) the meaning and content of the phrase " its previous decisions ". Bennion[30] has argued that

> "Article 42 (2) is intended to provide a suitable combination of certainty and flexibility in the enunciation and development of legal principles. Once the Supreme Court, as the highest court available to Ghanaians, has delivered itself of a proposition of law relevant to its decision in a particular case, that proposition is binding without modification in the High Court and the inferior Courts. It is also binding in principle on the Supreme Court itself, but the use in this occasion of the expression ' in principle ' is intended to indicate that the Supreme Court may in a particular case depart from its own previous decision if it considers that the decision was given per incuriam or should for any other exceptional reason not be followed."[31]

In accepting the learned author's explanation of the meaning of the phrase " in principle," Asante[32] has suggested that " exceptional reason " should include situations where the previous decision was wrong,[33] or where in the fullness of experience the decision proved " no longer responsive to the needs of the society." Asante has further argued that since there is a constitutional provision for judicial review of legislation in Ghana, a rigid adherence to precedent would have the undesirable effect of depriving the Supreme Court, in constitutional cases, of the power to change its mind about the meaning of an entrenched clause. This would leave the clauses more rigid than they need be. He bemoaned the ineptitude of resorting to constitutional amendment which in some cases requires a referendum. In a very informative survey the learned author reviewed the practice in six Commonwealth and ex-Commonwealth countries, bringing in the United States practice for good measure. The conclusion he came to was that apart from England and Malaysia, no other common law country still kept any doctrine of coercive judicial precedent in her final court of appeal. He concluded that this explains the insertion of the phrase " in principle " in the Ghana Supreme Court provision and that it meant no more than that the Court was at liberty to depart from a previous decision " when considerations of good policy so demand."

In this he is at one with Daniels.[34]

The contrary view has however, been put forward by Mr. Justice Ollennu.[35] He maintains that the Supreme Court is bound by its previous decisions. The learned judge's evidence for this startling proposition will be examined in the next section.

As to the meaning and content of " previous decisions," Professor Harvey in his inaugural lecture at the University of Ghana posed these questions:

> " If only the decisions of the Supreme Court are in future to be binding, what is the ' Supreme Court ' for this purpose? Is the Court as constituted under the Republican Constitution to be deemed to be a new court, so that only Republican decisions are fully authoritative? Or is a theory of antecedent and continuing existence to be applied?"

In an attempt to answer the above queries, Mr. Justice Ollennu has had this to say:

> " We may ask: is the term ' previous decisions of the Supreme Court ' to be limited strictly to decisions of that Court given after July 1, 1960, the date the Constitution and the Courts Act, 1960, C.A.9 came into effect? In other words, is it only a decision of the Supreme Court as established in 1960 which should be authoritative precedent, and all decisions of any other court whatsoever, be only persuasive? To answer that question we have to bear in mind that the Courts Act consolidated and reproduced in substance the essential features of the Courts Ordinance, Cap. 4, and the Court of Appeal Ordinance 1957, which itself reproduced the West African Court of Appeal Ordinance, Cap. 5; further that by creating the Supreme Court a final Court of Appeal, and the simultaneous repeal by the Constitution (Consequential Provisions) Act, 1960, C.A.8, of the Judicial Committee Act, 1833, and the revocation of the West African Court of Appeal Orders in Council, 1948-1957, and the Ghana (Appeal to Privy Council) Order in Council 1957 (L.N.215), the Supreme Court as established under the Constitution stepped into the shoes of and assumed the juris-

diction of both the Court of Appeal—the West African Court of Appeal and the Privy Council in so far as it affected Ghana and no more. That being the case, it is respectfully submitted that the authoritative decisions which, under Article 42, Section 4 of the Constitution, both the Supreme Court and the High Court are bound to follow, comprise and include decisions of the Privy Council in Ghanaian cases given prior to 1960, those made by the Privy Council under and by virtue of Section 16 of the Constitution (Consequential Provisions) Act, 1960, C.A.8, and it also includes decisions of the Court of Appeal, of the West African Court of Appeal, as well as decisions of the Former Full Court."

It must be recognised, however, that it is one thing to contend that the Ghana Supreme Court is absolutely bound by its previous decisions, and quite another to delimit the scope and content of these previous decisions. Thus, even if we accept the learned judge's contention about the meaning of " previous decisions," it could still be validly argued that all these decisions are binding in principle only, and the court may decline to follow any decision of any of its predecessors in functions if in its opinion the said decision no longer represents the law on any particular matter. Neither the Privy Council[36] nor the West African Court of Appeal[37] was absolutely bound by its previous decisions on points of law. In the Nigerian case of *Re Macaulay, Re Adadevoh* the West African Court of Appeal refused to follow its earlier decision in *re Williams*.[38] In the latter decision it had been held that as against a child of a marriage under the Marriage Ordinance, the issue of a valid customary marriage had no share in the father's property on his death intestate. In refusing to be bound by this earlier decision, Verity C. J. who read the judgment of the Court said :

" I am fully alive to the fact that grave inconvenience may arise from a judgment of this court in such a matter which reverses a view of the law which has been held for upwards of ten years, but when the court is faced with the alternative of perpetuating what it is satisfied is an erroneous decision which was reached per incuriam and will, if it be followed, inflict hardship and injustice upon generations in the future or of causing temporary disturbance of rights acquired under such a decision, I do not think we should hesitate to declare the law as we find it."[39]

In declaring the law as they found it their lordships refused to be bound by the Somefun decision.[40] Also in *Osumanu* v. *Amadu*,[41] the West African Court of Appeal declined to be bound by *Domprey* v. *Marfo*.[42] It was stated that the court was in principle bound by its previous decisions. Some exceptions were there laid down as follows :

(1) " The Court is entitled and bound to decide which of two con-
    flicting decisions of its own it will follow.

(2) The Court is bound to refuse to follow a decision of its own
    which, though not expressly overruled, cannot, in its opinion,
    stand with a decision of the Judicial Committee of the Privy
    Council or the House of Lords.

(3) The Court is not bound to follow a decision of its own if it is
    satisfied that the decision was given per incuriam."

As to the practice of the former Full Court and the former
Court of Appeal in Ghana, there does not appear to be any
authority for saying that they were absolutely bound by their
previous decisions.[43]

It is cold comfort to draw analogies to the practice in the House
of Lords as laid down in *London Tramways Co.* v. *London County
Council*.[44] There has been in recent years a growing volume of
protest[45] to the rigidity of precedent in the House as a result of
that decision. The recent observation of Lord Denning in *Ostime
v. Australian Mutual Provident Society*,[46] that

> " The doctrine of precedent does not compel your Lordships to
> follow the wrong path until you fall over the edge of the cliff.
> As soon as you find you are going in the wrong direction, you
> must at least be permitted to strike off in the right direction, even
> if you are not allowed to retreat your steps ",

characterises the general attitude against coercive precedent in the
House of Lords. Professor Goodhart has also recently said hard
things against this practice in the House.[47] The House has had to
give way to this weight of academic and judicial opinion. Mr.
Justice Ollennu's position, therefore, is necessarily a difficult one
to justify except one is compelled to do so by the express words of
the Constitution. If the framers of the Constitution wanted the
Supreme Court to be absolutely bound, they would have said so.
As has been amply stated in the Halsbury's *Laws of England*,[48]

> " It may be presumed: (1) that words are not used in a statute
> without a meaning and so effect must be given, if possible, to all
> the words used, for the legislature is deemed not to waste its
> words or say anything in vain,"

the use of the phrase " in principle " was therefore intended to
empower the Supreme Court to depart from a previous decision
under the circumstances discussed above.

As to whether the Supreme Court created under Article 41 (1)
of the Ghana Constitution was an entirely new court or only

succeeded to the assets and liabilities of the former court of appeal, Daniels has adumbrated the view that it was a new Court. He refers to the Speech[49] of Sir Arku Korsah, the then Chief Justice, made on the 4th July, 1960, which suggested that the Court so created was a new Court and the judges were the first judges of the Republic of Ghana. Daniels further draws a striking parallel with the position in Ireland as laid down in the Irish case of *Exham* v. *Beamish*[50] that the High Court established under the Irish Constitution was a new Court.

As has already been shown, this question is only collateral to the issue of binding precedent in the Supreme Court. It is, however, vital as far as precedent in the High Court and the Lower Courts goes, to know which decisions are binding on them.

Daniels' contention amounts to this: that the Supreme Court in Ghana has no predecessor. Only the decisions that were made after 1st July, 1960, by the said Supreme Court are binding on the Court itself and on the lower courts. Now, how descriptive of the true position is this suggestion? Bennion,[51] one of the draftsmen of the Ghana Republican Constitution and allied enactments, has explained that the provisions of the former Courts Ordinance Cap. 4 (1951), and the other enactments that regulated the Courts in Ghana had been so dismembered by suggested amendments that it became necessary to enact a new and comprehensive Courts Act, similar in scope to the English Judicature Acts 1873-5 and 1925, to replace the various enactments. This new Act was the Courts Act, 1960. Under it the Supreme Court became the final Court of Appeal, appeals to the Privy Council having been abolished. The various divisions of the High Court were unified in a new High Court, the Circuit and District Courts replaced the former Assizes and Chief Magistrates Courts.

The Local Courts were retained with certain jurisdictional amendments. It is astonishing in the extreme to read anything strikingly novel in this structure. Bennion went further to explain that the consequences of clearing the old judicial authority were thought to be so far-reaching (it might for instance deter investors if the law became uncertain!), that it was thought wiser to introduce an element of flexibility in the Supreme Court practice. It is therefore submitted with respect that Mr. Justice Ollennu's view about the scope of the " previous decisions " of the Supreme Court, is the better one.[52]

Judicial Precedent in Nigeria

It will not be necessary here to go over the same arguments as we had been in the case of Ghana as to whether or not Nigeria received the English doctrine of binding judicial precedent. We have sufficiently demonstrated that this aspect of the English common law is part of the received law of Ghana and this is equally true of Nigeria. The next important consideration is to investigate how judicial precedent has been applied in the Nigerian Courts. As in the case of Ghana we shall begin by looking at the history of law reporting in Nigeria and the structure of the courts.

Like in many other West African countries, law reporting in Nigeria has been a rickety structure. We must be quick to point out, however, that this sombre picture has been promptly improved by the timely emergence of the recent Nigerian Monthly Law Reports and the All-Nigeria Law Reports. More will be said about these later.

J. A. Otunba-Payne's Lagos Almanack (1875-1894) could be said to be the first attempt at any kind of law reporting in Nigeria. Here the first Nigerian Registrar of the Court in Lagos compiled among other things, some reports of what he considered to be important decisions of the courts in the Colony of Lagos up to 1894. These reports were the learned Registrar's summaries of such cases. Mention has already been made in another place of *P. A. Renner's Reports* and *H. W. H. Redwar's Comments on some Ordinances of the Gold Coast Colony*. We may add that these works are also relevant for a study of case law in Nigeria since the Gold Coast and Lagos Colonies were jointly administered between 1874 and 1884. It must also be added that the above attempts were neither official nor quasi-official efforts to keep records of decided cases.

Two curious instances of official law reporting can be found in the Old Record Book entitled: " Lagos: Reports of Certain Judgments of the Supreme Court, Vice-Admiralty Court and Full Court of Appeal (1884-1892) "—Law Reports (Colonial), Nigeria-A; and the " Trade Mark: Judgments " (1901-28). The judgments contained in each of these compilations related exclusively to the geographical area of the former Lagos Colony.

It was not until 1916 that the Judicial Department initiated a series of official law Reports, the Nigerian Law Reports. These run to twenty-one volumes, the last of which included cases decided in 1953. We must hasten to add that the standard of reporting could have been considerably higher.[53] Between 1933 and 1955 there were the West African Court of Appeal Reports. These included decisions on appeals from Nigeria. The Nigerian judiciary was regionalised in 1954 and each of the former three regions had its own law reports. There were also the Lagos High Court Reports and the Supreme Court Reports. In 1961 the Incorporated Council for

Law Reporting, a semi-official body was formed by the Federal Government of Nigeria under the chairmanship of the Federal Attorney-General, Dr. T. O. Elias and since 1962 there have been the All Nigeria Law Reports. It is a matter of profound regret that this initially hopeful venture has so far produced only three numbers, the 1961, 1962 and 1963 volumes and even these comprise mainly Supreme Court Judgments. It goes to its credit, however, that the standard of reporting is reasonably high and the indexing is very helpful.

In 1964, a group of private legal practitioners in Ibadan, Nigeria, inaugurated the new and most up to date series of reports in Nigeria. These are the Nigerian Monthly Law Reports.

We shall next be looking at the structure of the Courts in Nigeria. The Supreme Court established under Section III of the Republican Constitution is at the apex of the country's judicial pyramid. In each of the Regions and Lagos[54] there is a High Court with both original and appellate jurisdiction. Appeals lie from the High Courts to the Supreme Court. In all the Regions except the Northern Region there are Magistrates Courts with limited civil and criminal jurisdiction. The Customary Courts[55] in the Eastern, Mid-Western and Western Regions are at the base of the judicial system.[56] Appeals lie from the Customary Courts to the Magistrates or High Courts.

The position in Northern Nigeria was more complicated before the enactment of the Area Courts Edict, 1967. The Native Courts[57] were at the base of the judicial pyramid and there were five grades of native courts, namely, A, A-limited, B, C and D. Appeals from the A and A-limited native courts went to the High Court. But if the applicable law was Islamic Law, appeals from these courts went to the Sharia Court of Appeal. In cases of any doubt as to the law applicable, the case went to the Court of Resolution whose decision on questions of jurisdiction are binding on the High Court. Appeals from grades B, C and D native courts went to the Provincial Courts and thence to the High Court or the Sharia Court of Appeal. There are Magistrates Courts but their jurisdiction is limited to criminal matters,[58] their civil counter-parts are the District Courts. Appeals from the District and Magistrates Courts go to the High Court. One cannot help a feeling of dismay at this complex arrangement. It was no surprise to anybody therefore, when in a broadcast made on 11th February, 1966, the Military Governor of the then Northern Region put forward some proposals which if implemented would radically reform the Customary Court system of that Region. In fact in 1967, the Area Courts Edict[59] was enacted which repealed the Native Courts Law, 1956. For our purpose here two facets of the Edict require brief comment. Firstly the complex 5-tier system of native court structure has been demolished. In its place one has the Area Courts in three grades. These are the Grades 1, 2 and 3 Area Courts. There are also the Upper Area Courts.

Secondly the appeal system has been very considerably simplified. Appeals lie from any Grade of Area Courts to the Upper Area Court. Further appeals lie from the Upper Area Court to the Sharia Court of Appeal in cases involving Moslem law. In other cases appeal lies to the High Court.

As to whether or not the customary or Area Courts are bound by their previous decisions, there is no direct statutory or judicial authority either way. But as Allen has aptly pointed out,[60]

" No intelligent system would so crudely paralyse the indispensable instruments of analogy and parity of reasoning. Hence in all systems some degree of judicial uniformity is certain to exist and even to be applauded."

It is therefore likely that the customary courts will follow their decisions in previous cases where this is reasonable. The observation in *Yerenchi* v. *Akufo*,[61] a Ghana case, that " Native custom generally consists of the performance of the reasonable in the special circumstances of the case," appears to indicate that customary or native courts are not absolutely bound by their previous decisions. More will be said in another place about this observation of the former Chief Justice of the Gold Coast. It must be pointed out, however, that the fact that the decisions of the Customary Courts are not reported except those that go on appeal to the Superior Courts, will make a rigid adherence to precedent impracticable. The same is true of Magistrates Courts but where as in *Bentworth Finance (Nig.) Ltd.* v. *Akinboro & another*,[62] a Magistrates Courts decision lays an important legal principle it has high persuasive force. Both customary and Magistrates Courts are bound by the decisions of the High Court.

Precedent in the High Court of Nigeria has not yet been neatly covered by authority. It is of course clear that the High Court is bound by the decisions of the Supreme Court and its successors. In *Fagoji* v. *Kano Native Authority*[63] where the High Court of Northern Nigeria refused to follow the decision of the former West African Court of Appeal in *Gana* v. *Bornu Native Authority*,[64] the Federal Supreme Court of Nigeria as it then was, had this to say in a subsequent case:[65]

" There is no precedent for their (the High Court's) refusing to follow a previous decision of the West African Court of Appeal on the subject matter of the enquiry because they considered that the decision had been reached per incuriam. . . . With respect to the learned Chief Justice and other members of the court, it must be pointed out that it is not for an inferior court to say that a decision of the higher court was reached per incuriam; that is a privilege of the Higher Court after reconsidering its former decision, it is satisfied that the previous decision had been reached per incuriam. When the High Court found itself in such a position that it could not follow a previous decision of a higher court by which, according to the comity of courts, they are bound, the proper course, it appears, was for the High Court to have reserved question of Law under Section 20 of the Federal Supreme Court (Appeals) Act (this has been repealed), for the consideration of the Federal Supreme Court, in order to give that court which has taken the place of the West African Court of Appeal the opportunity of reconsidering the previous decision in the light of the question reserved with a view to giving a considered ruling on the question of law involved."

This attitude of the Supreme Court has been criticised by a learned author[66] on two grounds, the first of which is that the Northern Region High Court law has no provision for reservation of points of law in criminal cases. As a result the only course open to the accused would be by way of appeal and this can be an expensive business. Secondly, that if the High Court is free to choose one of two conflicting decisions of the Supreme Court or any of its predecessors, it follows that the High Court could also choose to comply with a statutory provision in preference to the decision of the Supreme Court where such Supreme Court decision was made in ignorance of the statute.

Nwabueze's first point is of course true of the Western, Mid-Western and Northern Nigeria High Court Laws. There are provisions for reserving points of law in criminal cases in the Eastern Nigeria and Lagos High Court Laws.

As to the learned author's second point it is respectfully submitted that the analogy to the High Court choosing one of two inconsistent decisions of the Supreme Court is fanciful in the extreme. Firstly, no attempt is made to distinguish between statutory provisions made before the decision of the case under consideration and those made after the case has been decided by the Supreme Court. Secondly, even if the Supreme Court decision was made in ignorance of an existing statute, it is only a matter of conjecture what the Court would have done if their attention was drawn to the provision. To allow the High Court the freedom to decline to follow a Supreme Court decision under the circumstances will strike at the very root of stare decisis and will inevitably undermine the comity of the courts. The opinion of the Supreme Court in the Bauchi[67] case is therefore the better one. The fact that some High Court Laws in Nigeria have no reservation provisions in criminal cases, does not make it less so. The appropriate remedy will lie in amending such High Court Laws to include reservation provisions.

The next important consideration is whether or not the High Court is bound by its previous decisions, and whether the decisions of the High Court in one Region binds the High Courts of the other regions including the deciding court. As we have noted earlier, the High Courts in Nigeria have both original and appellate jurisdiction. The decision of Brown, C.J. in the Northern Nigeria case of *Olawoyin* v. *Attorney-General of Northern Region*[68] has often been cited as authority for two propositions. The first is that the High Court is not bound by the decision of a judge of co-ordinate jurisdiction sitting at first instance. In his judgment the learned Chief Justice after reviewing the authorities had this to say:

> " It would therefore appear to be clear that while a judge sitting at first instance will accord great weight to a previous decision of a judge of co-ordinate jurisdiction and will only depart from it with reluctance and after the most careful consideration, he commits no breach of principle if he does—for he is not bound by it."[69]

The second proposition is that the High Court in Nigeria has the same powers as the English Divisional Court, if and when it exercises its appellate jurisdiction. Since the Divisional Court in England is bound by its previous decisions,[70] it follows that the High Court sitting as an appellate Court, is also bound by its previous decisions. In the course of his judgment in the Olawoyin case the learned Chief Justice said[71] in this connection:

> ". . . . I would refer to the judgment of Lord Goddard in *Nicholas* v. *Penny*[72] at the top of p. 473. *Nicholas* v. *Penny* applied the principles set out in *Young* v. *Bristol Aeroplane Company Ltd.*[73] to a Divisional Court. This seems to me to be important because in this Region (Northern Nigeria) the High Court sitting in its appellate jurisdiction is, in my opinion, analogous to a Divisional Court in England."

It is important to note that the *Olawoyin* case was affirmed on appeal to the Supreme Court,[74] although the said Supreme Court maintained discreet silence on the issue of precedent as expounded by Brown, C.J.

Park[75] has argued that the rule in Olawoyin's case can only be valid for the Northern Region since in its appellate jurisdiction the Northern High Court has a bench of at least two judges. In the other regions a single judge could exercise appellate jurisdiction. Another reason for this restriction is the fact that there are no sections in the High Court laws of the other regions corresponding to *section 35* of the Northern Nigeria High Court Law. The said section 35 empowers the Northern Nigeria High Court to adopt English practice and procedure in civil cases. The learned author further restricts the application of the rule in *Olawoyin's* case to civil causes and matters. One of his grounds for this is that Young's case on which Brown, C.J. based his analogy, was decided by the English Court of Appeal which court has no criminal jurisdiction. His other ground is that in *Fagoji* v. *Kano N.A.*[76] the Northern High Court refused to follow its previous ruling in *Jalo Tsamiya* v. *Bauchi N.A.*[77] both decisions being on criminal matters. The learned author concluded from these with approval that in criminal cases the Northern High Court even in its appellate jurisdiction is not bound by its previous decisions. Park finally suggests that the decisions of the High Court of a region are only of persuasive authority in another region but not binding. The fact that a particular decision was made by a High Court sitting in its appellate jurisdiction will enhance its persuasive force and no more.

Now, Park's reasons for restricting the application of the rule in *Olawoyin's* case are not at all convincing. Having conceded that English practice and procedure was introduced into Nigeria as part of the received common law, it is strange that the learned author still reads so much meaning into the absence of provisions for practice and procedure in the High Court laws of the other regions. As to his argument about the number of judges that can validly exercise appellate jurisdiction in the North, it is respectfully submitted that a legal system does not assess the importance of a decision only by counting the heads of the judges on the particular bench but also by the number of occasions on which a particular issue has been considered by the Superior Courts. On this latter principle, High Court appellate judgments are of equal judicial authority irrespective of the number of judges that decided the case. It is submitted therefore that the principle in Olawoyin's case should be of general application in all the High Courts in Nigeria.[78]

Park's authority for restricting the *Olawoyin* principle to civil cases is not a happy one. In *Fagoji* v. *Kano N.A.*[79] the Northern Nigeria High Court sitting in its appellate jurisdiction refused to follow its previous decision in *Jalo Tsamiya* v. *Bauchi N.A.*[80] because the latter decision was given per incuriam.[81] Brown, C.J., who read the judgment of the Court made it clear that he followed one of the exceptions to the rule in Young's case. This is seen in his dictum,

> " I think the matter is covered by a passage from the judgment of the master of the Rolls in *Young* v. *Bristol Aeroplane Company Limited* . . . ."[82]

As we have stated above the principle in Young's case and the exceptions thereto were applied by the Divisional Court in England in *Nicholas* v. *Penny*,[83] and this principle was also said to apply in the Northern Nigeria High Court sitting as an appellate court in the Olawoyin case. Park's limitation is therefore neither supported by the facts of the Fagoji case nor the practice of the Courts. It is submitted that the rule in Olawoyin's case applies to civil as well as to criminal causes and matters.

The authority of the decisions of one regional High Court in the courts of another region is not so clear. Undoubtedly these High Courts are established by different regional High Court laws although they all stem from the same constitutional authority and have the Supreme Court as the common appeal Court. It seems, however, that the decisions of one regional High Court will be only of persuasive authority in another regional High Court.[84]

Judicial Precedent in the Supreme Court of Nigeria

The Supreme Court established under *Section III* of the Republican Constitution is the final Court of appeal in the country. Its decisions are binding on all the other courts in Nigeria. There has recently been some speculation[85] as to whether or not the Supreme Court is bound by its own previous decisions. As was shown in the case of Ghana, " previous declarations " include the decisions of such other courts as the former Full Court, the West African Court of Appeal (in Nigerian appeals), and the former Federal Supreme Court. They also include Privy Council decisions on appeals from Nigeria.

Unlike the position in the Ghana Supreme Court, there is no constitutional provision for precedent in the Nigerian Constitution. It appears therefore that the Court can make up its mind whether or not to follow its previous decisions. There is authority for the view that the Supreme Court will not be rigidly bound by its previous decisions where the life of the subject is affected. Thus in *Maizabo* v. *Sokoto N.A.*[86] a homicide appeal from Northern Nigeria, the Federal Supreme Court as it then was, was faced with two of its previous declarations in *Jalo Tsamiya* v. *Bauchi Native Authority*,[87] and *Fagoji* v. *Kano Native Authority*,[88] in which later decisions it had been held that the High Court had no powers to substitute a verdict of manslaughter for that of murder where the accused has been rightly convicted by a native Court under Maliki Law even if the sentence could have been manslaughter if the defence of provocation had been considered. In remitting the Maizabo case back to the Northern High Court for a retrial, de Lestang, F.J., who read the judgment of the Court had this to say: [89]

> " Having regard, however, to the great importance of this matter and in particular since it affects the life of a subject, we felt it right to hear fresh arguments with a view to reconsidering, if necessary, the decisions of this court in the two cases under reference."

Later in his judgment he stated that the two previous decisions were wrong and were not to be followed. [90]

Unfortunately, precedent at the Supreme Court has not been a popular topic in the Supreme Court itself. It is astonishing that apart from the Maizabo case there has been no other direct judicial authority on precedent at the Court. The Maizabo case laid down that in cases of great importance and those in which the life of a subject is involved the court could reconsider a previous decision of its own.

A liberal construction of the phrase " cases of great importance " could cast the net so wide as to include all appeals to the Supreme Court. It might be an abuse of the Court's process to take pointless cases there. But if the Court intended this to be the effect of its dictum, it could have said so in so many words. It is respectfully submitted that all that the statement means is that as a matter of practice the court is bound by its previous decisions, but that the principle could be relaxed in certain cases. One of such cases is where the life of a subject is involved. We would also add constitutional cases and cases where the court is of the opinion that a previous decision was patently wrong.

The reason for the inclusion of constitutional cases in the category of " very important decisions " stems from the fact that Nigeria operates a written constitution whose amendment procedure is very complicated indeed. If therefore the courts feel absolutely bound by a previous decision in a constitutional case this will tend to make the constitution more rigid than it need be. To prevent this undesirable result the United States Supreme Court has adopted the position that they are free to overrule a previous decision of theirs if it is necessary, considering all the circumstances. Thus in the *Passenger Case*[91] Chief Justice Taney of the United States Supreme Court said:

> "I am quite willing that it be regarded hereafter as the law of this court, that its opinion upon the construction of the constitution is always open to discussion when it is supposed to have been in error, and that its judicial authority should hereafter depend altogether on the force of the reasoning by which it is supported."

To the same effect is the opinion of justice Brandeis in *Burret* v. *Coronado Oil and Gas Company*,[92] where he said:

> "Stare decisis is normally the wise policy, because in most matters it is more important that the applicable rule of law be settled than that it be settled right. . . . This is commonly true even where the error is a matter of serious concern, provided correction can be had by legislation. But in cases involving the Federal Constitution, where correction through legislative action is practically impossible, this court has often overruled its earlier decisions. The Court bows to the lessons of experience and the force of better reasoning, recognising that the process of trial and error, so fruitful in the physical sciences, is appropriate also in the judicial function.

Also in *Brown* v. *Board of Education*,[93] the United States Supreme Court overruled its previous decision on the constitutionality of "separate but equal" educational facilities for the negro and white Americans.[94] It might be said that the Brown case reflected the changed social and political climate of opinion in the United States in the 20th Century. This, of course, is the precise point we want to emphasise, that the Supreme Court in Nigeria should not be such a captive to binding judicial precedent as to be oblivious to changed social and other conditions in the country.

As to cases other than criminal and constitutional cases, it is submitted that the Nigerian Supreme Court should be able to overrule a previous decision which has been seen to be patently wrong. It is unnecessary for us to even short-list the factors that can make a previous decision wrong. Two of such factors must, however, be mentioned. One is where a previous decision of the Court was made in reliance on an English authority and the authority is later overruled by the English House of Lords. In such a case, barring any subsequent changes in English Statutory law on the issue, the Supreme Court should feel free to overrule its own previous decisions if need be. This is quite a different thing to say from the position that in every such case the Supreme Court must overrule the previous decision. As was aptly pointed out by Gavan Duffy,

P. in the Irish case of *Re Moore*,[95] after observing that he was not bound by the House of Lords decision of *Perrin* v. *Morgan*,[96]

> "I know no reason why I should not welcome a breath of fresh air from across the channel, particularly when it disturbs cobwebs spun in London and dutifully preserved with our borrowed collection of relics. . . . Stare decisis cannot mean persisting in error after the most authoritative judges of a particular precedent have demonstrated it to be both mischievous and misconceived."

Thus, faced with a similar situation, the Supreme Court in Nigeria should not feel bound by a previous decision. Such a situation was very narrowly averted by a House of Lords majority decision in *Murdock* v. *Taylor*[97] in which the principle of the right to cross-examine an accused on his previous criminal record if he testifies as to character was upheld by the House. This decision stamped the authority of the House of Lords on the Court of Criminal Appeal decision of *R.* v. *Ellis and Ellis*.[98] Meanwhile, in 1963, in the case of *R.* v. *Anyanwu*,[99] the Supreme Court had applied the principle as enunciated by the Court of Criminal Appeal in *R.* v. *Ellis*.[100] If the majority in the House of Lords had rejected the rule, it is not unlikely that their reasons for so doing would receive the careful attention of the Supreme Court in a subsequent case. It is submitted that the fact that the Anyanwu case was a criminal one is not a very important consideration. The same principle is equally applicable to a civil cause or matter.

The other factor that should influence the Court in declining to follow a previous decision should be one of the exceptions to the rule in *Young* v. *Bristol Aeroplane Company Limited*.[101] This is where a previous decision was given per incuriam, or as it has often been interpreted in ignorance of a relevant statute.

Allen[102] described this exception as

> "opportune in relaxing the bonds of precedent when they threaten to stop the circulation of the law's life-blood",

and it has been advocated that it be extended to the House of Lords. It is submitted that the Supreme Court in Nigeria could overrule a previous decision of its own when such previous decision was made per incuriam.[103]

NOTES

1. (1833) 1 C.L. and F. 527, at p. 546.
2. 1 Comm. 69.
3. *Police Authority for Huddersfield* v. *Watson* (1947) K.B. 842; *Young-*

husband v. *Luftig* (1949) 2 K.B. 354; *Moore* v. *Hewitt* (1947) K.B. 831; *Jeffrey* v. *Johnson* (1952) 2 Q.B. 8. But in *Nicholas* v. *Penny* (1950) 2 K.B. 466, the Court dissented from its previous majority decision in *Melhuish* v. *Morris* (1958) 4 All E.R. 98.

4. *Young* v. *Bristol Aeroplane Co.* (1944) K.B. 718, affirmed but not on the question of precedent in 1946 A.C. 163. But see A.L. Goodhart, " Precedent in the Court of Appeal " (1949) Camb. L.J. 349; and G. F. Peter Mason, " Stare decisis in the court of Appeal " (1956) 19 M.L.R. 136.

5. *London Tramway Co.* v. *London County Council* 1848 A.C. 375. The Lords have, however, relaxed the coercive nature of binding precedent in the House. See The Times (London), Wednesday 27th July, 1966. The announcement was made by Lord Gardner, L.C. on behalf of the law lords after the resolution had been taken by the House sitting quasi-judicially.

6. (1950) A.C. 379.

7. *Tumahole Bereng* v. *The King* (1949) A.C. 253.

8. (1939) 1 All E.R. 330.

9. (1946) A.C. 193.

10. (1882) 7 App. Cas. 829.

11. At p. 206.

12. (1938) A.C. 287.

13. (1926) A.C. 72.

14. See especially the judgment of the Board in the *Attorney-General for Ontario case* at pp. 206 et seq. Cf. *Re Transferred Civil Servants (Ireland compensation)* (1929) A.C. 242, where it was stated that " to suggest that . . . this Board is constrained blindfold to adhere to a decision based on a material error in fact, appears to be repugnant to good sense, and to attribute to the Board, as a court of final resort, an impotence which would be deplorable," at pp. 252 et seq.

15. See S. K. B. Asante, " Stare decisis in the Supreme Court of Ghana " (1964), University of Gh. L.J. 52; A. N. Allott, Judicial and Legal Systems in Africa, (London, Butterworths, 1962) pp. 21 et seq.; N. A. Ollennu, " Judicial precedent in Ghana " (1966) U.G. L.J. 139.

16. Para. 32 of the Courts Decree, 1966.

17. Para 87 (3) of the Courts Decree provides as follows " Every case pending before a Local Court immediately before the commencement of this Decree shall be continued and concluded by a District Court having jurisdiction over the area in which such Local Court was situated." Since no other provisions were made in the decree in respect of the jurisdiction of Local Courts, it is arguable that cases that were started in the Local Courts before the promulgation of the decree, will henceforth be started in the District Courts.

18. Para. 61 of the Courts Decree, 1966.

19. Paras. 32 and 33 of the Courts Decree, 1966.

20. Para. 26.

21. Para. 2.

22. 1 Comm. 69.

23. (1833) 1 CL & F. 527, at 546.

24. (1959) G.L.R. 50, at p. 53. This question is now purely academic in view of the Courts Decree, 1966.

25. 58, 15 and 84.

26. This practice and procedure was that of the High Court of justice in England.

27. N.L.C.D. No. 84 of 23rd September, 1966.
28. (1879-90) 13, Ch. D. 774. See particularly p. 784. See also *R.* v. *Benyon,* 41 Cr. App. R. 123 at p. 128, where a High Court judge on Circuit declined to follow a decision of another judge of the High Court in a Criminal matter, which had been given also on circuit four years previously. In *Forester* v. *Baker* (1910) 2 K.B. 636 at p. 638, a judge of the King's Bench Division refused to follow a previous decision of another judge of the King's Bench Division: *Skipper & Tucker* v. *Holloway* (1910) 2 K.B. 630. See the Ghana case of *Sasraku* v. *David* (1959) G.L.R. 7.
29. (1960) N.R.N.L.R. 53.
30. Bennion, *Constitutional law of Ghana* (London, 1962).
31. Op. cit. p. 173. It is interesting to note the similarity of approach between the current House of Lords practice on the subject on the one hand, and Bennion's explanation of the position in the Supreme Court of Ghana, on the other.
32. S. K. B. Asante, " Stare decisis in the Supreme Court of Ghana " (1964) 1 University of Ghana Law Journal, at p. 63.
33. Perhaps this means wrong in law. If so, then it is sufficiently covered under Bennion's " per incuriam " exception.
34. *Common Law in West Africa* pp. 183 et seq.
35. Speech to Sarbah Society, Supra See also University of Ghana Law Journal, (1966) p. 139.
36. It had amply been demonstrated above that this Board is not absolutely bound by its previous decisions: *Mercantile Bank of India* v. *Central Bank of India* (1938) A.C. 287.
37. *Re Herbert Macaulay* (1951) 13 W.A.C.A. 204.
38. 7, W.A.C.A. 156.
39. Op. Cit. at p. 310.
40. Supra. See also *Bambgose* v. *Daniel* (1952) 14, W.A.C.A. 111.
41. (1949) 12 W.A.C.A. 437.
42. (1948) 12, W.A.C.A. 349.
43. But analogies from Nigeria may suggest that these courts followed the W.A.C.A. practice in this matter: *Flione* v. *Oladipo* (1934) 11, N.L.R. 168; *Maizabo* v. *Sokoto N.A.* (1957) N.R.N.L.R. 133.
44. (1898) A.C. 373. (31) Lord Wright (1943) Camb. L.J. 144; Williams, Salmond, Jurisprudence (11th Ed.); Denning, *From President to Precedent* (1959).
45. (1960) A.C. 459 at p. 489.
46. (1960) A.C. 459 at p. 489.
47. (1963) 79, L.Q.R. 313. The binding nature of judicial precedent in the House of Lords has, however, been relaxed, as has already been mentioned. That court is no longer strictly bound by its former decisions on points of law, where, in its opinion, the previous decision was wrong. See The Times, Wednesday, 27th July, 1966.
48. 2nd Edition, Vol. 21 pp. 501-2.
49. Speech made at the Swearing-in of the Judges.
50. (1939) I.R. 336; Cited by Daniels, op. cit. See also Prof. Henchy. 25 M.L.R. 544.
51. *Constitutional Law of Ghana,* p. 173 et seq.
52. Ollennu's argument is equally valid for the practice in the Court of Appeal established under the Courts Decree, 1966.
53. Perhaps the sketchy nature of most of the reports follows from the

brief judgments of the bench. It may however have been more helpful if the arguments of Counsel were included. A good deal of the information in this sub-head is taken from Elias, Nigerian legal system, and B. O. Nwabueze, the machinery of Justice in Nigeria.

54. SS. 122 and 126 of the Republican Constitution.

55. In the Eastern Region these are divided into District Courts and County Courts. The County Courts are Customary Appeal Courts; Eastern Region Customary Courts Law. In the Western and Mid-Western Regions there are three grades of Customary Courts. The judges for the Grade A Customary Courts are Legal practitioners of at least seven years' standing. Cf. A decree of the Military Government in Nigeria (extra-Ordinary Gazette, Western Nigeria, January 26th, 1966) has abolished the Customary Courts in the Western Region. It is not yet clear whether this is intended as a temporary measure to insulate the customary courts from political control or necessarily increases the original jurisdiction of the Magistrate Courts.

56. See Allott, *Judicial and Legal Systems*, pp. 50 et seq.

57. Northern Nigeria Native Courts Law, Cap. 78. See also E. A. Keay and S. S. Richardson, *The Native and Customary Courts of Nigeria*, (London, Sweet & Maxwell, 1966).

58. Northern Nigeria Criminal Procedure Code Law, No. 11 of 1960.

59. Area Court Edict (1968) Benue Plateau State, No. 4 of 1968. See A. O. Obilade " Reform of Customary Court Systems in Nigeria under the Military Government," (1969) 13 J.A.L. 28.

60. *Law in the making* (7th ed.) p. 161.

61. Ren. 362 at p. 367, per Sir William Brandford Griffith, C.J.

62. B49/100, Suit No. 640/63. Lagos, No. 2 Court, Saturday, 6th day of July, 1963; a hire purchase case.

63. (1957) N.R.N.L.R. 57.

64. 14 W.A.C.A. 587.

65. *Jalo Tsamiya* v. *Bauchi N.A.* (1967) N.R.N.L.R. 73 at pp. 82-83.

66. *Nwabueze, Machinery of Justice*, p. 34 et seq.

67. Supra.

68. (1960) N.R.N.L.R. 53. See also *Agbalaya* v. *Bello* (1960) L.L.R. 190.

69. Supra at p. 58. See also *Flione* v. *Oladino* (1934) 11, *N.L.R.* 168.

70. *Police Authority for Huddersfield* v. *Watson* (1947) K.B. 842.

71. Supra p. 58.

72. (1950) 2 K.B. 466.

73. (1944) K.B. 718.

74. (1961) 1 All N.L.R. 245.

75. Sources, pp. 57 et seq.

76. (1957) N.R.N.L.R. 57.

77. Unreported decision of the Northern Nigeria High Court, Kaduna, 28th May, 1956.

78. In *Agbalaya* v. *Bello* (1960) L.L.R. 190 Sir Clement De Lestang C.J. says that the High Court is bound by its own appellate decisions (Lagos).

79. Supra.

80. Supra.

81. Sub. S.2 of S.40A of the Native Courts Ordinance was not considered by the Court.

82. Supra at p. 67.

83. (1950) 2 K.B. 466.

84. The position can become more acute with the introduction of twelve states and the resultant twelve judicial jurisdictions.
85. See B.O. *Nwabueze, Machinery,* pp. 32 et seq.; *Park, Sources* pp. 56 et seq.; *Brett, Stare decisis in Nigeria* (1965) N.B.J. 75.
86. (1957) 2 F.S.C. 13.
87. (1957) N.R.N.L.R. 73.
88. (1957) N.R.N.L.R. 84.
89. Supra, at p. 14.
90. (1849) 7 Hon. 283, at p. 470.
91. (1849) 7 Hon. 283, at p. 470.
92. (1932) 285 U.S. 393 at p. 406.
93. (1954) 347 U.S. 483.
94. (1947) I.R. 205.
95. (1947) I.R. 205.
96. (1943) A.C. 399.
97. (1965) 2 W.L.R. 425.
98. (1961) 1 W.L.R. 1064.
99. (1963) R.S.C. 54/1963.
100. Supra (1965) F.S.C. Nigeria Suit No. 54/63, Unreported.
101. (1944) K.B. 718.
102. *Law in the making* (7th Ed. 1964), p. 238.
103. We have not found it desirable to repeat our argument about judicial precedent in the Old West African Court of Appeal and the Judicial Committee of the Privy Council. These were sufficiently discussed in the section on the Supreme Court of Ghana, Supra.

PART II

VALID AGREEMENTS
TWO-PARTY SITUATIONS:

CHAPTER 4

THE NATURE OF AGREEMENT

The term " agreement " can be used to express three kinds of situations, namely :

1. The acts which create the relationship between the parties. It is used in this sense when B " agrees " to purchase a consignment of goods offered by A at a given price. Here A and B are said to be in " agreement."

2. A writing which if not itself such an act, is the evidence of such acts. A memorandum of a hire purchase agreement or a letter of acceptance of an offer to buy goods are such acts or evidence of such acts respectively of " agreement " between the parties.

3. The legal relations resulting from the operative acts. In this last sense, agreement is used to describe the legal consequence of the transactions between the parties. Thus as a result of what has transpired between A and B as given in our example above, B is under an obligation to pay A the agreed price of the consignment of goods and A has a duty to supply the goods. There is a legally enforceable " agreement " between the parties.

Agreement OR Contract?

Attempts to define agreement can be discussed under—

(a) those who contend that agreement is but an essential element of contract i.e. consent and little else, and

(b) those who define agreement in terms of the totality of our three uses as indicated above.

(a) Agreement defined as but an element of a contract:

The proposition that contract rests on agreement appears to begin with St. Germain's *Doctor and Student,* first published in 1523. At the commencement of Chapter 24, Book II, the student says that contract is the name given to bargains and sales " made by assent of the parties upon agreement between them," whereas an agreement containing several articles " is properly called a concord, but is also a contract." In explaining English law to the

Doctor the student distinguishes actionable promises i.e. those with a "*quid pro quo*" and those that are not so actionable because there was no "*quid pro quo.*" This narrower definition of contract as agreements with a "quid pro quo" was adopted in the first edition of "Termes de la Ley" published in 1527. Contract is there defined as a "bargain or covenant between two parties, where one thing is given for another which is called "quid pro quo."[1]

Blackstone also defined contract in terms of agreement although his exposition of contractual obligations was done in terms of forms of actions.[2] He defined contract as "an agreement, upon sufficient consideration to do or not to do a particular thing."[2]

The *American Restatement* of contracts defines agreement as "a manifestation of mutual assent by two or more persons to one another."[3] It goes further to assert that agreement has a wider meaning than contract, bargain or promise; that the word contains no implication that legal consequences are or are not produced, and that it applies to transactions executed on one or both sides, and those that are wholly executory.[4]

To the same effect is the statement of Holdsworth in his *History of English law*[4a] that "the essence of contract is agreement, and the essence of agreement is a union of wills." Holdsworth adds that this position was recognised by the English lawyers of the sixteenth century.

Judicial authority is not lacking for the approach that agreement is but an essential element of contract and little more. Thus in 1553 in the case of *Browning* v. *Beston*,[5] it was said of contract "the agreement of the minds of the parties is the only thing the law respects in our contracts"; and in 1551,[6] an agreement was defined as the "union, collection, copulation, and conjunction of two or more minds in anything done or to be done."

In relatively recent years this principle has been restated by eminent common law judges. Thus Lord Atkin in *Balfour* v. *Balfour*[7] has said, "there are agreements between parties which do not result in contracts within the meaning of that term in law." Also Bankes L.J. in *Rose Frank & Co.* v. *Crompton Bros.*[8] said: "there is, I think, no doubt that it is essential to the creation of a contract, using that word in its legal sense, that the parties to an agreement shall not only be *ad idem* as to the terms of their agreement, but that they shall have intended that it shall have legal consequences."

It may be pointed out that the exponents of what may rightly be described as a narrow view of agreement argue that there are other contracts, e.g. those contracts implied by law, where it is difficult to spell out an agreement between the parties. Where?, they would ask, can there be agreement in a circumstance as this one: " A walks into B's bookshop, collécts a copy of Cheshire's *Law of Real Property*, raises it for B to see him, and since he is in a hurry, goes away with the book intending to pay for it." A will be compelled to pay a reasonable price for the book, but where do we find the parties agreeing in the legal sense? Blackstone[9] attempted to answer this by arguing that the law implies that A agreed to buy the book at the marked price or the usual price or a reasonable price.

Secondly, the advocates of this view contend that fraud and mistake voids contracts even though there has been agreement. Chitty and Cheshire and Fifoot would prefer the use of the neutral term, " promise,"[10] since fraud or mistake do not have the same vitiating effect on a promise as on contract or agreement.

(b) Agreement defined as an alternative term to contract:

Attempts to define agreement as an alternative term to contract can be said to date as far back as West's Symbolaeography, published in 1590, where he says: " A covenant or agreement which hath cause is termed a contract, which is nothing else but an agreement with a lawful cause or consideration."[11] In the subsequent section of the same work he says, " the substance of all contracts consisteth in consent." This tendency was continued in the Statute of Frauds, 1677, section 4 of which provides for the " form " of " agreement that is not to be performed within the space of one year. This was cited as " contract not to be performed. . . ." in a seventeenth century case.[12]

Also in *Wain* v. *Warlters*, Lord Ellenborough decided that " agreement " was meant " in its proper and correct sense, as signifying a mutual contract on consideration between two or more parties.[13]

In the important case of *Rann* v. *Hughes*[14] decided in 1778, the Chief Baron delivering the opinion of the judges in the House of Lords said that, " all contracts are, by the laws of England, distinguished into agreements by specialty and agreements by parol." The Chancery Court also referred to deeds as agreements.[15] In *Alderson* v. *Temple*[16] counsel urged " that mutual consent is necessary to all contracts " although Lord Mansfield decided the case on other grounds.

Leake[17] following West,[18] Maine[19] and Austin[20] analysed contracts in terms of agreement. In this he is followed by Sir Frederick Pollock[21] and Sir William Anson.[22]

Critics of this approach have pointed to the lack of any real agreement in cases of acceptance of an offer by post where the offeror has withdrawn the offer but after the offeree had posted his letter of acceptance. In English law a contract has nevertheless been formed. It is pointed out with respect that this objection is not a strong one. Every legal system operates within the confines of certain rules. If English law regards acceptance by post as creating an agreement between the parties, the fact that it is called "agreement" instead of "contract" does not alter the principle involved.[22a]

It is further submitted that the word "agreement" has some added advantages. Taking obligations as a genus it is more convenient and responsive to better harmony to treat obligations created by agreement as one species and other obligations imposed by law as another. This approach will save both academic and judicial opinion from the futile attempts to imply a contract in order to impose liability. More will be said on this aspect of the question in another place.

Finally in Ghana and Nigeria where the laws are complicated by statutory recognitions of customary and Islamic laws, the term "agreement" removed as it apparently is from the technicalities of the term "contract" in English law, is obviously a more convenient mode of analysing contractual situations. As a learned author has aptly pointed out, "it is not a question of one view being correct and the other view being wrong; lawyers move within definitions of their own creation, and all we have to consider is consistency and convenience."[23]

In our enquiry the term "agreement" will be used in the following three senses, namely, as an act, as a memorandum or evidence of it, and as a legal consequence of what has transpired between the parties.[24]

Agreement, however, for legal purposes is not a state of mind but an act, and as an act it is a matter of inference from the conduct of the parties. Some legal systems set out to find out what in fact the parties willed or intended while some others draw an objective inference from the conduct of the parties. The English law of contract, deeply rooted as it is in *assumpsit* is dominated by the concept of bargain. Thus the English courts will find an agreement formed if in their opinion this was the intention of the parties and the consequences of their dealings.

This is clear from Lord Eldon's statement in *Kennedy* v. *Lee*,[25] when he said that his task was not "to see that both parties really meant the same thing (i.e. agreed) but only that both gave their assent to that proposition which, be it what it may, *de facto* arises out of the terms of their correspondence."

To the same effect is John Austin's position in his *Lectures*,[26] where after saying that " when we speak of intention of contracting parties, we mean the intention of the promisor or the intention of the promisee," added " or rather, the sense in which it is to be inferred from the words used or from the transaction or from both that one party gave and the other received it."

In Ghana and Nigeria the picture that emerges from an examination of the cases is an attempt to project the objective theory into the local laws of voluntary obligations. In accordance with this, if in the opinion of the court what has transpired between the parties does not satisfy the requirements of agreement under English law, the courts will not recognise any binding obligation. Thus in *Savage and others* v. *Uwechia*[27] a Nigerian appeal to the Judicial Committee of the Privy Council, the respondent claimed as against the trustees (appellants) of the will of one Rotibi, deceased, specific performance of an agreement made between himself and the deceased to convey certain properties at Onitsha (Eastern Nigeria) to him, and he tendered in support of his claim a copy of a document in the following terms:

" Promissory Note
£780 : — : —   Owerri
I promise to pay to Matthew Uwechia or order three months after date the sum of seven hundred and eighty pounds for value received or in default to convey to him all those messuages together with appurtenances thereto situate at No. 6 New Market Road in the township of Onitsha, to hold the same unto the said Matthew Uwechia or order in fee simple.

                                                (Sgd.) S. O. Rotibi."

Both the respondent and the deceased were natives of Nigeria and prima facie, native law will be presumed applicable except the parties intended or the nature of the transaction imported the application of any other law,[28] in this case, English law. Now, the above document is in a form that is common among natives as a means of charging property or of making conditional sales.[29] But both the Federal Supreme Court of Nigeria (as it then was) and the Judicial Committee held that the document was not a mortgage. The English case of *Tapply* v. *Sheather*[30] was cited as authority for this view. The Judicial Committee held further, reversing the Federal Supreme Court's finding in this respect, that there was no agreement to convey the property. The reason for this decision was said to be that the parties did not spell out the consideration; and " value received " was said to be too vague.

A learned editor[31] has remarked that the decision of their lordships may well have been right but for the wrong reasons. He suggested that the respondent ought to have relied on native law to prove the native mortgage but that in the absence of evidence in this direction English law would then be applicable as in fact it applied here.

It is submitted with respect that if the case were decided in a jurisdiction where the will of the parties to the transaction is given any emphasis, the *Uwechia* decision may well have gone the other way. To have refused the respondent his remedy on the technicality of the interpretation of " value received " was, again with respect fanciful in the extreme. The customary courts if they had jurisdiction to try the case (the amount involved excludes their jurisdiction) would undoubtedly have decided the case differently. Regard would have been given to what the parties set out to achieve.

NOTES

1. See also Noy's Maxims (1641) where a similar language is adopted.
2. *ii Comm. 442.*
3. (1932) Vol. 1, p. 5, S. 3. See also Indian Contract Act, 1872.
4. See also R. M. Jackson, " The Scope of the Term ' Contract ' " in (1937) 53 L.Q.R. 525 at p. 534 where he said " Agreement is used in a wide sense to signify an accord between two or more persons. An agreement in this sense is not necessarily a contract but it is said to be an essential element in every contract."—Ames 2 Harv. L.R. 15; Cheshire and Fifoot, *The Law of Contract* (6th ed. 1964), p. 20 and *Chitty on Contracts* (22nd ed.), p. 8.
4a. Vol. 8, p. 1.
5. (1553) Plowden, 140.
6. *Reniger* v. *Fogossa* (1551) Plowden, 17.
7. (1919) 2 K.B. 571 at p. 578.
8. (1923) 2 K.B. 261. See also *Carlill* v. *Carbolic and Smoke Ball Co.* (1893) 1 Q.B. 265 at p. 269 per Bowen, L.J.
9. *iii Comm. 161.*
10. Promise is also preferred by many American authors. See the Restatement of Contracts; Williston on Contracts. See also Section 2 of the Indian Contract Act, 1872 which uses the word " Promise."
11. Book 1, sects. 10 and 11.
12. *Anon (1698) Comb. 463,* cited by R. M. Jackson (1937) 53 L.Q.R. 525 at p. 529. See also Winfield (1939) L.Q.R. 499.
13. (1805) 5 East, 10.
14. (1778), 7 T.R. 350.
15. See *Abridgment of cases in Equity*, Chap. IV.
16. (1768) 4 Burr, 2235.
17. *Law of Contract* (1857).
18. *Symbolaeography* (1590).
19. *Ancient Law*, Chapter IX.
20. " Fragment—Quasi-contract and Quasi-delict "—printed in appendix to *Austin's lectures* (1863 ed.).
21. Pollock on Contracts (13th ed. P. H. Winfield, 1950), p. 6.

22. *Law of Contract* (22nd ed., Guest, 1964), p. 4.

22a. More will be said about the historical aspect of this question in our section on " acceptance ", post.

23. R. M. Jackson (1937) 53 L.Q.R. 525 at p. 534.

24. Where the word " contract " is used in our enquiry it is intended as an alternative to our use of the word " agreement." As almost all legislation and case law on the subject adopts the term " contract," it will not be desirable to substitute " agreement" wherever the word contract occurs.

25. (1817) 3, Mer. 441.

26. Lecture XXI, note 90. This approach to the interpretation of contract often called the objective approach is contrasted with the subjective approach which is prevalent in Continental legal systems. On the Continental approach, see K. W. Ryan, *An Introduction to the Civil Law* (1962) passim.

27. (1961) 1 W.L.R. 455; 105 Sol. J. 205; (1961) 1 All E.R. 830.

28. Eastern Nigeria High Court Law, Cap. 61, Section 28.

29. See Allott, *Essays,* pp. 275-282.

30. (1862) L.T. 298.

31. Allott (1961) 5 J.A.L. 104.

CHAPTER 5

OFFER AND ACCEPTANCE[1]

(i) OFFER

An agreement results from an accord of the wills of the parties either actually entertained or imputed as a matter of inference from their conduct. The common law system requires the exchange of declarations of will directed towards the same object and this is couched in the language of " offer " and " acceptance " or as some authors prefer to call it, " proposal " and acceptance. An offer has been defined as the " unilateral communication by one party to the other of his desire to conclude a contract (agreement) with that other."[2] An offer must be definite and unambiguous. Thus in the Ghana case of *Anglo-Guinea Produce Co. Ltd.* v. *George*,[3] where a definite offer to sell cocoa had been accepted by the plaintiffs, it was held that subsequent negotiations introduced by the plaintiffs did not affect the terms of the agreement. The facts of the case were as follows; on 9th February, 1924, the defendant sent the plaintiffs the following telegram:—" Offer you 550 bags cocoa now in store Nsawam delivered Accra 15/6 reply immediately." The plaintiffs replied the next day by telegram as follows: " We accept your offer 550 bags, subject immediate delivery." On the 11th February, the defendant rang up the plaintiffs and confirmed the agreement by telephone. On the same day the plaintiffs wrote the defendant saying " we confirm having accepted from you 550 bags of cocoa delivered Accra, subject to quality and weights satisfactory to us." On 13th February, the plaintiffs received the following telegram from the defendant:— " Regret owing to present position of the market, have decided not to sell forward " but the plaintiffs in their reply both by telegram and letter intimated that they were holding the defendant to his agreement. In a claim by the plaintiffs for £80:4:2d. damages for breach of the agreement the defendant contended that the delivery of the cocoa would constitute the offer and the payment of the price was an acceptance. Since there had been none of these in the negotiations there was no agreement between the parties. This argument was firmly rejected by Logan, Ag. C.J. who said at p. 145 that,

" When once there is a definite acceptance of the terms of an offer, further negotiations between the parties cannot, without the consent of both, get rid of the contract which has been made, though the subsequent correspondence may be used to show that the contract was not then completed."[4]

Also in the Nigerian case of *Arbuckle, Smith & Co. Ltd.* v. *Attorney-General*,[5] an appeal to the Nigerian Supreme Court from the judgment of Magistrate L. O. Lucas awarding damages to the respondents in an action for breach of agreement, the Commissioner for Lands (Lagos) wrote to the appellants offering them a choice of one of 60 years and 99 years leases, each term with conditions attached. Both terms were subject to the execution of a formal lease. The appellants in reply chose the 99 years lease and enclosed a cheque covering the consideration for it. A draft lease to the appellants was not returned to the Commissioner and the appellants' request for an extension of time to build was refused. In an action for damages for breach of the agreement the appellants took the point that the Commissioner's letter giving them the choice of one of two leases was not an offer and that there was no enforceable agreement. Both the court of first instance and the Supreme Court were not persuaded by this argument. It was held that there was an enforceable agreement and that the Commissioner's letter was a definite offer.

An offer may be made to a person, a specified or specifiable group of persons or to the public at large. Local judicial authority is very thin in this aspect of the law but the familiar English case of *Carlill* v. *Carbolic Smoke Ball Co.*[6] decided by the English Court of Appeal in 1893 has often been cited in both Ghana and Nigeria as authority for the theory that an offer to the public at large if definite can be the basis of an enforceable agreement. The Carlill case was followed in *Wood* v. *Letrik Ltd.*[7] In the latter case the defendants in an advertisement of their electric comb stated: " What is your trouble? Is it grey hair? In ten days not a grey hair left. £500 guarantee." The plaintiff claimed he had bought a comb and used it as directed, the only result being that the comb scratched his head and made him feel uncomfortable. He sued for and recovered the £500. Rowlatt, J. followed the Carlill case.[8]

The Carlill decision has come to be accepted by the American and Commonwealth Courts as the leading authority on offers by advertisements to the general public. *Goldthorpe* v. *Logan*[9] decided by the Ontario Court of Appeal in 1943 represents the general trend in this direction.

In that case the female appellant had some hairs on her face and wanted to have them removed. She saw an advertisement published in a newspaper by the defendant Anne Graham Logan in these terms: "Hairs . . . . removed safely and permanently by Electrolysis . . . No marks, No scars—Results Guaranteed." She went to the place of business stated in the advertisement and consulted the defendant's nurse, Kathleen Fitzpatrick, who assured her that her face would definitely be cleared and that the hair would be removed permanently and that the result was guaranteed. She then submitted to a number of treatments by electrolysis for the purpose of removing the hairs but the result was not satisfactory. Hairs continued to grow on her face in the same way as before, and in spite of the efforts of the defendants to remedy the condition. An action for breach of contract against the defendants was held to succeed. In course of his judgment Laidlaw, J.A. asked himself the questions: "What is the time, nature and construction of this advertisement?", and in answer had this to say:

> "It is a distinct communication by the defendant Logan to each and every member of the public. What intention did she possess and convey to such persons by the words she used? To ascertain that intention we may in this instance look at the surrounding circumstances. She was carrying on a business in which she appealed for public support and patronage. She required customers to buy services she desired to sell. She was a vendor seeking a purchaser. What she meant to say, and the sensible interpretation of her words is this: 'If you will submit yourself to my treatment and pay me (certain charges) I undertake to remove hairs safely and permanently by electrolysis and I promise to obtain a satisfactory result.' The effect in law of such a statement is to create an offer from the person by whom it is made to every person who is willing to accept the terms and conditions of it."[10]

It is submitted that the *Logan* case goes further than *Carlill* v. *Carbolic and Smoke Ball Co.*[11] What the latter case decided was that the deposit of £1,000 with a bank gave business efficacy to the promise to pay £100 for use of the Smoke Ball. Without the deposit the promise could have been a mere puff. This is evident from the judgment of Lindley, L.J. where he said: "We must first consider whether this was intended to be a promise at all, or whether it was a mere puff which meant nothing. Was it a mere puff? My answer to that question is NO, and I base my answer upon this passage: '£1,000 is deposited with the Alliance Bank, showing our sincerity in the matter.'" Thus what the Carlill case added to the 'reward' cases dating from the old English case of *Williams* v. *Carwardine*[12] decided by the King's Bench in 1833 was that where there was a specific amount as a guarantee the plaintiff will succeed. *Goldthorpe* v. *Logan*[13] goes further to make the defendant liable even if no specific circumstance led to the conclusion that the parties meant business. This, it is again submitted, is a healthy development. It is a bold judicial attempt to solve the problems posed by the age of automation where the public are invaded by door-to-door canvassers, by expanding business. It is the kind of solution that should appeal to the courts in Ghana and Nigeria if and when the question comes to be decided in a case.

Offers and invitations to do business distinguished

The Logan decision did not set out to and therefore could not resolve all the unanswered questions on offers to the public. There is still the familiar distinction between offers and invitations to do business. Thus although a railway time-table has been held to be an offer to all intending travellers and where a train service was permanently withdrawn without the necessary changes on the time-table within a reasonable time, a plaintiff who relied on it to his detriment recovered damages,[14] yet goods displayed and priced at shop windows have been held to be mere invitations to treat.[15] As has often been pointed out, the test of an offer is whether the offeror has completed his share of the formation of an agreement by finally declaring his readiness to undertake an obligation upon certain conditions, leaving to the offeree the option of acceptance or refusal.[16] Invitations to treat lack this finality in the offeror's declarations of readiness to be bound.

Familiar instances of invitations to treat are auction sales and goods priced at shop-windows or in a self-service store. Here again there are no local authorities in Ghana and Nigeria. There is, however, the English case of *Pharmaceutical Society of Great Britain* v. *Boots Cash Chemists (Southern) Ltd.*[17] decided by the English Court of Appeal in 1953 in which it was held that articles in a self-service store are not offers but mere invitations to treat. There is also the Transvaal case of *Crawley* v. *R*[18] the facts of which were as follows:

A tradesman advertised goods at a specified price. X entered the shop and persisted in demanding the goods at that price. The tradesman refused to deliver them and at last told X to leave the shop. X would not do so. He was prosecuted for, and convicted of unlawfully remaining on premises after being requested to leave them (an offence according to Transvaal law). Smith, J., who decided the case, said that extraordinary consequences would follow if every such advertisement was said to be an offer capable of acceptance by everybody who got into the shop. Sir Percy Winfield has suggested that the natural interpretation of the display of goods in a shop with a marked price upon them is that the

I

shopkeeper implicitly reserves to himself a right of selecting his customer. A shop, he said, is a place for bargaining, not for compulsory sales. The personality of the customer cannot be entirely eliminated. " If the display of such goods were an offer, then the shopkeeper might be forced to contract with his worst enemy, his greatest trade rival, a reeling drunkard, or a ragged and verminous tramp. That would be a result scarcely likely to be countenanced by the law."[19]

With regard to auction sales the distinction between offers and invitations to do business has arisen in three different respects. Firstly there is the question whether an advertisement that an auction sale will take place is an offer to the general public or a mere declaration of intention to hold the sale. In *Harris* v. *Nickerson*[20] an auctioneer advertised that certain goods, including office furniture, would be sold at a certain place on certain days. The plaintiff went to the sale but all the lots of office furniture in which he was interested were withdrawn and he sued the auctioneer to recover damages for his loss of time and expenses. It was held that the plaintiff's claim must fail as the advertising of the sale was a mere declaration of intention to hold a sale and not an offer which could be accepted to form a binding agreement. If the sale was not held the auctioneer was not bound to indemnify those who attended.

Secondly, is the auctioneer's request for bids an offer and a customer's bid an acceptance? This was answered in the negative in the English case of *Payne* v. *Cave*[21] where the defendant was the highest bidder at an auction sale but before the fall of the hammer had retracted his bid. It was held that he was entitled to do so as it is his bid which is the offer and not the auctioneer's invitation to bid. Now both *Harris* v. *Nickerson* and *Payne* v. *Cave* are pre-1874 decisions of English courts. We have already argued that pre-1874 decisions of English courts (in the case of Ghana) and pre-1900 decisions (in the case of Nigeria) were received into the two countries respectively. Both the *Harris* and *Payne* decisions are therefore part of the laws of Ghana and Nigeria. The position has been made statutory in Ghana.[22]

The third question is whether an advertisement that a sale will be without reserve constitutes an offer to the highest bidder. In Ghana, since the Sale of Goods Act, 1962,[23] the question has been answered in the affirmative. Section 4 (1) (d) states as follows:

" Where the sale is expressed to be without reserve the highest bona fide bidder shall be entitled to buy the goods at the price bid notwithstanding that the auctioneer refuses to accept his bid or to complete the sale."

The use of the words " bona fide " is very significant. It is meant to take care of situations where the seller bids in contravention of the conditions of sale, e.g. where the sale is without reserve. This happened in the English case of *Warlow* v. *Harrison*.[24] In that case an auctioneer had advertised that he would sell certain horses without reserve. Warlow bid 60 guineas for one of the horses whereupon the seller bid 61 guineas but Warlow refused to add anything. On the horse being knocked down to the owner, Warlow tendered the amount he bid and claimed the horse as the highest bona fide bidder. Although he was non-suited on other grounds there are dicta in the case which support the position as enacted in the Ghana Sale of Goods Act. The position as in *Warlow* v. *Harrison* has been described as curious by two learned authors[25] and has further been the topic of some academic controversy in relatively recent years.[26] There is little doubt, however, that the arrangement is not as inconsistent as it appears. Thus, while there is no obligation on an auctioneer to hold a sale according to an advertisement (barring fraudulent misrepresentation), when a sale has been held the auctioneer should be bound by his undertaking to sell to the highest bidder or to pay damages for the breach of guarantee.

The Western Nigeria Auctioneers Law (Cap. 9, 1959) is in similar terms to the Ghana Sale of Goods Act, 1962. Section 22 (5) has the following provision:

> " If the seller or any person employed by him or in his behalf shall bid at any sale contrary to any of the provisions of this section (i.e. without stating that he would so bid in the conditions of sale) any purchaser may refuse to fulfil his purchase, but the highest bona fide bidder shall be entitled, if he so elect, to have the land or goods at the price offered by him."

There are similar provisions in the Eastern and Northern Regions of Nigeria as well as in the Federal Sales by Auction Act which applies to Lagos.[27] These provisions have cleared any doubts created by the dicta in the decisions of English Courts[28] about the rights of the highest bona fide bidder at an auction sale without reserve to claim the property bid for, thus in both Ghana and Nigeria the fall of the auctioneer's hammer is no longer a vital element in the formation of the agreement as long as the statutory conditions are fulfilled. This, it is submitted, is a better position to adopt than the one taken in the Scottish courts where it has been held that no agreement is complete unless and until the auctioneer acknowledges the acceptance of the bid by the fall of his hammer even in cases of sales without reserve.[29]

As to the communication of an offer, the simple rule is that an offer is communicated when the offeree knows of it. This appears to be the universal practice.[30] There is no direct authority as to the legal effect of a communication of an offer to an agent. It has been suggested that in such a case the communication will be deemed to be communication to his principal only when the agent knows of the offer and has full authority to deal with the matters to which it refers.[31]

(ii) ACCEPTANCE

The acceptance of an offer is the act which completes the formation of the agreement.[32] There are of course two vital aspects of acceptance, namely, the fact of acceptance and the communication of acceptance to the offeror. The fact of acceptance need not detain us here. In English law the courts decide from the nature of the correspondence or other dealings between the parties whether or not there has been an acceptance of the offer. If in the court's opinion there has been a precise and unconditional adoption by the offeree of the terms of an offer, it will rule that there has been an acceptance. This attitude to acceptance of offers has also been adopted in the courts of Ghana and Nigeria. Thus in *Arbuckle, Smith & Co. Ltd.* v. *Attorney-General*[33] referred to above the Supreme Court of Nigeria ruled that the choice of a 99 years lease and an enclosed cheque sent to the Commissioner for Lands (Lagos) constituted an acceptance of the offer to take a lease. Where the nature of the correspondence leads to the only conclusion that the offeree meant to accept an offer made to him, the addition of superfluous words will not affect the agreement which results from the acceptance. This was the decision in the Ghana case of *Anglo-Guinea Produce Co. Ltd.* v. *George*[34] the facts of which were given above. Silence alone does not constitute an acceptance of an offer even if it is imposed by the offeree.[35] The authority of this rule in English law has been doubted by a learned author.[36]

On the communication of acceptance the general rule is that the offeror must know of the offeree's acceptance.[37] Thus in negotiations inter praesentes, i.e. face to face negotiations (which include acceptance by telephone) the offeror must hear the offeree's acceptance. In the English case of *Brogden* v. *Metropolitan Railway Co.*[38] decided by the House of Lords in 1877 both Brian, C.J. and Lord Blackburn stated that for a proposal to enter into an agreement to be enforceable there should be a communication of that acceptance to the proposer (i.e. the offerer). This principle was by inference restated by the House of Lords in the often discussed decision of *Entores Ltd.* v. *Miles Far East Corporation.*[39] It must be observed, however, that while the Brogden decision is part of the law of Nigeria being a pre-1900 decision of the House of Lords, it is of high persuasive force in Ghana. But the later case of *Entores Ltd.* v. *Miles Far East Corporation* is not binding on the Nigerian or Ghanaian courts though it is highly unlikely that it will not be followed in the courts of these countries—based as it is on expediency and the requirements of commerce.

Communication of acceptance by post either by letter or telegram presents a more difficult problem. The issue has been between those who contend that an acceptance is complete when the letter embodying the said acceptance is dropped into a post box (or in the case of telegrams when it has been sent to the post office), and those who argue that there has been no valid acceptance until the letter reaches the offeror.[40] The position in English law and in fact in the laws of Ghana and Nigeria is that stated in *Adams* v. *Lindsell.*[41] In that case the defendants wrote to the plaintiffs to offer to sell some wool and asked for a reply " in course of post ". The letter containing the offer was wrongly addressed and because of this the letter of reply was posted and received two days later than it would have been reasonable for the defendants to expect. On the day previous to the receipt of the letter of acceptance the defendants sold the wool to a third person but the letter of acceptance had been posted the day before the day on which the wool was sold. The plaintiff sued for the breach of the agreement. It was held that the plaintiff was entitled to recover as the agreement was concluded when the letter of acceptance was posted. This decision was followed by the English Court of Appeal in a later case,[42] but has been criticised in a recent article.[43] Without getting involved in the jurisprudence of the communication of acceptances by post, one takes leave to doubt the consistency of the rule in *Adams* v. *Lindsell* with the statute law relating to parcels by post in Ghana and Nigeria. *Section 3 of the Post Office Act, (Cap. 156, Laws of the Federation of Nigeria and Lagos, 1958)* which is in the same terms as the corresponding Ghana Ordinance[44] has the following provisions:

    (a) " a postal article shall be deemed to be in course of transmission by post from the time of its being posted at or delivered to, or taken delivery of by, the addressee or its being returned to the sender or otherwise disposed of under the provisions of this ordinance;

    (d) " the delivery of a postal article at the house or office of the addressee or to the addressee (or to his servant or agent or other person considered to be authorised to receive the article

> according to the usual manner of delivering postal articles to the addressee), and where the addressee is a guest or is resident at a hotel delivery to the proprietor or manager thereof, or to his agent, shall be deemed to be delivery to the addressee."

The combined effect of sub-sections (a) and (d) is that a postal packet is in transmission until it is delivered to the addressee or his agent (cases of return to the sender are excepted). It might be argued that this rule is for the purposes of liability in the event of the loss of a postal packet. But this contingency is provided for in section 10 of the Act which exempts the Government from liability howsoever caused. Postal Officers and postal departments are also exempted under this section except in cases of fraud or wilful default. Even if the argument for liability in the event of loss is valid, it does not invalidate our objection to the rule as laid down in *Adams* v. *Lindsell* to the effect that the addressee is deemed to have been communicated with when the sender posts a letter of acceptance. If the legislatures in Ghana and Nigeria intended this to be the position they could have adopted the wording of the Canadian Statute[45] which provides as follows :

> " Subject to the provisions of this Act and the regulations respecting undeliverable mail, mailable matter becomes the property of the person to whom it is addressed when it is deposited in a post office."

This, it is contended, is a re-enactment of the position in *Adams* v. *Lindsell* but not the provisions in Ghana and Nigeria. It is submitted that an acceptance by post in Ghana and Nigeria is not communicated to the offeror until the letter of acceptance is delivered to the offeror or his agent.[46] In this respect it is different from the English position.

(iii) TERMINATION OF OFFER OR ACCEPTANCE

Termination of offer

An offeror can of course change his mind and withdraw his offer. In English law such a revocation is only valid if there has been no acceptance of the offer in the meantime.[47] The position is simple enough in face to face negotiations. But in transactions conducted by correspondence as most are, the English courts take the view that an offer is revoked when the offeree has known or ought to have known of the revocation. Where, however, a letter of acceptance was posted before the offeree learnt of the revocation, it was held that an enforceable agreement had been formed and the revocation was of no legal effect.[48]

The question that arises is whether the Post Office provisions in Ghana and Nigeria have affected this principle of English law, and if so, to what extent? It has already been argued that the mere posting of a letter of acceptance does not in Ghana and Nigerian laws constitute communication to the offerer and consequently no acceptance is valid until communicated. Thus, as far as the offeror is concerned, there has been no acceptance until the offeree's letter has been delivered to him or to his agent. Consistently with this view it is further contended that a revocation of an offer will terminate the offer even if the offeree's letter of acceptance has been posted, provided that the said letter has not been delivered to the offeror or his agent before the revocation. Thus, while *Payne* v. *Cave* applies in Ghana and Nigeria (negotiations inter praesentes), *Routledge* v. *Grant* does not. (Letter of acceptance posted before letter of revocation was received).

Apart from revocation, an offer can also be terminated by the death of either of the parties,[49] by lapse of time[50] or by the failure of a condition precedent. In the Ghana case of *Pickard* v. *Innes & anor*[51] decided by the Full Court (as it then was) at Cape Coast in 1919, the defendants had offered to engage the services of the plaintiff as a mining surveyor in their mine provided that the plaintiff left his former employers on such terms as not to give offence to his general manager. The defendant's reason was that they were so dependent upon the graces of the general manager for the success of their own business that they dare not offend him. When the plaintiff sued for damages for breach of this agreement to employ him it was held that his failure to fulfil the condition precedent operated to terminate the offer of the defendants and that his action could not succeed. The Pickard case is, of course, not binding on the Nigerian courts but has very high persuasive force.[52]

It may be added that an offer can also be terminated by acceptance or rejection by the offeree.

Termination of acceptance

There is no direct judicial authority either way on whether or not an acceptance once given can be withdrawn in English law. A learned author[53] has suggested that such withdrawal is of no legal effect and he is supported in this view by a New Zealand decision.[54] The Scottish courts have, however, taken the view that such a withdrawal is only possible if it is received by the offerer either before the acceptance or contemporaneous with it, but not afterwards.[55] It is submitted that the Scottish solution is more consistent with the local laws of Ghana and Nigeria on acceptances and revocation by correspondence. The position is stronger still in cases of face to face negotiations. There is no reason, however, why the offeree should not be entitled to change his mind before the offeror has had time to do anything about the acceptance to his detriment. If one of the aims of the law of contracts is the fulfilment of the parties' reasonable expectations, it is not easy to see how this could be achieved by the proposed English and New Zealand solution of forcing obligations on reluctant, in fact, unwilling parties.

As to the death of either of the parties as terminating an acceptance there is no authority in English law for this view. In purely personal contracts, such as marriage or concert performance, it is difficult to see how death could not effectively terminate any acceptance. The same is true of acceptances to write a book.

(iv) OFFER AND ACCEPTANCE IN CUSTOMARY LAWS

The case for the existence of agreements as a distinct branch of customary law (which includes Islamic law) has already been argued. The next question that arises is whether customary law has any notion of offer and acceptance. In this as in many other aspects of the law there is a total lack of judicial or academic authority. Even in the native or customary courts an examination of the cases does not reveal any interest in these courts in the abstract concept of offer and acceptance, at least in the English or other extraneous law sense of the terms. Maine's editor has suggested in an analogous situation that this, like many similar embarrassments, has been occasioned by the error of " ascribing to the mental condition of an unformed society a faculty which pre-eminently belongs to an advanced stage of intellectual development, the faculty of distinguishing in speculation, ideas which are blended in practice."[56] Without joining issue with the learned editor, it is observed with respect that his suggestion over-simplifies the process. Surely in every system of law in which agreements are recognised and enforced, certain criteria are adopted in determining (1) whether there has been an agreement, and (2) what its legal effect is. A society is not any the less " formed " because it is not burdened with the minutiae of the extraneous law theory of offer and acceptance. In the Ghana case of *Baidoo* v. *Korkor & Anor*,[57] decided by the Kado Akwatia Local Court, the plaintiff claimed £50 damages for breach of marriage agreement from the defendants. The facts were that the plaintiff had given drinks and money to both the second defendant (the mother of the first defendant) and her relations for the purpose of taking their daughter as wife. The defendants had accepted both the drink and the money but had given the girl to another man in marriage having refused the plaintiff the girl's hand in marriage. The plaintiff's claim was dismissed with £20 costs!

Now, if this case had been decided in a court administering extraneous law and that law was intended by the parties to govern their obligations, there had obviously been an offer and an acceptance of the drinks and the money, for the object of taking the girl in marriage. If no specific performance could be ordered, at least damages could have been awarded, as was done in the Nigerian case of *Ugbomah* v. *Morah*.[58] The defendant would not have been allowed to accept the plaintiff's drinks and money, and then deny him the girl's hand in marriage. But customary law does not leave such emphasis on offer and acceptance for the purposes of the formation of agreements.[59]

Islamic law[60]

Maliki law recognises the concept of offer and acceptance. A contract, it is said, is a bilateral transaction and requires an offer (ijab) and an acceptance (kabul), and both are normally made in the same meeting or session (majilis) of the contracting parties. It is permissible to withdraw (ruju') the offer before there has been an acceptance.

Offer and acceptance can be expressed in the form of compliance with an order, such as, " sell me " and " I sell you herewith." In certain categories of transactions, no acceptance is necessary to create an obligation. Unilateral dispositions with immediate legal effect, such as the acquittance of a debtor, are examples of these.

NOTES

1. See *Pollock on Contracts* (13th ed.) 1950. *Chitty on Contracts* (22nd ed.) 1961, p. 19. *Restatement Contracts*, SS. 3-12; Winfield, " Some aspects of offer and Acceptance " (1939) 55 L.Q.R. 499; Nussbaum, "Comparative Aspects of the Anglo-American offer and Acceptance doctrine" (1936) 38 Colum. L.R. 290; Stimson, "Effective Time of an Acceptance" (1939) 23 Minn. L.R. 776 *S. 8 of the Indian Contract Act,* 1872; *Halsbury Laws* (3rd ed.), Vol. 8, p. 69. See also D. M. Evans, " The Anglo-American Mailing Rule " (1966) 15, I.C.L.Q. 553.
2. K. W. Ryan, *An Introduction to the Civil Law (1962)*, p. 42.
3. Gold Coast, Div. Ct. (1921-25), p. 143. See also *Attorney-General* v. *Otchere* (1957) 2 W.A.L.R. 238, where the plaintiff's letter giving an ex-civil servant a choice of returning a government-supplied vehicle or its value was construed to be an offer capable of acceptance by the defendant.
4. The learned judge relied on the authority of two English cases: *Lewis* v. *Nicholson*, 21 L.J.Q.B. 311, per Wightman, J. at p. 316 and *Bellamy* v. *Debenham* (1891) I, Ch. 412.

5. (1952) 20 N.L.R. 68.
6. (1893) 1 Q.B. 256. See particularly the judgment of Lindley, L.J. in the Court of Appeal.
7. *The Times*, January 13, 1932.
8. In the Ghana case of *Chikezie* v. *Ellie's Pools & anor* (1965) c.c. 137; Boison referred to the Carlill case with approval.
9. (1943) 2 D.L.R. 519. See also the Massachusetts Supreme Court case of *Bishop* v. *Eaton* (1894) 37 N.R. 665 (Massachusetts Supreme Court).
10. See J. B. Milner, *Cases and Materials on Contracts* (1963), p. 366.
11. (1893) 1 Q.B. 256.
12. (1833) 4 B. & Ad. 621; 110 E.R. 590. See also *Lockhart* v. *Barnard* (1845) 15 M. and W. 674; 153 E.R. 646, a case of joint reward for two persons who gave the information, and *Gibbons* v. *Proctor* (1891) 64 L.T. 594, a case of a police officer giving information as part of his duty. Cf. *Fitch* v. *Snedaker* (1868) 38 N.Y. 248 (New York Court of Appeals) where it was held that the plaintiff could not recover because he did not see the offer of the reward when he gave his information. It is submitted with respect that this restriction based as it is on assumpsit is undesirable.
13. (1943) 2 D.L.R. 519.
14. *Denton* v. *Great Northern Railway Co.* (1856) 5 E. and B. 860; 119 E.R. 701.
15. *Fisher* v. *Bell* (1961) 1 Q.B. 394.
16. Cheshire and Fifoot, *Law of Contract* (6th ed. 1964), p. 26.
17. (1953) 1 Q.B. 401.
18. (1909) T.S. 1105; L.L.R. 347 cited by Winfield 55 L.Q.R. 517.
19. See Winfield 55, L.Q.R., p. 518.
20. (1873) L.R. 8 Q.B. 286.
21. (1789) 3 Term Rep. 148.
22. Section 4 (1) (c): " Until such announcement is made any bidder may retract his bid. . . . See also S. 58 (2) of the English Sale of Goods Act, 1893.
23. Act 137 (1962).
24. (1859) 1 EL and EL. 309; 120 E.R. 925. See also *Spencer* v. *Harding* (1870) L.R. 5 C.P. 563.
25. Cheshire and Fifoot, *The Law of Contract* (1964), p. 29.
26. C. Slade, " Auction Sales of Goods without Reserve " (1952) 68 L.Q.R. 238; also L. C. Gower (1952) 68 L.Q.R. 457; and C. Slade (1953) 69 L.Q.R. 21.
27. S. 22 (5) Auctioneers Law Cap. 12 Laws of Eastern Nigeria: S. 22 (5) Auctioneers Law Cap. 10, Laws of Northern Nigeria and S. 22 (5) Sales by Auction Act, Cap. 187, Laws of the Federation of Nigeria and Lagos (1958).
28. *Warlow* v. *Harrison* (1859) 120 E.R. 925; *Spencer* v. *Harding* (1870) L.R. 5 C.P. 563; *Re Agra and Masterman Bank* (1867) 2 Ch. App. 391; *Johnson* v. *Boyes* (1899) 2 Ch. 73. See also *Adebaje* v. *Conde & ors* (1938) 14 N.L.R. 57.
29. *Fenwick* v. *Macdonald, Fraser & Co.* (1904) 6 F. (Ct. of Seas. 850). Cf. *Restatement of Contracts*, SS. 27.
30. Restatement of Contracts, SS. 23 states the position in American Law. Cf. Williston, *Contracts*, 3rd ed. SS. 34. In German law S. 130 of the B.G.B. is to the same effect and in French law the balance of the authorities supports this view. Planiol has in S. 986 the following: " la majorite des auteurs et les arrets decide que la volonte transmise au

loin produit son effet seulement lorsqu'elle parvient a la connaissance du destinataire." (Formation des contrats consensus), cited by Winfield, 55 L.Q.R., p. 503.

31. Winfield, " Some Aspects of Offer and Acceptance " (1939) 55 L.Q.R. at p. 504.

32. See P. S. Atiyah, *Introduction to the law of Contract*, Oxford, 1962, p. 35.

33. (1952) 20 N.L.R. 68.

34. Gold Coast, Div. Ct. (1921-25) 143.

35. *Felthouse* v. *Bindley* (1862), 11 C.B.N.S. 869. In the United States silence in some cases is deemed to be an acceptance of an offer. See *Restatement of Contracts* (1932) S. 29 comment (a) " Even silence may sometimes be effective as a mode of acceptance." See also S. 72 (1).

36. Atiyah, op. cit., p. 37.

37. The reward cases and other unilateral agreements are excepted. Here the communication of acceptance is not necessary.

38. (1877) 2 App. Cas. 666 (House of Lords). See also S. 4 of the Indian Contract Act, 1872 which states : " The communication of a proposal is complete when it comes to the knowledge of the person to whom it is made. The communication of acceptance is complete : as against the proposer, when it is put in a course of transmission to the person to whom it is made, so as to be out of the power of the acceptor, when it comes to the knowledge of the proposer. . . ." On the American system see *Restatement, Contracts* S. 72; *Williston, Contracts*, 3rd ed. 1957, S. 70; Corbin, *Contracts* (1950) SS. 67 and 73. See also Art. 130 (1) of the B.G.B.

39. (1955) 2 Q.B. 327.

40. See Winfield, " Some aspects of offer and Acceptance " (1939) 55 L.Q.R. 499; Nussbaum, " Comparative aspects of the Anglo-American offer and acceptance doctrine " (1936) 38 Colum. L. Rev. 920; Stimson " Effective time of an acceptance " (1939) 23 Minn. L. Rev. 776: *Uniform Law on the Formation of Contracts for the International Sale of Goods* (1964) I.C.L.Q. 553. On the application of the rule to telegrams, see the U.S. case of *Watson* v. *Paschall* (1913) 93 S.C. 537.

41. (1818) 1 B & Ald. 681.

42. *Household Fire and Carriage Accident Insurance Co. Ltd.* v. *Grant* (1879) 4 Ex. D. 216.

43. D. M. Evans, supra.

44. Post Office Ordinance, Cap. 214, Laws of the Gold Coast (1951), S. 3; Re-enacted in Post Office Act, 1963 (Act 194), S. 44 (2).

45. Post Office Act, S. 39 (Revised Statutes of Canada, 1952, Cap. 212).

46. We are not here concerned with the merits or demerits of what have been called " complete on posting " and " complete on delivery " rules. We agree with Ryan that the criterion should be commercial efficiency. Although German, Scottish and French writers have made much of the correctness of their solution, i.e. " complete on delivery " there is no evidence that the English rule has occasioned any injustice. See Ryan, op. cit., p. 44.

47. (1789) 3 T.R. 148.

48. (1828) 4 Bing 653 Options to keep offers open for a given period will be discussed under " Form and Consideration " infra.

49. *Dickenson* v. *Dodds* (1876) 2 Ch. D. 463.

50. *Ramsgate Victoria Hotel Co.* v. *Montefiore* (1866) L.R. 1 Ex. 109.

51. Gold Coast, F. Ct. (1919) 12

52. This is especially so since the judges of the then Gold Coast Colony were ex-officio members of the Full Court of Nigeria. This was equally true of the Nigerian judges vis-à-vis the Gold Coast Full Court. See *Van Berkel & Co.* v. *Netherlands Distilleries,* Gold Coast F.C., 1926-29, p. 400.

53. *Benjamin on Sale,* 8th ed., p. 83.

54. *Dunmore (Countess)* v. *Alexander* (1830), 9 sh. (Ct. of Sess.) 190. Although the facts of this case reveal that two letters, and not a letter and a subsequent telegram were involved, it is submitted that the same principle is applicable provided the letter or telegram of revocation is received before or contemporaneous with the letter of acceptance.

55. *Wenckheim* v. *Arndt* (N.Z.) 1 J.R. 73 cited by Cheshire & Fifoot—p. 44.

56. Sir Henry Maine, *Ancient Law* (ed. Firth), 1963, p. 305.

57. Ghana, Eastern Region Local Court Returns for 1963, Suit No. 469/63.

58. (1940) 15 N.L.R. 78.

59. The importance of form in customary agreements is discussed below.

60. See J. Schacht, *An Introduction to Islamic Law,* Oxford, Clarendon Press, 1964, pp. 145 et seq.; Abdur Rahim, *Muhammedan Jurisprudence* (1910) p. 61; L. Milliot, *Droit du Musulman,* S.641. See generally J. N. D. Anderson, " The Future of Islamic law in British Commonwealth Territories," (1962) 27, Law and Contemporary Problems, 617.

CHAPTER 6

FORM AND CONSIDERATION

In this chapter we shall be attempting to answer the question, what parts do form and consideration play in the creation of legally enforceable agreements in Ghana and Nigeria? We shall first of all look at the position in English law which, it has been suggested in some quarters,[1] is the same as the law in Nigeria, and finally, the actual state of the law in Ghana and Nigeria.

Form

In English law an agreement must either be executed in a certain form or there must be present some consideration moving from the promisee to the promisor.[2] The most common form has been the use of the seal, and when this is present the law does not stop to ask if there has been consideration. Consideration is presumed.[3] The origin and history of the seal in English law need not detain us here.[4] It is enough to mention that when its use was imported into England from the courts of Frankish Kings, only few persons in high positions had a seal. In the course of its development, however, the seal has changed its character. From a piece of wax impressed with a device of an elaborate kind and individual to the owner of the device it has become a paper disc stuck to or printed on a document opposite the square reserved for signature. In the words of Pollock and Maitland, " the law of the great has become the law of all."[5]

It has been suggested that use of a seal of this description has lost its value and that its abolition as a privileged category of agreements is long overdue.[6] In fact in 1937 the English Law Revision Committee in their *6th Interim Report*[7] suggested that any written agreement not providing for consideration should be valid even without a seal. The English Law Commission set up under the Law Commissions Act, 1965 has " contracts under seal " as one of its subjects for re-examination.[8] The seal has also been abolished in many jurisdictions in the United States of America.[9]

Now, there is no doubt that *Rann* v. *Hughes* which stamped the authority of the House of Lords on the division of agreements into those under seal and those by parol is part of the law of Ghana and Nigeria, being a pre-1874 decision of the English House of Lords.

It must be pointed out however, that the statement about the division of agreements in that case was obiter and was not necessary for the decision.[10] It is suggested that the distinction in many American jurisdictions between business transactions and gifts is more in keeping with the needs of commerce than that between agreements with seal and those without.

Consideration

Consideration is necessary in all agreements except those under seal. Various theories have been put forward as to its origin. Holmes[11] thought that it arose from the *quid pro quo* of the action of debt; Fifoot found it in the bargain theory of agreements in English law[12] and Holdsworth has suggested that it arose from the tortuous nature of the action of assumpsit, the detriment being the damage resulting from the breach of the obligation.[13] Lord Mansfield's[14] attempt to approach consideration on moral grounds has not been accepted in English law. Pollock's definition in terms of " an act or forbearance or the promise thereof, which is offered by one party to an agreement and accepted by the other, as an inducement to that other's act or promise,"[15] has been more generally followed. English law has come to accept the position that an informal agreement not supported by consideration cannot be enforced by the courts. It has generally been assumed that this is also the law in Nigeria[16] and to some extent in Ghana.[17] So much protest has however been raised at the continued existence of this requirement as an element of enforceable informal agreements that it bcomes vital to look again at the juristic basis of its application in Ghana and Nigeria. Some of the relevant questions to be answered are: (i) is consideration part of the received laws of Ghana and Nigeria? (ii) If so, has it been changed or modified in any way or ways?, and finally (iii) does the doctrine require any further changes or modification? We shall attempt the answers seriatim.

(i) *Is the doctrine of consideration part of the received laws of Ghana and Nigeria?*

In order to answer the question we have to look at the facts of the familiar case of *Rann* v. *Hughes*[18] in which the English House of Lords have been said to have laid down the doctrine as part of the law of England. In that case:

> John Hughes owed £938 to a creditor, but before paying it he died, leaving an estate of over £3,000. His widow Isabella Hughes took out letters of administration to his estate, and took possession of his assets. She promised to pay to the creditor the sum of £938

which her late husband owed; but she did not say that she would pay it personally out of her own money nor was this promise put in writing to satisfy the Statute of Frauds. Presumably she meant to pay it from her late husband's estate. She failed to keep her promise and the creditor sued her not as an administratrix but against her personally.

Lord Mansfield, following his previous decision in *Pillans* v. *Van Mierop*[19] in 1765, held that she was personally liable. But the Exchequer Chamber and the House of Lords held that she was not. Now, there were three possible bases for the decision of the House of Lords, namely, (a) that it was never alleged nor proved that the defendant promised to pay personally; (b) that any such promise would have to be in writing to satisfy the Statute of Frauds, 1677, but none was alleged nor proved from the evidence; and finally, (c) that there was no consideration to support the promise. All these three points were argued before the House. The judges who advised the House on the case said that such a promise was unenforceable because there was no consideration to support it, but according to the reporter, the House held the promise to be unenforceable because it was not alleged nor proved to be in writing.[20] It is remarkable that both judicial and academic opinions have proceeded on the basis that the opinion of the judges was accepted by the House. It is very respectfully submitted that there is no evidence to support this assumption. It may be argued, however, that in English law this objection cannot be a strong one since the House of Lords have in subsequent cases reaffirmed the doctrine in unambiguous terms.[21] It may be argued further that these subsequent cases, some of which were pre-1874 decisions are parts of the laws of Ghana and Nigeria. Our answer to this is that if the doctrine is supposed to be based on the decision in *Rann* v. *Hughes* and the House of Lords have purported to follow it because of binding precedent, then the Ghanaian and Nigerian Courts should feel free to interpret the *Hughes* Decision in a different way. This position is made stronger still by cases where injustice would result from following the interpretation placed on that case by the House of Lords. The fact that the Ghanaian[22] and Nigerian[23] courts have hitherto felt bound by these decisions does not alter the principle one bit. Our answer to the question posed above, i.e. is consideration part of the received laws of Ghana and Nigeria is a doubtful " yes."

(ii) *Has the doctrine of consideration been changed or modified in any way or ways in Ghana and Nigeria?*

We are not concerned here with the attempts of English law

through the laws of agency and trusts to neutralise some of the worst excesses of the doctrine of consideration. It is enough to mention these casually and to add that the law of bailment belongs to a different category from that of agreements, solely because of the absence of consideration in the former (however, some cases of bailment arise from an existing contractual situation e.g. hire-purchase). In order to answer the above question effectively we shall take a look at some of the more important facets of consideration. Six of them have been commonly recognised by the courts, namely:

(a) An informal agreement must be supported by a consideration;[24]

(b) The consideration must move from the promisee and not otherwise;[25]

(c) Consideration must not be past;[26]

(d) Options to keep offers open are not enforceable except they are supported by consideration;[27]

(e) A promise to forgo part of a debt is not enforceable except it is supported by consideration;[28] and

(f) Performance of an act or the promise to perform an act is not sufficient consideration if the act is already enjoined by some legal duty.[29]

We shall examine the local authorities on each of these in turn to determine if there have been any modifications of the doctrine in Ghana and Nigeria.

(a) An informal agreement must be supported by consideration:

In spite of the doubts we expressed on the authority of the English case of *Rann* v. *Hughes*,[30] the courts in both Ghana and Nigeria have adopted the English law attitude of looking for consideration in every informal agreement. In the Ghana case of *Hamilton* v. *Mpoley*.[31] decided by the Ghana Full Court (as it was then) in 1921, the plaintiff claimed a refund of a loss of £118:10s. from the defendant. The transaction was evidenced by what was called a "note of hand" and one of the points argued for the defendant was the absence of consideration to support the loan. This argument was upheld both by the Court of first instance and the Full Court. The three judges who decided the appeal were unanimous that the absence of consideration was fatal to the plaintiff's claim. To the same effect is the judgment in the *Colonial Bank* v. *Bellon*[32] where their Lordships of the then Gold Coast Full Court dismissed

the plaintiff's appeal also on the ground of absence of consideration. The plea of estoppel based on section 55 of the English
Conveyancing Act, 1881 did not avail the plaintiff. It is remarkable
that the Ghana Contract Act, 1960,[33] which has been acclaimed as
progressive by some learned authors,[34] has done nothing about this
aspect of the doctrine of consideration. It is submitted however,
on the basis of our earlier contention on the authority of *Rann* v.
Hughes, that the Supreme Court of Ghana is free to enforce agreements intended by the parties to have legal effect even without the
requirement of a consideration.

The Nigerian Courts have adopted a similar attitude to that of
the courts in Ghana. The Privy Council Appeal of *Savage & ors.* v.
Uwechia,[35] turned on the absence of consideration. In the case of
Akenzua II v. *Benin District Council,*[36] Thomas, J., after holding
that the evidence disclosed no consideration whatsoever moving
from the plaintiff added:

> " It is rather odd, in these circumstances that the plaintiff could
> imagine that he could become the licensee in perpetuity of a very
> vast area of land within which to exploit timber by the passing
> of the council's resolution simpliciter, and without giving any
> consideration whatsoever."[37]

The facts of this case were that the plaintiff had as President of
the Benin District Council played some part in recovering five
pieces of forest areas from a timber exploiting company. The
plaintiff later appealed to the council to allow him exploit one of
the five areas in order to augment his poor salary and this permission was granted by a resolution of the council, later signed by the
plaintiff as chairman. The resolution was subsequently revoked
by the council in accordance with its standing orders and the
plaintiff sued for the breach of the agreement as per the resolution.
The court held, among other grounds, that there was no consideration to support the council's original promise and the action was
dismissed.[38]

Thus in Nigeria as in Ghana the courts have always been very
willing to refuse to enforce agreements not supported by consideration.

    (b) Consideration must move from the promisee and not
       otherwise:

It is a cardinal rule of the English law of contract that consideration must move from the promisee.[39] Thus where A writes a book
for B and asks B to pay C, C cannot enforce the payment since

K

he has given no consideration. The fact that he may have been a party to the agreement does not affect the general principle.[40] This aspect of the doctrine of consideration has been adopted by the Nigerian courts without question. In *Cardoso* v. *The Executors of Doherty*[41] the plaintiff had assisted the deceased testator in obtaining some loans which were secured with mortgages on several landed properties. The testator had expressed the wish that the plaintiff should reside in one of the houses so secured without any payment of rent. On the strength of this wish the executors had written to the plaintiff a letter in these terms:

> " Dear Sir,
>
> I am directed by the Board of Executors to inform you that the Board has decided to dispose of all the properties mortgaged by you, excepting your property No. 23, Bamgbose Street, which the Board has decided to reserve for your occupation, to remain in, all your life time.
>
> Yours faithfully,
Signed Albert E. Carrena,
Secretary to the Board."

On the strength of this letter the court below granted the plaintiff an injunction as against the executors, against his eviction during his life-time, by realising the mortgages on the property. A strong West African Court of Appeal consisting of Kingdon, Petrides C.J.J. and Graham Paul. J. allowed the appeal of the executors on the ground among others, that there was no consideration moving from the plaintiff to the executors to support the promise made in the letter and that the wish of the testator was not such consideration. The court said (at page 80) of the judgment:

> " It is clear upon the plaintiff's statement of claim that his case before the court below was not based on any valuable consideration having passed from him in regard to the letter of 10th August, 1935. In paragraph 5 he specifically states that it was in consideration of the wishes of the deceased that the executors wrote the letter on which he founds. That is not in law a valuable consideration."

It is submitted with respect that this is a clear instance of the doctrine of consideration being used to frustrate the intentions of the parties. Surely the letter of 10th August from the board of executors was intended as a business transaction binding on the board. To deny the plaintiff his remedy on such tenuous technicality, leaves the merits of the doctrine very questionable.

In Ghana this aspect of the doctrine has been abolished by statute. Section 10 of the Contracts Act, 1960 provides as follows:

" No promise shall be invalid as a contract by reason only that the consideration therefor is supplied by someone other than the promisee."

There has not been any local post-1960 decision on this section of the Act but it is clear from the wording that if the *Cardoso* decision were before the Ghana courts today, the judgment might well go the other way.

(c) Consideration must not be past:

This was laid down in the English case of *Roscorla* v. *Thomas*,[42] and was argued on behalf of the defendants in the Nigerian case of *Akenzua II* v. *Benin District Council*,[43] to which reference has already been made. We are not concerned here with the quasi-contractual action of *quantum meruit* or *quantum valebant* in cases where " request " can be proved.[44] It is enough to mention that the *Roscorla* decision was followed in the West African Court of Appeal decision from Ghana of *U.T.C.* v. *Hauri*.[45] The latter decision has been cited by two learned authors as part of the law of Nigeria.[46]

Commercial practice and convenience has however, forced the hands of the legislatures in both Ghana and Nigeria to create exceptions to this rather undesirable doctrine. Thus section 27 (1) of the Nigerian Bills of Exchange Act,[47] which is in similar terms to the Ghana statute on the same subject, provided that:

" 27 (1) Valuable consideration for a bill may be constituted by (a) any consideration sufficient to support any simple contract; (b) an antecedent debt or liability. Such a debt or liability is deemed valuable consideration whether the bill is payable on demand or at a future time."

Thus in cases of negotiable instruments, even past consideration will be considered good or valuable consideration.[48]

(d) An option to keep an offer open is not enforceable against the offeror except it is supported by consideration:

The decision in *Routledge* v. *Grant*[49] has often been said to have laid down this principle. In that case the defendant offered to purchase the plaintiff's house and gave him six weeks to decide whether to accept or reject the offer. The defendant purported to withdraw his offer before the six weeks had expired and in an action for breach of agreement by the plaintiff who accepted after the withdrawal of the offer but within the six weeks period, it was held that there was no consideration for the option. This state of the law has been heavily criticised and its abolition had been recommended in 1937 in England.[50] It has in fact been abolished in Ghana by Section 8 (1) of the Contract Act, 1960:

> " (1) A promise to keep an offer open for acceptance for a specified time shall not be invalid as a contract by reason only of the absence of any consideration therefor."[51]

No similar provision exists in Nigeria and although local judicial authority on this aspect of the law is rather thin, it is not unlikely that the Nigerian courts will prefer to follow the rule in *Grant's* case.

(e) A promise to forgo part of a debt or any liability is not enforceable except it is supported by consideration:

This facet of the doctrine covers situations where a creditor agrees to accept part of a debt as discharge for the whole and where an obligor agrees to waive any other legal right. The orthodox theory as far as this goes in English law is that there must be a consideration to support the waiver if it is to be legally enforceable. Thus if X agrees to accept £800 from Y out of a debt of £1,000 on the same day and place as stipulated in the original agreement, the waiver is not enforceable except there is consideration for it.[52] Also if A agrees to deliver goods to B within eight weeks and later requests for extension of time to deliver, B could still sue for breach of the agreement unless the waiver at the time of delivery was supported by valuable consideration.[53] This rule was restated by the Court of Exchequer in *Sibree* v. *Fripp*,[54] in which case Baron Alderson, in re-examining the whole position, laid bare the fanciful and tenuous nature of its practical application. The House of Lords nevertheless gave their approval to the doctrine in 1884 in the curious case of *Foakes* v. *Beer*.[55] The severe impact of this rule in English law has however been diminished by what Lord Cairns described as the " broad rule of justice " in *Hughes* v. *Metropolitan Railway Co.*[56] applied and extended by Bowen L.J. in *Birmingham Band Co.* v. *London and North-Western Railway*[57] and expounded into a general doctrine by Denning J. (as he then was) in the famous case of *Central London Property Trust Ltd.* v. *High Trees House Ltd.*[58] In the Hughes case the appellants gave the respondent six months' notice to repair but before the notice expired opened negotiations for the purchase of their lease. These negotiations were broken off and when six months had passed from the service of the notice, the appellant brought an action of ejectment. The House of Lords held that the respondents were entitled to relief in equity as the negotiations had the effect of suspending notice, which would not expire until six months had passed from the time when the negotiations were discontinued. In the High Trees case it was laid down that when parties enter into an arrangement which is intended to create legal relations and in pursuance of such arrangement one party makes a promise to the other which he knows will be acted on and which is in fact acted on by the promisee, the promise is binding on the promisor to the extent that it will not allow him to act inconsistently with it, although the promise may not be supported by consideration in the strict sense. The *High Trees* principle, however, is only valid as a defence and does not create any new right of action.[59]

This position has been substantially adopted as the state of the law in Nigeria. In the recent case of *Ajayi* v. *R. T. Briscoe (Nigeria) Ltd.*[60] the defendant by two hire-purchase agreements, hired eleven lorries from the plaintiffs on the terms that the balance of the purchase price after payments of deposits, was to be paid by stated instalments ending on January 30th, 1957. On July 12th, 1957 the hirer wrote the plaintiffs (owners) complaining about inadequate repair facilities for the lorries and requesting a suspension of the payment of instalments until the lorries were back in active service after repairs. The plaintiffs granted this request in their letter dated 22nd July, 1957, in these terms:

" Dear Sirs,

We are in receipt of your letters of July 5 and 12 and are indeed very sorry to hear about the troubles you have had with your fleet of Seddon Tippers. We hope very soon to be able to put at your disposal, the service of our engineer and on completion of our workshop in Apapa we should be able to give you proper service for your Seddon vehicles in the time to come.

Please rest assured that we do regret the inconvenience and loss you have been put to and we confirm herewith that we are agreeable to your withholding instalments due on the Seddon Tippers as long as they are withdrawn from active service.

Yours, faithfully,
Signed B. A. Heidermann,
A/G Manager."

The defendant having sent in eight of the lorries, these were repaired by the plaintiffs who thereafter tried to advise him to collect them and resume payment of the instalments. All efforts in this direction having failed, the plaintiffs sued him for the arrears of instalments in November, 1957. The defence of fraud, on which the defendant relied was dismissed by Onyeama J. who heard the case at the High Court. On appeal to the Nigerian Supreme Court, the defendant relied on the plaintiffs' letter as raising an estoppel against their insisting on the terms of the agreements. This defence was also dismissed by the Court and this decision was affirmed by the Judicial Committee. Their lordships went further to delimit the scope of the doctrine of promissory estoppel as follows: (a) that the party relying on the estoppel must have altered his position; (b) that the promisor can resile from his promise on giving reasonable notice, which need not be formal, giving the promisee a reasonable opportunity of resuming his position, and (c) that the promise only becomes final and irrevocable if the promisee cannot resume his position. Since there was no evidence to show that the defendant had re-organised his transport system on the basis of three instead of eleven lorries, but on the contrary he could have resumed his original position on the notice he was deemed to have received, the doctrine did not avail him. The plea therefore failed.

In Ghana, however, this rule which had its origin in *Pinnel's* case has been abolished by statute. Section 8 (2) of the Contract Act, 1960 provides that :

> " 8 (2) A promise to waive the payment of a debt or part of a debt or the performance of some other contractual or legal obligation shall not be invalid as a contract by reason only of the absence of any consideration therefor."

It could be argued that this subsection is only a statutory recognition of the existing position of the law in England, and that it does not create any new rights of action that did not exist before the enactment of the statute. Its logical limits would then be the rule in *Combe* v. *Combe*.[61] But this approach to the interpretation of the provision is open to serious objections. Firstly the volume of academic and judicial dissent from the rule in *Pinnel's* case has been quite considerable. The Ghana Legislature could hardly have intended to perpetuate such a position in statutory form. Secondly, the whole tenor of Part III of the Contract Act leads to the only conclusion that the legislature in Ghana intended to modify various aspects of the doctrine of consideration. The preceding section (i.e. subsection 8 (1)) made options to leave offers open for acceptance, enforceable even without being supported by consideration. Finally, but not with any emphasis, the sidenotes to section 8 has the following: " Certain contracts to be valid despite lack of consideration."

It is therefore submitted with respect that the subsection creates a new right of action and that *Combe* v. *Combe* could well be differently decided in Ghana.[62]

(f) Performance of an act or the promise to perform an act is not sufficient consideration if the act or the promise is already enjoined by some legal duty:

This rule covers situations where the plaintiff's performance or promise to perform an act is already imposed by a previous agreement[63] or a public duty.[64] It is distinguished from cases where the act or promise is already imposed by an agreement previously made not between him and the defendant but between himself and a third party. In the latter case, English law finds sufficient consideration in the plaintiff's act or promise[65] but in the former, enforcement is denied the plaintiff on the basis of the absence of consideration.[66] An attempt to reconcile the two conflicting streams of authority has been made on the basis that the third party might derive some benefit or satisfaction from the plaintiff's performance or promise, while a party to the agreement could legally enforce it against the plaintiff thereby making his eventual performance nothing more than what he is legally bound to do. It is submitted with respect that this distinction is more ingenious than practical. It is difficult to see the difference in A promising X that he will perform his agreement with B, and his making the same promise to B himself. Here again the Ghana Contract Act has improved on the state of the law. Section 9 of the Act provides that:

"9. The performance of an act or the promise to perform an act may be sufficient consideration for another promise notwithstanding that the performance of that act may already be enjoined by some legal duty, whether enforceable by the other party or not."

The above section should thus be a welcome relief to the Ghana courts who will be spared the unpleasant task of looking for tenuous distinguishing features in order to hold a defendant liable, as was done in the English decision of *Hartley* v. *Ponsonby*.[67] There is, however, no similar provision in Nigeria but it is hoped that the situation will not be in its present unsatisfactory state much longer.

Our answer to the question posed at the beginning of this subsection i.e. whether the doctrine of consideration has been changed or modified in any way in Ghana and Nigeria, is in the affirmative in the case of Ghana. In the case of Nigeria all the existing evidence points to a too-ready desire to follow English authority.

(iii) Does the doctrine of consideration require any further changes or modification?

The pros and cons of the doctrine of consideration have engaged the attention of judicial and academic opinion for upwards of two centuries.[68] Some have advocated its total abolition,[69] some feel that any legal system without it should promptly invent one,[70] others are satisfied with the removal of some of its more objectionable manifestations.[71] We do not consider it desirable for our purpose here to add to so heavily documented a topic. We do however associate our views with those of the latter group of thinkers for the vital reason that the doctrine is so much part of the law, not only of contracts but of property and trusts, that its total abolition will be tantamount to burning down a house in order to roast a particular pig. If the doctrine is abolished, the law will still have to cater for such situations as total failure of consideration, the test of reasonableness in agreements in restraint of trade, the differences in treatment between purchasers for value and volunteers, the meaning of holders for value in bills of exchange, and the important distinction between gifts and business transactions.[72] It is not enough to accept ready-made answers to some of these problems from the civil law or Roman-Dutch law systems without accepting the whole basis of their own concept of agreement. The latter course would for instance mean the importation of the notarial form in gifts as in French law.[73]

What we propose to do here is to spotlight such aspects of the doctrine of consideration as we feel are unsuitable in Ghana and Nigeria, having regard to the existence of laws other than English law.

As has been pointed out by a learned author in a recent article, " customary law defies the kelsenite dichotomy between the realm of ought and the domain of ' is '."[74] The doctrine of consideration on the other hand has as one of its tenets the rule that moral consideration is no consideration.[75] It is easy to see the glaring injustice that will result from a rigid application of this rule. In the Nigerian case of *Odufunade* v. *Rossek*,[76] decided by the Supreme Court in 1960, the defendant undertook to pay the plaintiff ten per cent commission on the purchase price of his lease if the plaintiff would introduce anybody that would eventually take an assignment of the lease. The plaintiff brought the property to the attention of the Chief Federal Lands Officer (Lagos), who later arranged for a compulsory acquisition of the land and the defendant was adequately compensated for his interest. He however refused to pay the agreed ten per cent commission to the plaintiff who therefore sued for it. The learned trial judge relied on Lord

Watson's statement in *Toulmin* v. *Millar*[77] that in order to found
a legal claim for commission, there must be a contractual relation
between the introduction and the ultimate transaction on sale "
and decided that a compulsory acquisition was a negation of contract and therefore no commission was payable to the plaintiff.
The judgment was affirmed by the Nigerian Supreme Court. The
statement of their Lordships of the Supreme Court emphasises the
point we are trying to make here. Bairamian F.J. who read the
judgment after discussing the English authorities on the subject
added:

> " A commission of ten per cent is high. It shows how anxious the
> defendant was to get rid of his interest and it was the wit of
> the plaintiff in speaking to the Federal Lands officer which led to
> his getting the property off his hands at what was no doubt a
> fair price. A little generosity on his part would have been
> welcome, but that must be left to him."[78]

There is little doubt that this decision is rather hard on the
plaintiff. It is curious that in this case neither the plaintiff nor the
court considered the applicability of customary law to the transaction. It is contended that in cases such as this, miscarriages of
justice could be averted by emphasising the intention of the parties.
Here they clearly intended that the plaintiff would be entitled to
commission on a disposition of the defendant's interest in the
property. To have denied this to the plaintiff on a technical rule is,
it is submitted with respect, patently unfair. If the stipulated commission was too high, the Court could impose a reasonable sum.

As we have already pointed out, we have no serious objection to
the continued requirement of consideration as an element of a
valid agreement. We contend, however, that the doctrine must shed
its technical nature and be but evidentiary of a transaction. The
payment of " aseda " or " ntrama " in Ghana customary laws[79] or
" oji " in Ibo customary law,[80] is not burdened with the same
technicalities as we find in the English doctrine. These are but
evidence of the fact that the parties meant business. It is submitted
that this should be the role of consideration in an integrated law
of agreements in Ghana and Nigeria.[81]

Form and consideration in customary law

> Customary agreements are not entirely destitute of certain forms.
> The sale or other disposition of land in the respective tribes in
> Ghana and Nigeria is attended with elaborate formalities,[82] the
> absence of some of which would be fatal to the validity of the
> transaction. Marriage also must conform to certain set forms.[83]
> Money-lending transactions[84] and bailments[85] in customary law

have been said to require certain given forms to be valid and enforceable. A learned author[86] has justified these formal requirements in land and marriage transactions on the basis of the peculiarities of property and family laws. Nwabueze would dispense with formalities in other customary agreements.

While agreeing with his later suggestion, one would, however, add that the aim of the law should be to simplify property transactions and that the requirements of rigid form are hardly a step towards this goal. There is of course, the need for certainty. As has already been suggested in connection with agreements under seal, we feel that " form " should not go to the " essential validity " of an enforceable agreement in customary law.

There is still the question whether or not customary law knows anything like the doctrine of consideration.[87] Nwabueze[88] has deduced from the dearth of evidence on the enforcement of executory agreements in customary law, the conclusion that there was no such thing as consideration in the law. The learned author however concedes that the issue as to the existence or otherwise of executory agreements in customary law is by no means resolved. The recent judgment[89] of Ollennu J. in the Ghana Land Court, to the effect that specific performance is a recognised customary remedy, stresses the inconclusive nature of the argument. Now, although it is correct to assert that consideration in its imported technical sense was unknown to traditional customary agreements, it is equally true to say that in all systems of customary law there was a type of " earnest " which gave customary transactions business efficacy. Although these went by different names in differenct places[90] the role they played was strikingly similar. It is submitted with respect that it is futile to search for the attributes of the English doctrine of consideration in a customary transaction. The role of the " earnest " is to validate and give business touch to a transaction.[91] It also facilitates the proof of the existence of an obligation. This later function is the precise role that we prescribed for any doctrine of consideration in our preceding sub-head. It may be added that in Islamic law the conclusion of a contract is essentially informal. Only the literal meanings of certain technical terms such as *safka* (striking hand upon hand) reflect former symbolic acts.

NOTES

1. See McNeil & Rains, *Nigerian Cases and Statutes on Contract and Tort* (London, Sweet & Maxwell, 1965), p. 15.
2. *Rann* v. *Hughes* (1778) 4 Bro. Parl. Cas. 27.

3. See no. (2) supra.
4. Pollock and Maitland, *History of English Law*, vol. II 2nd ed. passim.
5. Op. cit., p. 216.
6. See Walter Stern, "Consideration and Gift" (1965) 14 I.C.L.Q. 675. In Kenya the Law of Contract Ordinance (No. 43 of 1960) provides that no contract shall be void or unenforceable by reason only that it is not under seal.
7. (1937) Cmd. 5449, cf. (1937) I.M.L.R., p. 97.
8. *First Programme of the Law Commission*, 1965, p. 7.
9. See William J. Lloyd, "Consideration and the Seal in New York," 46 Col. L.R.I. See also *Restatement, Contracts*, S. 116.
10. For the facts of this case see infra.
11. *Common Law*, Chapter 7.
12. *History and Sources of the Common Law (Contract & Tort)*, p. 398.
13. *History of English Law*, vol. III, p. 3.
14. *Pillans* v. *Van Mierop* (1753) 3 Burr. 1663. See also *Hawkes* v. *Saunders* (1782), 1 cowp. 289.
15. *Pollock on Contracts* (13th ed. 1950), p. 8.
16. McNeil and Rains, *Nigerian Cases and Statutes on Contract and Tort*, pp. 15 et seq.
17. *Walkden and Co.* v. *Kwamin* (1923-25) Div. Ct. 24. *Hamilton* v. *Mpoley* (1921) F.C. 78.
18. (1778) 4 Bro. Parl. Cas. 27.
19. (1765) 3 Burr. 1663.
20. See 4 Bro. Parl. Cas., headnote, p. 27.
21. *Eastwood* v. *Kenyon* (1840) 11 Ad. & El. 438; *Bunn* v. *Guy* (1803) 4, East, 190.
22. See *Mue* v. *Nyumutei* (1926-29) Div. Ct. 93; *Colonial Bank* v. *Bellon* (1923-25) F. Ct. 176.
23. See *Savage & ors.* v. *Uwechia* (1961) 1 W.L.R. 455.
24. *Eastwood* v. *Kenyon*, supra.
25. *Dunlop* v. *Selfridge*, supra.
26. *Eastwood* v. *Kenyon*, supra. Cf. cases of negotiable instruments.
27. *Routledge* v. *Grant* (1828) 4 Bing, 653.
28. *Foakes* v. *Beer* (1884) 9 App. Cas. 605.
29. *Stilk* v. *Myrick* (1809) 2 camp. 317.
30. (1778) 4 Bro. Parl. Cas. 27.
31. (1921) F. Ct. 78.
32. Gold Coast (1923-25) F. Ct. 176. See also *Aryeh* v. *Thompson* (1926-29) F. Ct. 354; *Mue* v. *Myumtei* (1926-29) Div. Ct. 93. Cf. the recent case of *Adjabeng* v. *Kwabia* (1960) G.L.R. 37 where the Ghana Supreme Court held that inadequacy of consideration was no ground for avoiding a sale.
33. Act 25.
34. See Daniels, *Common Law in West Africa* (1964). Read (1961) 5, J.A.L. 48.
35. (1961) 1 W.L.R. 455.
36. (1959) W.R.N.L.R. 1.
37. See op. cit. at p. 5.
38. See also S. 3 of the Mercantile Law (Amendment) Act, 1856 (19 & 20 Vict. Cap. 97), which provides that consideration should appear upon the face of the document by which it is to be proved. (Amended in

Ghana by Act 25). See per Tindal, C.J. in *Laythorpe* v. *Bryant* (1836) 2 Bing. (N.C.) 735.

39. *Dunlop* v. *Selfridge* (1915) A.C. 847.
40. See Cheshire and Fifoot, *Law of Contract* (6th ed. 1964), p. 65.
41. (1938) 4 W.A.C.A. 78.
42. (1842) 3 Q.B. 234.
43. (1959) W.R.N.L.R. 1.
44. See *Lampleigh* v. *Brathwaite* (1615) Hob. 105.
45. (1940) 6 W.A.C.A. 148.
46. McNeil and Bains, *Nigerian Cases and Statutes on Contract and Tort*, p. 21. It has already been pointed out that Ghana decisions, though they are of high persuasive force in Nigeria, are not binding on the Nigerian courts.
47. Cap. 21 (Laws, 1958). See also S. 25 (1) of the *Ghana* Bills of Exchange Act, 1961 (Act 55) repealing and substantially re-enacting the Gold Coast Bills of Exchange ordinance (Cap. 195) Laws of the Gold Coast, 1951. An acknowledgement of a statute-barred debt which revives the original debt without further consideration could be taken as another exception to the rule, but Pollock has argued that this is only a procedural device. Since the Infants Relief Act, 1874, is not a statute of general application in Ghana (it came into force on 7th August, 1874, i.e. after 24th July, 1874, the effective date of the reception of English law in Ghana) it could be argued with some force that an acknowledgement of a liability by an infant after the age of 21 will be enforceable against him and that this is another exception to the rule in Ghana. This will of course not be true of Nigeria.
48. For cases on this statute see: for Ghana *Yeboah* v. *Adane* (1921-25) Div. Ct. 75; *Colonial Bank* v. *Bellon* (1923-25) F. Ct. 176. On Nigeria see *Savage* v. *Uwechia*, supra.
49. (1828) 4 Bing, 653, see also *Cooke* v. *Oxley* (1790) 3 T.R. 653.
50. *Sixth Interim Report of the Law Revision Committee* (1937), Cmd. 5449, pp. 23-24 and p. 31.
51. *Act 25*. It is not unlikely that the Ghana Legislature were influenced by the American example as found in the *Restatement, Contracts*, S. 45. See also *Section 3 of the Swiss Federal Code of Obligations*: "Where a person offers to another to enter into a contract and fixes a time limit for acceptance of the offer the person is bound by his offer until the expiration of the time limit."
52. Pinnel's case (1602) 5 Co. Rep. 117a.
53. See Lord Denning, "The way of an iconoclast" (1959-63) J. of Soc. of Public Teachers of Law, at p. 78.
54. (1846) 15 M. and W. 23.
55. (1884) 9 App. Cas. 605.
56. (1877) 2 App. Cas. 439.
57. (1888) 40 Ch. D. 268.
58. (1947) K.B. 130; (1956) 1 All E.R. 256. This position was achieved through the equitable doctrine of quasi-estoppel, sometimes called promissory estoppel. It extends the common law doctrine by including as binding, representations of intention meant to create or alter legal relations. The scope of the rule was delimited by the House of Lords in *Tool Metal Manufacturing Co.* v. *Tungsten Electric Co. Ltd.* (1955) 2 All E.R. 657.
59. (1951) 2 K.B. 215. See particularly the judgment of Denning, L.J. (as he then was).

60. (1964) 3 All E.R. 556.
61. (1951) 2 K.B. 215 cf. *D & C Builders* v. *Rees* (1966) 2 W.L.R. 288.
62. No decision in the Ghana courts has been based on this subsection.
63. *Collins* v. *Godefroy* (1831) 1 B. and Ad. 950.
64. *Stilk* v. *Myrick* (1809) 2, Camp. 317.
65. *Shadwell* v. *Shadwell* (1809) 9 C.B.S. 159. See also A. G. Davis, "Promise to perform an existing duty" (1937) 6 Camb. L. Journal 203; Hamson, "The reform of consideration" (1938) 54 L.Q.R. 233; Shatwell, "The doctrine of consideration in the modern law" 1 Syd. Law. Rev. 324.
66. *Stilk* v. *Myrick*, supra. c.f. *Hartley* v. *Ponsonby* (1857) 7 E. and B. 872 where the plaintiff succeeded because he had performed on request more than he was legally bound to do.
67. (1857) 7 E. and B. 872.
68. See among others, Sir Frederick Pollock, 6 Harv. L.R. 389; Lord Wright, *Legal Essays and Addresses*, passim; A. L. Goodhart, "Blackmail and consideration" (1928) 44 L.Q.R. 436; Holdsworth, *History of English Law*, vol. III, p. 48; Ames, "Two theories of Consideration" (1899) 12 Harv. L. Rev. 29; N. Newman, "Doctrine of Cause" (1952) 30 Can. B.R. 662.
69. Lord Wright op. cit. especially at p. 375; see also B. O. Nwabueze, "Integration of the law of contracts" (1964) and Sir Kenneth Roberts-Wray, "The adaptation of imported law in Africa" (1960) 4 J.A.L. 66.
70. See Walter Stern, "Consideration and gift" (1965) 14 I.C.L.Q. 675.
71. Law Revision Committee, 6th Interim Report, Cmd. 5449 (1937); Hamson (1938) 54 L.Q.R. 233; A. L. Denning, "The Way of an iconoclast" (1959-63) Journal of Soc. of Public Teachers of Law, 77; Cheshire and Fifoot, *Law of Contract* (6th ed. 1964), pp. 57-92.
72. See J. F. Wilson, "The problem of the enforcement of promises in Anglo-American law" (1958) 32 Tul. L. Rev. 371; D. E. Allen, "An equity to perfect a gift" (1963) 69, L.Q.R. 238.
73. Walter Stern, op. cit., p. 677.
74. S. K. B. Asante, "Interests in land in the customary law of Ghana—A new appraisal" (1965) 74 Yale, L.J. 848.
75. *Eastwood* v. *Kenyon* (1940) 11 Ad. & El. 438. Cf. Lord Mansfield in *Pillans* v. *Van Mierop* (1765) 3 Burr. 1663 who thought that consideration should merely be evidentiary which would include moral consideration.
76. (1960) F.S.C. 358.
77. (1887) 58 L.T. 96.
78. *Addaquay* v. *African Association* (1910) Ren. 586 where the plaintiff was denied his agency commission because of fraud.
79. On "ntrama" and "guaha" see the decision of Ollennu, J. in the Ghana case of *Donkor* v. *Asafe* (1960) G.L.R. 187; also the Ghana Court of Appeal decision in *Angmor & Co.* v. *Yiadom III & anor* (1959) G.L.R. 157; on gifts see *Amo* v. *Ntwiaah* (1965) C.C. 172; *Semua* v. *Foriwaa* (1960) G.L.R. 256; on aseda see Allott, *Essays*, pp. 231 and 256; J. M. Sarbah, Fanti Customary law, pp. 74-75.
80. See S.N.C. Obi, *Ibo Law of Property* (London, 1963), p. 113; M. Green, *Ibo village affairs* (London, 1947), Chapter 4. On the Yorubas, see P. C. Lloyd, Yoruba Land law, pp. 68-69.
81. See also *The future of law in Africa*, Allott (ed.) 1960, p. 40.
82. In Ghana: J. M. Sarbah: *Fanti customary law*, pp. 42, 74-75. R. S. Rattray, *Ashanti law and constitution* (London, 1956), p. 358; J. B.

Danquah, *Akan Laws and Customs,* 212-233; N. A. Ollennu, *Customary land law in Ghana* (London, 1962), pp. 109-110; *Adai* v. *Daku* (1905) Ren. 417; *Adjuah* v. *Wilson* (1926-29) F. Ct. 261; *Norquaye* v. *Malm* (1959) G.L.R. 368. In Nigeria: J. O. Field, "Sales of land in an Ibo community" (1945) Man, vol. XLV. No. 47; C. K. Meek, *Land law and customs in the colonies* (1946), p. 162; P. C. Lloyd, *Yoruba land law* (London, 1962), p. 68; S. N. C. Obi, *Ibo law of property* (1963), p. 114.

83. *In re Sapara* (1911) Ren. 605; *Kofi* v. *Agbote* (1959) G.L.R. 305.

84. *Hughes* v. *Davies* (1909) Ren. 550.

85. *Ansa* v. *Sackey* (1923-25) F. Ct. 113.

86. B. O. Nwabueze, "Integration of the law of contract," p. 14.

87. On form in Islamic law, see J. N. D. Anderson (1959) 3 J.A.L. 152. On Islamic agreements generally, see (1958) 33 New York University L. Rev. 917.

88. Op. cit., p. 14.

89. *Kwame* v. *Fio,* 1960, May 9th H. Ct. (Lands Division) (1960) G.L.R. 119.

90. On the terms used in the Ghana systems, see Allott, *Essays,* pp. 243, 256; in Nigeria see Obi, op. cit., p. 114; Lloyd, op. cit., p. 220.

91. See the Ghana cases of *Poku* v. *Ntow* (1965) c.c. 165, where it was held that "aseda" gives business efficacy to native transactions; *Angmor* v. *Yiadom* (1959) G.L.R. 157 where "guaha" was said to be indispensable to the validity of customary sales of land and "ntrama" in transactions over personalty; *Kramo* v. *Kuma* (1965) c.c. 21 where "aseda" given and shared by the family was held to validate the appointment of a successor.

CHAPTER 7

INTENTION TO CREATE LEGAL RELATIONS

In English law the consensus of the parties and the presence of consideration do not exhaust the essential requirements of an enforceable agreement.[1] The parties must also have intended to create or to alter any existing legal relations. If from the nature of the transaction or the wording of the agreement the courts are of the opinion that the parties intended to be bound in honour only, they will not enforce the obligation. The decided cases in the English courts tend to indicate the existence of a dual standard in this aspect of the law. In domestic transactions the courts go on the presumption that the parties did not intend to create legal relations[2] but this can be rebutted by the actual dealings between them.[3] In commercial transactions the presumption is that the parties intended to create legal relations[4] but this can be rebutted by the actual insertion of an " honour clause."[5]

The courts in Ghana and Nigeria have not yet worked out any set of applicable rules in this sub-branch of the law. It is clear that only *Dalrymple* v. *Dalrymple*[6] and the *McGregor* decisions form part of the imported law of Nigeria,[6] and that only the former is part of the law of Ghana.[7] *Jones* v. *Vernon's Pools Ltd.* has been followed in the Ghana case of *Chikezie* v. *Ellie's Pools & Anor.*[8] It may however be argued that this decision was based on a local statute. Regulation 3 of the Football Pools Regulations 1964 (L.I. 358) made under section 11 of the Football Pools Authority Act 1961[9] (Act 78), provides as follows:—

" It is a basic condition of the sending in and the acceptance of every coupon that it is intended and agreed—

(a) that the conduct of the Football Pools and everything done in connection therewith and all arrangements relating thereto (whether mentioned in these regulations or to be implied), and

(b) that any coupon and any agreement or transaction entered into or payment made by or under it,

shall not be attached by, or give rise to any legal relationship, rights, duties or consequences whatsoever or be legally enforceable or the object of litigations; but that all such arrangements, agreements, or transactions are binding in honour only on all parties."

119

In the *Chikezie* case the plaintiff alleged that in April 1963, he won £2,660:11:6. on a football coupon No. 974788, which he filled in duplicate and presented to the defendants who were sub-agents of Zetters International Pools Ltd. for transmission to London through the Ghana Pools Authority, third parties to the action. The plaintiff alleged that the defendants negligently failed to send the original of his coupon to London, and were therefore liable to him for the amount claimed which represented his winnings if the coupon had been sent in. It was held by Boison J. at Accra that the handing in and the acceptance of the coupon did not create any enforceable legal relationships and that the transaction was binding in honour only. The court relied on Regulation 3 of the Football Pools Authority Regulations.

This decision raises afresh the issue of the value of " honour clauses " whether statutory or otherwise in agreements that are otherwise legally enforceable. The position in Ghana is further complicated by the provision in Section 2 (4) of the parent enactment (the Football Pools Authority Act):

" 2 (4) The authority[10] may enter into agreement with any person for the operation of football pools and the agreement shall provide for the retention of a share of the profits accruing to that person from the operation of the football pools:
Provided that no agreement executed by the authority shall be valid unless the same shall have been executed with the consent in writing of the minister first had and obtained."

There is no doubt that any agreement that is valid under the above sub-section will be enforceable in the courts. There is no provision to the contrary in the Act itself. It is curious therefore that while the authority or any of their agents can enforce their obligations against each other, an investor is denied this right under the regulations. It is respectfully submitted that such a situation is bound to produce absurd results. If the courts will assist the authority or any agent, there is no logic or justice in their refusing the same assistance to the clients on whose investments the others depend for their continued existence as going concerns. It is further submitted that the " honour clause " in agreements should be treated no differently from other provisions that are against public policy. This argument is given greater weight by the actual sums involved in many of these transactions. An agreement that involved upwards of £2,000 in countries like Ghana and Nigeria should invite the scrutiny of the courts rather than their present judicial abstinence.

As regards domestic agreements the attitude of the courts in

Ghana does not seem to be very clear. The case of *Eliza Morris* v. *John Monrovia*[11] appears to indicate a willingness on the part of the courts to apply any existing customary rule where the parties are natives. In that case the plaintiff and the deceased John Weatu, were both Kroos from Liberia. They had cohabited for some years but were not actually married. The plaintiff's action was against the administrator of the estate of John Weatu, claiming a house which she alleged was built on their joint contributions, or £94 being the sum she had contributed. The trial judge found the contribution proved and allowed the claim for £94. This was reversed by the Ghana Court of Appeal on the ground among others, that the plaintiff had not established her case—for an intention to create a loan transaction rather than an outright gift. In course of his judgment Sawrey-Cookson J. referred with approval to the " sarwie " custom described by Sarbah in his book[12] and added that if the parties were Fantis, he would have applied this custom.[13] The custom, however, does not cover cases where the parties are validly married. It is possible to argue that in the latter case such an agreement would be enforced.[14] There does not appear to be any local Nigerian decision on this aspect of the law. It is hoped that the English rule in domestic transactions will be adopted. The nature of the agreement should determine its binding nature or otherwise.

NOTES

1. In the United States Professor Williston of Harvard has felt that a third requirement is superfluous. He has argued that the courts enforce an agreement if there is consideration, that the common law does not require any positive intention to create a legal obligation as an element of contract, see Williston, *Contracts,* (L. 57) s. 21, p. 39. Cf. Cheshire & Fifoot *Contract,* p. 93. See also R. Tuck, " Intent to contract and mutuality of assent " (1943) 21 can. B. Rev. 123. Cf. Lord Stowell in *Dalrymple* v. *Dalrymple* (1811) 2 Hagg. Con. 54 at p. 105.

2. *Balfour* v. *Balfour* (1919) 2 K.B. 571, see also the Court of Appeal (England) decision of *Spellman* v. *Spellman* (1961) 2 All E.R. 498 where the Balfour principle was applied. See particularly the judgment of Scrutton, L.J. in *Rose and Frank* v. *Crompton* (1923) 2 K.B. 261 at p. 288.

3. *McGregor* v. *McGregor* (1888) 21 Q.B.D. 424, a case of cross-assaults between husband and wife; *Simpkins* v. *Pays* (1955) 3 All E.R. 10; and *Parker* v. *Clark* (1960) 1 All E.R. 93.

4. *Carlill* v. *Carbolic Smoke Ball Co.* (1893) 1 Q.B. 256; see particularly Lord Phillimore in *Rose and Frank* v. *Crompton* in the House of Lords (1925) A.C. 445 at p. 455.

5. *Jones* v. *Vernon's Pools, Ltd.* (1938) 2 All E.R. 626; *Appleson* v. *Littlewood, Ltd* (1939) 1 All E.R. 464. The rule in these groups of

L

cases has been criticised by the learned editors of *Law Reform Now* (London, 1963), p. 64.

6. Both are pre-1900 decisions of English courts.

7. Being the only pre-1874 decision in this group of cases.

8. (1965) C.C. 137.

9. No similar regulations have been made under the Nigerian Pool *Betting Control Act*, 1961 (No. 69 of 1961).

10. That is, the authority established by the Act to provide for the organisation and control of football pools transactions in Ghana.

11. (1930) 1 W.A.C.A. 70. In this case the courts applied the imported law requirement of intention to create legal relations. See also *Odum* v. *Banson* (1965) C.C. 177.

12. *Fanti customary law*, p. 42 has the following: " A woman living in concubinage cannot sue the man with whom she is so living for any maintenance, nor can her family or parents sue the man for any satisfaction or maintenance. Whatever is given or entrusted by a man or woman, to the person with whom he or she is living in concubinage, cannot be reclaimed on any consideration whatsoever . . . if a man therefore will not be properly and honourably married to a woman but will for his own purpose keep her and live upon her labour, she is at liberty to terminate the immoral relation at any time she pleases, and she shall not be liable to return to him anything whatsoever he may have given or entrusted to her for safe keeping, sale, or any purpose whatsoever." Cf. *Ansa* v. *Sackey* (1923-25) F. Ct. 113 where a refund of trading debts was ordered where the transactions took place after termination of the concubinage.

13. The result of the case would have been the same, anyway.

14. See *Ayer* v. *Kumordzie* (1965) C.C. 45.

PART III

VALID AGREEMENTS:
MORE THAN TWO PARTIES

INTRODUCTORY NOTE

In the preceding part we dealt with the creation of valid agreements where two parties are involved. In this part we shall be looking at agreements with more than two parties. These will be treated in three sections, namely:

(i) agreements between two parties where a third party is affected. Privity of agreements will be discussed under this subheading;

(ii) agreements between two parties where one or both are represented by a third. This has often been treated under the heading of agency; and finally,

(iii) agreements between two parties where one or both subsequently transfer to a third. These are of course the familiar topics of assignments and negotiability.

CHAPTER 8

PRIVITY[1]

It is a general rule of English law that a contract affects only those who are parties to it. Nobody can obtain the benefit or bear the burden of an agreement to which he is a stranger. The injustice that would result and has in fact resulted from the rigid application of this rule has driven English judicial and academic opinion to invent exceptions to its operation.[2]

There are also several statutory exceptions.[3]

Two aspects of the rule, namely, attempts to confer benefits on a third party and attempts to impose the burden of an agreement on a stranger have been recognised. The two facets of the rule constitute the English doctrine of privity of agreements.[4]

Like the doctrine of consideration to which reference has already been made, the critics of the rigid application of the doctrine of privity have been so vocal and its impact has so besmeared all notions of justice that one takes another look at the authorities to satisfy oneself that it is or not part of the received laws of Ghana and Nigeria. The recent decision of the Nigerian Supreme Court in *Chuba Ikpeazu* v. *African Continental Bank Ltd.*[5] and its general impact on the law of third party rights in Nigeria, underlines not only the need but the urgency of such exercise.

Benefit

The old but leading case of *Crow* v. *Rogers*[6] decided in 1724 has often been said to lay down the rule that no stranger to an agreement can enforce any right under it, even if the agreement was made for his benefit.

In that case John Hardy owed the plaintiff £70 in return for a promise by Hardy that he would convey his house to the defendant. The plaintiff was a stranger to the agreement and could not enforce it. On the other hand where a father intended to cut down some oak trees to make provision for his children (including the plaintiff), and the defendant promised his father that if he spared the trees, he (the defendant) would give his sister (the plaintiff) £1,000, it was held that the plaintiff could enforce this promise.[7]

The authority of *Dutton* v. *Poole* was seriously questioned in the

126

later case of *Tweddle* v. *Atkinson,* and in 1915 the House of Lords restated the rule that no stranger to an agreement can enforce any benefit under it, in rather strong terms.[8]

Lord Haldane's words represent the true position as their Lordships saw it then. He said:

> " In the law of England certain principles are fundamental. One is that only a person who is a party to a contract can sue on it. Our law knows nothing of a *jus quaesitum tertio* arising by way of contract. Such a right may be conferred by way of property, as for example, under a trust, but it cannot be conferred on a stranger to a contract as a right to enforce the contract in personam."[9]

Since *Dunlop* v. *Selfridge,* there has been a fierce jostle for exceptions and the line of reasoning which has its genesis in the Exchequer Chamber decision of *Dutton* v. *Poole* is still very much alive. A recent decision of the (English) Court of Appeal, later affirmed by the House of Lords, restates the absurd results that will follow from a rigid adherence to the rule of privity. In the words of Salmon, L.J., " no system of jurisprudence should permit what was manifestly such a monstrous injustice."[10]

In the *Beswick* case, the deceased had conveyed his coal business to his nephew, in consideration for his promising to pay him £6 10/- weekly for the rest of his life and after his death, to pay his widow £5 weekly for her life. The nephew (defendant) kept to the terms of the agreement during his uncle's life but on his death refused to pay the widow as specified in the agreement or at all. Arrears of £175 accrued. The widow (plaintiff) then sued personally and as an administratix of her late husband's estate, for the arrears and for future regular weekly payments of £5 as provided for in the agreement. Vice Chancellor Burgess in the Chancery Court of the County Palatine of Lancaster decided in favour of the defendant, relying on the judgment of Wynn-Parry, J. in re *Miller's Agreement.*[11]

But a strong Court of Appeal reversed this decision. In a penetrating review of the authorities Lord Denning (M.R.) reaffirmed his views on the subject as revealed in *Smith and Snipes Hall Farm* v. *River Douglas Catchment Board,*[12] *and Drive Yourself Hire Company (London) Ltd.* v. *Strutt,*[13] to the effect that third parties could sue if the agreement was made for their benefit. Dankwerts, L.J. added that section 56 (1) of the law of Property Act, 1925 has " dealt *Tweddle* v. *Atkinson*[14] the mortal wound it well deserved."[15] A leader in " The Times " described the Beswick decision as a " belated triumph of the jus quaesitum tertio," but as has been noted above, the House of Lords refused to be drawn into a discussion of this principle since the appeal was disposed of on other grounds.

Position in Nigeria

Now, what is the position in Nigeria? It is clear that the post-1900 decisions of the English Courts are not part of the imported law of Nigeria. On this principle we are left with the two lines of authority, namely, the *Crow* v. *Rogers*,[16] and *Tweddle* v. *Atkinson*[17] theory, and the *Dutton* v. *Poole*[18] theory of third party rights. The former appears to have no place for the enforcement of third party rights while the latter makes substantial concessions where there is a clear case of intended benefit for the stranger. The trend of local judicial authority, however, supports the former theory of privity.[19] In *Chuba Ikpeazu* v. *African Continental Bank Ltd.*,[20] the appellant, a leading legal practitioner in Nigeria at the time, was the second defendant in a claim for £28,013. 19. 10d. by the respondent bank. The first defendants, Emodi Brothers, had admitted liability and were no longer taking part in the action. The two grounds of claim against the defendant (appellant) were (i) that he was a partner in the said Emodi Brothers; and (ii) that he guaranteed the loan to the partnership. Our concern here is with the second ground of claim. This was based on a deed between the appellant and William Emodi. By this deed William Emodi transferred the business of Emodi Brothers to the appellant in consideration for the appellant's promise to guarantee his overdraft from the respondent bank. The deed was deposited with the respondent bank. The appellant's defence, among others, was that the bank were strangers to the deed and could not sue on it. The trial judge at Onitsha (Eastern Nigeria) treated the deed as a guarantee and allowed the claim against the appellant. On appeal the Supreme Court held that:

(i) generally a contract cannot be enforced by a person who is not a party, even if the contract is made for his benefit and purports to give him the right to sue upon it;

(ii) the position is stronger with regard to contracts under seal; unless a person is named as a party to the deed, he cannot maintain an action upon it. The only exception to this rule relates to indentures made about land which was introduced by Section 5 of the Real Property Act, 1845, to enable a stranger to a deed to take advantage of a benefit to him in the deed.

The 4th and 5th grounds do not concern us here. The Supreme Court thus allowed the appeal; relying as their Lordships admitted they were, on the authority of *Dunlop* v. *Selfridge*.[21] Three aspects of the *Ikpeazu* decision deserve some re-examination. Firstly, although their Lordships of the Supreme Court discussed with approval, the rule in *Tweddle* v. *Atkinson*,[22] as seen in the first ground of their decision, the other line of authorities stemming from *Dutton* v. *Poole* were never cited nor argued.

It is therefore still open to argument whether the *Ikpeazu* case has said the last word on third party benefits in the Nigerian Law of agreements. It is respectfully submitted that it has not.

Secondly, their Lordships noted Section 5, of the Real Property Act, 1845[23] as the only exception to the rule that no stranger to an agreement can enforce its terms. There are, of course, other statutory exceptions to the rule. Section II of the Motor Vehicles (Third Party Insurance) Act[24] empowers third parties under certain circumstances to enforce insurance provisions made in their favour. Section 2 of the Third Parties (Rights Against Insurers) Act,[25] has similar provisions. Section II of the Married Women Property Act, 1882, an act of general application, and Section 29 of the Bills of Exchange Act[26] are other instances of exceptions to the rule of privity. It is clear therefore that as far as statutory exceptions go, their Lordships' specific mention of Section 5 of the Real Property Act, 1845 is but representative of the others.

Thirdly, there are other recognised exceptions to the rule of privity which are part of the received law in Nigeria. One of them is where there was an intention to create a trust in favour of the stranger. This concept of the trust as an exception to the rule was recognised by Lords Haldane and Dunedin in the *Dunlop* v. *Selfridge* decision on which their Lordships of the Supreme Court of Nigeria heavily relied. Its history, however, is much older than the Dunlop decision.

In *Tomlinson* v. *Gill*,[27] J. G. died intestate. The defendant, Robert Gill, promised the deceased's widow, Catherine, that if she would allow him to be joined with her in letters of administration to be issued in respect of her husband's estate, he would make good any deficiencies of assets to pay debts. Accordingly joint administration was taken out, and action was taken by the deceased's creditors to enforce the undertaking which the defendant had given. It was held that the creditors were entitled to the benefit of the contract made, since the widow had entered into it as trustee for them.

This principle was later applied by the English House of Lords in *Walford's case*,[28] an action on a charter party. *Lloyds* v. *Harper*,[29] an action on behalf of third parties, is also to the same effect. Now, both the *Tomlinson* and *Lloyd's* cases are pre-1900 decisions of English courts and therefore part of Nigerian law. It is therefore remarkable that Ademola, C.J.N., in the *Ikpeazu* decision, rejected counsel's submission for the bank in these terms:

" Counsel for the bank agreed that the bank was 'not a party to the document (i.e. the agreement) and cannot sue on it, but he said that this is so at common law. In equity, he submitted that as the document is a compromise document prepared for the benefit of the bank, it (the bank) can sue on it on the theory of trusteeship. Counsel has not referred to any case for likening the bank to a *cestui que trust*, nor explained how the recital of a representation made by the appellant to William Emodi, that he had guaranteed the debt, can be read as the contract of guarantee given by the appellant to the bank; and we do not know of any decided case which supports his submission. . . ."[30]

It is very respectfully submitted that there is no lack of judicial authority for the theory of trust as an exception to the rule of privity. It is sad that these cases were not cited or argued before their Lordships.[31]

Finally, neither counsel for the bank nor a strong Supreme Court[32] raised any finger of protest against the unjust results that will follow any rigid application of privity. Their Lordships were unanimous in accepting the doctrine as enunciated by the House of Lords in *Dunlop* v. *Selfridge*. It is curious, however, that the massive literature of dissent against privity could not persuade the Supreme Court to the contrary. Neither the American approach as contained in section 133 of the *Restatement of Contracts*,[33] nor the Ghana solution,[34] held out any attraction to their Lordships. Perhaps the court relied on Parliament to abolish privity if it wanted to. It is, however, observed with respect that it was not by reliance on Parliament that Lord Hardwicke, Lord Mansfield and Lord Atkin made their reputations as judges. If the heroic age of judicial exploits is past in English law (Lord Denning's judgments suggest the contrary), it is by no means so in Nigeria.

Position in Ghana

The position in Ghana is now governed by Section 5 (i) of the Contract Act, 1960 (Act 25) which is as follows:

" 5 (i) Any provision in a contract made after the commencement of this Act which purports to confer a benefit on a person who is not a party to the contract, whether as a designated person or as a member of a class of persons, may, subject to the provisions of this part (i.e. part ii), be enforced or relied upon by that person as though he were a party to the contract."[35]

No local decision has been based on this provision but it is clear that a similar provision in Nigeria could have covered the *Ikpeazu* decision.

Burden[36]

The other leg of the doctrine of privity is that nobody shall be liable under an agreement to which he is a stranger. On the face of it, this appears a salutary rule, for life would be rather unbearable if liabilities were imposed on persons not party to an agreement. English law has, however, made special concessions here to land matters. A restrictive covenant runs with the land and can be enforced against a third party who has knowledge of the restriction.[37]

Outside land matters, two kinds of cases under this leg of privity have been recognised by the courts. The first is the attempt to impose restrictions on the sale of goods, and the second is the attempt to restrict the use of chattels.

Restrictions on the sale of goods

In English law this has taken the form of manufacturers or vendors restricting the sale or retail prices of goods supplied to their dealers. Any provision in an agreement to this effect is not enforceable by the courts.[38] An exception to this rule was made by Section 25 of the Restrictive Trade Practices Act, 1956, which permitted the individual (but not collective) enforcement of such terms against persons who acquired such goods for purposes of resale in the course of business and with notice of the conditions. Section I of the Restrictive and Resale Prices Act, 1964 has made void contractual provisions between a supplier and a dealer so far as they purport to establish, or provide for the establishment, of minimum prices to be charged on resale of the goods in the United Kingdom.

It is interesting to contrast the position in English law with the law in Ghana on this subject.

Section 5 (2) (a) of the Ghana Contract Act, 1960[39] provides as follows:

" 5 (2) Subsection (i) (i.e. right of third parties to sue) does not apply to—

(a) a provision in a contract designed for the purpose of resale price maintenance, that is to say, a provision whereby a party agrees to pay money or otherwise render some valuable consideration to a person who is not a party to the contract in the event of the first mentioned party selling or otherwise disposing of any goods, the subject matter of the contract, at prices lower than those determined by or under the contract."

Thus in Ghana the common law position has been given statutory form. It is doubtful, however, if this represents any major improvement of the law on the subject, rather than an attempt to project the arm of the state into agreements between private persons. Neither the courts nor the legislatures in Nigeria have applied their minds to the problem of restrictions on sale of goods. In Nigeria, therefore, the courts are still free to make up their minds.[40]

Restrictions on the use of chattels

" Reason and justice seem to prescribe that, at least as a general rule, where a man, by gift or purchase, acquires property from another, with knowledge of a previous contract, lawfully and for valuable consideration made by him with a third person, to use and employ the property for a particular purpose in a specified manner, the acquirer shall not, to the material damage of the third person, in opposition to the contract and inconsistently with it, use and employ the property for a particular purpose in a specified manner, seller."

This dictum of Knight-Bruce in *De Mattos* v. *Gibson*,[41] based on the extension to chattels of the rule in *Tulk* v. *Moxhay*,[42] has been very much discredited in English law.[43] It was, however, followed by the Privy Council in the Canadian appeal of *Lord Strathcona Steamship Co. Ltd.* v. *Dominion Coal Co. Ltd.*[44] It is submitted that the *De Mattos* decision and not the *Port Line* variation of it, is part of the laws of Nigeria and Ghana.[45] The position in Ghana is made clearer by the fact that this is not one of the exceptions to third party rights as provided for in Section 5 (I) of the Contract Act, 1960.

NOTES

1. See Prof. Corbin, "Contracts for the benefit of third parties" (1930) 46 L.Q.R.; 12; Glanville Williams, "Contracts for the benefit of third parties" (1944) 7 M.L.R. 123; F. E. Dowrick, "A jus quaesitum tertio by way of contract in English law" (1956) 19 M.L.R. 374; M. P. Furmstin, "Return to Dunlop v. Selfridge?" (1960) 23 M.L.R. 373; S. Chaffee Jnr., "Equitable servitudes on chattels" (1928) 41 Harv. L. Rev. 945-1013; E. C. S. Wade, "Restrictions on User" (1928) 44 L.Q.R. 51; Lord Denning, "The Way of an Iconoclast (1959-63) Journal of The Society of Public Teachers of Law," p. 77; see also the Interim Report of the Law Reform Committee, Comnd. 5449 (1937).
2. e.g. where equity imputes the creation of a trust—*Dutton* v. *Poole* (1678) 3, Lev. 210; Banker's Commercial Credit cases, see Denning, supra at p. 81; *Guaranty Trust Co. of New York* v. *Hannary & Co.* 1918 2. K.B. 623; *Malas* v. *British Imex Industries Ltd.*, (1958) 1 All E.R. 262; cases of agency are *sui generis*.

3. S. II of the Married Women Property Act, 1882; S. 29 of the Bills of Exchange Act, 1882; S. 14 (2) of the Marine Insurance Act, 1906; SS. 47 and 56 (I) of the law of Property Act, 1925; S. 36 of the Road Traffic Act, 1930.

4. In French law this was formulated as the doctrine of relativity; Buchland and McNair, *Roman law and common law*, 2nd ed. pp. 214-217.

5. (1965) N.M.L.R. 374, for the facts, see infra.

6. (1724) I stra. 592.

7. *Dutton* v. *Poole* (1678) 2 Lev. 210. It has often been thought that *Tweddle* v. *Atkinson* (1861) I. B.E.S. 393, overruled *Dutton* v. *Poole*, but this is doubtful in view of the fact that *Dutton* v. *Poole* is the decision of the court of Exchequer Chamber. The objection is not however a strong one for purposes of English law since the House of Lords decision of *Dunlop* v. *Selfridge* supports the Atkinson decision.

8. (1915) A.C. 847. See the judgment of Lord Haldane at p. 853.

9. Supra at p. 853.

10. *Beswick* v. *Beswick* C.A.; The Times, 23rd June, 1966. See also the comment on this case that " The common law of England stands alone among modern systems of law in its rigid adherence to the view that a contract should not confer any rights on a stranger to the contract, even though the sole object may be to benefit him." See (1966) 3 All E.R. 1 (CA); (1967) 2 All E.R. 119 F. For the decision at first instance see (1965) 3 All E.R. In the House of Lords the decision of the Court of Appeal was affirmed but on the ground of Mrs. Beswick suing in her capacity as administratrix and not in her personal capacity. Lord Reid, one of the Judges in the House on this case stated " . . . for the purposes of this case I shall proceed on the footing that the commonly accepted view is right." This is of course the view that only parties to a contract can enforce its terms. See p. 1201 of Report.

11. (1947) ch. 615.

12. (1949) 2 K B. 515.

13. (1954) I Q B. 250; 275.

14. Supra.

15. It is remarkable that no reference was made in this case to the House of Lords decision in *Dunlop* v. *Selfridge*, (1915) A.C. 847 which is the leading case on third party rights. It could be argued however that the volume of protest against the rigid application of privity might dissuade their Lordships of the House of Lords feeling bound by the later case. See *The Times*, 27th July, 1966.

16. (1724) I. Stra. 592.

17. (1861) I B L S. 393.

18. (1678) 2 Lev. 210.

19. See *John Holt & Co. Ltd.*, v. *Alhaji Jafa'aru* (1958) N.R.N.L.R. 29.

20. (1965) N.M.L.R. 374.

21. (1915) A.C. 847 *Tweddle* v. *Atkinson* was also discussed at length and the rule in that case was approved of by their Lordships.

22. Supra.

23. 8 & 9 Vict.

24. Cap. 126, Laws of Nigeria (1958).

25. Cap. 196, Laws of Nigeria (1958).

26. Cap. 21, Laws of Nigeria (1958).

27. (1756) Amb. 330, see also *Re Flavell* (1883) 25 Ch. D 89, where the same rule was applied. But see *Re Schebsman* (1944) Ch. 83 where it was refused.
28. *Les Affreteurs Reunis Societe Anonyme* v. *Leopold Walford (London) Ltd.,* (1919) A.C. 801.
29. (1880) 16 Ch. D. 290.
30. Op. cit. at p. 379.
31. Apart from the theory of trust, other recognised exceptions to the privity rule are bankers' commercial creditors—see C. V. Brown, *The Nigerian Banking System,* Glasgow, 1966 passim; agency—will be discussed in a subsequent section.
32. Composed of Ademola C. J. N. Brett, Bairamian, Onyeama and Ajegbo JJ. S.C.
33. See also *Article* 1029 of the *Quebec Civil Code* which is to the same effect. Even the *Civil Code of the USSR* has a similar provision in Article 167—see translation by Kiralfy, 1966.
34. See infra. See particularly Section 6 of the Ghana Contract Act.
35. The exceptions to this provision will be discussed later.
36. See particularly E.C.S. Wade, " Restrictions on User " (1928) 44 L.Q.R. 51; on the Privy Council decision in the *Strathcona case* (1926) A.C. 108; and Z. Chaffee, Jnr.; " Equitable servitudes on Chattels " (1928), 41, Harv. L. Rev. 945.
37. *Tulk* v. *Moxhay* (1848) 2 Ph. 774. The scope of the rule in this case has been restricted to instances where the plaintiff retains some land that will be affected by the breach of the covenant.
38. *Taddy* v. *Sterious* (1904) I Ch. 354 i.e. against a stranger to the agreement. The *Taddy* case was on restrictions on tobacco prices.
39. Act. 25.
40. Since the *Taddy* decision is a post-1900 English decision, it is submitted that the courts in Nigeria are still free to enforce resale prices on third parties; but the *Ikpeazu* case suggests a negative answer.
41. (1858) 4 De G. & J. 276 at p. 282.
42. (1848) 2 Ph. 774.
43. See *Port Line Ltd.* v. *Ben Line Steamer Ltd.* 1958 2 Q.B. 146, at p. 166, per Diplock, J. See also E.C.S. Wade (1928) 44 L.Q.R. 51 C.F. Cheshire and Fifoot, *Law of Contract,* (6th Ed. 1964) p. 396.
44. (1926) A.C. 108.
45. See also *Messageries Imperiales Co.* v. *Baines* (1863) 7, L.T. 763. These are all pre-1874 decisions of English courts. The Port Line case was decided in 1958.

CHAPTER 9

AGREEMENTS BETWEEN TWO PARTIES WHERE ONE IS OR BOTH ARE REPRESENTED BY A THIRD, i.e. AGENCY[1]

Although a person cannot by an agreement with another confer rights or impose liabilities upon a third, yet he may represent another, as being employed or otherwise authorised by him, for the purpose of bringing him into legal relations with a third. As was stated by Tindal, C. J. in the old case of *Wilson* v. *Tumman* :[2]

> "That an act, done for another, by a person not assuming to act for himself, but for such other people, though without any precedent authority whatever, becomes the act of the principal, if subsequently ratified by him, is the known and well established rule of law. In that case the principal is bound by the act, whether it be for his detriment or his advantage, and whether it be founded on a tort or a contract."

Bowstead has defined agency as the relationship that exists between two persons one of whom, the principal, expressly or impliedly consents that the other, the agent, similarly consenting, should represent him or act on his behalf.[3] One of the unique advantages of the doctrine of agency is of course, that it tempers the rigidity of the doctrine of privity of contracts.[4] Agency is of especial significance in the laws of Ghana and Nigeria for two reasons. Firstly, after the abolition of the slave trade in the nineteenth century, the primary interest of Europeans in the West African coast was other forms of trade. Several European companies extended their operations to West Africa and local personnel were recruited either as servants or as agents.[5] This explains the relative wealth of local case law on the subjects of master and servant, guarantees, and agency. For our purpose here, it emphasises the need for an examination of the concept of agency in the two territories. The second reason is that family property is still very much part of the laws of Ghana and Nigeria. The language of agency has been used in examining the position of the family head in relation to family property.[6] Agency is of course a comprehensive word used to describe both the relationship between the principal and the agent on the one hand, and the rights and liabilities of third parties on the other. While we are concerned with both these aspects of the subject, our emphasis will be on the latter for the obvious reason that it is this facet of the problem that has mostly exercised the courts in Ghana and Nigeria.

(A) CREATION

Five modes of creating the relationship of principal and agent have been recognised in English law namely (i) by an actual or implied authority to contract given by the principal to the agent:[7] (ii) by the principal's ratification of an agreement entered into by the agent on his own behalf but without his authority:[8] (iii) by an ostensible authority conferred by the principal on the agent even though no actual authority has been given:[9] (iv) by a legal presumption in the case of a married woman cohabiting with her husband:[10] and finally (v) by an implication of law in cases of necessity.[11]

Only the first three modes of the formation of agency have been the subjects of local judicial decision in Ghana and Nigeria. We shall be examining these seriatim.[12]

(i) *Actual or implied authority*

Generally, no special form is necessary for the creation of agency. It has been suggested that professional agents e.g. solicitors, should insist on a written appointment to clear them from any suspicion of champerty.[13] There is however, no direct judicial authority for this view.[14] An authority to execute a sealed document must also be by deed. In the Nigerian case of *Abina & two others* v. *Albert Farhat*,[15] the plaintiffs were landlords and the defendant was their tenant, paying rent on monthly basis on the premises let to him by the plaintiff's father (deceased). On being given notice to quit, the defendant alleged that the terms of his lease with the plaintiffs had not expired. It turned out that the lease relied on by the defendant was granted by one Ogunala, an agent of the deceased father of the plaintiffs but who had authority to collect rents and not to grant leases. The deed was executed by Ogunala. Relying on *Berkeley* v. *Hardy*,[16] Carey J. held that the plaintiffs were not bound by the lease and awarded judgment against the defendant. On the other hand, in the Ghana case of *Cole* v. *Jead*,[17] a lease executed under seal by an agent who was not authorised to execute documents under seal, was held valid for the reason that the lease being for a term of less than three years could have been made in writing not under seal. The fanciful nature of the requirement of the seal for appointments to execute sealed documents, is demonstrated very clearly by the fact that where the deed is executed by the agent in the presence of the principal, the authority could be by mere words or even signs.[18] The logical inference from this state of affairs is that the law strives to fulfil the intentions of the parties and in this case, words and signs go to portray the intention on the part of the principal to be bound. It is remarkable therefore that in *Berkeley* v. *Hardy*[19] a document not under seal did not avail the agent. It is respectfully submitted that the continued insistence on the seal as the only alternative to words and signs is too restricted a view and causes hardship in individual cases. It obviously did cause hardship in the *Farhat* and *Berkeley* cases.

Authority could also be implied from the circumstances of the individual employed. It has been said that every agent has implied authority to act in accordance with the reasonable customs and usages of the particular place, trade, or market where he is employed.[20] In *Real and Personal Advance Co.* v. *Phalempin*[21] it was held that a hospital matron has implied authority to pledge the credit of the hospital committee for meat supplied to the hospital. The latter case is of course, not part of the law of Ghana, but there is little doubt that it will be followed by the Ghana courts.[22]

(ii) *By Ratification*

The relationship of principal and agent is also created where A adopts the act of B who purported to contract on his behalf either without any authority whatsoever or in excess of any existing given authority. In such a case the principal is said to have ratified the act of the agent and he is as liable under the agreement as if the agent had his authority in the first instance. Thus in the Ghana case of *Bank of British West Africa Ltd.*, v. *Adams*,[23]

The Vasarnet Cocoa Company Limited appointed one Briscoe its Attorney to mortgage its premises to the Bank of British West Africa Limited in security for a loan of £7,500. The Mortgage, however, was executed (in 1920) not in the form of a mere security for the repayment of £7,500, but in the form of a continuing security covering the Accra overdraft. The £7,500 was repaid. In 1922 the company gave the defendant Barnett a debenture and, in 1923 a mortgage over the company's premises, subject to any subsisting mortgages in favour of the bank. In 1924 the bank obtained judgment against the company for £9,105 2s. 11d. and costs in respect of the Accra overdraft, but this judgment was not satisfied. The company having gone into liquidation, and

Barnett and Adams (the receiver and manager appointed under the debenture) being in occupation of the premises, the bank sued them for possession under its mortgage and obtained judgment in the Divisional Court. On Appeal to the Full Court, it was argued for the defendants that since Briscoe's authority was limited to mortgaging the property for an overdraft of £7,500 and, this amount had been paid off, the company was no longer liable to the bank under the deed. Michelin, J. who read the judgment of the Full Court easily dismissed this argument, holding among other things, that there was evidence that the company had ratified the execution of the mortgage to the bank, and that, as the judgment for the amount of the overdraft had not been satisfied, the mortgage subsisted not withstanding the repayment of the £7,500.

The operation of the principle of ratification is however confined to certain defined limits. Firstly, the agent must have contracted as an agent and not as principal. The recent case of *Foloshade* v. *Duroshold*,[24] decided by the Nigerian Supreme Court is authority for this view. In that case the plaintiff sued the defendant for recovery of possession of a certain piece of land. It happened that in 1926 and 1927 someone whom the plaintiff alleged was the agent of the vendors who later sold to the defendant, sold the land to one Alfa from whose next of kin the plaintiff purchased the property in 1949. There was in 1955 a purported ratification of the 1926-27 transaction and this was said to have been recited in the 1949 deed. But in 1952 the owner had sold and conveyed the said land to the defendant who went into possession in 1956. The court found as a fact that the landlord did not authorise the 1926-27 transaction and consequently found for the defendant. On appeal to the Federal Supreme Court, it was argued inter alia on behalf of the plaintiff that the 1955 deed of ratification by the owner dated back to the sales of 1926-27 which therefore preceded the 1952 transaction. On this submission, Ademola, C. J. F. had this to say:

> " I will deal with the first submission that the ratification dates back to 1927 and 1926. We were referred to the definition of ratification at page 1476 in the *Dictionary of English law* by Lord Jowitt. It is defined thus: ' Ratification: Confirmation: agency may be created by ratification where A purports to act as agent for B either having no authority at all or having no authority to do that particular act, the subsequent adoption by B of A's act has the same legal consequences as if B had originally authorised the act. But there can be no ratification unless A purported to act as agent, and to act for B, and in such a case

B alone can sue.' The definition cannot by any stretch of the imagination, in my view, apply to the present situation. . . ."[25]

The Supreme Court thus affirmed the judgment of the court of first instance and the plaintiff's appeal was dismissed.[26]

The second requirement is that the alleged agent must have contracted for an existing and ascertainable, though not necessarily a named principal. In English law pre-incorporation contracts of companies have been avoided on the basis that the promoters contracted as agents of a non-existent principal.[27] There has been some doubt as to the effect of contracts made conditional on the registration of the company on a specified date. One view has been that such contracts are binding on the company when eventually incorporated.[28]

In Nigeria the law on the subject of non-existent principals with regard to companies, was stated by Sowemimo, J. in the recent case of *Caligara* v. *Sartori & Co. Ltd.,*[29] as follows:

> " The law is that a company is not bound by its contracts purported to be entered into on its behalf by its promoters or other persons before its incorporation. The company cannot, after incorporation, ratify or adopt any such contract because there is in such cases no agency, and the contract is that of the parties making it."

In that case an action against a company for the sum of £800 raised by its promoter before its incorporation was dismissed by the court.[30] In the Ghana case of *Panagiotopoulos* v. *Plastico Ltd.,*[31] it was also held that a company is not bound by contracts purporting to be made on its behalf by its promoters or other persons, before its incorporation. It is clear, however, that this decision no longer represents the law on the subject. Section 13 of the Companies Code, 1963 (Act 179), provides as follows:

> " 13 (i) Any contract or other transaction purporting to be entered into by a company prior to its formation or by any person on behalf of the company prior to its formation may be ratified by the company after its formation; and thereupon the company shall become bound by and entitled to the benefit thereof as if it had been in existence at the date of such contract or other transaction and had been a party thereto."

> " (2) Prior to ratification by a company the person or persons who purported to act in the name or on behalf of the company shall, in the absence of express agreement to the contrary, be personally bound by the contract or other transaction and shall be entitled to the benefit thereof."

In this respect, therefore, Ghana law diverges from the Nigerian and English law on the subject. It is submitted that the Ghana provision is productive of fairer results than the principle as restated by Sowemino, J. in the *Caligara* case. The third essential of the principle of ratification is that the principal must be competent to make the agreement both at the time the agent purported to act on his behalf and at the time of the ratification. Again in the case of companies, it has been held that a company cannot ratify an agreement that is *ultra vires* its Articles of Association.[32] There has been some doubt as to the effect of this doctrine on Section 5 of the English Companies Act, 1948.[33] The latter Act is not a statute of general application and therefore not part of Nigerian law. There is no corresponding provision in the English Companies Act, 1929 on which the Nigerian Companies Act (cap. 37, Laws of Nigeria, 1958) was substantially based. It appears therefore that the principle laid down in *Ashbury Railway Carriage and Iron Co. v. Riche* is still very much part of Nigerian law on the subject. In that case the directors of the appellant company agreed to purchase a concession for making a railway in Belgium. This company had no powers to do so under their memorandum of association. It was held that such an agreement was *ultra vires* and void as it was of a nature not included in the memorandum and as such could not be ratified even by the whole body of shareholders.

In Ghana the combined effect of Section 25 of the Companies Code, 1963, is that a company incorporated under it can make any agreement it likes, subject to the rights of certain specified persons to apply for a court order to set aside such agreements on several given grounds. The court has a discretion in the matter of setting aside an agreement.[34] Thus, although Section 25 (1) prohibits the making of agreements that are *ultra vires* the regulations of a company, Section 25 (3) provides as follows:

> " 25 (3) Notwithstanding subsection (i) of this section, no act of a company and no conveyance or transfer of property to or by a company shall be invalid by reason of the fact that such act, conveyance or transfer was not done or made for the furtherance of any of the authorised businesses of the company or that the company was otherwise exceeding its objects or powers."

It appears therefore that an *ultra vires* agreement could be ratified by a company in Ghana, subject to the safeguards contained in Sections 25,[35] (4) 210,[36] 218,[37] and 247.[38]

The case of *Adjaye v. Kufuor*[39] was an instance of a principal purporting to ratify the act of his agent when he lacked competence at the time of such ratification. The facts of that case were that one Gharbin, the "linguist" of Omanhene Kofi Adjaye was authorised to give evidence on behalf of his Omanhene. Gharbin did give the evidence, but at the end of the trial, he further executed a bond for an appeal on behalf of his principal. It appears from the facts that he had no authority to execute a bond of appeal. The Omanhene purported to ratify the execution of the bond, but at the time of the alleged ratification the statutory period allowed for the bringing of appeals had expired. It was held that he had no capacity to ratify and that the appeal was out of time without leave and therefore null and void.[40]

(iii) Ostensible authority, or agency by estoppel

Where any person, by words or conduct, represents or permits it to be represented that another person has authority to act on his behalf, he is bound by the acts of such other person with respect to anyone dealing with him as an agent on the faith of such representation, to the same extent as if such other person had the authority which he was represented to have.[41] Thus in the law of agency, appearance is equated to reality. The Privy Council has restated this principle in the following words in connection with the sale of goods:

> " To permit goods to go into the full possession of another, with all the insignia of possession thereof and of apparent title, and to leave it open to go behind that permission so given and accompanied, and upset a purchase of the goods made for full value and in good faith, would bring confusion into mercantile transactions and would be inconsistent with law and with the principles so frequently affirmed, following *Lokbarrow* v. *Mason* (1787) 2 T.R. 63."

This was in the leading case of *Akotey* v. *Commonwealth Trust & anor.*[42] Here the plaintiff (respondent) had consigned some cocoa to the second defendant but there was no agreement as to the price of the goods. The second defendant having got hold of the delivery documents, consigned the goods to the appellants to pay off an antecedent debt. There was no fraud on the part of the appellants. In action for the price of the cocoa or its return, the trial court found for the defendants but this was reversed by the Full Court. On a further appeal to the Judicial Committee of the Privy Council, the judgment of the Full Court was set aside and it was held that the plaintiff (respondent) was bound by the dealings of his ostensible agent.[43]

(B) RIGHTS AND LIABILITIES OF THE PARTIES:

Having discussed the various modes of creating agency as

recognised by the courts in Ghana and Nigeria, we shall next examine the rights and liabilities of the parties involved in any given transaction. Now, agency has both internal and external aspects. The internal aspect is the relationship between the principal and the agent, while the external facet is the rights and liabilities of third parties. A third party for our purpose here is of course, anyone other than the principal and the agent, with whom the said agent contracts on behalf of the said principal and with his authority

(i) *The Internal aspect of agency*

We are not here concerned with the rights and duties of the various categories of general and special agents.[44] Fascinating as this aspect of the problem is, we feel that it is outside the scope of a general discussion of agreements. It is rather an aspect of the contractual and fiduciary nature of the relationship that we propose to explore. Remuneration of the agent by the principal and the liability of the agent to " account " will be here discussed. Firstly, remuneration.[45] The right of an agent to be remunerated for his services is founded upon an express or implied agreement between the parties. We are here concerned with express provisions in such agreements. Most of such provisions take the form of commissions. In English law the payment of commission depends on the express terms of the agreement,[46] and such terms are strictly construed by the courts.[47] It is an implied term of the agreement that the agent will not wrongfully be deprived of his commission by the principal.[48] A fraudulent agent loses his commission in relation to the same transaction.[49]

Judicial authority in both Ghana and Nigeria tends to indicate a total adoption of the English position. Thus in the Nigerian case of *Odufunade* v. *Rossek*,[50] to which reference has been made in another connection, the agent lost in his action for ten per cent commission against the principal because the event stipulated in the agreement did not occur. In that case instead of an assignment of the lease, which was stipulated in the agency agreement, the property was compulsorily acquired by the Nigerian Federal Government. It has already been shown that this was a very narrow construction of the provision in the agreement. An attempt to justify this approach has been made by the analogy of agency commission agreements to insurance contracts, where the insurers are only liable for the specific risks insured against. It is submitted, however, that such analogy is rather improper for two reasons. Firstly, while insurance contracts are *uberimmae fidei*, agency agreements are not. Secondly, while in certain cases the assured could reclaim his premiums on a void policy, no such consideration is extended to the agent in cases of commission agreements.

The Ghana case of *Mercer* v. *Anglo-Guinea Produce Co.*[51] is authority for the view that it is an implied term of the agreement that the principal will not wrongfully deprive the agent of his commission. In that case the plaintiff (appellant) entered into an agreement with the defendant (respondent) company to be their cocoa purchasing agent. The company was to advance sums up to £1,500 from time to time to enable the plaintiff purchase the cocoa and there was provision for the payment of commission on the purchases. The transaction was secured with a mortgage of the plaintiff's landed property. In fact no such advances were made and no commission was paid. The plaintiff later had his property reconveyed to him. The defendants blamed this on the state of the market. In an action for the breach of the agreement, the trial judge decided in favour of the defendants. On appeal, the Full Court reversed the decision, thus deciding in favour of the plaintiff (appellant). After a review of the authorities, Sir Phillip Crampton, C. J. who read the judgment of the court, stated the law as follows:

> "These cases[52] lay down the principle that the courts will not imply conditions not expressed in the contract. In the present case there is an express agreement to give employment; there are clear admissions that the employment was not given, from which it follows the plaintiff was deprived of the opportunity of earning commission, and by the retention of his title deeds by the defendants that he was deprived of the means of entering into contracts with other firms."[53]

The court relied for their decision, on the authority of *Turner* v. *Goldsmith*.[54]

Finally, in *Addaquay* v. *African Association*,[55] the point that arose was the circumstances under which an agent would lose his right to commission. The plaintiff in that case was an agent of the defendants both for the purchase and shipping of produce, and the sale of other goods. He was to be paid commission on both transactions. It was a term of the agreement that the plaintiff should not sell goods on credit without substantial security. The plaintiff had made substantial profits in the produce business but had also sold goods on credit without security. In an action for the payment of his commission, the defendants counterclaimed for the sales on credit and on the alternative pleaded that the breach of the clause of the agreement disentitled the plaintiff to any commission. The two problems posed by this case were

(i) Under what circumstances will provisions in an agreement containing several clauses be severed?; and

(ii) What factors will deprive the agent of his commission? The answers to the two questions as provided by Kennedy, J. in *Hippisley* v. *Knee*[56] were adopted by their Lordships of the Ghana Court of Appeal (as it then was). In the *Hippisley* case, Kennedy, J. said:

> "I agree with my Lord that this is not one of the cases in which it would be just to deprive the agent of his agreed remuneration as well as his secret profit. I feel it is difficult to lay down any definite rule upon the subject with confidence, but I would venture to suggest the following, that where the agent's remuneration is to be paid for in the performance of several inseparable duties, if the agent is unfaithful in the performance of any one of those duties by reason of his receiving a secret profit in connection with it—and here I use the word ' unfaithful ' as including a breach of obligation without moral turpitude—it may be that he will forfeit his remuneration. . . . but where the several duties to be performed are separable as to my mind they are in the present case, the receipt of a secret profit in connection with one of those duties would not, in the absence of fraud, involve the loss of remuneration which had been fairly earned in the proper discharge of the other duties."

Accordingly their Lordships held that the plaintiff was entitled to his commission in respect of the produce transactions. It was made sufficiently clear that fraud would have disentitled him to any such commission.

We shall next examine the fiduciary nature of the relationship. Our discussion here will be centred on the agent's obligation to render accounts to his principal. Our choice here has been determined by the divergence of the customary law position in Ghana from the English and in fact Nigerian law on the subject. In an investigation such as this, the familiar but unresolved issue of the duty of the family head to render accounts to his members, assumes new importance. The family head in relation to family property has been discussed in the language of agency by some writers. In a recent lecture, Allott has stated : " The English law of agency is also relevant and some of its principles have infiltrated into modern analysis of the powers and responsibilities of the head of the family."[57]

It may be observed that this is particularly true of the agent who is also a principal for certain purposes. Most writers on African laws are agreed on the fiduciary nature of the position of the family head. Sarbah in his Fanti Customary law has said: " In this country the head of the family holds family possessions in trust for himself and the members of his family,"[58] while Danquah has also said: " The highest English term which describes the office of an Akan patriarch is ' trustee ', a trustee, however, who is himself one of the *cestui que trust*."[59] To the same effect is Elias' position in his *Nigerian land law and customs* as follows: " The head of the family is, like the chief, a trustee-beneficiary of family lands."[60] In this, both Coker[61] and Ollennu[62] are also in agreement.

Now, a fiduciary in English law is under a duty to keep accurate accounts in respect of the transaction for which he is appointed. He has to furnish periodical information on the state of the accounts to his beneficiaries and in any case, must do so on demand.[63] We shall be looking at the positions in the customary laws of Ghana and Nigeria.

Ghana

The often quoted statement of Sarbah[64] on the powers of the family head, like the dead and buried forms of action in the common law, has haunted the Ghana courts on the accountability of the family head. In dealing with his powers of disposition of family property, the learned author emphasised the immunity of the head from any action for account.[65] It is remarkable that this incidental statement on a general discussion of the powers of the family head, has been accepted and acted upon by the Ghana courts since 1924. Thus in the case of *Pappoe* v. *Kweku*,[66] it was laid down by the Full Court that no junior member of the family can claim an account from the head. This was a case where the brother of the deceased sued for an account of his late brother's estate, letters of administration of which estate had been granted to the family head. The court having ruled that the grant of letters of administration does not necessarily oust the application of native law, proceeded to lay down that the plaintiff had no right to sue the head for account. The language of Gardner Smith, J. who read the judgment of the court left little doubt on the matter.

" In my opinion," he said, " the learned Chief Justice was justified in finding that native law applies and that it is a general principle of native law that the personal property of a deceased head passes to his successor (subject to certain obligations to support the other members of the family) and that an action for an account is unknown to native law."[67] In *Abude* v. *Onanor*[68] the West African Court of Appeal extended the scope of the head's immunity from account from an action by a single member of the family to even a group of family elders. In that case an action for account by the elders of the Labadi Stool against the Ga Mantse was held not to lie. It was restated by the court that neither a chief nor the head of a family can be sued for account either of state or of family funds.

In 1953, the West African Court of Appeal had yet another opportunity of reconsidering the justice of the immunity of the family head from account. This was in the case of *Fynn* v. *Gardiner.*[69] The facts were that one R. A. Harrison had made a valid gift of his land to three of his maternal relations on whose death the land became family property.[70] The plaintiffs (appellants) were the grandchildren of the said R. A. Harrison and they sued the family head, (i) for a declaration that they were joint-tenants with the other members of the family of the said property left by their late father; and (ii) for an account of the proceeds from dealings with the land. The Native Court decided both issues in their favour, but both the Land Court and the West African Court of Appeal reversed this ruling of the Native Court, holding in favour of the defendants. Foster-Sutton, P., who read the court's judgment, restated the position in these words:

> "We indicated, during the course of the arguments, that in our opinion, the Native Court erred in ordering an account. It is a well settled principle of native law and custom that junior members of a family cannot call upon the head of the family for an account. Their remedy is to depose him and appoint another head instead."[71]

Perhaps their Lordships were rather influenced by the vital fact that among the Akans, children are not members of their father's family, and do not inherit his property on intestacy. It is, nevertheless, curious that the opinion of a Native court on the matter was lightly disregarded by the appeal court.[72]

It must be mentioned, however, that the Ghana Courts have allowed actions for account in cases where the agent was only a caretaker of the family property and not the family head. Thus in *Nelson* v. *Nelson,*[73] where some of the children of a deceased native brought an action for account against a brother of theirs who had been appointed by the deceased, on his death-bed, to look after their interests in his estate, it was held that an action for an account lay against him. The court emphasised the fact that the defendant was only a caretaker and not the family head. A later decision of the West African Court of Appeal restated this principle in unambiguous terms.[74] In that case, Kingdon, C.J. had this to say:

> "Turning now to the claim for an account, the appellant has protested that the office of caretaker cannot be thrust *ex post*

facto upon a person in the way the judgment thrusts it upon the appellant and his brother Louis before him. Perhaps the term 'Caretaker' is, strictly speaking, a misnomer, but it is a term which is commonly used in this country to mean the member of the family, not necessarily the head, who acts as agent for the family in conducting its affairs. The trial judge found, and I see no reason to differ, that the defendant and his brother, Louis, before him were caretakers in the sense I have indicated, though not heads of the family. They as the literate members of the family, naturally managed the family's affairs rather than the illiterate plaintiffs, who entrusted the family affairs to members most capable of managing them. It would, I think, be inequitable and contrary to well-recognised native custom to deprive the illiterates of their claim to enforce their rights even after a period of years."[75]

Nigeria

In Nigeria, the trend of academic and judicial opinion is that the family head is liable to account. Among the Yorubas, both Coker[76] and Lloyd[77] are of the opinion that the Yoruba family head is but *primus inter pares,* and that the courts will interfere to restore the rights of any member who acts in good time[78] and in good faith.[79] Thus in *Mariana Lopez* v. *Domingo Lopez and Others,*[80] Combe, C.J. ruled that where there has been a persistent refusal by the head of a family, or by some members of the family, to allow other members of the family to enjoy their rights under native law in family land, the court has exercised, and will continue to exercise, its undoubted right to make such order as will ensure that members of the family shall enjoy their rights. Although it could be argued that this principle may only be applicable to Yoruba law for which the case is authority, there is support for the view that it also applies among the Efiks[81] of Eastern Nigeria and among the Ibos.[82]

(ii) *External aspects of agency*

This is of course the rights and liabilities of third parties. An agreement made by an agent on behalf of a principal creates rights and duties between the principal and the third party, and in some cases, between the agent and the third party. We shall be examining these situations and in the above order.

Principal and third party

The principal is bound to the third party by the terms of an agreement made by his agent on his behalf and with his actual or apparent authority. This position appears to have been accepted by the courts in Ghana and Nigeria as the true state of the imported law of agency. *Raccah* v. *Standard Company of Nigeria*[83] was an action against the defendant company by the plaintiff for the cost of produce bought by the defendants through their agent. It happened that by the time the transaction was entered into, the agent's authority had been terminated by the defendants but this fact was not made known to the plaintiff who therefore acted in the belief that the agent had authority to contract. The defendants were held liable. Also, in *Cole* v. *Jead*,[84] a lease granted by an agent was held binding on his principal, and in *Abban* v. *Appiah*,[85] an execution sale of the plaintiff's property with the connivance of his agent was held binding on him. The fact that the agent did not act in good faith did not, in the court's opinion, affect the rights of third parties. But the principal is not liable where the agent acted outside the scope of his authority. In the *Raccah* case, the purchase of produce was within the scope of the agent's authority. The fact that the authority had been terminated without the third party's knowledge, did not make the matter less so. But in the recent Nigerian case of *Obaseki* v. *African Continental Bank & ors*[86] the plaintiff brought an action against the defendant bank for the specific performance of an agreement to purchase land. The alleged purchase was at an auction sale, one of the conditions of which was that " the highest bidder shall be the purchaser subject to the approval of the mortgagee " i.e. the approval of the bank. The branch manager of the bank had purported to approve the sale. In fact he had no authority to do so under the Articles of Association of the bank and the Articles were registered in the usual way under the local Companies Act.[87] Under the Articles, only the board of directors had the power to approve such a transaction. It was held by the Nigerian Supreme Court, affirming the decision of the trial court, that the defendants were not liable on the ground that the act was outside the scope of the authority of the defendant's agent.[88] Similarly, the third party's liability on the agreement is to the principal and he alone can sue the third party. This was the decision in the Ghana case of *Nyamfe* v. *Amoako & Another*.[89] In this case, one Wilson supplied the plaintiff with money for the purchase of cocoa. Consignments were made to Wilson in a lorry owned by the first defendant and driven by the second defendant. One of the consignments got lost and in an action by the agent (plaintiff) for the price of the cocoa, the court held that the plaintiff was a mere agent and could not sue since he had no property in the goods consigned. It was added that the property in the goods vested in Wilson immediately they were delivered to the carrier. The trial judge, Howes, J., quoting

Lord Alvanley, C.J. in *Dutton v. Solomonson*,[90] stated at page 88 as follows:

> " If a tradesman order goods to be sent by a carrier, though he does not name any particular carrier, the moment the goods are delivered to the carrier, it operates as a delivery to the purchaser; the whole property immediately vests in him; he alone can bring an action for any injury done to the goods; and if any accident happen to the goods, it is at his risk."

The agent must, however, have contracted as an agent, otherwise the third party is not liable.[91] When the agent has so contracted on behalf of a principal, even an undisclosed principal can sue the third party.[92]

Agent and third party

Although the principal is normally liable to the third party under an agreement made by the agent, there are instances where the agent himself can sue and be sued by the third party under the agreement. The instance of an agent who contracts as a principal has already been mentioned. In such a case he and not the principal is liable to the third party.[93] The agent is also liable if this was the intention of the parties. This is particularly true of agents representing foreign principals. In this aspect of the law, the Ghana Courts have moved from the position as recognised in the English case of *Armstrong v. Stokes*[94] and followed in the Ghana case of *Essien v. Boyan*[95] to the current position in English law as represented by *Miller, Gibb & Co. v. Smith & Tyre Ltd.*[96] In the *Essien* decision, the Divisional Court at Cape Coast ruled that,

> " the court is always prepared to hold (in the absence of evidence to the contrary) that in a contract between a native producer and a shipping agent, there is always an implied contract that the agent shall pay in case the principal abroad fails to pay."

This presumption of the agent's liability in cases of foreign principals has been said to be no longer good law.[97]

Between 1959 and 1960 the Ghana Court of Appeal had two opportunities of ruling on the matter of the agent's liability where foreign principals are involved, and on the two occasions, decidedly resolved the matter in favour of the intention of the parties. Firstly, *British West African Insurance Services v. Abdilmasil.*[98] In that case the plaintiffs were the Ghana agents of Gresham Fire and Accident Insurance Society, a company registered in the United Kingdom, and under a power of attorney from the latter company had wide powers of representatiton in these terms:

"to appear and represent the Society in any court or courts of law or equity in the said territories[99] aforesaid and there to sue or be sued and to answer, defend and reply to all matters and causes touching and concerning the premises, or any action or actions, suit or suits, matter or thing that may be sued or prosecuted by or against the society touching or concerning the premises, and, for that purpose or any other purpose, to accept on behalf of the society service or process and notices required to be served on the society, and to submit on behalf of the aforesaid and also to do, say, pursue, implead, seize, sequester, arrest, attach and imprison and out of prison again to deliver."

The defendant had obtained judgment for £8,154 3s. 5d. against the Gresham Insurance Society, and this amount was still unpaid. Relying on the agent's power of attorney, the defendant obtained a writ of fi.fa. against the plaintiffs' stores for this sum, and although the plaintiffs later paid this amount by cheque, their stores had, in the meantime been sealed off by the defendant's agents for four days. In an action for trespass by the plaintiffs based on fi.fa., the point that arose was whether or not the execution of the process on the plaintiffs' property was proper. On this, the Court of Appeal, affirming the judgment of Smith, J., held:

"that where agents in this country of a firm in the United Kingdom are virtually identified with their principal, where full and wide powers are given to the former by the latter's power of attorney, where the whole business is in the hands of the local agents, and where the latter own property in this country, it would be wrong and unjust that the agents should be permitted to tell a judgment-creditor in this country to collect the debt in London."[100]

The second case was *Sackey* v. *Fattal*.[101] Here, the fact that the plaintiff had got into direct communication with Japanese principals of the defendants (agents) did not in the opinion of the court, affect the personal liability of the Ghana agent to the plaintiff. Relying on the authority of the English case of *Dramburg and Another* v. *Pollitzer*,[102] Ollennu, J. (as he then was), held that there was a clear intention to make the local agent liable. After a review of the authorities, the learned judge continued:

"Counsel's final submission was that, by her act in writing to the defendant's principals to complain about the goods, the plaintiff elected to treat the principals as the persons liable on the contract, the agent's liability if any, ceased. But this is also shown, by the book to which he referred in support, to be a question of fact depending on each case."

" In *Dramburg and anor* v. *Pollitzer*,[103] it was held that an order placed with, and accepted by, an agent of foreign manufacturers formed a contract between the customer and the agent. It was further held that a letter written by the customer to the foreign manufacturers after a breach of that contract had been committed, did not constitute an election by the customer to treat the manufacturers as principals. In my opinion, that case is very similar to the present one in many respects.[104]

The *Fattal* decision was affirmed on appeal by the Ghana Court of Appeal.[105]

NOTES

1. See *Bowstead on Agency*, 12th ed., by E. J. Griew (1959) passim; *Halsbury's laws*, 3rd ed., pp. 145-246; W. Muller-Freienfels, "The undisclosed principal" (1953) 16 M.L.R. 299; F. E. Dowrick, "The relationship of principal and agent" (1954) M.L.R. 24. See also G. H. L. Fridman, *The law of Agency* (1960); Stoljar, *The law of Agency* (1961).

2. (1843) 6 M.C.G. 236, at p. 242.

3. Op. cit., p. 1. See also *American Restatement, Contracts*, S. I, in the Indian Contract Act, 1872, S. 182 an agent is defined as "a person employed to do any act for another or to represent another in dealings with third persons."

4. Cf. Sir Fredrick Pollock's comments on the case of *Cooke* v. *Eshalby* (1887) 12 App. Cas. 271, in (1888) 3 L.Q.R. 359. Pollock regretted the impact of the doctrine of the undisclosed principal on the theory of privity of contracts.

5. See J. D. Fage, *An Introduction to the History of West Africa*, Cambridge, 3rd ed., 1962, p. 11; K. O. Dike, *Trade and Politics in the Niger Delta* (Oxford, 1956), pp. 97 et seq. *Wilson* v. *Tumman* supra, being a pre-1874 English decision is part of the imported laws of Ghana and Nigeria.

6. See Allott, " Family Property in West Africa: its juristic basis, control and enjoyment." See also S. K. B. Asante (1965) 14 I.C.L.Q. 1144.

7. *Pollock* v. *Stables* (1948) 2 Q.B. 765.

8. *Bolton Partners* v. *Lambert* (1888) 41 Ch. D. 295. See also *Keighly, Maxsted & Co.* v. *Durant* (1901) A.C. 240.

9. This is the same as agency by estoppel. *Pickering* v. *Busk* (1812), 15 East, 38. See also Partnership Act, 1890, S. 5 (England).

10. *Debenham* v. *Mellon* (1880) 5 Q.B.D. 394.

11. *Harrison* v. *Grady* (1865) 13, L.T. 369. The question of capacity will be discussed under defective agreements infra.

12. It is likely, however, that in the 4th and 5th modes of formation the courts in Ghana and Nigeria will follow English authority. This will be particularly true in Ordinance Marriages.

13. See *Bowstead on Agency*, p. 32.

14. See, however, *Lord* v. *Kellett* (1833) 2 Myl & K.I.; *Allen* v. *Bone* (1841) 4 Beav. 493.

15. (1938) 14 N.L.R. 17.

16. (1826) 8 D & R. 102. In this case there was writing but not under seal.
17. (1939) 5, W.A.C.A. 92.
18. *R.* v. *Longnor* (1833) 4 B & AD. 647.
19. Supra Section 53 (i) of the law of Property Act, 1925 (England), which requires a lease for more than three years to be in writing provides that an agent who signs for a principal in these cases must also be appointed in writing.
20. *Anson's law of Contract,* 22nd ed., 1964, p. 526 (1893) 9 T.L.R. 569.
21. (1893) 9 T.L.R. 569.
22. e.g. S. 18 (i) of the Ghana Auction Sales Ordinance, Cap. 196, empowers auctioneers to sue for the price of goods sold. It is obvious that an auctioneer who so sues will be entitled to a refund of the cost of the action reasonably incurred.
23. (1926-29) F. Ct. 215. On Nigeria, see *Foloshade* v. *Duroshola* (1961) All N.L.R. 87.
24. (1961) 1 All N.L.R. 87.
25. Op. cit. at p. 90. But see the Ghana case of *Lokko* v. *Konklofi* (1907) Ren. 450, where a chief's acquiescence was taken to be ratification.
26. Apparently the plaintiff could sue the vendor for damages on a total failure of consideration. Any tort action might be statute-barred.
27. *Kolner* v. *Baxter* (1866) L.R. 2 Ch., p. 174, see especially Erle, C.J. at p. 183, where he said, " There must be two parties to a contract and the rights and obligations which it creates cannot be transferred by one of them to a third person."
28. See Cheshire and Fifoot, *Law of Contract,* 6th ed., 1964, p. 406.
29. (1961) 1 All N.L.R. 534; see also *Newborne* v. *Sensolid* etc. (1953) 1 All E.R. 708.
30. The Nigerian Companies Act, Cap. 37, laws of Nigeria (1958), appears to be silent on pre-incorporation contracts.
31. (1965) C.C. 96, decided by Apaloo, J.S.C. at Accra, H. Ct., 5th March, 1965, unreported.
32. (1875) L.R. 7 H.L. 653.
33. See W. B. P. Holt (150) 66 L.Q.R. 493; L. C. B. Gower (1951) 67, L.Q.R. 41.
34. S. 25 (4) of the Companies Code, 1963.
35. Application to the court by any member of the company, or the holder of any debenture secured by a floating charge over all or any of the company's property, or by the trustee of the holders of any such debentures.
36. Legal liability of directors for exceeding their powers.
37. Application by certain members for remedy against oppression. Here the oppression is the ultra vires act.
38. Application for winding up.
39. (1926-29) F. Ct. 147.
40. It is remarkable that in this case an authority to execute an appeal bond was not implied from a general authority to represent the Omanhene at the trial. If the role of the linguist in customary law is similar to that of counsel in the imported law, it is difficult to justify this limitation of his authority. On the implied authority of barristers and solicitors, see *Bowstead on Agency,* pp. 65-66.
41. See Bowstead, op. cit., p. 10.
42. (1923-25) F. Ct. 78. See also *Nanka-Bruce* v. *Laing and the Commonwealth Trust Ltd.* (1923-25) F. Ct. 89. (Ghana) of the Nigerian case of *Abina & ors.* v. *Farhat* (1938) 14 N.L.R. 17, where the plea failed.

43. Other aspects of this case will be discussed under "defective agreements" infra. See also the Nigerian case of *Raccah* v. *Standard Co. of Nigeria* (1922) 4 N.L.R. 48 where apparent authority was successfully pleaded.
44. On this see *Bowstead on Agency,* pp. 48-108; R. Powell, *The Law of Agency,* 2nd ed., London, 1961, pp. 295-377; S. J. Stoljar, *The Law of Agency,* London, 1961, pp. 267-326.
45. In both Ghana and Nigeria certain enactments make provisions for the remuneration of agents. See among others for Ghana: Legal Profession Act, 1960 (Act 32), SS. 30-42; Auctions Ordinance (Cap. 196); S. 140 of the Companies Code, 1963. For Nigeria, see Legal Practitioners Act, 1962, SS. 10 and 11; Auctioneers Law (Cap. 9); Western Region, 1959.
46. *Biggs* v. *Gordon* (1860) 8 C.B. (N.S.), 638, cited by Bowstead, op. cit. at p. 123.
47. *Toumlin* v. *Miller* (1887) 58 L.T. 96; see also *Ackroyd and Sons* v. *Hasan* (1960) 2 W.L.R. 810.
48. *Turner* v. *Goldsmith* (1891) 1 Q.B. 544; see also *Warren & Co.* v. *Agdeshman* (1922) 38 T.L.R. 588. But cf. *Rhodes* v. *Forwood* (1876) 1 App. Cas. 356, where the House of Lords refused the agents (appellants) any remedy for loss of business.
49. *Hippisley* v. *Knee* (1905) 1 K.B. 1. In this case it was stated that the auctioneers would have lost their commission if there had been fraud.
50. (1960) F.S.C. 358.
51. (1922) F. Ct. 114, cf. *Ankrah* v. *The German West African Trading Co. Ltd.* (1905), Ren. 400, where the court was not prepared to imply the payment of commission. See also the Nigerian case of *Nigerian Sweet & Confectionary Co. Ltd.* v. *Tate & Lyle (Nigeria) Ltd.* 380/1964—S. Ct.—Unreported.
52. The cases referred to were: *Taylor* v. *Caldwell* (1863) 3 B. & S. 826; *Oriental S.S. Co.* v. *Taylor* (1893) 2 Q. B. 518; *Rhodes* v. *Forwood* (1876) 1 App. Cas. 276; and *Holford* v. *Acton Urban District Council* (1898) 2 Ch. 240.
53. Op. cit. at p. 117.
54. In that case an agreement to pay commission for five years was enforced by the court despite the fact that the factory where the goods were to be manufactured had been burnt down.
55. (1910) Ren. 586.
56. (1905) 1 K.B. 1.
57. "Family Property in West Africa: Its juristic basis, control and enjoyment." Lecture delivered at the School of Oriental and African Studies, Univ. of London, during the 1965-66 academic session. See also S. K. B. Asante (1965) 14 1. C.L.Q. 1144 at p. 1146.
58. (2nd ed. 1904), p. 89. See also pp. 65-66.
59. *Akan laws and customs* (1928), p. 205.
60. 3rd ed. 1960, p. 143.
61. *Family Property Among the Yorubas* (1st ed., 1958), p. 154.
62. *Principles of Customary Land laws in Ghana* (162), p. 46. See also Bensi-Enchil Ghana land law (London, 1964), and P. C. Lloyd, "Family Property among the Yorubas" in (1959) 3 J.A.L. 105 at p. 110.
63. See Prof. Hanbury, *Modern Equity* (6th ed., 1952), p. 343.
64. J. M. Sarbah, *Fanti Customary law* (2nd ed., 1904), p. 90.

65. On this question there is divergence of views between Sarbah and Danquah. The latter feels that the head is liable to account to the elders of the family. See J. B. Danquah, *Akan laws and Customs.* Judicial support is, however, on Sarbah's side.
66. (1923-25) F. Ct. 158.
67. Ibid. at p. 161. See also *Villars* v. *Baffoe* (1909) Ren. 549. It is hard, however, to see how the support referred to by his Lordship in the *Pappoe* case can be enforced short of action for account.
68. (1946) 12 W.A.C.A. 102.
69. (1953) 14 W.A.C.A. 260.
70. For this view of the law, see Sarbah (2nd ed., 1904), p. 90.
71. At p. 261.
72. Two views to rationalise the head's immunity from account have been put forward. One is that the chief or head of the family cannot be sued in his own court and that it would detract from the dignity of the head to be called to account. This view has been based on the religious background of the office of the head. For this see R. S. Rattray, *Ashanti law and Constitution* (London, 1956), Ch. XXV; and, S. K. B. Asante (1965), 14 1. C.L.Q., p. 1151. It is submitted, however, that the whole tenor of the modern economic rise in the value of land militates against this privilege and that it has outlived its usefulness. The other view, that of Ollennu in his *Principles of Customary land law in Ghana* (1962), p. 137, has been based on the procedural difficulties of bringing a representative action against the family head, since he is the only person allowed to sue on behalf of the family. For the opposite view on this see, Asante, op. cit., pp. 1170-71; see also G. R. Woodman, " The alienation of family land in Ghana " (1964), Univ. of Ghana L.J. 23. Woodman is of the opinion that the rise in the economic value of land calls for a reappraisal of the head's immunity to account.
73. (1951) 13 W.A.C.A. 248.
74. *Ruttmern & ors.* v. *Ruttmern* (1937) 3 W.A.C.A. 179.
75. Op. cit. at p. 180. Is this equally applicable to a literate family head?
76. *Family Property among the Yorubas* (1st ed., 1958), p. 149.
77. " Family Property Among the Yoruba " (159) 3 J.A.L. 105, at p. 110.
78. Thus where a member waited for 40 years before bringing the action, the court refused to entertain it: *Kosoko* v. *Kosoko* (1937) 13 N.L.R. 131.
79. Where the action is brought with a view to embarrassing the occupant of the family head, the courts will refuse to lend their aid—*Kosoko* v. *Kosoko,* supra.
80. (1924) 5 N.L.R. 47 at p. 50.
81. *Archibong* v. *Archibong* (1947) 18 N.L.R. 117. Apart from the present writer's discovery of this fact during his field work, the whole structure of the Ibo political organisation militates against status and privilege which immunity symbolises.
82. See M. I. Jegede, " The position of head of a family in relation to family property; is he a trustee in the English sense?" (1966) 7 Nigerian Bar Journal, p. 21.
83. (1922) 4, N.L.R. 48. For powers of family head to bind the family, see infra, pp. 492 et seq.
84. (1939) 5 W.A.C.A. 92.
85. (1926-29) Div. Ct. (Ghana) 175. See also the recent Nigerian case of *Onwuegbu & anor* v. *African Insurance Co. Ltd.* (1965) N.M.L.R. 248,

where it was held that the principal was liable even where the agent misappropriated premiums collected on behalf of the said principal. See *MacGillivra on Insurance*, 5th ed., vol. I, p. 295.

86. (1966) N.M.L.R. 35. See also *Wiaboh* v. *Woodin* (1896) Ren. 124, and *King* v. *Freres* (1926-29) F. Ct. 1.
87. Cap. 37, Laws of Nigeria (1958).
88. It is arguable on behalf of the plaintiff that this provision in the conditions of sale (i.e. for the approval of a third party) where the auction sale was without reserve, is inconsistent with the provision of the Sales by Auction Act, Cap. 187, S. 22 of which empowers the highest bidder to sue for the article offered for sale. On the other hand the parties could be said to be in *pari delicto* since they contracted in the knowledge of the provisions of the Act. See *K. Chellaram & Sons Ltd.* v. *Messrs. Costain (West Africa) Ltd.* (1957) 2 E.N.L.R. 10, where the principal was held not liable for the agent's forgery.
89. (1926-29) Div. Ct. 87.
90. (1803) 3 Bos. & Pul. at p. 584.
91. *Makanjiola* v. *Olupitan* (1958) W.R.N.L.R. 165.
92. *Sam* v. *Cape Coast Boating Co.* (1904) Ren. 306.
93. *Makanjiola* v. *Olupitan,* supra.
94. (1872) L.R. 7 Q.B. 598, see p. 605.
95. (1911) Ren. 614.
96. (1917) 2 K.B. 141.
97. Powell, *The Law of Agency* (2nd ed.), p. 252; *Anson's law of Contract* (22nd ed., 1964), p. 564. But cf. Hudson (1957) 35 Can B. Rev. 336; (1960) 23 M.L.R. 695.
98. (1959) G.L.R. 188; affirmed (1960) G.L.R. 107.
99. In this case, Ghana.
100. Op. cit. at p. 189.
101. (1959) G.L.R. 169, affirmed (1959) G.L.R. 176.
102. (1873) 28 T.L.R. (N.S.) 470 cited by Ollennu, J. in the *Fattal* case, supra.
103. (1873) 28 T.L.R. (N.S.) 470.
104. Op. cit., p. 175.
105. (1959) G.L.R. 176. Although this aspect of agency has not agitated the Nigerian courts as much as the courts in Ghana, it is likely, however, that the trend in the courts of the latter territory will be followed in Nigeria if and when the matter arises for decision.

CHAPTER 10

AGREEMENTS BETWEEN TWO PARTIES WHERE ONE OR BOTH SUBSEQUENTLY TRANSFER TO A THIRD

The parties to an agreement may under certain circumstances drop out and others take their place. In this section we shall be examining the circumstances under which contractual rights and liabilities can be transferred to third parties. These will be discussed under the sub-headings of assignments and negotiability.[1]

(a) *Assignments*[2]

This is the transfer of contractual rights and liabilities to a third party with or without the concurrence of the other party to the agreement. Such transfer could be by the acts of the parties to the contract or by operation of law. It is by operation of law in cases of the death or bankruptcy of one or both of the contracting parties. In English law, certain rights are not assignable, namely, a mere right to sue for damages,[3] a bare right of action,[4] salaries of public officers paid out of public funds,[5] the alimony granted to a wife,[6] and the benefits under social security legislation.[7] Some rights in action have been made assignable by statute. Examples are legion, but specific mention could be made of bills of lading,[8] policies of life[9] and Marine Insurance,[10] shares in a company,[11] negotiable instruments,[12] patents[13] and copyright.[14]

Similar statutory provisions have been made in Ghana[15] and Nigeria[16] for the transfer of the benefits over things in action.

What we propose to do here is to focus our attention on the different ways of effecting a valid assignment. For this purpose we shall be examining the voluntary transfer of contractual rights, then the transfer of contractual liabilities, and lastly, assignments by operation of law.

1. VOLUNTARY TRANSFERS OF CONTRACTUAL RIGHTS

Before 1875 English law adopted the view (consistent with its theory of privity of contracts) that a chose in action[17] was not assignable at common law.[18] The courts of chancery, however, did recognise and enforce the rights of an assignee, provided the right assigned was an equitable right. A legacy or a share in a trust fund are examples of such equitable rights. An equitable assignee could sue the debtor without joining the assignor. An equitable assignment of a legal right, however, could only be enforced against the debtor, if the assignor was joined, and the chancery courts would compel the assignor to lend his name to the assignee for purposes of an action against the debtor.[19] This was the position in England until the enactment of the Judicature Act, 1873, which came into force on 1st November, 1875.

Section 25 (6) of this Act provides as follows:

> " Any absolute assignment by writing under the hands of the assignor (not purporting to be by way of charge only) of any debt or other legal chose in action of which express notice in writing shall have been given to the debtor . . . shall be and be deemed to have been effectual in law (subject to all equities which would have been entitled to priority over the right of the assignee if this Act had not passed) to pass and transfer the legal right to such debt or chose in action from the date of such notice."

The effect of this provision was to empower the assignee of any thing in action to sue the debtor in his own name without joining the assignor, subject of course to the fulfilment of the conditions laid down in the section. It did not, however make assignable such other things as were not transferable before the passing of the Act, nor did it replace equitable assignments. It rather supplemented the latter.[20] The present position in English law is governed by *Section 136* of the *Law of Property Act, 1925.* which is a substantial re-enactment of the older provision.

The position in Ghana

Now, the Judicature Act, 1873 is not a statute of general application in Ghana.[21] Consequently the imported law of Ghana is the pre-1875 English law on the subject. Accordingly Ghana law did not recognise legal assignments, and there must be a consideration to support an equitable assignment since equity will not aid a volunteer.

The anomalous nature of this state of the law was very obvious. The Contract Act,[22] 1960, has however, effected some necessary changes. Section 7 of this Act provides as follows:

> " 7 (i) Subject to any rule of law, and subject to any contrary intention appearing from any transaction giving rise to any legal rights, a person may, after the commencement of this Act, assign a legal right to another person as hereinafter specified.[23]

7 (ii) An assignment, whether given for consideration or not, of a vested legal right, transfers the full right and interest therein to the assignee and extinguishes the right and interest therein of the assignor if—

(a) it is absolute and not by way of charge only; and
(b) it is in writing and is signed by the assignor or his agent; and
(c) written notice thereof is given to the debtor or other person against whom the right is enforceable."

The significance of section 7 (i) of the Act is to exclude from the application of the section, cases in which the parties intended the application of any other law. Thus it could be argued that an assignment under customary law need not comply with the provisions of section 7 (ii). So far no local judicial decision has turned on the interpretation of section 7 (i). It is contended, however, that customary law assignments are outside its scope.

Section 7 (ii) is a substantial re-enactment of the provisions of Section 136 of the English Law of Property Act, 1925 which hitherto was not applicable to Ghana. Under the subsection, a valid assignment must be absolute, must be in writing, and the debtor must have been notified in writing. A purported assignment of a conditional right operates as a promise to assign the right if and when the condition occurs.[24]

In the recent case of *C.F.C. Construction Co.* v. *G.N.C.C. and Anor*[25] decided by Apaloo, J.S.C. at Accra, the High Court had to consider the interpretation of Section 7 (ii) and (iii) of the Contract Act. In that case, the plaintiff obtained judgment against a certain Presec Ltd. for £1,247 4s. 5d. with costs. Presec arranged to pay this debt at the rate of £1,000 per month but defaulted after paying three instalments. The Ghana Division of Public Construction (hereafter called D.P.C.) owed the Presec Ltd. some money as a result of a building contract carried out by the latter company for the former. The debt under the contract was to become due six months after October 10th, 1961 (the date of the making of the building contract). Certain deductions were to be made by the D.P.C. for repairs. The defendants were the successors of the D.P.C. i.e. as creditors of Presec Ltd. In May, 1962 (i.e. after the contract debt had become due), Presec Ltd. wrote to the defendants purporting to assign any amount due to them (Presec) to the plaintiffs. A copy of this letter was given to the plaintiffs. In September, 1962, Presec Ltd., went into liquidation and in October, 1962, the defendants paid £6,227 to the provisional liquidator, the assignment of May, 1962, notwithstanding. The plaintiffs sued for the sum of £10,227 being money due to Presec Ltd. which had been validly assigned to them; basing their claim on section 7 (ii) of the Contract Act 1960.

On behalf of the defendants it was argued (a) that the purported assignment of May, 1962 was only a conditional assignment and therefore was not enforceable under Section 7 (ii) of the Contract Act; (b) that the defendants as debtors had not given their consent to the said assignment and therefore were not bound by its terms; and finally (c) that no sum certain was assigned since the amount owed was subject to deductions for repairs and defects.

The court lightly rejected all these arguments, holding firstly, that the May assignment was an unconditional transfer of Presec Ltd's interest in the contract debt. Secondly (and it is curious that it was ever argued for the defendants), that the consent of the debtor was not necessary for a valid assignment under the sub-section. Thirdly, that there was sufficient certainty about the said assignment, being the whole amount due to Presec Ltd. The fact that the sum might be diminished by valid counterclaim or set-off did not operate to make the sum any less certain. Finally, since the assignment was unconditional, and of a right vested in interest, it did not operate as a promise to assign under section 7 (iii) of the Act. English judicial authority based on the 1873 legislation was cited with approval.[26]

Under Section 7 (iv):

" An assignment, whether given for consideration or not is valid notwithstanding that it does not comply with all or any of the requirements of subsection (ii) but—

(a) no right so assigned shall be enforced or relied upon against the debtor or other party against whom the right is enforceable unless the assignor is a party to any proceedings in which it is sought to be enforced or relied upon, or unless the court is satisfied that it would be impossible or

(b) no such assignment shall prejudice the debtor or other person against whom the right is enforceable unless he has written notice thereof."

What the above sub-section has done has been to elevate to the status of a statutory provision the English rules relating to equitable assignments. The assignee can sue the debtor but the assignor must be made a party to the action. It is submitted that this statutory fusion of law and equity is a step in the right direction. It is curious in the extreme that although equity and law are administered in the same courts since 1875, the dichotomy has remained in English law. The Ghana provision, again in this respect, is an improvement on the English position.

Section 7 (v)[27] of the Act makes provision for the priority of assignments. It states as follows:

> " Where there are two or more assignments in respect of the same debt or right, a later assignee shall have priority over an earlier assignee if the debtor or other person liable has not received written notice of the earlier assignment at the time when the latter assignment was made."

It must be observed that if this provision was intended to be the rule in *Dearle* v. *Hall*[28] in statutory form, then there is room for considerable improvement in the drafting. If however, it means what it says, then its merits are very highly questionable. *Dearle* v. *Hall* decided that where there are two or more assignments in respect of the same debt or right, priority dates from the date of notice to the debtor. Now, the date of such notice need not be that on which the assignment was made. The Ghana provision, however, tends to suggest that a later assignment takes priority over an earlier one if the earlier assignee had not given notice to the debtor on the date the subsequent assignment was made. It is the making of the subsequent assignment not notice to the debtor that gives it priority over the first. The absurd results that follow from a literal interpretation of the provision have been emphasised by a learned commentator.[29]

Finally, Section 7 (vi) of the Act provides that the assignee takes subject to equitable defences at the time when the debtor received notice of the assignment.

The position in Nigeria.

It has already been noted that in Nigeria there are five separate jurisdictions namely, Federal, Northern Region, Eastern Region, Western and Mid-Western Regions.[30] The English Judicature Act, 1873 is a statute of general application in all but the Western and Mid-Western Regions, where all the relevant statutes of general application within the region's legislative competence have been substantially re-enacted as part of their statutory laws.

Thus although Section 25 (vi) of the Judicature Act, 1873, regulates assignments in the Federal Territory, Northern and Eastern Regions, this is not the case in the Western and Mid-Western Regions. In the two latter regions the Property and Conveyancing Law,[31] makes similar provisions to Section 136 of the English Law of Property Act, 1925.[32] It must be added that unlike the Ghana enactment, priority of successive assignments under the Western Nigeria legislation dates from notice and not from the time the assignment was made[33]. Policies of insurance are excluded from the provisions of the section.[34]

2. VOLUNTARY TRANSFER OF CONTRACTUAL LIABILITIES

It is a trite assertion in English legal parlance that a promisor cannot assign his liabilities under an agreement, and conversely, that a promisee cannot be compelled by the promisor or by a third party, to accept any but the promisor as the person liable to him under an agreement.[35] This general statement is, however, subject to some exceptions. The method of novation has already been mentioned. Mention has also been made of the transfer of the burden of restrictive covenants in land matters.[36] Here we are concerned with a situation where B can validly transfer his liability to C under an agreement with A in such a way that A would look to C for the performance of the obligation, and such performance discharges B. This has often been called the doctrine of vicarious performance and there have been doubts as to its being an aspect of assignments at all.[37] The Latin maxim, *qui facit per alium facit per se* has often been prayed in aid of the doctrine.

The limits of the doctrine in English law were laid down by Lord Greene in *Davies* v. *Collins*,[38] in these words:

> " Whether or not in any given contract performance can properly be carried out by the employment of a sub-contractor, must depend on the proper inference to be drawn from the contract itself, the subject matter of it and other material surrounding circumstances."

In both Ghana and Nigeria there is a dearth of local judicial or statutory authority on this branch of the law. The Ghana contract legislation is silent on the assignment of contractual liabilities, providing rather for the transfer of contractual rights. It is likely however, that the courts in both countries will follow the decisions of English courts on the subject.

3. ASSIGNMENTS BY OPERATION OF LAW

This is the transfer of contractual rights and liabilities to a third party as a result of the death or bankruptcy of any of the contracting parties. The position in English law is regulated by The Law Reform (Miscellaneous Provisions) Act, 1934[39] in cases of death, and the Bankruptcy Act, 1914[40] in cases of insolvency. Neither of these Acts is of general application in either Ghana or Nigeria.[41] The former Act has, however, been substantially re-enacted in Ghana and some jurisdictions in Nigeria.[42] Thus sections

22-24 of the Ghana Civil Liability Act (Act 176) provide for the survival of causes of action vested in or subsisting against a deceased person in the same terms and subject to the same conditions[43] as the English statute on the same subject. To the same effect are Sections 3-5 of the Nigerian (Federation) Civil Liability (Miscellaneous Provision) Act (No. 33 of 1961) and Section 3 of the Northern Nigeria Civil Liability (Survival of Actions, Tortfeasors and Contributory Negligence) Law (N.R. No. 20 of 1957).[44]

The position on the bankruptcy of one of the parties to an agreement is regulated in Ghana by the Insolvency Act, 1962 (Act 153), and the Companies Code, 1963 (Act 179)[45] in the case of registered companies. The Insolvency Act provides for the passing of the assets of an insolvent to an official Trustee (Section 37), the diligent administration of the business of the insolvent by the said official trustee (Section 45) and the disclaimer within a given period, of any onerous assets (Section 51).

Now, in Nigeria the English statute of 1914 or its subsequent amendments do not apply, and there is judicial authority for the view that even the Full Court of Nigeria had no Bankruptcy jurisdiction.[46] It is not clear from the *McIver* case whether or not the English Bankruptcy Act, 1883, a pre-1900 English statute, is of general application in Nigeria. The better view seems to be that it is. It is submitted however, that the Nigerian Law on this subject is most uncertain. In view of the importance of the topic in the supply of credit and other aspects of economic development it is further contended that swift legislative action along the lines of the Ghana statute is long overdue.[47]

4. NEGOTIABLE INSTRUMENTS

These are specialised kinds of assignments and are easily distinguishable from other types of assignable contracts.[48] An instrument is said to be negotiable when any person who has acquired it in good faith and for value can enforce the contract contained in it or the right of property of which it is evidence, against the person originally liable on it, although the person from whom he acquired it may have a defective title or none at all.[49] Quite apart from the importance of negotiable instruments in commercial transactions generally, they are particularly vital in an investigation of the law of obligations in Ghana and Nigeria because of their impact on native customary notions of credit. In this as in some other aspects of the law the conflict between customary and imported laws is most apparent.

Origin and history[50]

The origin and history of negotiable instruments in English law need not detain us here. It suffices to mention that they arose from a custom of the merchants responding to a need for the simplification of the giving of credit. Originally part of the law merchant, negotiable instruments are now mainly regulated by the English Bills of Exchange Act, 1882 and allied enactments.[51] Cheques,[52] Bills of Exchange,[53] and promissory notes[54] have been recognised by statute as categories of these instruments. But these have been said not to be exhaustive. The categories are not closed.[55]

Negotiable instruments in Ghana and Nigeria

In both Ghana and Nigeria statutory provisions similar to those contained in the English Bills of Exchange Act, 1882, have been made with regard to certain negotiable instruments. Section 1 of the Ghana Bills of Exchange Act, 1961 (Act 55) which repeals and substantially re-enacts Section 3 of the former Bills of Exchange Ordinance[56] (of the then Gold Coast), defines a bill of exchange as " an unconditional order in writing addressed by one person to another, signed by the person giving it, requiring the person to whom it is addressed to pay on demand or at a fixed or determinable future time a sum certain in money to or to the order of a specified person, or to bearer." Provisions about negotiability of bills are made in sections 6 and 29. Cheques[57] and promissory notes[58] are also regulated in the same enactment. A promissory note is there defined as " an unconditional promise in writing made by one person to another signed by the maker, engaging to pay, on demand or at a fixed or determinable future time, a sum certain in money, to or to the order of, a specified person or to bearer." Other statutory provisions for negotiability in Ghana and Nigeria have been made in relation to share certificates and share warrants,[59] bank notes[60] and to a very limited extent, bills of lading.[61]

It is in relation to promissory notes and allied documents that the conflict between the customary and imported laws has been most apparent and it is this conflict that we propose to examine here.

Promissory notes are of course an imported law device for the convenience of commerce. Thus if A wants to raise a loan from B, this could be achieved by A giving B a promissory note undertaking to repay the amount which must be certain, at a definite or determinable future time. In the Nigerian case of *Savage* v. *Uwechia*[62] to which reference was made in an earlier part,[63] a document in the following terms :

" —Promissory Note.

£780: Owerri

I promise to pay Matthew Uwechia or order three months after date, the sum of seven hundred and eighty pounds for value received or in default to convey to him all those messuages together with appurtenances thereto situate at No. 6, New Market Road, in the township of Onitsha to hold the same unto the said Matthew Uwechia or order in fee simple—

Signed S. O. Rotibi."

was said by the Nigerian Supreme Court and the Judicial Committee of the Privy Council to be a promissory note within the definition of Section 3 of the Nigerian Bills of Exchange Act. Such a note could be transferred by B to C by an endorsement in blank[64] or by a special endorsement,[65] and in any such case A is then liable to C on the note. It is this idea of negotiability that underlines the commercial importance of the promissory note or any other negotiable instrument.

Traditional customary law, on the other hand, knew of no writing. In fact the absence of writing has been said to be one of its basic features.[66] The later decades of the 19th and early 20th centuries, however, witnessed the introduction of writing as evidence of customary law transactions. The decided cases on this head in both Ghana and Nigeria are legion.[67] But writing, although it helped solve the problem of proof in customary law transactions, created the equally difficult problem of a confusion between customary law and imported law matters. The fact that customary law, unlike the imported law, was not burdened with too many technicalities and refinements intensified rather than alleviated the conflict between the two. The attempts made by the law in Ghana and Nigeria to resolve this conflict will be examined in another Part.[68] Here we are concerned with the existence or otherwise of negotiability in customary law, with special reference to promissory notes. It is of course clear from the existing statutory and judicial authorities that no specific provision is made for the recognition of negotiability in the customary laws of either Ghana or Nigeria. It could however, be argued that no specific enactment on this head is necessary in view of the fact that customary law is already statutorily recognised in both countries, and customary promissory notes, if proved to exist, will come under this umbrella. This latter view however, militates against the tenor of the Bills of Exchange Acts in Ghana and Nigeria both of which define bills of exchange (which include promissory notes) in more or less exhaustive terms. The definition restricts their operation to the conditions specified in the Acts. " I (2) An instrument which does not comply with these conditions or which orders any act to be done in addition to the payment of money, is not a bill of exchange."[69]

No saving was made for customary law transactions. This could have been inserted if it was intended by the legislatures of the two countries.[70] Thus in the Ghana case of *Hamilton* v *Mpoley*,[71] a customary "note of hand" written for the parties by a local catechist was held not to be a promissory note because no consideration for the note was proved. Also in *Renner* v. *Thensu*[72] an I.O.U. between natives was held not to be a promissory note. In the latter case Gardner Smith J. the appeal judge, relied on the authority of the English case of *Gould* v. *Coombe*,[73] where the distinction between an I.O.U. and a promissory note was laid down. The intention of the parties as to the law applicable was never argued before his Lordship in the *Thensu* case. The decision appears to have been based on the assumption that the parties intended their obligations to be governed by English law. This of course, was a curious assumption to make in view of the fact that both parties were natives and there was nothing in the nature of the transaction to suggest the automatic application of English law. Customary law (in this case, Fanti Customary law; the parties from their names being presumably Fantis) recognises the giving of loans[74] and the fact that this transaction was put into writing does not make it less so. Four points must be emphasised here. Firstly, that the restricted definition allowed by the Bills of Exchange Acts in Ghana and Nigeria has driven the courts to look for imported law characteristics in transactions that would otherwise be governed by customary law. The result of the *Thensu* case where the plaintiff had to forfeit £250 out of a loan of £400 emphasises the hardship that has befallen litigants as a result of this statutory shortcoming.

Secondly, that any statutory regulation of commercial matters (in this case promissory notes) should necessarily take into account the practice that has been recognised in native customary law transactions which form the dominant sector in numerical, though not in economic force.

Thirdly, that customary transactions are not burdened with the minutiae of technicalities and distinctions as exist in the imported law. This simplicity is not a shortcoming but a virtue that could well improve the general law in the interest of harmony in any future attempt at the integration of the law on the subject. Finally, that such an integration is vital to the uniformity of the law on commercial matters both in Ghana and in Nigeria.

It is remarkable that no decided case in the courts of Ghana or Nigeria has dealt with the negotiability of customary promissory notes. The existing authorities are confined to suits on such notes by either the creditors themselves or their representatives. An examination of the records of several customary courts in Ghana and Nigeria[75] has revealed that the bulk of the documents involved in commercial dealings among natives are either receipts or other forms of acknowledgement of indebtedness. The I.O.U. is in regular use. No special form is adhered to but the intention to be bound is often clear on the face of the document. No instances were found of negotiability in the imported law sense, but a creditor could transfer an I.O.U. or a receipt to a third party, say a son or a nephew and such a son or nephew could proceed to collect the amount involved from the debtor. Such a transfer does not, however, unlike the position in the imported law, cure any defect on the face of the I.O.U. or receipt. In fact the transferee of the note does not sue in his own right but in that of the original creditor and if the debtor (or acceptor) refuses to pay, he has no means of compelling him to do so. This reluctance of the courts to recognise the negotiability of customary notes is assignable to two causes. In the inferior or customary courts this is because this idea is entirely alien to all customary notions of credit, and in the superior courts, most of the notes involved do not conform to the existing statutory requirements on bills of exchange. The inadequacy of these provisions has been sufficiently argued above.

Assignments and Negotiability in Islamic law[76]

The Islamic institution of the *Hawala*, has functional similarities to the imported law concept of assignment. Literally, *Hawala* means " transfer " or a mandate to pay; that is, X, who owes something to A, charges B to pay the debt. It could also be an assumption of X's debt by B. It is a condition for a valid Hawala that X has a claim against B which is equal to or higher than his liability to A. The claim could be for the return of an object which has been improperly taken by B. Also, there need not be any liability owed by X to A. The essence of the Hawala is that X mandates A to collect a debt or other liability from B, and this creates an obligation on B towards A. The acceptance by A of the Hawala extinguishes any obligation that X may have owed to A in respect of which the Hawala was made. The obligation can only be revived if B died bankrupt or denied the existence of the Hawala.

Performance by B towards A extinguishes X's claim against B only if the Hawala was concluded with specific reference to the obligation in issue. It is not extinguished if the Hawala was conditional. It is obvious from the above role of the Hawala that it is a much less complicated method of extinguishing or transferring an obligation than the common law theory of assignments.

Another Islamic institution, the *suftaja*, has been said to be the predecessor of bills of exchange. It has been defined as " a loan of money in order to avoid the risk of transport." The difference between the *Hawala* and the *Suftaja* in our example above is that the obligation of B towards X, which in the case of *Hawala* is normally supposed as already existing, is, in the case of the *suftaja*, created on purpose by a payment which X makes to B. This is, of course, construed as a loan of money from which the donor derives no counter-value, which is against the principle of the sharia. The *suftaja* is, however, reprehensible but not *fasid* (invalid).

NOTES

1. The allied topic of novation, i.e. the elimination of one agreement and a substitution by another, has often been distinguished from both assignments and negotiability. Novation is a substitution by mutual agreement of the parties, while an assignment is a unilateral substitution of a stranger for one of the parties. For novation in Nigerian law, see *G. B. Ollivant & Co.* v. *Effioms Transport & anor* (1934) 2 W.A.C.A. 91.
2. See Marshall, *The Assignment of choses in Action* (1950); S. J. Bailey, " Assignment of Debts in England " (1931) 47, L.Q.R. 516; I (32) 48 L.Q.R. 248; 547, Fuller, *Basic Contract*, pp. 580-2; on Islamic law, see J. Schacht, *Introduction to Islamic Law*, Oxford (Clarendon Press, Ch. 20).
3. *May* v. *Lane* (1894) 64 L.J. Q.B. 236.
4. *Deffries* v. *Milne* (1913) I Ch. 98.
5. *Wells* v. *Foster* (1841) 8 M & W. 149.
6. *Re Robinson* (1884) 27 Ch. D. 160.
7. National Insurance Act, 1946, *s. 32.*
8. Bills of Lading Act, 1855, *s. 1.*
9. Policies of Assurance Act, 1867, *s. 1.*
10. Marine Insurance Act, 1906, *s. 50 (2).*
11. Companies Act, 1948, *s. 73.*
12. Bills of Exchange Act, 1882.
13. Patents Act, *s. 74 (4).*
14. Copyright Act, 1956, *s. 36.*
15. For Ghana see Bills of Exchange Act, 1961 (Act 55) ss. 85 and 27, Bills of Lading Act, 1961 (Act 42) s. 7 (i) Copyright Act, 1961 (Act 85) *s. 10*; Companies Code, 1963 (Act 179) Part J, ss. 95-102; Merchant Shipping Act, 1963 (Act 183) *s. 20*; Insurance Act, 1965 (Act 288) *s. 50* and Social Security Act, 1965 (Act 279) *s. 26.*
16. For Nigeria, see Marine Insurance Act (No. 54 of 1961) s. 51 (i). But s. 77 (i) (b) of the Merchant Shipping Act (No. 30 of 1962) prohibits the assignment of wages before they have been earned. See also the Companies Ordinance (Cap. 37, Laws, 1958) *ss. 30-31* Exchange Control Act (Cap. 63, Laws, 1958) *ss. 18* and *28.*

17. We would prefer the use of the phrase "things in action" to the common but inelegant phrase "Chose in Action."
18. The common law, however, adopted the device of "powers of attorney," novation, and suing the debtor in the assignor's name and with his consent, in order to effect valid transfers of contractual rights.
19. See *Row* v. *Dawson* (1749) I Ves. Sr. 331, 27 E.R. 1064 per Lord Hardwicke, L.C. ". . . and although the law does not admit an assignment of a chose in action, this court does."
20. See *Pollock's Principles of Contract* (6th ed., 1896), pp. 204-213.
21. The Act was not in force till 1st Nov. 1875. See the Ghana case of *Colonial Bank* v. *Bellon* (1923-25) F. Ct. 173, where the Ghana Full Court held that the Act was not applicable in Ghana.
22. Act 25.
23. This subsection is peculiar to the Ghana enactment. There are no corresponding provisions in either the English Law of Property Act, 1925 or the Western Nigeria Property and Conveyancing law, Cap. 100 (laws, 1959) *s. 150*. It is submitted that this saving for customary assignments is a welcome variation.
24. Section 7 (iii).
25. (1965) C.C. 13.
26. On the first argument for the defendants, see *Brice* v. *Bannister* (1878) 3 Q.B.D. 569; *Buck* v. *Robson* (1878) 3 Q.B.D. 686. On the second, see *Brandt* v. *Dunlop Rubber Co.* (1905) A.C. 454, see also *Accra Perfumery Co. Ltd.* v. *Thomas* (1947) 12 W.A.C.A. 160 where the assignor had to be joined in an action by the assignee of part of a debt.
27. See J. S. Read (1961) 5 J.A.L. 48.
28. (1828) Russ I.
29. See Read op. cit., p. 49.
30. On its creation in 1963, the Mid-Western Region inherited the laws of Western Nigeria. Perhaps this may be described as a secondary reception of law in the region, the primary one being on January 1st, 1900, the date of reception for the whole country.
31. S. 15 (i), Cap. 100, Laws of Western Nigeria (1959) Revision.
32. 15 and 16 Geo. v. C. 20.
33. S. 150 (i) of the Property and Conveyancing Law, supra.
34. S. 150 (ii) of the Property and Conveyancing Law, supra.
35. *Robson & Sharpe* v. *Drummond* (1831) 2 B. & Ad. 303; 109, E.R. 1156.
36. *Tulk* v. *Moxhay* (1848) 2 Ph. 774; see p. 133, supra.
37. See Cheshire and Fifoot, *Law of Contract* (6th ed., 1964), pp. 451-452. The argument has been that since B is still liable to A under the agreement until performance by C, all that the doctrine of vicarious performance entails is the delegation of performance and not its outright assignment. There is, of course, a lot of force in this point of view. (22) (1945) 1 All E.R. 247 at p. 250.
38. (1945) 1 All E.R. 246 at p. 250.
39. 24 & 25 Geo. 5 41 S. I. See particularly S. I (i) (b) on actions for breach of promise to marry. The general rule is that rights and liabilities under a contract pass, on the death of a party to the agreement, to his personal representatives.
40. As amended by the Bankruptcy (Amendment) Act, 1926 (16 & 17 Geo. 5 C. 7).
41. But see S. 205 of the Nigerian Companies Act, Cap. 37, Laws (1958) which provides for the application of English Bankruptcy rules in

winding up of insolvent companies. See also *Halliday* v. *Alapatira* (1881) N.L.R.I.; and S. 99 of the Ghana Companies Code.

42. The Federal Territory and the Northern Region. See also S. 44 of the Eastern Nigeria Co-operative Societies Law, Cap. 28 Laws of the Eastern Region (1963) consolidation.

43. e.g. where a cause of action survives for the benefit of a deceased person's estate, the damages recoverable are not to include any exemplary damages, and in the case of a breach of promise to marry, they are to be limited to such damage if any, to the estate of the deceased as flows from the breach of promise to marry.

44. Since there are no corresponding statutory provisions in both the Eastern and Western Regions of Nigeria, it could be argued with some force that the common law position, i.e. contractual rights and liabilities vesting in the personal representatives of the deceased with exceptions as to personal contracts, as laid down in *Stubbs* v. *Holywell Railway Co.* (1867) L.R. 2 Ex. 311, applies in the two jurisdictions.

45. See Part U, ss. 246-261 of the Companies Code (Ghana).

46. This was stated by speed Ag. C.J. in the case of *Fairley, Ltd.* v. *McIver* (1900) I.N.L.R. 37 at p. 48, see also *Callendar Sykes & Co.* v. *Colonial Secretary of Lagos* (1891) App. Cas. 60 where it was held that colonial courts having no bankruptcy jurisdiction cannot act as auxiliaries to the court of Bankruptcy in England.

47. See the arguments of Allott in "Legal Development and Economic Growth in Africa" in *Changing Law in Developing Countries* (ed. J. N. D. Anderson) (London, 1963), p. 194, particularly pp. 201-207.

48. Negotiable instruments differ from other assignable contracts in the following respects:
    (i) They are transferable by delivery, i.e. the contract contained in them is;
    (ii) No notice need be given to the debtor of the transfer;
    (iii) The right or contract embodied in them cannot be transferred without the instrument itself;
    (iv) A bona fide transferee for value will get a good title even though the title of his transferor was defective—see ss. 29 and 38 of the English Bills of Exchange Act, 1882.

49. See Earl Jowitt, *The Dictionary of English Law* (London, 1959), p. 1216. See also *Crouch* v. *Credit Foncier* (1873) L.R. 8 Q.B. 374, and *Goodwin* v. *Roberts* (1875) L.R. 10 Ex. 337 at p. 346.

50. See the judgments of Blackburn, J. in *Crouch* v. *Credit Foncier* (1873) L.R. 8 Q.B. 344; Cockburn, C.J. in *Goodwin* v. *Roberts* (1875) L.R. 10 Ex. 337 at p. 346; Kennedy, J. in *Bechuanaland Exploration Co.* v. *London Trading Bank* (1898) 2 Q.B. 658 at p. 678.

51. These enactments which date from the Bills of Exchange Act (1697) 9 Will 3 C. 17, were consolidated in the 1882 legislation.See also the Cheques Act, 1957, and the Currency and Bank Notes Act, 1954.

52. 5 & 6 Eliz. II, c. 36.

53. 45 & 46 Vict., c. 61.

54. 45 & 46 Vict., c. 61.

55. But the category of negotiable instruments in English law is not closed, see *London Joint Stock Bank* v. *Simmons* (1892) A.C. 201.

56. Cap. 195, Laws of the Gold Coast (1951). See also S. 3 of the Nigerian Bills of Exchange Act, Cap. 21 of the Laws (1958); which is in the same terms as the Ghana provision.

57. S. 72. See also S. 73 of the Nigerian enactment, supra.

o

58. S. 82 of the Ghana Act and S. 83 in Nigeria.
59. In Ghana, see S. 54 of the Companies Code, 1963 (Act 179) subject to the provisions of S. 95 of the same Act. For Nigeria, see S. 39 (2) (i) of the Companies Ordinance, Cap. 37 (1958) Laws.
60. For Ghana, see Ss. 14 and 17 of the Bank of Ghana Act (Act 182) and for Nigeria see Ss. 17 and 21 of the Central Bank of Nigeria Ordinance, Cap. 30 (1958) Laws.
61. For Nigeria, see S. 4 of the Carriage of Goods by Sea Ordinance, Cap. (1958) Laws.
62. (1961) I.W.L.R. 455. P.C.
63. p. 277, supra.
64. i.e. writing the name of the transferor and delivering the note to the transferee.
65. i.e. writing the name of a special transferee and delivering the note to the said transferee.
66. See Allott, *Essays*, p. 62.
67. For a comprehensive study of this problem in relation to land matters, see Allott, *Essays*, Ch. 10, and the Appendix at pp. 275-282. For cases on the law of obligations in particular see *Benson* v. *Hortons* (1926-29) Div. Ct. 75 (Ghana) I.O.U. and promissory notes distinguished in certain cases; *Hughes* v. *Davies & anor.* (1909) Ren. 550.—loan transaction between reputed concubines; *Renner* v. *Thensu & ors.* (1926-29) F. C. 498 (Ghana)—promissory note and I.O.U. discussed *Aradzie* v. *Yandor & anor.* (1922) F. C. 91—promissory note between native chiefs; *Hamilton* v. *Mpoley* (1921) F. Ct. 78—note of hand distinguished from negotiable instruments.
68. See Part 7.
69. Ghana Bills of Exchange Act, 1961 S. 1; see S. 3 of the Nigerian Bills of Exchange Ordinance, Cap. 37 (1958).
70. As was done in S. 14 (i) of the Ghana Contract Act, 1960, on contracts of guarantee.
71. (1921) F. C. 78.
72. (1926-29) F. C. 498.
73. (1845) 135 E.R. 653. Some of the distinctions are that a party may recover the amount of an I.O.U. upon the action of account stated— *Payne* v. *Jenkins* (1830) U C & P. (Nisi Prius) 324; that the considera- tion for an I.O.U. is examinable—*Rainsford* v. *Eager* (1853) 3 I.C.L.R. 120 cited in *Renner* v. *Thensu*, supra.
74. See *Fynn* v. *Quassie* (1873) Ren. I. where it was held that interest is chargeable on customary loans. Prof. Schapera records similar trends among the Tswana in his " Concepts and Procedures in African law ", Jan. 1966 as follows: As early as 1915 Ngwaketse courts were accept- ing promissory notes as confirmation of debt, and in 1937 relatively complex written agreements were being made among the Kgatla by small groups of men for sharing the cost and use of boreholes in grazing areas—p. 6.
75. This was the personal experience of the writer when he conducted researches into the customary court records in Eastern Nigeria in 1961, and during his field work in customary and superior court records in Ghana and Nigeria in 1965.
76. The information on this aspect of Islamic law is substantially based on Professor Schacht's very informative work—*The Introduction to Islamic Law* (Oxford, 1964), pp. 148 et seq.

PART IV

DEFECTIVE AGREEMENTS

INTRODUCTORY NOTE

As we pointed out in the introductory chapter, one of our chief considerations in this work is to lay down a basic structural mould into which any detailed materials on obligations created by agreement may be poured. In furtherance of this we have given separate treatment to valid agreements involving (1) two parties[1] and (2) more than two parties.[2] These are agreements in which there are no defects initial or supervening other than breach itself. In this chapter we shall be looking at defective agreements. This is, of course, the whole question of the differing effects of defective contracts, i.e. void, voidable, unenforceable and illegal agreements. One advantage of this treatment is that it enables one to deal with normal contractual situations unencumbered and undistracted by considerations of defects. This, it is submitted, produces a cohesion denied the law of agreements under the conventional treatment. The other advantage lies in the field of remedies. By separating valid from defective agreements it will be appreciated that the only remedies generally given for defective contracts are restitutionary remedies.

A third advantage is that the term " defective " has the added merit of encompassing all agreements containing some vitiating element without resorting to the confusing definitions of void, voidable, unenforceable and illegal as is done in the orthodox treatment of the subject. These four terms are intended to describe the various legal effects of holding an agreement to be defective.

Three facets of this category of agreements will be investigated. Firstly we shall be looking at situations in which there are defects in reaching an agreement. This will mainly be concerned with cases of inadequate consent (more usually called mistake), misrepresentation and non-disclosure, and duress and undue influence.

The second group of cases are those on defects in the validity of an agreement. The problem of incapacity, informality, illegality and infringement of public policy will be examined under this subhead. Finally there are defects due to impossibility of performance. Here we shall be reviewing cases of initial impossibility and supervening impossibility.

CHAPTER 11

DEFECTS IN REACHING AN AGREEMENT

(a) *Inadequate consent*

The English law of contracts is riddled with massive literature[3] on the effects of what is often called " mistake " on the formation of agreements. The doctrine of mistake is bedevilled with imprecise terms such as common, mutual and unilateral mistakes. It is said to be common when both parties to an agreement make the same mistake about a subject matter, e.g. an agreement to buy and sell goods which, unknown to the parties have already perished. It is mutual when the parties misunderstand each other's intentions about the subject matter. An example is where A intends to sell a 10 horse-powered engine while B is offering to buy an 8 h.p. engine.[4]

In unilateral mistake, only one of the parties is under any misapprehension about the subject matter. The other is not.[5] A close study of the authorities has revealed, however, that most of the cases on the doctrine of mistake could have been decided on the basis of inadequate consent.[6] Thus, where the plaintiff and the defendant contracted to buy and sell a consignment of cotton arriving in a ship called " The Peerless," the plaintiff intending the December ship and the defendant, the September ship, what the courts have to decide is whether or not there has been adequate consent to support an agreement.[7] In determining whether or not there has been adequate consent, the courts will have regard to the intentions of the parties as evidenced in the dealings between them. It is totally unnecessary for this purpose to resort to the jurisprudential distinction between mutual and unilateral mistakes.

There is a dearth of local judicial authority in Ghana and Nigeria on cases of inadequate consent. *Tay* v. *Williams*[8] was an action by the plaintiff for the specific performance of an agreement to sell a piece of land to him by the defendant. The plaintiff had offered to buy the whole piece of land while the defendant accepted the offer on the understanding that he was selling only part of the land. It was held by the Ghana Full Court, affirming the judgment of the Divisional Court that the plaintiff could not enforce the agreement since there was no real consent on the part of the defendant to sell the whole land. In *U. T. C.* v. *Tetteh & 2 ors,*[9] the Ghana Divisional Court at Sekondi was to decide whether the defendant's (1) illiteracy and (2) ignorance of the nature of the document to which he appended his signature, absolved him from liability under a guarantee bond. It was found as a fact that the said signature had been obtained on the pretext that the defendant was signing merely as a witness to the principal debtor's signature. In fact the defendant had signed a guarantee bond and had been sued on it by the plaintiff. It was argued on behalf of the said plaintiff that the defendant was negligent in that he did not acquaint himself with the contents of the document before he signed it; and secondly, that the document was read over to the defendant before his signature was obtained (words which appeared at the foot of the document before the space for signature).

The court was to decide whether there had been adequate consent to form the basis of an agreement between the parties. If the plaintiff's allegation (of the document being read to the defendant) was proved, this would be a strong evidence in favour of the defendant's consent. On this aspect of the case, his Lordship relied on a long series of authorities to the effect that where an illiterate person executes a document any other party to the document who relies upon it must prove that it was read over and interpreted to the illiterate party and that he fully appreciated the meaning and effect of the said document before he signed it.[10] On this test it was held that the plaintiff had failed to prove that the guarantee was both read to the defendant and that he fully appreciated its meaning before he signed it. On the question of negligence, his Lordship relied on the English decision of *Carlisle & Cumberland Banking Co.* v. *Bragg,*[11] where it was held on similar facts that the negligence of the defendant signing a document without enquiry would only involve him in liability in cases of negotiable instruments.

Since the *Tetteh* case was an action on a guarantee bond, the defendant was held not liable.

On the other hand, in another case where the defendant pleaded that he signed a promissory note on the understanding that it was a bail bond, it was held by the Ghana Full Court that he was liable on the promissory note. The Court argued that a bail bond is normally signed in a court room and not in a bedroom where the promissory note was found to have been signed. The court ruled that this was not a case of inadequate consent.[12]

The Nigerian case of *Abraham* v. *Chief Oluwa*[13] raised the issue of the plaintiff's right to recover some money paid for the purchase of a piece of land which already belonged to the said plaintiffs before the purported sale. The facts were that the plaintiffs (the Grand United Order of Oddfellows, Faith Lodge No. 4198, Lagos) had in 1917 purchased a piece of land in the then colony of Lagos from a vendor who himself purchased from a holder of a crown grant. There was no conveyance deed executed in pursuance of the 1917 transaction. In 1943 the defendant, believing that the land belonged to Chief Oloto, attached it under a writ of fieri facias, and its sale was advertised. The plaintiff put up a caution notice warning all persons against purchasing the land. He also informed the defendant that the land belonged to the lodge. The sale was nevertheless carried out and the plaintiffs purchased it in the belief that their former title was defective. In this action they sought to recover the sum paid in the execution sale on the ground that there could be no agreement to purchase what was already one's own property.[14] In other words there was no consent to pay the purchase price in the execution sale.

Baker J. who decided the case, quoted with approval the following passage from *Kerr's Fraud and Mistake*:[15]

> " If two parties enter into an agreement with reference to a supposed state of things and it turns out by mutual mistake of the parties, the supposed actual state of things does not in fact subsist, the consideration for the agreement fails, and the agreement is subsequently void."[16]

It was held that the plaintiff could recover the £68 he had paid towards the execution sale since the agreement on which the payment was based, was defective.

Inadequate consent could also be brought about by a mistake in the identity of one of the contracting parties. In *K. Chellaram & Sons Ltd.* v. *Messrs. Costain (West Africa) Ltd.*[17] the defendants were accustomed to obtaining goods from the plaintiffs on credit. An unidentified person fraudulently obtained goods from the plaintiff company by using some of the defendants' order forms, which he had somehow acquired, and by forging the signature of the defendants' accountant. The rogue had made away with the goods and the plaintiffs sued the defendants for the price. It was argued for the plaintiffs that they had relied on the defendants' order forms and not on the forged signature of the rogue, to their detriment. It is curious however, that so much weight should have been left on this argument in view of the fact that the plaintiffs were suing in contract and not for deceit.[18] The argument was lightly dismissed by the Enugu High Court (Eastern Nigeria). The defendants had, on the other hand, pleaded that they never ordered any goods from the plaintiffs, and in any case, had not received the goods, the subject matter of the action. It was held that there was no agreement between the plaintiffs and the defendants and that the action could not succeed.[19]

On its facts, the *Chellaram* decision can be said to be a logical though a hard one on the plaintiffs. It is doubtful if a contractual action could succeed even against a bona fide purchaser for value without notice, of the goods. Presumably in such a case, the plaintiffs could sue in tort for the return of the goods or their value.

We can now attempt a general principle in cases of inadequate consent. The rationale of these cases is that where the dealing between the parties does not provide any basis for erecting an agreement between them, the courts will hold that there is no contract and any remedy that the plaintiff might have will lie in tort or in restitution.

(b) *Misrepresentation and non-disclosure*

Statements made by one party to an agreement may induce the other to contract, thus negativing full consent.[20] Such a statement might be fraudulent, negligent or innocent. If it is false and induces the contract, it operates as a misrepresentation. Silence or non-disclosure might in certain circumstances constitute a misrepresentation. These circumstances include

(i) Where the silence distorts a positive representation:

(ii) Where the contract requires the utmost good faith or as it is more often called, uberrimae fidei; and

(iii) Where a fiduciary relationship exists between the contracting parties.

In this sub-section we shall be examining cases of inadequate consent brought about by the misrepresentation of one of the parties to an agreement. In English law certain conditions must be satisfied before a representation will operate as a misrepresentation. These are that there must be a false representation;[21] it must be a representation of fact and not merely of opinion;[22] it must be intended to be acted upon by the other party to the agreement;[23] and finally, the representation must induce the contract.[24] These conditions have also been accepted in both Ghana[25] and Nigeria.[26] It is however in the nature of remedies available to the victim of a misrepresentation that the law is not so clear both in England[27] and in Ghana and Nigeria.

Where the misrepresentation is fraudulent

The general effect of an operative misrepresentation is to make the agreement voidable at the suit of the party misled. Where the misrepresentation is coupled with a fraudulent intent, the victim of the fraud has an additional remedy in an action for deceit against the party guilty of the fraud. In many cases, however, the party committing the fraud is not always in a position to make good the defendant's loss, having in the meantime resold the goods to a third party. Where such subsequent purchaser is also guilty of the fraud, the plaintiff can still avoid the transaction. But where the subsequent purchaser is a bona fide purchaser for value without notice of the defect in the title to the goods, and purchases before the plaintiff disaffirmed the contract, the subsequent purchaser has good title. The issues involved in a case of fraudulent misrepresentation were fully discussed in the Privy Council appeal from Ghana of *Nanka-Bruce* v. *Laing & Anor*.[28] The facts were that

> The first defendant, Laing, had obtained 300 bags of cocoa from the plaintiff (appellant) on the representation that he was purchasing for a company called the Tin Areas Ltd. In fact Laing had no intention to resell to the said company. On receiving the way bills for the cocoa he transferred them to the second defendants to whom he was indebted on a previous transaction. Laing had purported to buy from the plaintiff (appellant) at the cost of 59 shillings a bag, but sold to the second defendants at 42 shillings a bag, who subsequently sold at 45 shillings a bag. In the present action the plaintiff sued for the return of the goods or their value.

Three issues were to be resolved by the court. Firstly, whether or not there was adequate consent on the part of the plaintiff (appellant) to transfer the title in the goods to Laing in pursuance of a contract of sale. In resolving this the court had to consider the past business dealings between the plaintiff and the first defendant. It was found as a fact that on past occasions the first defendant had obtained goods on credit from the plaintiff. The court therefore ruled that there was sufficient intention to conclude a contract of sale although such consent was induced by Laing's fraudulent misrepresentation.[29]

Secondly, whether or not the plaintiff had elected to affirm or disaffirm the contract before the subsequent transfer to the second defendants. On this the court quoted with approval the following passage from *Addison on Contracts*:[30]

> " If a vendor has parted with the possession of goods in fulfilment of a contract of sale, obtained by fraud on the part of the purchaser, the contract is voidable, but he cannot, after the goods have been resold and passed into the hands of a bona fide subpurchaser, disaffirm the contract, and annul the title of the latter

to the property (*White* v. *Garden*).[31] But, if the relation of the vendor and the vendee does not subsist between the original owner and the person who commits the fraud, and the goods have been obtained by false pretences, in such a way as not to transfer the property in them, and have been afterwards disposed of to a bona fide purchaser by sale not in market overt, the latter does not acquire a title to the goods as against the person who has been defrauded. (*Kingsford* v. *Meny*);"[32]

It was found that the plaintiff had affirmed the contract after the transfer to the second defendants. It was therefore too late for him to avoid its terms.

Finally, whether or not the second defendants were party to the fraud of the first defendant who had already been convicted. The court determined this final question in the negative. It was held that the plaintiff could not recover the goods or their value from the second defendants who were innocent purchasers for value without any notice of the fraud. This decision was affirmed both by the Ghana Full Court and the Judicial Committee of the Privy Council.[33] Their Lordships came to a similar conclusion in the earlier decision of *Akotey* v. *The Commonwealth Trust Ltd., & Laing.*[34] On whom the onus of establishing fraud lies, the Divisional Court at Sekondi (Ghana), held in *Dr. Masters* v. *Maclean*[35] that the burden lies on the party who says that he was induced by fraud to enter into a contract, to prove the fraud; that the representee must show at the time when he entered into the contract, he was deceived by the false representations. If, when he enters into the contract, he knows the real facts, he is not deceived. Finally, it was also held that it is not enough to show that the representee had the means of knowledge, even though the means were supplied to him by the representor; it must be shown that he actually knew.

In the *Masters* case the defendant's counterclaim for damages for fraudulent misrepresentation was dismissed since he had not discharged the onus of proving fraud as set out above.[36] The fact that the plaintiff's means of knowledge could have discovered the fraud cannot avail a fraudulent defendant. In the Nigerian case of *Sule* v. *Aromire*,[37] the defendant had fraudulently represented to the plaintiff that he was the rightful owner of certain premises and had purported to convey the said premises to him. The plaintiff could have discovered the true facts if he had examined a High Court Judgment in respect of the land which was in fact the property of a third party. In an action to set aside the conveyance and recover the price paid on grounds of fraudulent misrepresentation, it was argued for the defendant that the plaintiff could have discovered the true facts if he had made enquiries; since he had waived such enquiries, his action did not lie. This submission was overruled by the Nigerian Supreme Court. It was held, among other things, that as the plaintiff was misled by the defendant's fraudulent misrepresentation, it was no defence for the latter that the plaintiff might have found out the truth if he had made enquiry, and the plaintiff was entitled to annulment of the sale and a refund of the purchase price.

The victim of a fraudulent misrepresentation is also entitled to an action for damages as an alternative to rescission or annulment. The curious case of *Josephine Jola Martins* v. *Adenugba*[38] was a claim for damages against the defendant for fraudulently misrepresenting to the plaintiff that they were legally married and thereby inducing her to live with him as wife for three years. The facts were that the plaintiff had agreed to marry the defendant, and on an appointed day they had both gone to a Marriage Registry for the marriage. The defendant alone went in to see the Registrar and on coming out, made the plaintiff believe that the marriage was concluded and showed her a marriage certificate which he claimed to have obtained from the Registrar. In fact the whole affair was staged and the plaintiff had only gone into the Registrar's office to have a chat with a friend. Three years afterwards the plaintiff discovered the hoax and in the ensuing action claimed £150 damages for the fraud. Brooke, Ag. C. J. awarded her £50 damages for the deceit.

A plea of fraudulent misrepresentation can also be a defence to an action for specific performance of an agreement induced by the misrepresentation. In *Sackey* v. *Ashong*,[39] the court refused to sustain the plea because it was found as a fact that there had been no such fraudulent misrepresentation.

Where the misrepresentation is negligent

The test of liability for negligence in English law is whether or not the defendant owed the plaintiff a duty of care, that the duty has been breached and that the plaintiff has suffered damage. For purposes of liability for negligent misstatements the House of Lords has held that such a duty exists in cases of fiduciary relationship.[40] Attempts to expend the scope of the liability under the rule in *Donoghue* v. *Stevenson*[41] did not meet with much success. But in the recent decision of *Hedley Byrne & Co. Ltd.* v. *Heller & Partners Ltd.*,[42] liability for negligent misstatements has been said to lie

" where it is plain that the party seeking information or advice was trusting the other to exercise such a degree of care as the circumstances required, where it was reasonable for him to do that, and where the other gave the information or advice when he knew or ought to have known that the inquirer was relying on him."[43]

In the lucid words of Lord Pearce,

> " There is also, in my opinion, a duty of care created by special relationships which, though not fiduciary, give rise to an assumption that care as well as honesty is demanded."[44]

Thus it can be said that the modern basis for liability for negligent misstatements in English Law is the existence of a fiduciary relationship between the parties and the extension of that relationship as laid down in the *Hedley Byrne* decision. The remedies available to the victim of a negligent misstatement are similar to those obtainable by the plaintiff in an action based on fraudulent misrepresentation, except that in the former, an action for deceit may not lie.

There are no local judicial authorities in this aspect of the law in Ghana and Nigeria. It is likely however that the Courts in the two countries will follow the rule in *Hedley Byrne* when the matter arises for decision.[45]

Where the misrepresentation is innocent

A false representation may be neither fraudulent nor negligent. In such a case the misrepresentation is said to be innocent. The Common Law accorded no relief to a victim of an innocent misrepresentation unless such a misrepresentation had become a term of the contract.[46] In equity, however, such a victim could obtain a rescission[47] of the agreement or set up the misrepresentation as a defence to any action for specific performance of the agreement.[48]

No damages are obtainable in an action for misrepresentation unless there was fraud or negligence.[49]

Four limits to the right to rescind have been recognised in English Law. Firstly, the victim of an operative misrepresentation has a choice between affirming the contract and repudiating it. If he affirms the contract, the right of rescission is lost.[50] Secondly, restitutio in integrum must be possible.[51] That is, that it must be possible to restore the pre-contract position of the parties. Thirdly, where third parties have acquired bona fide rights under the agreement the right to rescind is lost.[52] Finally under the rule in *Wilde* v. *Gibson*[53] for land and *Seddon* v. *North Eastern Salt Co. Ltd.* [54] for other contracts, the right to rescission is lost when the contract is executed. The rule in the latter decision has been very heavily criticised and it is doubtful if it will be followed in the Courts of Ghana and Nigeria.[55]

Non-disclosure

The circumstances under which silence or non-disclosure can operate as a misrepresentation, have already been mentioned.[56] In English Law, instances where non-disclosure is a ground for relief can be found in contracts of insurance, agreements for the sale of land, contracts preliminary to family settlements; agreements for the allotment of shares in a company, suretyships and partnerships, and finally, cases involving parties in a fiduciary relationship.[57]

In Ghana and Nigeria, however, most of the cases under this sub-head have been concerned with suretyships. The principle established by the cases is that there must be a full disclosure of all facts likely to affect the judgment of the intending surety. Thus in the Nigerian case of *John Holt & Co. Ltd.* v. *Oladunjoyce,*[58] the defendant as surety executed a bond guaranteeing up to £400 the fidelity of an employee of the plaintiffs under his contract of service. Before this the employee had been employed in the same sort of job (i.e. produce buying) by the plaintiffs and as a result of his previous work he had defaulted to the amount of £600. It was in order to recoup themselves for this loss of £600 that the plaintiffs proposed to finance him in further work of the same kind under the safeguard of the defendant's indemnity bond. The plaintiffs' agent told the defendant that the employee had worked for them before and was a good produce-buyer. It was not disclosed that the employee had defaulted in his previous dealings with the plaintiffs. In a claim against the defendant for the sum of £304 19s. 6d. being the shortage in the employee's account, the defendant set up the non-disclosure of the existing liability of £600 as his defence. It was argued for the plaintiff company that there was no obligation upon them to disclose the employee's state of accounts without enquiry from the defendant, and that unless the concealment was fraudulent the surety could not escape liability under the bond. On this submission by the plaintiffs, Graham Paul, J. who decided the case had this to say:

> "I have considered the authorities quoted and my view upon them is that the contract of suretyship is in general not a contract where uberrima fides is demanded of the person in whose favour the guarantee is given, as it is demanded for instance of the assured in contracts of assurance. But it is a fidelity guarantee, as distinct from a guarantee of a bank overdraft, it comes very near what I may term the uberrima fides class of contract. As it is put

in the judgment of Foy, J. in the case of *Davis* v. *London &
Provincial Marine Insurance Co.*,[59] " very little said which ought
not to have been said, and very little not said which ought to
have been said, would be sufficient to prevent the contract being
valid." . . . Upon this point after considering the facts of this
case and the authorities, I am of opinion that for the plaintiffs'
agent to represent to a prospective surety that the principal was
a good produce-buyer was inconsistent with the fact that as a
result of his buying for the firm with the firm's money or goods
there was a balance of £600 for which he could not deliver
produce and which he could not pay except by being launched
on a fresh enterprise with fresh credit by the plaintiffs."[60]

It was held that the plaintiff could not recover.

On the other hand in *U.A.C.* v. *Jazzar*[61] where the defendant
guaranteed the principal's account with the plaintiffs for up to
£200, without being informed of a debit balance of £12 in the said
principal's account, it was held that the plaintiffs were under no
obligation to disclose the principal's indebtedness in the absence of
inquiry. The non-disclosure was held not to amount to a misrepresentation such as would entitle the defendant to avoid the
contract. It is remarkable that the *John Holt* case decided three
years earlier, was neither cited nor argued before his Lordship.
An attempt to distinguish the former from the latter decision can
be made on the basis that in the *U.A.C.* case there was no suggestion that the principal was unable to meet his indebtedness or had
in any way committed default, both of which circumstances were
present in the *John Holt* case.

The U.A.C. decision also lays down that the nature of a particular transaction determines whether a fact not disclosed is such that
it is impliedly represented not to exist. This aspect of the matter
was elaborated on in *Ode* v. *J. F. Sick & Co. and ors.*[62] In this case
the first defendants employed the plaintiff's brother as an unsecured
salesman, and, having found him to be short in his stock to the
amount of £650, closed the shop and declined to open it or continue his employment without security. The plaintiff was the
principal debtor's sister and had agreed to secure the brother in the
defendant's employment by a mortgage of her premises. No notice
was given of the previous indebtedness nor did the defendant make
any inquiries. The amount of the security was not limited. A few
months later the principal's stock was short by £68 and the plaintiff having refused to make good the shortage, the defendants
purported to exercise their right of sale under the mortgage. In the
ensuing action the plaintiff sought an injunction to restrain the sale.
It was argued on her behalf that the non-disclosure of the existing

liability of her brother to the defendants absolved her from her obligation under the guarantee. The Court found as a fact that the plaintiff knew of the defendants' closure of the brother's shop and the non-continuance of his employment in the absence of security. In the Court's view, these should have put the plaintiff on her enquiry but this she did not do. It was therefore held that in the circumstances the first defendants were not under any obligation to inform the surety of the existence of the indebtedness of the employee at the time of the guarantee and that the surety was liable for his past and subsequent indebtedness to the defendants. The injunction was therefore refused.

But in another case where the subsisting indebtedness was recited in the guarantee deed and the sureties undertook to guarantee any subsequent losses in the account, an action based on the past debit balance of the employee was held not to lie against the sureties.[63]

(c) *Duress and undue influence*

In the two preceding sub-sections we have been examining instances of defects in reaching an agreement, brought about by inadequate consent and misrepresentation. We shall next be discussing cases where the consent of one of the parties is not a free consent because of the presence of some form of compulsion. This is of course the whole problem of duress and undue influence.

Duress

It is a trite statement that a party cannot be held to an agreement unless he is a free agent. He is not free when the consent has been extracted by some compulsion. This compulsion has often been called duress. Legal duress, however, is a narrow concept in the common law. It has been defined to mean actual violence to the person.[64] It is not enough to plead that the duress was of a person's goods.[65] Although there is as yet no local judicial authority in Ghana and Nigeria on the scope of duress, it is hoped that the Courts will not confine its operation to actual violence or threats of violence to the person. A plea of duress of goods ought to be a ground for avoiding an agreement.

Undue influence

The scope of this equitable doctrine was restated by Lindley, L.J. in *Allcard* v. *Skinner*[66] as follows:

> " In a Court of equity if A obtains any benefit from B, whether under a contract or a gift, by exercising an influence over B which in the opinion of the Court, prevents B from exercising an

independent judgment in the matter in question, B can set aside the contract or recover the gift. Moreover in certain cases the relation between A and B may be such that A has peculiar opportunities of exercising influence over B. If under such circumstances A enters into a contract with B, or receives a gift from B, a Court of equity imposes upon A the burden, if he wishes to maintain the contract or gift, of proving that in fact he exerted no influence for the purpose of obtaining it."[67]

Thus there are two facets of the doctrine namely where the circumstances point to the fact that the mind of one of the parties dominated that of the other so as to affect his independent judgment; and where the relationship between the parties is such as to raise the presumption of undue influence. In the former case the onus is on the party alleging that there has been an undue influence to prove it,[68] while in the latter, undue influence is presumed until rebutted.

The latter category of decisions is concerned with cases where the party alleging the undue influence reposes confidence in the other party to the transaction as a result of the relationship between them. In English law such relationships have been recognised between parent and child,[69] solicitor and client,[70] medical man and patient,[71] trustee and cestui que trust,[72] spiritual adviser and his flock,[73] and fiancé and fiancée.[74] The presumption of undue influence is rebutted when it is proved that the party in whom confidence is reposed (often called a fiduciary), has not concealed any material fact from the party affected, and that the latter was in a position to take an independent decision.[75]

In *Victoria Williams & Ors* v. *Franklin & Ors*,[76] the Nigerian Supreme Court was to rule on the validity of a sale to a solicitor by his client. The respondent was a solicitor practising in Lagos. In 1929 Cole purchased lands in Lagos and the respondent acted as his solicitor in that transaction and in other collateral transactions concerning those lands up to 1938. In 1938 Cole experienced certain financial difficulties and tried to sell the land by public auction for £150 subject to an existing mortgage (to the value of £130) but did not succeed. The respondent then offered to buy the land, subject to the mortgage, for £150 and Cole sold it to him. When in 1938 Cole died, the respondent acted for his family (the appellants) in obtaining letters of administration of his estate. The respondent was in possession of the land in issue and exercised absolute ownership over it for twenty years and the appellants raised no objection. In 1948 when the Lagos Executive Development Board acquired the land and proposed to pay the necessary compensation to the respondent, the appellants brought

P

an action to set aside the sale of the lands, and for a declaration that any compensation on the land was payable to them and not to Franklin. It was argued on their behalf that the relationship of solicitor and client existed between the deceased Cole and the respondent; that this raised a presumption of undue influence, that the respondent had not rebutted the presumption; and that the purported sale was voidable at their instance.

The learned trial judge found against them on all the above points, holding that

(a) there was a sale by Cole to the respondent in 1938;

(b) at the time of the sale the relationship of solicitor and client did not exist between the parties; and that

(c) a fair price had been paid for the land.[77]

On appeal to the Federal Supreme Court, the appellants' contention that a relationship of solicitor and client existed between Franklin and the deceased Cole at the time of the transaction, was upheld. Unsworth, F. J. who read the Court's judgment referred to the English case of *Allison* v. *Clayhills*[78] with approval and continued:

" In considering whether in any particular transaction any duty exists such as to bring the ordinary rule into operation, all the circumstances of the individual case must be weighed and examined. Thus, a solicitor may by virtue of his employment acquire a personal ascendancy over a client and this ascendancy may last long after the employment has ceased, and the duty towards the client which arises out of any such ascendancy will last as long as the ascendancy itself can operate. Again, a solicitor may by virtue of his employment acquire special knowledge, and the knowledge so obtained may impose upon him the duty of giving advice or making a full and proper disclosure in any transaction between himself and his client, though such transaction may take place long after the relationship of solicitor and client in its stricter sense had ceased to exist. And there may be other circumstances which may impose a duty on a solicitor, which duty may continue to exist after the relationship of solicitor and client in the strict sense has ceased."[79]

The Court found that the present case came within the residual category of " other circumstances which may impose a duty." It was held further, following the Privy Council decision of *Mac-Master* v. *Byrne*,[80] that independent legal advice is not in such circumstances an absolute pre-requisite to such a transaction. In this case the fact that two members of the Cole family were present when the transaction was completed, was sufficient to fulfil the requirement of independent advice.

On the question of the reasonableness of the price, the Court found, after examining all the surrounding circumstances,[81] that £150 was a reasonable price for the property. It was also found that the respondent disclosed to Cole all the relevant information about the property, which was all the duty imposed on him by the law as a fiduciary. The appeal was dismissed.

What the *Franklin* decision has achieved is the laying down of a sounder basis for rebutting any allegation of undue influence without the former rigid requirement of independent legal advice as laid down in the earlier English authorities. It is hoped that this test will be applied in the Ghana Courts when the question arises for decision.[82]

NOTES

1. See Part II supra.
2. See Part III supra.
3. See among others: J. F. Wilson " Identity in contract and the Pothier fallacy " (1954) 17 M. L. R. 515-529; J. Unger " Identity in contract and Mr. Wilson's fallacy " (1955) 18 M. L. R. pp. 259-270; G. Williams " Mistake as to party in the law of contract " (1945) 23 Can. Bar. Rev. pp. 271 and 380; C. J. Slade " The myth of mistake in the English law of contract " (1954) 70 L. Q. R. 385; P. S. Atiya & F. A. R. Bennion " Mistakes in the construction of contracts " (1961) 24 M. L. R. 421; K. O. Shatwell " The supposed doctrine of mistake in contract: A comedy of errors " (1955) 33 Can. Bar. Rev. 164; G. Williams " Mistake and rectification in contract " (1954) 17 M. L. R. 154.
4. See Cheshire & Fifoot, *Law of Contract* (6th ed. 1964) p. 188.
5. See *Hartog* v. *Colin and Shields* (1939) 3 All E.R. 566.
6. In cases of *res extincta* and *res sua* the agreement is in effect since one cannot contract to purchase what does not exist or what already belongs to him.
7. *Raffles* v. *Wichelhaus* (1864) 2 H & C 906.
8. (1912) Ren. 691.
9. (1965) Current Cases (Ghana) No. 92. See also *Ansah* v *Amalgamated Banket Areas* (1938) 4 W.A.C.A. 81.
10. *Pagay* v. *Toku* (1894) Sarbah's F. L. R. 89; *Graves* v. *Ampimah* (1905) Ren. 318; *Fisher* v. *Hammond* (1926-29) Div. Ct. 217; *Waya* v. *Byroughy* (1958) 3 W.A.L.R. 413; *Yiadom* v. *Angmor*, (1959) GLR. 157 at p. 160; *Dadzie* v. *Kokofu*, Sup. ct. 13/2/61 unreported; *Manidu* v. *Aban & anor.* (1965) current cases, 10. See also *U.A.C.* v. *Apaw* (1936) 3 W.A.C.A. 114.
11. (1911) 1 K.B. 459.
12. *Hamilton & anor.* v. *Addu* (1923-25) F. Ct. 47.
13. (1944) 17, NLR. 123.
14. The plaintiffs relied on the old English decision of *Cooper* v. *Phibbs* (1887) L.R. 2 H.L. 149. a decision on similar facts.
15. 6th ed. pp. 623-624.

16. See also *Stapylton* v. *Scott* (1807) 13 Ves. J. 417; *Robinson* v. *Dickenson* (1827) 3 Russ. 399.
17. (1957) 2 E.R.L.R. 10.
18. Even if the action had been framed on deceit the plaintiffs would still have had to establish and prove a duty of care owed them by the defendants.
19. The English authorities of *Hardman* v. *Booth* (1863) I H & Co. 803; and *Cundy* v. *Lindsay* (1878) 3 A.C. 459, were freely cited by the court.
20. We are not here concerned with statements which have become terms of the contract. The construction of contractual terms will be discussed in the next part. See infra, p. 283.
21. *Keates* v. *Lord Cadogorn* (1851) 10 C.B. 591.
22. *Anderson* v. *Pacific Fire and Marine Insurance Co.* (1872) L.R. 7 C.P. 65.
23. *Peek* v. *Gurney* (1873) 6 H.L. 377.
24. *Horsfall* v. *Thomas* (1862) 1 H & C. 91.
25. *Nanka-Bruce* v. *Laing & Anor.* (1923-25) F. Ct. 89 P.C.
26. *Josephine Jola Martin* v. *Adenugba* (1946) 18 N.L.R. 63.
27. See The English Law Report Committee 10th Report, *Cmnd.* 1782 (1962). See also the Representation Act, 1966.
28. (1923-25) F. Ct. 89 P.C.
29. Thus if it had been found that there was no such intention to pass the property in the goods, there would have been no contract. See *Fowler* v. *Hollins* (1872) L.R. 7 Q.B. 616.
30. 11th ed. p. 594.
31. (1851) 30 L-J. C.P. 166.
32. 26 L-J. Ex. 83; see also *Henderson* v. *Williams* (1895) 1 Q.B.D. 521.
33. At p. 101 of the report.
34. (1923-25) F. Ct. 78.
35. (1921-25) Div. Ct. 110.
36. This was an action for the arrears of instalments on the sale of a medical practice. The defendant's counterclaim for damages or for rescission on grounds of fraudulent misrepresentation was dismissed. Cf. *Ankramah* v. *Kitcher* (1926-29) F. Ct. 366 where the plaintiffs were not allowed to plead their own fraud to defeat a conveyance.
37. (1951) 20 N.L.R. 20. See also *Sackey* v. *Ashong* (1956) I.W.A.L.R. 108.
38. (1946) 18 N.L.R. 63.
39. (1956) 1 W.A.L.R. 108. Cf. *Henderson* v. *Jolaosho & Ors.* (1926) 6 N.L.R. 19, where the Nigerian Full Court also refused a plea of misrepresentation on the ground that the respondent was not induced by it to enter into the agreement, in this case, as a co-surety.
40. *Nocton* v. *Lord Ashburton* (1914) A.C. 932.
41. (1932) A.C. 562.
42. (1964) A.C. 465.
43. Per Lord Reid at p. 486.
44. Op. cit. at p. 539.
45. In the Nigerian case of *Sodino* v. *Coker & Ors.* (1932) 11 N.L.R. 138, the Divisional Court allowed a claim for the rescission of a sale on the ground of the auctioneer's misdescription of the area.
46. *Kennedy* v. *Panama, etc. Royal Mail Co. Ltd.* (1867) L.R. 2 Q.B. 580.
47. *Lamare* v. *Dixon* (1873) L.R. 6 H.L. 414.
48. See (47) supra.
49. See the Ghana case of *Dr. Masters* v. *Maclean* (1921-25) Div. Ct. 110.
50. *Long* v. *Lloyd* (1958) 1 W.L.R. 753.

51. *Armstrong* v. *Jackson* (1917) 2 K.B. 822.
52. *Babcock* v. *Lawson* (1880) 5 Q.B.D. 284.
53. (1848) 1 H.L.C. 605.
54. (1905) 1 Ch. 326.
   55 L.Q.R. 90; M. Howard, "The rule in Seddon's case" (1963) 26 M.L.R. 272; *Tenth Report of the Law Reform Committee*, 1962 Cmnd. 1782, S. 6. The decision in the *Nigerian* case of *Sule* v. *Aromire* (1951) 20 N.L.R. 20, tends to support the view that the rule in Seddon's case is part of the Law of Nigeria.
55. See H. A. Hammelmann, *Seddon* v. *North Eastern Salt Co.* (1939).
56. See p. 177 supra.
57. For the position in English Law, see Cheshire & Fifoot, *Law of Contract* (6th ed. 1964) pp. 230-234; *Anson's Law of Contract* (22nd ed. 1964) pp. 232-240.
58. (1936) 13 N.L.R. 1.
59. (1878) 8 Ch. D. at p. 475.
60. Op. Cit. at pp. 3-4.
61. (1939) 15 N.L.R. 67 affirmed (1940) 6 W.A.C.A. 208.
62. (1939) 15 N.L.R. 4. Cf. *Pettiford* v. *May* (1937) 13 N.L.R. 138, where the non-disclosure of the interest due on a promissory note absolved the surety from liability.
63. *J. F. Sick & Co.* v. *Ilo & Anor.* (1939) 15 N.L.R. 34.
64. *Seear* v. *Cohen* (1881) 45 L.T. 589.
65. *Skeate* v. *Beale* (1840) 11 Ad. & El. 983.
66. (1887) 36 Ch. D. 145.
67. Op. cit. pp. 181, 183.
68. *Williams* v. *Bayley* (1866) L.R. 1 H.L. 200.
69. *Bainbridge* v. *Browne* (1881) 18 Ch. D. 188.
70. *Wright* v. *Carter* (1903) 1 Ch. 27.
71. *Mitchell* v. *Homfray* (1881) 8 Q.B.D. 587.
72. *Beninfield* v. *Baxter* (1886) 12 App. Cas. 167.
73. *Allcard* v. *Skinner* (1887) 36 Ch. D. 145.
74. *Re Lloyds Bank, Ltd.* (1931) 1 Ch. 289.
75. Before the Privy Council decision of *MacMaster* v. *Byrne* (1952) 1 All E.R. 1362, it used to be thought that the weaker party must have obtained and acted on an independent legal advice. That requirement is not part of the law of Nigeria. See infra.
76. (1961) 1 All N.L.R. 218.
77. The learned judge's fourth and final reason for the decision is not relevant to the discussion on undue influence.
78. (1907) 97 L.T. 709.
79. At p. 222.
80. (1952) 1 All E.R. 1362.
81. e.g. the value of the property at the time of the transaction and the fact that at an auction sale the propery had been withdrawn because all the offers made were less than £150.
82. See also the Privy Council appeal from Sierra Leone of *Patience Johnson* v. *Williams* (1935) 2 W.A.C.A. 248, which was concerned with the relationship of a medical man and his patient. Here also the presumption of undue influence was successfully rebutted by evidence. The result of a successful plea of undue influence is to make the agreement voidable at the instance of the weaker party. But delay is fatal to the plea. The rights of bona fide third parties may defeat a belated claim.

CHAPTER 12

DEFECTS IN THE VALIDITY OF AN AGREEMENT

Although the consent of the parties might be present, some other factors may still operate to render the agreement defective. These include incapacity, informality, illegality and the infringement of public policy. In this and succeeding chapters we shall be investigating these factors and in the above order.

(i) Incapacity[1]

So far we have been discussing agreements the parties to which are under no disability to conclude a valid contract. The defect in the validity of an agreement may, however, be due to the fact that legal policy has not recognised in one or both parties the capacity to make a binding agreement. Obvious instances of incapacity in English law are infants, lunatics and drunkards, corporations, and to some extent, the Crown. Since the enactment of the Married Women (Restraint upon Anticipation) Act, 1949, there are no longer any contractual restraints on married women in English law.

In Ghana and Nigeria two aspects of the subject are of striking importance. The first is the capacity of infants to make agreements and the second is the vital question of the capacity to make a valid alienation of family property.

Infancy

The Common Law has recognised twenty-one as the age of contractual capacity.[2] Anyone under that age is designated as infant and is in general exempted[3] from liability for his contracts. The exceptions to this rule were infants' contracts for necessaries. These have been defined to include food, clothing, lodging, apprenticeship (and education) and service. Two categories of infants' contracts not for necessaries were recognised by the common law. The first were those in which the infant acquired an interest of a permanent or continuous nature. Examples are shares in a company or interest in land. These were binding on the infant until he avoided them either during infancy or within a reasonable time after attaining his majority. The other category of agreements were those not of a continuous or permanent nature. These were not binding on the infant unless he ratified them within a reasonable time after majority. This was the position before the enactment of the Infants Relief Act, 1874,[4] the provision of which rendered absolutely void the latter category of agreements made by infants. Mention must also be made of *Section* 2 of the *Sale of Goods Act.* 1893 which provides that where necessaries are sold and delivered to an infant or to a person who by reason of mental incapacity or drunkenness is incompetent to contract, he must pay a reasonable price therefor. In other words, if in the opinion of the court the contract price was not a reasonable price, the court will substitute their price for that of the parties.

Two facets of the above position deserve some comment. Firstly, the age of majority as accepted by the common law is arbitrary and bears no relation to the realities of actual life or the requirements of commerce. It has occasioned so much injustice in the English law of contract that a large volume of protest has developed against the plea of infancy based on it.[5] Two cases typical of the point we want to illustrate will be discussed. *Cowern* v. *Nield,*[6] was an action against an infant who was a hay and straw merchant. The plaintiff had ordered some clover and hay from him and had paid £35.19.0. to cover the price. The defendant delivered the clover but as this was not fit for the purpose for which it was required, the plaintiff rejected it. The infant took back the clover. He did not deliver any other goods to the plaintiff nor did he refund the £35.19.0. (or any part of it) already paid for the goods. An action for damages for the breach of contract or alternatively for the £35.19.0. as money had and received on a total failure of consideration was defeated by the defence of infancy. The County Court judge who tried the action at first instance had rejected the plea of infancy, but this was overruled on appeal by the Court of King's Bench. In effect the defendant kept both the money and the clover.

Also in *Mercantile Union Guarantee-Corporation Ltd.* v. *Ball,*[7] the infant defendant aged 20 was a haulage contractor. He bought a lorry on hire purchase from the plaintiffs for £666 and this was found to have been used in his business. He paid his instalments regularly until his business was adversely affected by increased tax when he could not keep up with the payments. The plaintiffs sued for the arrears of instalments but a plea of infancy was upheld by the court as a defence to the action. A learned author has had this to say on the *Cowern* and *Ball* decisions:

> " If we imagine that in these two cases the infant defendants had
> a wife and children, the absurdity of the rule becomes perhaps
> ever more glaring. To regard a person who has the responsibility
> of providing food, clothing and shelter for a family of four or
> five as an infant lacking capacity to enter into trading contract
> has hardly anything in reason to commend it. If he orders food
> for himself and his family, the law will hold him liable to pay a
> reasonable price therefor, but the same law will refuse to enforce
> a trading contract from which he derives the wherewithal to pay
> for the food."[8]

We are respectfully in agreement with the comments of the learned
author. It may be added that neither customary nor Islamic law
requires the age of twenty-one for contractual capacity.[9] Both
systems regard puberty as the age of contractual capacity.[10] Also
section 29 of the Eastern Nigerian *Co-operative Societies Law*[11]
restricts contractual incapacity for infants to those made by people
under 18 years of age. We do of course accept the position that a
limit must be imposed on the capacity of people of tender years to
make valid agreements. But it is submitted that the common law
position of twenty-one is unrealistic in English law and totally
unsuitable to the Ghana and Nigerian Societies. It is suggested
that instead of the common law requirements, 18 years should be
substituted with a proviso that if the infant is between the ages of
16 and 18, married and/or is in any business, he should be treated
for the purposes of contractual capacity as if he had attained his
majority.[12]

The second facet of the English position that deserves comment
is the effect of infants' contracts. It is clear from the authorities
that all the infants' contracts made absolutely void by the *Infants
Relief Act, 1874*, were merely voidable before the enactment of
the statute. Now, this enactment is not a statute of general application in Ghana since it was not in force in England until 7th
August, 1874, a fortnight after 24th July, 1874.

The Ghana case of *Sey* v. *Abadoo*[13] was decided on the common
law position on infants contracts. Secondly, the Sale of Goods Act,
1893 is not applicable to Ghana, being a post-1874 statute of the
United Kingdom Parliament not made expressly applicable to
Ghana. Section 2 (2) of the Ghana Sale of Goods Act, 1962 (Act
137) however provides as follows:

> " 2 (2) where necessaries are delivered to a person under an
> agreement which is void because of that person's incapacity to
> contract he shall be bound to pay a reasonable price therefor."

Since infants' contracts are not void but voidable in Ghana, it is submitted that the above provision does not cover contracts by infants. It is still arguable therefore that in cases where necessaries are sold to infants they will be expected to pay the contract (as opposed to a reasonable) price.[14]

In Nigeria, the case of *Labinjoh* v. *Abake*[15] is authority for the view that the Infants Relief Act, 1874, is an Act of general application in force in Nigeria. This makes the effect of infants' contracts in Nigeria similar to what it is in current English law. The injustice of this position has already been observed. Here it may be added that section 29 of the Eastern Nigerian Co-operative Societies law provides that the minority or under-age of any person duly admitted as a member of any registered society shall not debar that person from executing any instrument or giving any acquittance necessary to be executed or given under that law or the regulations made thereunder. It further provides that it shall not be a ground for invalidating or avoiding any such contract entered into by any such person with the society, and any such contract entered into by any such person with the society either as principal debtor or as surety, shall be enforceable by or against such person notwithstanding his minority or under-age. There are similar provisions in the Western and Northern Nigerian Co-operative Societies laws.[16]

Thus, in cases covered by the co-operative societies laws, the provisions of the Infants Relief Act, 1874, as to the effect of certain infants' contracts, do not apply in Nigeria except perhaps in the Federal territory of Lagos.

Capacity to make a valid alienation of family property[17]

A book on contractual obligations is hardly the proper place to explore the vast and complicated subject of the law of property generally, or its special branch, the laws governing family property, even if one were qualified to undertake it.[18] On the other hand any discussion of the law of agreements in Ghana and Nigeria that does not contend with the perennial problem of who has capacity to alienate or otherwise deal with what property, and the legal effect of any purported alienation, is so much the poorer for it. In this sub-section, therefore, we shall be taking a brief look at the question of capacity to alienate family property. This will be followed by a more detailed discussion of the legal effect of any purported dealing in family property by its members. Two preliminary points must, however, be made. Firstly, that although the above sub-title might indicate a discussion on the capacity to alienate family property generally, our discussion here will be centred on land and land matters. This treatment does not detract from the importance of forms of family property other than land.

It rather underlines the interminable nature of the argument on who has capacity to deal with what land. Secondly, that the exclusion of other forms of property, e.g. individual and stool or state property is deliberate. While the former are governed by the rules on general contractual capacity which we have already discussed,[19] the latter is in many respects similar to family property except where, as is the case in present-day Ghana, there are new statutory regulations. Such provisions will of course be mentioned at the appropriate place.

Capacity to alienate family land

" The next fact which it is important to bear in mind in order to understand the native land law is that the notion of individual ownership is quite foreign to native ideas. Land belongs to the community, the village or the family, never to the individual. All the members of the community, village or family have equal right to the land, but in every case the chief or headman of the community or village, or head of the family has charge of the land, and in loose mode of speech is sometimes called owner. He is to some extent in the position of a trustee, and as such holds the land for the use of the community or family. He has control of it and any member who wants a piece of it to cultivate or build a house upon, goes to him for it. But the land so given still remains the property of the community or family. He cannot make any important disposition of the land without consulting the elders of the community or family and their consent must in all cases be given before a grant can be made to a stranger."

This passage quoted from Chief Justice Rayner's report on *West Africa Land Tenure*[20] was fully endorsed by the Judicial Committee of the Privy Council in the leading Nigeria appeal of *Amodu Tijani* v. *Secretary, Southern Nigeria*,[21] but it has of course been overtaken by events in many vital respects.[22] Individual " ownership " for instance, is no longer as foreign as it used to be. The question of ownership even if this was a convenient word for the discussion of African land law, need not detain us here.[23] It is enough to say that as far as control and alienation of family property goes, Rayner's statement is still substantially the current legal position.[24] That is to say that it is only the family that has competence to deal with its property in any way that the law permits. No single individual has capacity to alienate family land. Sarbah has said that:

" Neither the head of the family acting alone nor the senior members of the family acting alone, can make any valid alienation or give title to any family property whatsoever."[25]

This position has been found to be of general application in both Ghana and Nigeria.[26]

The logical conclusion from the above position would seem to be that every member of the family would be consulted in any dealing with family property.[27] But such a requirement would be absurd even if it were possible to bring together under one roof all the members of any given family at any given time. There would still be the complication created by the impossibility of ascertaining the views of infants and patients—mental and physical. Needless to mention the paper work involved in having to provide places for the signatures of upwards of 300 family-members in order to validate a particular conveyance for, say, a plot to build a house on. Common sense therefore suggests, and the law has long accepted the principle of representation for purposes of alienating or otherwise dealing with family land. "Management committee,"[28] "family council,"[29] "family land committee"[30] have variously been accepted as competent authorities for the purpose of dealing with family land. A regular feature of these bodies is that each of them is made up of the family-head,[31] his elders and the principal members of the family. The criteria for determining who is a principal member varies from one society to the other, but in general, these are the sub-heads of the different branches of the family. It is this body that has the capacity to alienate family land. Neither the head alone nor the principal members alone can effect a valid alienation of family land. There are scores of judicial and academic authorities in both Ghana and Nigeria to support this assertion.[32]

Some exceptions to the general rule have, however, been recognised. Firstly, among the Gas (Accra, Ghana) *Vanderpuye* v. *Botchway*[33] decided that the consent of the children of a Ga six-cloth marriage was vital to the validity of any alienation of the property owned by their deceased father which on his death had become family property. Thus in this category of family property the management committee would seem to include such six-cloth marriage children for purposes of valid alienation.

A second exception has been suggested by a learned author to the effect that if a member of a family has a personal right in family property distinct from the communal interest of the family, no alienation of the said property without his consent would be valid.[34]

Thirdly, Woodman[35] has cited *Kwan* v. *Nyieni*[36] to support the view that the court would allow any member of a family to sue to preserve the family character of property "where the head and principal members are deliberately disposing of family property in

their personal interest, to the detriment of the family as a whole."
This latter exception is not so much a question of the management
committee lacking capacity to alienate family land as that of their
misusing their capacity to so alienate.[37]

A contrast could be drawn between the position of the family
head on the one hand and the sole trustee in English law on the
other. Thus, while a trustee has the legal estate vested in him and
can transfer a valid title to the purchaser without joining the beneficiary,[38] the family head has no such powers of alienation over
family land. Also, an analogy of the family managing committee
to the board of directors of an incorporated association, is equally
inapposite since the latter can transact business in the absence of
(and even in opposition to) its managing director.[39]

The legal effect of a purported alienation of family land without the necessary authority

It is now necessary for us to advert to the effect in law of a
purported alienation of family land. There has of course been a
considerable divergence of judicial and academic opinion on
whether a purported sale or other form of alienation without the
necessary consents is a nullity from its inception or valid until
avoided by one of the parties. This is the whole question of the
agreement being void or voidable. In the former case no title
passes to the purchaser while in the latter the transaction passes a
defeasible title. According to Bentsi-Enchill, any alienation without
the necessary consents is void *ab initio* and no title passes to the
purchaser since nobody can convey to another what he himself
has not got. He states in his book:

> " There are two seemingly conflicting lines of decision on this
> point. It is submitted here, however, that the sounder view is that
> contained in the line of decisions which hold that title does not
> pass, i.e. that a purported alienation is void or invalid where the
> transfer is not the act of the " management committee " and that
> the principle of the seemingly conflicting line of cases can be
> reconciled with this position on satisfactory grounds."[40]

And Ollennu has said, to the same effect, that

> " Any conveyance made by the occupant of the stool alone, or
> the head of the family alone, is null and void *ab initio*, and any
> alienation made by the principal members alone without the
> occupant of the stool or head of the family is likewise null and
> void *ab initio*."[41]

In Nigeria Elias has also subscribed to the theory that such sales are void. He said in his book,[42] referring to the effect of such sales among the Yorubas:

> " But if a family member purports to alienate any portion of the family land without the consent or approval of the others, the purported alienation is a nullity and the purchaser from him has a void and not merely a voidable title. It is on this principle that all the cases of attempted sale or mortgage of family land by an unauthorised member thereof have been held to be void transactions."

Lloyd came to the same conclusion about the legal effect of sales without the concurrence of the family among the Ijebus (Yoruba)[43]

On the other hand while Asante[44] holds the view that such sales are voidable, Allott,[45] Woodman,[46] Obi[47] and Coker[48] have argued that such a sale could be either void or voidable depending on the circumstances of each transaction. Coker's mode of distinguishing between void and voidable sales (that this depends on what the vendor purports to be selling) tends to stand alone.

Before going on to discussing the cases, one must want to know what difference it makes to the purchaser's title whether the alienation is void or voidable. If A sells family land to B without the necessary consents, what difference does it make to him that the court adjudges his title void or voidable? There is of course the theoretical difference that in the first instance no title passes to him while in the latter he acquires a title which can be defeated. But for practical purposes B will keep the land if in the former case the family are guilty of acquiescence[49] and in the latter if they did not act timeously.[50] Another theoretical distinction between the two instances is that in the former the intervention of the right of a third party does not affect the validity or otherwise of the title under the maxim *nemo dat quod non habet,* while in the latter the agreement cannot be avoided if in the meantime a third party has acquired a bona fide interest in the subject matter. Again, for practical purposes no local judicial authority in either Ghana or Nigeria appears to have been decided on this distinction. It has been suggested by a learned author that in such a case notice, actual or constructive, might defeat the family's claim to set the transaction aside.[51] Where, on the other hand, B in our example above knew of the family's interest in the land but nevertheless proceeded to purchasing from A without further inquiries, the family can recover. This was the decision in the Ghana case of *Insilhea* v. *Simons.*[52] It may well be that the onus of establishing acquiescence in void transactions is heavier than in cases where the agreement is merely voidable. In *Abbey* v. *Ollennu*[53] where the defendant had purchased land from a vendor who subsequently had no title to convey, Foster-Sutton, P, quoted with approval the following passage from the judgment of Fry, J. in *Willmott* v. *Barber*: [54]

> " It has been said that the acquiescence which will deprive a man of his legal rights must amount to fraud, and in my view that is an abbreviated statement of a very true proposition. A man is not to be deprived of his legal rights unless he has acted in such a way as would make it fraudulent for him to set up those rights. What then are the elements or requisites necessary to constitute fraud of that description? In the first place the plaintiff must have made a mistake as to his legal rights. Secondly, the plaintiff must have expended some money or must have done some act (not necessarily upon the defendant's land) on the faith of his mistaken belief. Thirdly, the defendant, the possessor of the legal right, must know of the existence of his own right which is inconsistent with the right claimed by the plaintiff. If he does not know of it he is in the same position as the plaintiff, and the doctrine of acquiescence is founded upon conduct with a knowledge of your legal rights. Fourthly, the defendant, the possessor of the legal right, must know of the plaintiff's mistaken belief of his rights. If he does not, there is nothing which calls upon him to assert his own rights. Lastly, the defendant, the possessor of the legal right, must have encouraged the plaintiff in his expenditure of money or in other acts which he has done, either directly or by abstaining from asserting his legal rights. Where all these elements exist, there is fraud of such a nature as will entitle the court to restrain the possessor of the legal right from exercising it, but in my judgment nothing short of this will do."[55]

Thus in void transactions only acquiescence which amounts to fraud could defeat the title of the family to the land while in voidable agreements fraud is not a necessary element. Ordinary lapse of time would operate to defeat the family's right to set the deal aside.[56]

We shall now look at the trend of judicial opinion on the legal effect of an alienation of family land without the necessary consents. A study of the cases in both Ghana and Nigeria has revealed a neater division into two streams of authority than has often been recognised. The courts appear to operate on the basis that where the family head either alone or with the consent of a majority or minority of the members of the " management committee " alienates family land, the transaction is voidable at the instance of any member of the family; but any alienation without the consent of the head of the family is void *ab initio*. It will be seen below that what Bentsi-Enchill describes as apparently conflicting streams of authority are reconcilable on the principle we have enunciated above. This is as true of Nigeria as it is of the position in Ghana. We shall be discussing the cases under two headings, namely, where the family head is a party to the alienation, and where he is not a party to the transaction.

Where the family head is party to the transaction

Here the transaction is voidable but not void. Thus, in the Nigerian case of *Aganran* v. *Olushi & ors*,[57] a case about the sale of family land at Badagry (Nigeria), the said sale had been carried out by the family head, Chief Ajope without the concurrence of key members of the family. In an action to set aside the sale by the said member of the family, the Full Court held (Pennington, J. dissenting) that the sale of family land without the consent of all necessary members thereof is invalid under local law and custom, but it is voidable and not void. The claim was refused on the ground of the plaintiff's delay in bringing the action. Also in *Adeniji & anor*. v. *Disu & ors*.[58] the plaintiff sought to set aside a sale of family land on the ground that his concurrence was not obtained when the alienation was carried out. It appears from the report that the family head was party to the transaction. The Nigerian Federal Supreme Court, affirming the judgment of Jobling, J. (at the Lagos High Court) held that the sale was voidable and not void. The effect of a purported alienation of family property by the head but without all the necessary consents, was also in issue in the recent decision of the High Court of Western Nigeria. In that case[59] the family head (Mogaji) had sold a portion of the family land with the concurrence of only three out of sixteen branches of the family. The plaintiffs sought to set aside the sale on the ground that their consent had not been obtained. It was argued for the defendants that they had been constituted the family council and could alienate family land without consulting the other members of the family. The granting of such powers to the defendants was stoutly denied by the plaintiffs. It was held " that under native law and custom, family land can only be validly alienated by the head and principal members of the family, otherwise such alienation will either be void or voidable; that if the principal or other members of the family alienate family land without the consent of the head, such alienation is void *ab initio*, but if the head alienates it either alone or with the consent of members who are not all the principal members such alienation is voidable."

In Ghana there is a long line of judicial authorities to support the view that an alienation of family land by the head but without all the necessary consents, is voidable. In *Bayaidee* v. *Mensah*[60] the family head had sold family land without the consent of the family members, in fact against the opposition of those members. In an action to set aside the sale after fourteen years, the Full Court held that the transaction was voidable but that the plaintiffs were guilty of delay and could not impugn the sale. Hutchinson, C.J. came to a similar conclusion in *Assraidu* v. *Dadzie*[61] where the family head had given out family land to the defendant without the consent of the plaintiff. The West African Court of Appeal also considered the effect of such sales in *Manko & ors.* v. *Bonso & ors.*[62] Here the head of the family had sold a house belonging to the family without the concurrence of the principal members. In an action to set aside the sale their Lordships quoted with approval the following passage from *Bayaidee* v. *Mensah*:[63]

> " Now although it may be, and we believe it is, the law that the concurrence of the members of the family ought to be given in order to constitute an unimpeachable sale of family land, the sale is not itself void, but is capable of being opened up at the instance of the family, provided they avail themselves of their right timeously and under circumstances in which, upon the rescinding of the bargain, the purchaser can be fully restored to the position in which he stood before the sale."[64]

Accordingly it was held that the sale was voidable and not void but the plaintiff's claim was dismissed on grounds of delay.[65]

Where family head is not a party to the alienation

In such a case the transaction is void *ab initio*. In the Nigerian case of *Chief Obanikoro* v. *Chief Suemu & ors,*[66] the plaintiff's action was for the setting aside of the lease of family property given without his consent. The plaintiff was the family head. It was held by the Divisional Court at Lagos that the lease was void *ab initio*. Also in *Oshodi* v. *Aremu,*[67] a case about the person entitled to receive compensation on a piece of land being compulsorily acquired by the Lagos Executive Development Board, the first claimant relied on an execution sale in which he purchased the land as the property of the Oloto family. The second claimant relied on a conveyance made to him by a member of the Oloto family who in turn had been given the said land as an outright gift by the then family head. It was found as a fact that the said gift was not made with the consent and concurrence of the members of the Oloto family and that the sale on which the second claimant relied was carried out without the necessary consents. Two issues were to be resolved by the court, firstly, whether the family head could validly make a gift of family land without the consent of the principal members of the family, and secondly, the legal effect of the purported sale to the second claimant. On the first question, the trial court held that the second claimant had not discharged the onus of proving any native custom that permits family heads to make an outright gift of family land without the consent of the principal members of the family.[68]

Such a gift was therefore invalid. If the gift was invalid the land retained its family character. Accordingly, on the second question it was held that the purported sale of the land without the consent of the head was void and of no effect. The first claimant had a better title. This decision was affirmed on appeal by the West African Court of Appeal.

The Ghana Courts have also accepted the position that any alienation of family land without the consent of the head of the family is void. *Agbloe* v. *Sappor*[69] was a conveyance by four out of the six principal members of the family, to the purchaser. The family head was one of the members left out. The alienation was held to be void *ab initio*. This principle was also applied in the later case of *Owiredu* v. *Moshie*[70] where it was held by the West African Court of Appeal that a lease of family land that was given without the consent of the family head was not binding on the family.

The position in Ghana since 1960

After independence in 1957 the Government of Ghana pledged itself to a rapid industrialisation of the country and the advancement of agriculture.[71] Security of title to land was considered vital to each of these objectives.[72] Accordingly in 1960, *The Land Development* (*Protection of Purchasers*) *Act*[73] was passed, the object of which was to give the Courts some discretion in any actions seeking to set aside any alienations of land where some building or other development had taken place on the said land.

Section 1 (i) of the Act provides:

" 1. (i) Where

(a) a person (in this section referred to as ' the purchaser ') has taken a conveyance of land in a prescribed area at any time after 31st December 1944 (whether before or after the date on which the area became a prescribed area), and

(b) the purchaser or a person claiming through him has in good faith erected a building on the land, and

(c) proceedings are brought to obtain a possession order in rela-

Q

tion to the land on the ground that a person other than the purchaser or a person claiming through him is entitled to the land,

the court, where it considers that if this Act had not been passed the possession order would fall to be made by reason that the conveyance taken by the purchaser did not operate to confer on him the title to the land, but that to make the order would cause hardship and injustice to the person against whom it would fall to be made, may, instead of making the possession order, make an order providing that the conveyance taken by the purchaser shall be deemed for all purposes to have operated to confer on him the title to the land."

Section 1 (2) also empowers the court to order the payment of any additional sum to the vendor where an order under *Section* 1 (i) would occasion any hardship on the said vendor or anybody claiming through him.[74] Conveyance in the interpretation section of the Act includes transfer under customary law.

What *Section 1* of the Act has achieved has been to add a link to the existing chain of defences of the purchaser in an action to set aside any dealings in land. Thus apart from delay and acquiescence the purchaser could also plead that he has set up some buildings on the land in order to defeat a plaintiff's claim. The effect of this provision would seem to be that if a case like *Nelson* v. *Nelson*[75] were to be retried in the Ghana courts after 1960, the decision (as far as possession of the land in dispute is concerned) might well go the other way.

It must be conceded that this provision is a progressive step in the direction of securing titles to land. It is obviously a necessary remedy to the situation vividly described by the West African Court of Appeal in a Nigerian case as follows :

" The case is indeed in this respect like many which come before the court; one in which the Oloto family either by inadvertence or design sell or purport to sell the same piece of land at different times to different persons. It passes my comprehension how in these days, when such disputes have come before this court over and over again, any person will purchase land from this family without the most careful investigation, for more often than not they purchase a law suit, and very often that is all' they get."[76]

But with respect, one takes leave to doubt whether the Ghana enactment strikes sufficient balance between the needs of society for security of tenure on the one hand and the prevention of fraudulent dealings in land on the other. The effect of the first section of the Act appears to be that if A without authority alienates family land to B and B has set up some building on the said land, A's family, C cannot annul the transaction. It is not enough to argue that Section 34[77] of the Land Registry Act, 1962 (Act 122) makes the alienation by A an offence under the Act, since the effect of Section 32[78] of the same enactment (Land Registry Act, 1962) makes saving for proceedings under the Land Development (Protection of Purchasers) Act, 1960 (i.e. the Act under reference). Much will depend on how the courts will use their discretion under Section 1 of the 1960 enactment.

Section 2 of the 1960 enactment provides as follows:

" 2 (i) Where

(a) a person (in this section referred to as ' the purchaser ') took a conveyance of land in a prescribed area at some time after 31st December, 1944 and before the date on which the area became a prescribed area, and

(b) the purchaser, or a person claiming through him, in good faith erected a building on the land, and

(c) a possession order was made in relation to the land in proceedings finally disposed of before the date on which the area became a prescribed area, and was so made by reason that the conveyance taken by the purchaser did not operate to confer on him the title to the land, the person against whom the possession order was made may, at any time within twelve months after the date on which the area became a prescribed area, apply to the High Court for an order under this section.

2 (ii)

If the court considers that the making of the possession order caused hardship and injustice to the person against whom it was made, the court may make an order setting aside the possession order and providing that the conveyance taken by the purchaser shall be deemed for all purposes to have operated to confer on him the title to the land:

Provided that an order under this subsection shall not be taken to render unlawful anything done in the period before the making of the order or to found a claim for mesne profits or other compensation in respect of occupation during that period."

It is further provided[79] that if the making of the court's order would in itself occasion hardship to anybody who in the meantime had obtained possession before the passing of the enactment, the court may order the payment of compensation by the purchaser as a condition to his obtaining a reconveyance, provided that such compensation shall not exceed the aggregate of twice the price of the land at the time the original conveyance was made and the value of the development that had taken place on the land since the original possession order. Where, however, the rights of third parties have intervened between the making of the possession order and the application under the 1960 enactment, the court may order the third party to pay such compensation to the original purchaser as they may deem just.[80] Section 3 of the Act makes provision for payment by instalments.

It would appear that the recent Ghana Court of Appeal decision of Kwan v. Nyieni[81] is covered by Section 2 (2) of the 1960 enactment. It will be recalled that in that case the defendant had to surrender possession of the family land sold to him without the necessary consents and that the court ordered the payment of £900 from the land to reimburse the purchaser for the original price he paid for the land.[82]

Bentsi-Enchill[83] has suggested that a better way of securing the title of the purchaser of family land is a system of registering all family heads and any subsequent successors with the Probate Registry and also registering the names of the members of a management committee with the Registrar of titles to land. It will be the duty of the family to keep the list of the members registered at the Land Registry, up to date. Any purchaser or prospective purchaser should satisfy himself of the rightful owners of any piece of land by searching the Land Registry for the members of the managing committee (thereby being in a better position to obtain their consents), and ascertaining who the family head is at the Probate Registry. When a purchaser has fulfilled these two conditions any alienation can hardly be avoided on grounds of lack of the necessary consents and a better balance will be struck between the needs for security of title and the protection of the family. Apart from the obvious problem of having to register managing committees in respect of each bit of family property in Ghana, it is submitted that the learned author's proposal is a better solution than the enactments already discussed.[84]

In this respect mention must be made of the Nigerian Registered Land Act, 1964[85] which has some provisions not found in the Ghana Registered Land Act (Act 22). Under the Nigerian Act the Registrar may register the names of all the members of the family as being proprietors of the property together with the size of their shares therein, and if the number of those entitled to the property is more than twenty, he may register the names of such of them as are put forward as their representatives.[86] Section 12 of the Act provides for the settling of names of the members of the family as well as their shares. In cases of disagreement as to the size of the shares the land will be registered as family land.

Thus, Section 12 (4) provides:

> "If no agreement is reached, the adjudication officer shall record the land as family land, and when so recorded it shall have the effect of a caveat under this Act and no dealing with the land may be registered until such time as the family representatives are ascertained."

Under Section 4 (3) of the Registration of Titles Act (Cap. 181), the Federal Public Service Commission has power to appoint Assistant Registrars of Titles who will be responsible for the register of Titles.[87]

NOTES

1. For the current position in English law on contractual capacity, see Cheshire & Fifoot, *Law of Contract* (6th ed., 1964), pp. 347-374: *Anson's Law of Contract* (22nd ed., 1964), pp. 173-206: *Halsbury's Laws* (3rd ed.), vols. 9, p. 4; 29, 374-384; 34, 24-25, 439-440.
2. In Islamic law the capacity of the parties is an important factor in determining the validity of an agreement. The law requires the parties to have attained the age of discretion in order to enter into a valid contract. In gratuitous acts, the immaturity of the donor is fatal to the validity of the gift. See Milliot, *Obligations*, s. 792.
3. i.e. a plea of infancy would avoid the contract. Such an agreement was therefore voidable.
4. 37 & 38 Vict. Cap. 62, see also the Betting and Loans (Infants) Act, 1892 (England) which renders void any negotiable instrument given in respect of a void loan. Such an instrument cannot be enforced against an infant even after majority.
5. See P. Winfield, "Necessaries under the Sale of Goods Act, 1893" (1942) 58 L.Q.R. 82; P. S. Atiyah, "The Liability of Infants in Fraud and Restitution" (1959) 22 M.L.R. 270; Treitel, "The Infants Relief Act, 1874" (1957).
6. (1912) 2 K.B. 419.
7. (1937) 2 K.B. 498.
8. B. O. Nwabueze, "Integration of the Law of Contracts." Paper presented to Institute of African Studies, University of Ife, August, 1964—at p. 8.
9. *Labinjoh* v. *Abake* (1924) 5 N.L.R. 33.
10. The ages of 15 and 16 have been freely mentioned. It may be remarked that *Fafawa* v. *Kano N. A.* (1958) N.L.R. 64, which Mr. Nwabueze cited as the authority for this proposition in Islamic law, was concerned with infancy for the purposes of criminal evidence. Milliot uses

maturity without defining it in terms of years. See s. 792 of his *Obligations*.

11. Cap. 28, Laws of Eastern Nigeria (1963).

12. See also the *Uganda Contract (Amendment) Act*, 1964, where a minor or infant is defined as any person under 18 years of age.

13. (1885) Ren. 65.

14. In the *Sey* case it was, however, found as a fact that the defendant was already reasonably well supplied and the plaintiff could not recover the price of the goods.

15. (1942) 5 N.L.R. 33.

16. See s. 27 of the Western Nigeria Co-operative Societies Law, Cap. 26 of 1959; and s. 29 of the Northern Nigeria Co-operative Societies Law, No. 9 of 1956.

17. See particularly K. Bentsi-Enchill, *Ghana Land Law, an Exposition, Analysis and Critique* (London, 1964), pp. 41-79; S. K. B. Asante, "Interests in Land in the Customary Law of Ghana" (1965) Yale Law Journal, 848; A. N. Allott, *The Ashanti Law of Property* (1966); T. O. Elias, *Nigerian Land Law and Custom* (1953), pp. 173 et seq.; S. N. Obi, *Modern Family Law in Southern Nigeria* (London, 1966); G. B. A. Coker, *Family Property among the Yorubas* (2nd ed., 1966), pp. 94 et seq.

18. There are several works in Ghana and Nigeria on this aspect of the law. See among others: C. K. Meek, *Law and Authority in a Nigerian Tribe* (London, 1937); S. N. C. Obi, *Ibo Law of Property*; Casely-Hayford, *Gold Coast Native Institutions* (1903); J. B. Danquah, *Akan Law and Customs* (1928); R. S. Rattray, *Ashanti Law and Constitution* (1929); A. N. Allott, *Essays in African Law* (1960); Polly Hill, *Migrant Cocoa-farmers of Southern Ghana* (1961); N. A. Ollennu, *Customary Land Law in Ghana* (1962).

19. There has been some doubt as to the ambit of the recent Ghana Administration of Lands Act, 1962 (Act 123). S. 8 provides as follows: (i) "Any disposal of any land which involves the payment of any valuable consideration or which would, by reason of its being to a person not entitled by customary law to the free use of land involved the payment of any such consideration, and which is made (a) by a stool (b) by any person who, by reason of his being so entitled under customary law, has acquired possession of such land either without payment of any consideration or in exchange for a nominal consideration, shall be subject to the concurrence of the minister and shall be of no effect unless such concurrence is granted." It does not seem that the alienation of any possessory title by a native would require presidential consent to be valid. This result would be anomalous in view of the exclusion of family land.

20. (1898).

21. (1921) 2 A.C. 399, per Viscount Haldane at pp. 404-405.

22. This was recognised in the recent Privy Council decision of *Kote* v. *Asere Stool*, Privy Council Appeal No. 31 of 1959 (unreported) where Lord Denning discussed the modern trends in rights and interests in land. Cf. Allott in (1961) 5 J.A.L. 180. Asante in the article to which reference has already been made, supra, attributes the changes to (a) the growth of commercial agriculture (b) the emergence of revolutionary attitudes towards the alienation of land (c) the influence of English juristic ideas and (d) the decline of traditional authority.

23. On this see the interesting dialogue between Allott and S. R. Simpson on the definition of absolute ownership in (1961) 5 J.A.L. pp. 99; 145-150. On ownership in English law, see H. Honore, "Ownership" in " Oxford Essays in Jurisprudence " (ed. Guest, 1961) p. 107.

24. A distinction must be made between the absence of any incentives to sell land (which is a matter of opinion) and the inalienability of land (which is factual). Conventional discussion of the alienation of land has often confused the former with incapacity to alienate. See for instance T. O. Elias, " Nigerian Land Law and Custom " (1953) p. 172. "There is perhaps no other principle more fundamental to the indigenous land tenure system throughout Nigeria than the theory of inalienability of land." But at 178 he notes the buying and selling of land in the Chad area; G. B. A. Coker, Family Property among the Yorubas, (1st ed. 1958) p. 40, " Strict and orthodox native law and custom does not recognise the sale of land and the literature on this point is abundant." See also to the same effect p. 94 (2nd ed. Coker); K. A. Busia, The Position of the Chief in the Modern Political System of Ashanti (1952) p. 43: "The idea that the land belonged to the ancestors made the Ashanti unwilling to sell his land." J. B. Danquah, Akan Laws and Customs, p. 212: "Tradition has it that absolute alienation of land was until recent times not generally practised by the Akan people. . . . An absolute sale of land by an Akan was therefore not simply a question of alienating realty; notoriously it was a case of selling a spiritual heritage for a mess of pottage, a veritable betrayal of ancestral trust, an undoing of the hope of posterity." Cf. C. K. Meek, Land Law and Custom in the Colonies; and Law and Authority in a Nigerian Tribe, where instances of sale of land among the Akwapim (Ghana) and Ibos (Nigeria) were described by the author—see S. K. B. Asante (1965) I.C.L.Q. 1143.

25. Fanti Customary Law p. 79.

26. See N. A. Ollennu, Principles of Customary Land Law in Ghana (1962) p. 126; K. Bentsi-Enchill, Ghana Land Law, (1964) p. 44; A. N. Allot, Ashanti Law of Property (1966) p. 146; G. R. Woodman, " The Alienation of Family Land in Ghana " (1964). I Univ. of Ghana L. Journal, p. 23; P. C. Lloyd, Yoruba Land Law (1962) p. 82; G. B. A. Coker, Family Property among the Yorubas (1966) p. 66; A. E. W. Park, " A Dual System of Land Tenure, the Experience of Southern Nigeria " (1965) J.A.L. p. 1.

27. In fact Obi suggests that this was a strict requirement in traditional family law, op. cit., p. 66.

28. Bentsi-Enchill, op. cit. p. 44.

29. Foko v. Foko & Ors. (1965) Nig. M.L.R. 3.

30. Obi, op. cit. p. 66.

31. Among the Yorubas, he is called the " Mogaji " and among the Ibos, the " Okpala " or " Okpara " or " Okwara."

32. In Ghana see Agbloe v. Sappor (1947) 12 W.A.C.A. 187; Nelson v. Nelson (1951) 13 W.A.C.A. 248; Owiredu v. Moshie (1952) 14 W.A.C.A. II; Honger v. Bassil (1954) 14 W.A.C.A. 569, Sasraku v. David (1959) G.L.R. 7. In Nigeria: Foko v. Foko & ors (1965) N.M.L.R. 3; Adebubu v. Makanjuola (1944) 10 W.A.C.A. 33; Adewuyin v. Ishola (1958) W.R.N.L.R. 110; Essan v. Faro (1947) 12 W.A.C.A. 135; Onasanya v. Shiwoniku (1960) W.R.N.L.R. 166. In each of these cases what was in issue was the validity of the authorised body acting for and on behalf of the family.

33. (1951) 13 W.A.C.A. 164 ct. p. 168, reversed by Privy Council (1956) 2 W.A.L.R. 16.

34. Allott, *Essays*, pp. 305-306. Cf. G. R. Woodman, infra, who although he accepts the principle guiding Allott's exception, rejects Allott's authority in *Lawani* v. *Tadeve* (1944) 10 W.A.C.A. 37, describing the latter case as an unusual decision. See also T. O. Elias, *Nigerian Land Law and Custom*, (1953) p. 213, where the Lawani decision was described as a case of some difficulty. There is no doubt that *Beyeden* v. *Bekoe*, unreported judgment of Jackson, J. Land Court Accra 31/3/52 and *Agbloe* v. *Sappor* (1947) 12 W.A.C.A. 187, support Allott's general thesis.

35. "The alienation of family land in Ghana" (1964) Univ. of Ghana L. Journal 23 at p. 28.

36. (1959) G.L.R. 67 at p. 73.

37. There has been some doubt as to whether a management committee must be unanimous to effect a valid alienation of family land or whether a majority decision was enough. *Allotey* v. *Abrahams* (1957) 3 W.A.L.R. 280 supports the view that a majority decision will validate the sale. Ollennu adds that such a majority must include the family head (Customary Land Law in Ghana, p. 128). On the other hand, *Bassil* v. *Honger* (1954) 14 W.A.C.A., 569; *Kwan* v. *Nyieni* (1959) G.L.R. 67, and the Nigerian cases of *Esan* v. *Faro* (1947) 12 W.A.C.A. 135 and *Foko* v. *Foko & ors.* (1965) Nig. L.R. 3, tend to suggest that the decision must be unanimous.

38. See *Snell's Principles of Equity* (25th ed. 1960) p. 228. But in *Appiah* v. *Dansoa* (1954) Accra Land ct. 12/10/54 Mayo Plange, J. decided that the family head has capacity to effect a valid transfer without obtaining anybody's consent provided that such transfers lapse after his death. This decision appears, however, to stand alone and is unlikely to be widely followed.

39. See L. C. B. Gower, *The Principles of Company Law* (2nd ed. 1957) pp. 129 et seq. See also Allott, "Family Property in West Africa: its juristic basis, control and enjoyment" 1966, p. 9, where similar analogies were drawn by the learned author. Cf. Harrigan C.J. in *Agbloe* v. *Sappor* (1947) 12 W.A.C.A. 187, where the learned Chief Justice likened the family head in Ewe law to a trustee in English law for purposes of determining where the legal estate vests.

40. *Ghana Land Law*, p. 50.

41. *Customary Land Law in Ghana*, p. 128.

42. *Nigerian Land Law and Custom* (2nd ed. London, 1953) p. 196. Elias however, discussed *Aganran* v. *Olushi* (1907) 1, N.L.R. 66, *Oshodi* v. *Balogun* (1936) 2 All E.R. 1632 where similar agreements were said to be voidable.

43. P. C. Lloyd, *Yoruba Land Law* (London C.U.P. 1962) p. 169.

44. S. K. B. Asante, "Interests in Land in the Customary Law of Ghana— A New Appraisal" (1964-65) 74 Yale Law Journal, 848.

45. *Essays*, pp. 304 et seq.

46. G. R. Woodman, "Alienation of Family Land in Ghana" (1946) I University of Ghana Law Journal, p. 23. The learned author discussed four types of agreements for sale or other alienation of family land. These are sales by the head alone, sale with consent of majority of principal members; sale with consent of minority of family members; sale by members without head's consent. Only the last example was said to be void ab initio. The others were voidable.

47. S. N. C. Obi, *Modern Family Law in Southern Nigeria* (London, 1966) p. 66.
48. C. B. A. Coker, *Family Property among the Yorubas* (2nd ed. 1966) pp. 96 et seq. See also p. 323.
49. *Abbey* v. *Ollennu* (1954) 14 W.A.C.A. 567.
50. In *Bayaidee* v. *Mensah* (1878) Sarbah F.C.L. 171, the Gold Coast Full Court had this to say: " Now although it may be, and we believe it is the law, that the concurrence of the members of the family ought to be given in order to constitute an unimpeachable sale of family land, the sale is not in itself void, but is capable of being opened up at the instance of the family, provided they avail themselves of their right timeously and under circumstances in which, upon rescinding the bargain, the purchaser can be fully restored to the position in which he stood before the sale. This is obviously not the case where, as here, the purchaser has possessed for a series of years (14 years) an un-disputed ownership, has cultivated and improved the land and estab-lished a house upon it. We are of opinion that whatever right of im-peaching the sale the family possessed is barred by their acquiescence and the plaintiff's continued course of undisturbed possession." See also *Insilea* v. *Simons* (1899) F.L.R. at p. 105.
51. Allott, *Essays*, p. 305 of the Nigerian case of *Ajose* v. *Harworth*.
52. (1899) Sar. F.L.R. 104.
53. (1954) 14 W.A.C.A. 567.
54. 15 Ch. D. at p. 105.
55. At p. 568.
56. *Assraidu* v. *Dadzie* (1890) Sar. F.C.L. 174. See also *Oshodi* v. *Balogun & ors* (1936) 4 W.A.C.A. I where the court refused a plea of acquies-cence to defeat the title of the family to certain lands.
57. (1907) 1, N.L.R. 66. See also *Ofondu* v. *Onuoha* (1964) Nig. monthly L.R. 120.
58. (1957) 3 F.S.C. 104.
59. *Foko* v. *Foko & ors* (1965) Nig. monthly law Reports 3. See also *Raji Saka* v. *Asiatu*, Sup. Ct. Suit No. 479/1950, unreported where the Nigerian Supreme Court came to a similar conclusion. See *Banigo* v. *Banigo* (1942) 8 W.A.C.A. 148; *Onwuka & anor.* v. *Abiriba Clan Council & ors* (1956) 1 E.R.N.L.R. 17. In the latter case the fact that the plaintiffs descended from slaves did not affect the issue of their consent to the sale of family land.
60. (1878) Sar. F.C.L. 171.
61. (1890) F.C.L. 174.
62. (1936) 3 W.A.C.A. 62.
63. Supra.
64. Op. cit. at p. 63. See further *Orasanmi* v. *Idowu* (1959) 4 F.S.C. 40; *Awau Ajoke* v. *Olateji* (1962) L.L.R. 137.
65. The cases of *Nelson* v. *Nelson* (1951) 13 W.A.C.A. 248; *Owiredu* v. *Moshie* (1952) 14 W.A.C.A. 11, *Honger* v. *Bassil* (1954) 14 W.A.C.A. 569 and *Kwan* v. *Nyieni* (1959) G.L.R. 67 have been cited as instances where the courts held alienations of family land without the necessary consents to be void irrespective of the fact that the family head was a party to each of the transactions. An examination of the cases, how-ever, reveals that they could well have been decided on the basis that the agreements were voidable and that the plaintiffs had acted timeously. In the *Nelson* case, the sale was said to be invalid and was set aside because the plaintiffs did not acquiesce in the alienation; in the

Owiredu decision the family head was in fact not a party to the transaction; in *Honger* v. *Bassil*, the plaintiffs although they were said to be the descendants of slaves had acted timeously to protect their rights to avoid the lease: and also in the *Nyieni* case the plaintiffs had acted in time. It must be conceded however, that the courts in some cases confuse the terms void and voidable while many others prefer the term " invalid " to describe the legal effect of the transactions. Cf. G. B. A. Coker, *Family Property among the Yorubas* (2nd ed. 1966) p. 323: it is submitted that the references to " recitals " and " parcels " are only relevant if English form of conveyancing is used.

66. (1925) 6 N.L.R. 87.

67. (1952) 14 W.A.C.A. 83. See also *Ekpendu & ors.* v. *Erika & ors.* (1959) 4 F.S.C. 79.

68. Cf. the Ghana case of *Appiah* v. *Dansoah* (1954). Unreported judgment of Mayo Plange J. (Accra Land Court, 12/10/54) where it was held that such estate will be valid during the life of the family head.

69. (1947) 12 W.A.C.A. 187.

70. (1952) 14 W.A.C.A. 11. See also *Insilhea* v. *Simons* (1899) Sar. F.L.R. 104; *Bary Barnes* v. *Chief Quasie Atta* (1871) Sar. F.C.L. 169; *Allotey* v. *Abrahams* (1957) 3 W.A.L.R. 280; *Akinwumi* v. *Sappor* (1958). Unreported judgment delivered in the Land Court, Accra, December 5 1958; *Nunekpeku* v. *Ametepe*, cited by Ollennu in *Customary Land Law in Ghana* (1962).

71. W. B. Harvey, *Law and Social Change in Ghana*, (Princeton University Press, 1966) Chapters 6 and 7.

72. See also Allott, " Legal Development and Economic Growth in Africa," [in] *Changing Law in Developing Countries* (ed. J. N. D. Anderson, 1962) p. 194

73. (Act 2) 1960.

74. Provided that the additional sum to be paid by the said purchaser does not exceed twice the price of the land at the time the original conveyance was executed.

75. (1951) 13 W.A.C.A. 248.

76. *Ogunbamibi* v. *Abowaba* (1951) 13 W.A.C.A. 222, per Verity Ag. P. at p. 223. See also *Olowu* v. *Oshinubi* (1958) L.L.R. 21.

77. Section 34 of the Land Registry Act, 1962, (Act. 122) provides as follows: " Any person who knowingly—

(a) purports to make a grant of a piece of land to which he has no title: or

(b) purports to make a grant of a piece of land without authority: or

(c) makes conflicting grants in respect of the same piece of land to more than one person, shall be guilty of an offence which shall be a second degree felony and may, in addition to any other punishment that may be imposed upon him, be liable to pay an amount of twice the value of the aggregate consideration received by him."

78. This section provides as follows:
" (i) where proceedings to which the Land Development (Protection of Purchasers) Act, 1960, and the Farm Lands (Protection) Act, 1962 apply are instituted in any court, the registrar of the court shall give notice of the proceedings to the Chief Registrar who shall adjourn consideration of any matter affecting the land which is the subject of the proceedings until the conclusion of the proceedings." Subsection (2) Empowers the Chief Registrar to amend the register accordingly.

79. S. 2 (3) of the Land Development (Protection of Purchasers) Act, 1960, (Act. 2).

80. Section 2 (5) of the Act.

81. (1959) G.L.R. 67.

82. The Farm Lands (Protection) Act, 1962 (Act 107) makes similar provisions in respect of agricultural lands. There are no enactments in any of the Nigerian jurisdictions corresponding to the provisions in Ghana.

83. *Ghana Land Law* (1964) pp. 57 et seq.

84. In respect of Stool lands and lands in the Northern Territories of Ghana, see the Administration of Lands Act, 1962, which consolidated the provisions of the Akim Abuakwa (Stool Revenue) Act, 1958, Ashanti Stool Lands Act 1958, Stool lands Control Act, 1959, and the Stool Lands Act, 1960. The 1962 enactment vests title to all such lands in the President; transfers without the consent of the minister (to whom the President delegates his functions) is void and anybody entering into such an agreement commits an offence under the Act. On who has the right to grant concessions see the Concessions Act, 1962 (Act. 124) and the Minerals Act, 1962 (Act 126).

85. No. III of 1964. This repeals the Registration of Titles Act, cap. 181 but its operation is confined to the Federal Territory.

86. S. II (3) (a) of the 1964 enactment.

87. This power was exercised in the Assistant Registrars of Titles Notice (Appointment), of 31st January, 1964 by the Public Service Commission. —See Laws of the Federal Republic of Nigeria (1964 annual supplement) p. B. 33.

CHAPTER 13

AGREEMENTS AFFECTED BY INFORMALITY[1]

In this section we shall be examining agreements the defects in which have been occasioned by the failure of the parties to comply with certain formal requirements. The importance of this category of agreements in Ghana and Nigeria can hardly be overemphasised. Quite apart from the cleavage between the provisions of the general law and the various customary laws with regard to the requirements of writing for certain agreements, there are also the differences in the general laws of the various jurisdictions in the two countries brought about by local legislative action. Another unique feature of this category of agreements is that while the defects in the contracts we have already treated go to nullify or modify the consent of the contracting parties (by making the contract void *ab initio* or voidable), agreements affected by informality are perfectly valid but are unenforceable through the agency of the courts.[2]

We shall be investigating the positions in both the customary and imported laws.

The position in customary law

Discussion on the formal requirements of enforceable agreements has often been centred on the importance of writing. On this assumption it has always been asserted that customary law knows no formal requirements in the making of agreements. It must be admitted that traditional customary law knew no writing and it would be preposterous if writing was considered a vital element in agreements concluded under any of its systems.

In fact suretyship and land agreements both of which required writing in the imported law, were perfectly enforceable in customary law in the absence of any form of writing. In the Ghana case of *Kwesi Johnson* v. *Effie*[3] it was aptly remarked by Foster-Sutton, P. that " a conveyance forms no part of a sale by native law and custom." It would also be curious if customary law which regulates the transactions of predominantly illiterate populations should require writing to make their agreements enforceable.[4]

Having said this, the fact that no system of customary law in either Ghana or Nigeria has been found to be entirely devoid of certain formal requirements, has got to be faced. Marriage contracts, suretyship agreements and agreements for the sale of or other dealing in land are attended by elaborate formalities. This aspect of the subject has been fully discussed above.[5]

Where writing is used in customary law transactions it does not go to make the agreement enforceable but facilitates proof of the existence of the obligation. Although the distinction between evidence of the existence of an agreement and the enforceability of the said agreement is a fine one in customary law terms,[6] it is clear that the absence of writing would not make the agreement any less enforceable to the court. In this respect the gap between customary law and the imported law is apparent since in the latter, with the possible exception of the equitable doctrine of part performance, any agreement which is required by law to be in writing is unenforceable except it was in written form.

Position in the imported law

At common law writing was not an essential requisite for the validity or enforceability of agreements. This position was however altered by statute in 1677 when the Statute of frauds required certain types of agreements to be in writing or evidenced by a memorandum. The relevant sections of the statute in this respect are sections 4 and 17. Section 4 provides as follows:

" No action shall be brought whereby to charge any executor or administrator on any special promise to answer damages out of his own estate; or whereby to charge the defendant upon any special promise to answer for the debt, default or miscarriage of another person; or to charge any person upon any agreement made upon consideration of marriage; or upon any contract or sale of lands, tenements or hereditaments or any interest in or concerning them; or upon any agreement that is not to be performed in the space of one year from the making hereof; unless the agreement upon which such action shall be brought, or some memorandum or note thereof, shall be in writing and signed by the party to be charged therewith or some other person thereunto by him lawfully authorised."

The section therefore required writing for five categories of agreements, namely,

    (i) a promise by an executor or administrator;

    (ii) a promise to answer for the debt, default or miscarriage of another person, i.e. a contract of guarantee or suretyship;

    (iii) an agreement made upon consideration of marriage;

(iv) an agreement for the sale of land or any interest in land; and

(v) an agreement that is not to be performed within one year from the making thereof.

Section 17 as subsequently amended by the Sale of Goods Act (England) 1893[7] added a 6th category to the above list. These are agreements for the sale of goods of up to or above ten pounds, provided the buyer has not in the meantime accepted the goods or part thereof, or given something in earnest or in part payment of the price.[8] Now, this enactment (i.e. the Statute of Frauds) is of course a pre-1874 statute of general application in England and is therefore part of the imported laws of Ghana and Nigeria. It has been found to be in force in the two latter countries.[9]

But the provisions of section 4 of the Act and section 17 (as amended by section 4 of the Sale of Goods Act 1893 (England)) had been the subject of considerable academic and judicial criticism in England.[10] The current English law position with regard to those categories of agreement covered by the two enactments, is contained in section 40 of the Law of Property Act 1925 and sections 1 and 2 of the Law Reform (Enforcement of Contracts) Act, 1954. While the former enactment retains writing for land agreements, the latter retains agreements of guarantee or suretyship among those agreements that will be unenforceable except they are in writing.

The position in Ghana

The position in Ghana and the various jurisdictions in Nigeria appears to be more complex. Section II of the Ghana Contracts Act, 1960 (Act 25) provides as follows:

" Subject to the provisions of any enactment, and to the provisions of this Act, no contract whether made before or after the commencement of this Act, shall be void or unenforceable by reason only that it is not in writing or that there is no memorandum or note thereof in writing."

What this section has achieved has been the restoration of the position in English common law before the enactment of the Statute of Frauds in 1677. The saving for the provisions of any enactment is intended to remove any doubts there might well be in cases of moneylending transactions, hire-purchase agreements and insurance contracts all of which are governed by different enactments.

The Ghana legislation goes further to provide as follows:

" Section 4 (i)

Any agreement made before or after the commencement of this Act whereby a person (hereinafter in this part called ' the guarantor ') guarantees the due payment of a debt or the due performance of any other obligation by a third party shall be void unless it is in writing and is signed by the guarantor or his agent, or is entered into in a form recognised by customary law."

" Section 14 (ii)

Any promise or representation made after the commencement of this Act, relating to the character or credit of any third person with the intent that that third person may obtain credit, money or goods, from the person to whom the promise or representation is made, shall be void unless it is in writing and is signed by the party to be charged therewith or his agent."

Sections 4 and 17 of the Statute of Frauds (except land contracts) are expressly repealed.[11]

Thus, as far as agreements concerning land are concerned, Section 4 of the Statute of Frauds, 1677, is still part of the law of Ghana. This section was in issue in the recent case of *Moubarak* v. *Duke Banson*.[12] This was an indemnity action for £1,700 from the defendant who counterclaimed for

(a) £1,200, representing his 10 per cent commission for negotiating the sale of plaintiff's premises for £12,000 in 1954. The prospective purchaser had made a part-payment of £2,000;

(b) £200 being expenses incurred by the defendant in connection with the negotiation for the sale of another premises of the plaintiff. This expenditure was proved; and

(c) £42.19.6 which was a debt due to the defendant from one J. K. Ghana, payment of which the plaintiff had guaranteed but which, the defendant claimed, had not in fact been paid. The guarantee was not in writing.

On the first head of counter-claim Djabanor, J., who tried the case at Cape Coast (Ghana), held that the agreement was unenforceable since there was no memorandum to satisfy the Statute of Frauds, 1677. The payment of the £2,000 by the prospective purchaser was not considered to constitute sufficient act of part-performance to take the case out of the statute. This holding also disposed of the defendant's second head of counter-claim. On the third head of counter-claim the court ruled that the guarantee was unenforceable since there was no writing to satisfy the provisions of Section 4 of the Statute of Frauds.

It is curious, however, that the learned judge preferred to base his ruling on the third head of counter-claim, under the Statute of Frauds when the position is neatly covered by Section 14 (i) of the Contracts Act, 1960 and the provisions of this section of the Contract Act apply to agreements made before or after the commencement of the Act. It is submitted with respect that the counter-claim under head (c) above is not unenforceable but void and that the relevant provision governing the transaction is Section 14 (i) of the Contracts Act, 1960 (Act 25), and not Section 4 of the Statute of Frauds, 1677, which had been repealed by the said Section 14 (i) of the later enactment.

Having said this, some comment will be made on two peculiar facets of Section 14 of the Ghana legislation. The first is the saving for customary law transactions. This recognition of the duality of legal rules (according each its validity within its proper law) is a progressive step in the harmonisation of these rules with a view to perhaps eventual unification. As was pointed out by Boison, J. in the recent case of *Hamid Arab* v. *Norgah,*[13] " it will be most unreasonable, inequitable, and productive of hardship— if the provisions of the Statute of Frauds were applied to transactions between illiterates."[14]

The second facet of the provision is the legal effect of noncompliance with the section. Under the Statute of Frauds, such an agreement would be perfectly valid but could not be enforced by the courts as a result of its informality. But it could still be used as a defence to an action for the return of money or other property that passed under the contract.[15] The Ghana provision, however, makes the agreement absolutely void in default of compliance. This view is, of course, consistent with those of Blackstone as contained in the third Book of his Commentaries (Comm. iii, 157-8) and was adopted by Lord Abinger in *Carrington* v. *Rootes*[16] in the following words:

> " The meaning of the Statute is, not that the contract shall stand for all purposes except that of being enforced by action, but it means that the contract shall be altogether void."

But this view of the provisions of the Statute of Frauds had been questioned in the later case of *Leroux* v. *Brown*[17] and specifically overruled by the House of Lords in *Maddison* v. *Alderson*[18] in 1883. The effect of the Ghana provision is, however, different. Thus, if A gives an oral guarantee to B on behalf of C, and gives his car as security for the guarantee, B will not be allowed to set up the oral guarantee in any action by A for the return of the car or its value. It can be argued that the intention of the legislature in making the provision is the protection of inexperienced people from being led into undertaking obligations which they did not fully understand; and also to avoid the contingency of unscrupulous persons asserting that credit had been given on the faith of a guarantee which the surety had no real intention of giving. On the other hand, the whole object of the requirement of writing is the evidenciary value of the document in proving that there was such a guarantee (having had regard to all the surrounding circumstances). Though it did not comply with the requirement of the enactment with regard to writing, it will be anomalous not to recognise such an agreement for purposes of a defence to an action based on it. For instance if A in our example above, gave his land as security for the oral guarantee, there is no reason why B cannot set up the guarantee as a defence to an action for trespass brought against B by A. The effect of the Ghana provision, however, is to render the transaction absolutely void thus invoking the maxim *ex turpi causa non oritur actio*. It is submitted that the better rule is that which denies informal agreement the agency of the courts for purposes of enforcement, leaving them valid for other purposes.

Federal Territory of Lagos, Western Nigeria and Mid-Western Nigeria

The position in Ghana with regard to the legal effect of non-compliance with statutory requirements as to writing, is in marked contrast to the state of the law in the Federal Territory of Lagos, Western and Mid-Western Nigeria. Part two of the Law Reform (Contracts) Act, 1961[19] (which applies only to the Federal Territory of Lagos), has repealed Section 4 of the Statute of Frauds, 1677 and also Section 4 of the Sale of Goods Act, 1893 with respect to agreements made after the commencement of the operation of the enactment. Section 5 of the Act provides as follows:

" 5 (i) This section applies to—

(a) every contract for the sale of land;

(b) every contract to enter into any disposition of land being a disposition that is required by any enactment to be made by deed or instrument in writing or to be proved in writing;

(c) every contract to enter into any mortgage or charge on land; and

(d) every contract by any person to answer to another person for the debt, default or liability of a third person.

S.5 (2): No contract to which this section applies shall be enforceable by action unless the contract or some memorandum

> or note in respect therefor is in writing and is signed by the party to be charged therewith or by some other person lawfully authorised by him."

Thus, although writing is still required for land agreements and contracts of guarantees, non-compliance with these formalities will only render the agreement unenforceable and not void. Also while the Ghana enactment applies to contracts made before or after the coming into force of the Act, the Law Reform (Contracts) Act, 1961, applies only to agreements made after the passing of the statute.[20] On the other hand, both the Ghana and the Nigerian Acts (i.e. Federal Territory) make savings for agreements concluded under customary law. These will be valid according to their proper law irrespective of non-compliance with the requirement of writing.

The Western Nigeria Contracts Law,[21] which is also in force in the Mid-Western Region, has similar provisions to the Law Reform (Contracts) Act, 1961, with regard to the categories of agreements that require writing, and the legal effect of non-compliance with the provisions of the Act. There are, however, two vital points of departure from the Federal legislation. The first is that the Western Nigeria Contracts Law, like the Ghana enactment on the subject, applies to agreements made before or after the commencement of the operation of the Act.

Secondly, the Western Nigeria enactment has no saving for customary law agreements. Apparently these have to be in writing if the courts are to enforce their terms. It is not clear, however, if such a radical alteration of the customary law position can be inferred from the drafting omission. It can be argued, of course, that as statutory provisions take precedence over customary law rules, all agreements that come within the ambit of the contracts law must comply with its provisions, customary or imported law transactions notwithstanding. The position may well be anomalous if the provisions were rigidly applied by the courts.

The position in Eastern and Northern Nigeria

In both these two regions Section 4 of the Statute of Frauds, 1677 and Section 4 of the Sale of Goods Act, 1893 are still in force. One is startled at the vast difference it makes to the enforceability of an agreement to conclude a contract in one region of Nigeria rather than in another. The effect of the continued operation of the two statutes of general application in the two regions of Nigeria, is that the following categories of agreement still require writing for their enforceability:

(a) a promise by an executor or administrator;

(b) a promise to answer for the debt, default or miscarriage of another person;

(c) an agreement made upon consideration of marriage;

(d) a contract for the sale of land or any interest in land;

(e) an agreement that is not to be performed within one year from the making thereof; and

(f) a contract for the sale of goods of the value of ten pounds or upwards—unless the buyer has accepted and actually received part of the goods so sold or has given something in earnest to bring the contract or in part-payment.[22]

Agreements that do not comply with these formalities are unenforceable but are not void. Customary agreements are excluded. These are still enforceable in the absence of writing in view of the provisions in the High Court Laws of the two regions empowering the courts to observe and enforce the observance of customary laws in appropriate cases. The distinction between this position and the state of the law in Western Nigeria lies in the fact that while customary law rules take precedence over a corresponding stipulation in a statute of general application this is not true of local enactments. These supersede any inconsistent rule of customary law in the absence of any specific saving for the latter.

It need hardly be argued that the state of the law in Eastern and Northern Nigeria could do with prompt legislative attention,[23] Any legislation in the two regions or any of them should avoid the Ghana provision as to the legal effect of non-compliance with the stipulations, and the Western Nigeria omission to include savings for customary law transactions. It is submitted that there is no pressing need for any integration of the customary and imported law rules in this aspect of the law. The enforceability of transactions ought to be determined according to their proper law.[24]

NOTES

1. See B. O. Nwabueze, "The Integration of the Law of Contracts." Paper prepared for the Conference on the Integration of Customary and Modern Legal Systems, Ibadan, 24-29 August, 1964.
2. Cf. Blackstone iii, 157-8 who felt that such agreements are void. But see *Leroux* v. *Brown* (1852) 12 C.B. 801.
3. (1953) 14 W.A.C.A. 254 at p. 256. Also in *Alake* v. *Awawu* (1932) II N.L.R. 39 it was held that an oral gift of land under customary law was

effective to pass the title thereto to the donee. See also *Malomo* v. *Olusola* (1954) 21 N.L.R. I; *Griffin* v. *Talabi* (1948) 12 W.A.C.A. 371, and *Nelson* v. *Nelson* (1951) 13 W.A.C.A. 248.

4. The prevalent use of writing in modern customary law transactions with particular reference to land matters is fully investigated by Allott, see *Essays*, " Writing and Title to Land in Ghana," pp. 242 et seq. See also our discussion on the place of writing in determining the parties' intention as to the law applicable to their transactions—post pp. 275 et seq. On illiterates and writing see Nwogugu (1968) J.A.L. 27.

5. See form and consideration, supra; p. 101.

6. Under the Illiterates Protection legislation in Ghana and Nigeria an illiterate can adduce evidence to prove what actually transpired between him and the third party even if this contradicts the document on which a third party relies. This privilege is not open to a literate third party dealing with an illiterate person. See *U.A.C. of Nigeria Ltd.* v. *Edems & Ajayi* (1958) N.R.N.L.R. 33; *S. C. O. A. Zaria* v. *Okon* (1960) N.R.N.L.R. 36.

7. *S. 4.*

8. Other types of agreement that require writing to be enforceable include moneylending transactions under the Moneylenders Acts; Hire-purchase agreements; marine insurance agreements.

9. For Ghana, see *Johnson & Anor.* v. *Golightly* (1923-25) Div. Ct. 88; *George* v. *Afari & Anor.* (1926-29) Div. Ct. 195; *Hamid Arab* v. *Norgah* (1965) Current Cases, 138; *Moubarak* v. *Duke Banson* (1965) Current Cases, 68. For Nigeria, see *Alake* v. *Awawu* (1932) II N.L.R. 39.

10. See Lord Wright, *Legal Essays and Addresses*, p. 226; Holdsworth, *History of English Law*, vol. vi, pp. 369-97; Law Reform Committee Report, April, 1953 Cmd. 8809.

11. S. 19 of the Contract Act, 1960 (Act 25). The Sale of Goods Act, 1893 (England) was never a statute of general application in Ghana.

12. (1965) Ghana Current Cases, No. 68.

13. (1965) Ghana Current Cases No. 138. This was a horse-selling transaction and the defendant had argued that as the price was higher than £10 the agreement was unenforceable since there was no writing.

14. The courts had long recognised this principle in land matters, see *Nelson* v. *Nelson* (1951) 13 W.A.C.A. 248.

15. But cf. the case of *Carrington* v. *Rootes* (1837) 2 M & W, 148 where it was held that a plaintiff could not rely on an agreement that did not comply with the provisions of the Statute of Frauds, in an action for trespass.

16. (1837) 2 M & W. 248 at p. 255.

17. (1852) 12 C.B. 801.

18. (1883) 8 App. Cas. 467; see particularly p. 488.

19. No. 64 of 1961 SS. 5 (6) and 7 (i).

20. S. 7 (3).

21. No. 25 of 1959. See also S. 5 of the *Sale of Goods Law*, Cap. 115, Laws of Western Nigeria, which repeals S. 4 of the *Sale of Goods Act*, 1893 (England) in respect of agreements for the sale of goods whose value is up to or above ten pounds.

22. Items (a)—(e) are contained in S. 4 of the *Statute of Frauds*: while item (f) is contained in S. 4 of the *Sale of Goods Act*, 1893.

23. Nwabueze has argued that any requirement of writing in an integrated law of contract in Nigeria should not apply to illiterates. We would

agree with the author that writing should not be imposed as a necessary element in customary law transactions. As long as the duality between customary and imported law transactions continues to operate, an illiterate who chooses to contract under the rules of the imported law ought to be subject to its doctrinal implications. Illiteracy should not be made to assume the posture of a privileged status. Any cases of hardship to an illiterate party to a transaction will be taken care of by the *Illiterates Protection* legislation which has been re-enacted in all the jurisdictions in Ghana and Nigeria. The suggestion that writing should be abandoned as a necessary element of a limited category of agreements in an integrated law of contract, is a startling proposition and runs against the modern customary law trend which is fast adopting the use of writing, particularly for purposes of facilitating the proof of the existence of obligations. It is submitted that the removal of the requirement of writing for such transactions as land agreements, guarantees, moneylending and hire-purchase transactions will create more problems than it will purport to solve.

24. The local judicial authority on this branch of the law can be grouped under two broad sub-heads, namely
    (i) Sufficiency of writing for purposes of the Acts; and
    (ii) Exceptions to the unenforceability or void rule.

Under (i), see *Hamilton* v. *Mensah* (1937) 3 W.A.C.A. 224, where a receipt containing the particulars of a transaction was considered sufficient compliance with the Statue of Frauds; *Akenzua II* v. *Benin District Council* (1959) W.R.N.L.R.I., where a council resolution which under the council's rules could be revoked after 6 months was held not to constitute such a memorandum; *Okoleji* v. *Okupe* (1939) 15 N.L.R. 28, where the Nigerian Supreme Court held that an auctioneer's receipt at a sale by private treaty was not such a memorandum. See also *Basma & Ors.* v. *Weeks* (1948) Privy Council Appeal No. 45. Under (ii), see: *Alake & Lawal* v. *Awau* (1932) 11 N.L.R. 39, gift of land by illiterate, held statute does not apply; *Hamid Arab* v. *Norgah* (1965) Ghana Current cases, 138, claim by illiterate for balance of account in a horse-dealing transaction, held the statute did not apply. Cases under the equitable doctrine of part-performance are also exceptions to the unenforceability rule *Sackey* v. *Ashong* (1956) W.A.L.R. 108.

The courts have also drawn a distinction between cases of oral waiver and rescission of the obligation of an agreement on the one hand, and oral variation of agreements on the other. The former need not be in writing while the latter are unenforceable unless they are put in writing. See *John Holt & Co.* v. *Lafe* (1939) 15 N.L.R. 14; *U.A.C.* v. *Argo* (1938) 14 N.L.R. 105.

CHAPTER 14

AGREEMENTS AFFECTED BY ILLEGALITY[1]

The defect in the validity of an agreement could arise from the fact that it comes within a class of contracts which are absolutely prohibited by law, or whose mode of formation or performance are strictly laid down by the law but the latter restrictions have not been observed by the parties or any one of them. It must be stated that it is in this category of agreements that the freedom of contracting parties to make whatever agreements they please, is up against its most obvious limitations. This is, of course, as it should be, and it will be argued in a later chapter that the interference has not gone far enough. The major problem in Ghana and Nigeria as in other developing countries is economic development. This spans all aspects of life in a society. The law should be an instrument of channelling and charting the course of this development, and cannot therefore be left to the wasteful process of accidental changes as happened in the more developed countries. The proscription or regulation of certain types of agreements is one way of fulfilling this function. In this section we are concerned with the investigation of the extent to which the parties' freedom of contract has been limited by both the common law and statute, and the legal effect of purported agreements that do not comply with the rules.

Classification of illegal agreements

In English law illegal agreements are easily divisible into two broad groups of common law and statutory illegality.[2] The former group consists of six main types of agreements, namely:

    (i) a contract to commit a crime, a tort or a fraud on a third party;

    (ii) an agreement that is sexually immoral;

    (iii) an agreement that is to the prejudice of the public safety;

    (iv) an agreement that is prejudicial to the administration of justice;

    (v) a contract that tends to corruption in public life; and

    (vi) a contract to defraud the revenue.

The latter group is made up of agreements which are expressly or impliedly prohibited by statute.

In Ghana and Nigeria, however, criminal law has been codified and most of the common law offences in English law are statutory in the two former territories. Thus, apart from that category of agreements, e.g. an agreement to commit a tort, which is still illegal under the common law, the bulk of the case law in the two countries (i.e. Ghana and Nigeria) is concerned with varying degrees of statutory prohibition.

Distinction between agreements which are illegal by statute and those that are merely void by statute

A vital distinction between those contracts which are illegal by statute and those that are merely void but not illegal, must be recognised. The importance of this distinction lies in the field of remedies available to the parties and will be discussed in some detail in a later subsection.[3]

Here we are concerned with those statutes which have declared the making of certain types of agreements to be void without also making such contracts illegal. Such an intention in a statute could be express or implied. An example of an express provision is found in the Ghana Sale of Goods Act, 1962. Section 8 (3) of this Act (which deals with the fundamental obligations of the seller) provides:

> " Any provision in a contract of sale which is inconsistent with, or repugnant to, the fundamental obligation of the seller, is void to the extent of the inconsistency or repugnance."

Also Section 67 of the same Act which regulates hire-purchase agreements states as follows:

> " Any provision in a hire-purchase contract whereby the seller or any person acting on his behalf is authorised to enter upon any premises for the purpose of taking possession of the goods, or is relieved from liability for any such entry, is void."

To the same effect is the provision of Section 21 of the Ghana Lotteries and Betting Act, 1960[4] which makes gaming and other wagering agreements void.[5] Section 5 (2) of the Ghana Contract Act, 1960 (Act 25) is an instance of an enactment rendering an agreement void by implication. This subsection which deals with exceptions to the rule as provided for in Section 5 (i) of third-party rights in contracts, provides as follows:

" S. 5 (2)

Subsection (i) does not apply to—

(a) a provision in a contract designed for the purpose of resale price maintenance, that is to say, a provision whereby a party agrees to pay money or otherwise render some valuable consideration to a person who is not a party to the contract in the event of the first-mentioned party selling or otherwise disposing of any goods, the subject matter of the contract, at prices lower than those determined by or under the contract;[6] or

(b) a provision in a contract purporting to exclude or restrict any liability of a person who is not a party thereto."[7]

The effect of this sub-section is that any provision in an agreement to sell goods at certain minimum prices, is void. The position is the same in the case of any provision in a contract to exclude or restrict any liability of a person who is not a party to the said contract.

Statutory illegality

There does not appear to be any general rule for distinguishing a statute which makes any contract void or makes it illegal. It is a question of interpretation from the general tenor of a particular enactment and of any given provision. In many cases an absolute prohibition is followed by a penalty clause for any default. In such a case the agreement is said to be illegal. Under the Ghana Moneylenders Ordinance,[8] Section 18 (i) prohibits the employment of agents or canvassers by moneylenders, while Section 18 (2) imposes a fine of twenty pounds on any agent or canvasser who accepts a commission from a borrower for purposes of introducing him to a lender. Any such commission agreement will therefore be illegal. The Nigerian case of *Patience Kasumu* v. *Baba Egbe*[9] concerned the interpretation of Section 19 of the Moneylenders Ordinance which imposed a penalty for failure to keep certain records of a moneylending transaction. The transaction was held to be illegal.[10] Also section 38 of the Ghana Pawnbrokers Ordinance prohibits in absolute terms the taking of certain articles in pawn. These include " linen or apparel, unfinished goods, or materials entrusted to any person to wash, scour, iron, mend, manufacture, work up, finish or make up." The penalty for taking any of the articles in pawn is double the cost of the said article. Any such pawning transaction will therefore be illegal.[11]

Another mode of determining an illegal agreement is the peremptory nature of the wording of the enactment prohibiting it.

Section 14 (i) of the Ghana Auction Sales Ordinance is an example of this kind of provision, thus

> " 14 (i) No sale by auction of any land shall take place until after at least fourteen days' public notice thereof has been made at the headquarters town of the district in which the land is situated, and also at the place of the intended sale. . . ."

A penalty is also provided for any breach of this provision.[12]

Kinds of Statutory illegality

The legislature, in enacting any legislation in this aspect of the law, often has any one or more of the following objectives in view, namely:

(i) the absolute prohibition of the making of certain types of agreements;

(ii) the regulation of a particular trade or profession;

(iii) the protection of a particular class of people or the general public; and

(iv) the protection of revenue.

Agreements to do any act prohibited under any of the criminal codes in Ghana and Nigeria; partnerships or co-operative societies carrying on business without complying with statutory requirements as to maximum or minimum numbers respectively; and any other agreements that constitute a breach of any absolute prohibition in an enactment, will come under the first head. Under the second head we have such enactments as those regulating the professions, namely, legal practitioners,[13] medical practitioners,[14] and pharmacists.[15]

Other enactments regulate such businesses as pawnbrokers,[16] moneylenders,[17] auctioneers[18] and mercantile agents.[19]

Under the third head we have most of the enactments under (ii) and also the Illiterates Protection legislation in Ghana and the various jurisdictions in Nigeria. Finally, the Crown Lands Ordinance and the other enactments which require some payment to be made to the Government (local or central) form the bulk of the legislation under the fourth head.

It will be demonstrated presently that the enormity of any given agreement (i.e. the degree of the illegality) depends on which of the four sub-heads above that the legislature intended to emphasise. Thus there is a vital distinction between the rights of a defaulting lender under the Moneylenders Ordinance in Nigeria or Ghana (which form of agreement is absolutely illegal under the laws of the two countries) and the rights of a lessee of Crown lands who obtains a lease without the lessor obtaining the necessary governmental consents.[20]

In the former the legislature intended to protect borrowers from the hazard of unlicensed and indiscreet lenders. Thus any transaction by an unlicensed lender is absolutely illegal and void.[21]

In the latter, however, the intention of the legislature was to keep direct control over dealings in land. Any dealings in land without their consent is not absolutely illegal in the same sense as in moneylending matters, but is subject to the government acting to annul the transaction. Until such annulment, therefore, the lessee can remain in possession till the expiration of the lease.

Legal consequences of a breach of statutory prohibition or of other statutory regulation

The general rule here is that the courts will not enforce any transaction that arises from a breach of the law. This has often been put in the Latin maxim *ex turpi causa non oritur actio*. Thus, if two highwaymen disagree over the division of their booty, the courts will not lend their aid to the aggrieved party.[22] Also, where A pays B a sum of money to kill C, the latter act being an offence under the criminal codes of Ghana and Nigeria, A cannot recover the amount paid if B fails to carry out the assignment.[23]

Subsidiary to the above general rule is the position that the courts will not entertain an action by the offender to recover an indemnity against the consequences of his criminal act. To allow such an action would be to defeat the objects the criminal law is intended to serve. It would constitute a negation of the personal nature of punishment for an offence. It cannot be said in any ordinary sense to deter other criminals, where an offender is allowed to recover any fines he had paid in a court, through a civil action for enforcement of indemnity. The retention of capital punishment in Ghana and Nigeria further complicates any support there might be for allowing any indemnity for criminal acts. The practice of insurance appears to be an exception to this rule but even here the position is far from clear. Thus, although the courts in *Haseldine* v. *Hosken*[24] refused to enforce an indemnity against the insurers of a solicitor on the ground that champerty on which the solicitor's liability was based, was an offence, the position was different in the later case of *Tinline* v. *White Cross Insurance Association Ltd.*[25]

In the latter action the plaintiff had paid damages for negligence in a motor accident claim. It had been found that his negligence was so gross as to amount to manslaughter. It was held in a civil action for the claim against the insurance company that the defendants were liable. An attempt to reconcile the two cases could be made on the basis that while champerty is an offence in which intention is a vital element, negligence arises from inadvertence and the law recognises this distinction by allowing recovery in the latter case.

In Ghana and Nigeria, however, champerty is not an offence under any of the criminal codes. In both countries legal practitioners are allowed to sue for the recovery of their fees and in Nigeria the Legal Practitioners Remuneration Committee[26] makes regulations on inter alia, agreements between practitioners and clients with respect to charges. There is no prohibition against a practitioner taking a proportion of the proceeds of any action as part of or all his fees. It is unlikely therefore that the *Haseldine* case will be followed in either Ghana or Nigeria on its facts. But the principle, i.e. that the courts will not help any person to get reparation for the consequences of his own culpable criminal act, will be applied. The *Tinline* case, on the other hand, has a better chance of being followed in the two countries since the Ghana *Motor Traffic Ordinance*,[27] the Nigerian *Road Traffic Ordinance*[28] and the *English Road Traffic Act*, 1930, have similar provisions with regard to driving offences.[29]

The second general rule about the legal consequences of a breach of statutory prohibition or of other statutory regulation, is that where the parties are equally at fault the position of the defendant is an enviable one, i.e. *in pari delicto potior est conditio defendentis*. This, of course, logically follows from the first one. If the courts will not entertain the action, they certainly cannot order the restitution of any property or the refund of any money that passed as a result of the transaction. But like most other maxims, this one is imprecise and is hedged round with many exceptions.[30] We shall be looking at the exceptions presently. For the maxim to operate, the parties must have formed an intention to break the law either in the formation or in the performance of the agreement.[31] In Ghana and Nigeria the maxim has operated to deprive moneylenders of any sums lent in breach of the moneylenders legislation. Thus, in *Fashina* v. *Odedina*,[32] it was held that a moneylender could not recover the sum of £285.5.0. being the balance of a loan which contravened Section 13 on the rate of interest chargeable on such loans. The breach constituted an offence under Section 14 (i) of the Ordinance.

Breaches of the provisions of the Illiterates Protection Acts in Ghana and Nigeria have also come under the maxim. Section 3 of the Nigerian (Lagos) Enactment[33] provides as follows:

" Any person who shall write any letter or document at the request, on behalf, or in the name of any illiterate person shall also write on such letter or other document his own name as the writer thereof and his address; and his so doing shall be equivalent to a statement—

(a) that he was instructed to write such letter or document by the person for whom it purports to have been written and that the letter or document fully and correctly represents his instructions; and

(b) if the letter or document purports to be signed with the signature or mark of the illiterate person, that prior to its being so signed it was read over and explained to the illiterate person, and that the signature or mark was made by such person."

Section 4 provides for a penalty of £50 fine or 6 months' imprisonment for any failure to comply with the said section. This was in issue in the case of *U.A.C. of Nigeria Ltd.* v. *Edems & Ajayi*.[34] In that case the second defendant was a guarantor to the plaintiffs' company on the groundnut account of the first defendant. The second defendant being an illiterate, the bond was to comply with the provisions of the Illiterates Protection Ordinance, i.e. it was to be read over to the illiterate, interpreted and explained to him before obtaining his thumb-print. The second defendant had pleaded his illiteracy and ignorance of the terms of the bond. In a claim for £300 from the said second defendant being his liability under the bond, Smith, J. held at the Kano High Court (Northern Nigeria) that the company could not recover. The reason for the decision was the non-compliance with the provision of the section.

In the latter case of *S.C.O.A.* v. *Okon*,[35] the Nigerian Federal Supreme Court extended the class of illiterates to include a person who could sign his name and read figures but who was not sufficiently literate to understand the meaning and effect of the document he is signing. Such a person has to be treated as an illiterate for purposes of Sections 3 and 4 of the Ordinance. The facts of the case were that the appellant company claimed the sum of £200 from the respondent as a surety guaranteeing the repayment of any shortages of a third party in the event of the latter being employed by the company, up to the amount of £200. The letter, though signed by the respondent, was written by the appellant's manager. The letter was not read over to the respondent before he signed, nor did he ask for it to be read to him. His evidence was that he understood the figure of £200 which he saw in the document, but that he signed it believing that he was witnessing a written transaction between the appellant company and the third party. In dismissing the appellant's case the Supreme Court held that the failure to comply with Section 3 of the Illiterates Protection Ordinance was fatal to their claim. It was further held in *Patterson Zochonis & Co. Ltd.* v. *Gussau*[36] that a person who is literate in, say, Arabic but illiterate in English is an illiterate in relation to a document written in English.[37]

Other enactments which have received similar construction by the courts under the *in pari delicto* maxim include the Auctioneers legislation in Ghana and Nigeria;[38] the Ghana Sale of Goods Act;[39] and the Ghana Rent (Stabilization) legislation.[40]

Limits on the application of the *in pari delicto* rule

The first is, of course, that there has to be a *delictum* before anybody can be party to it. Thus, if the object of the enactment was not to prohibit the formation of a particular type of agreement but, say the protection of revenue, the plaintiff can recover under the contract. In the Nigerian case of *Harry* v. *Martins*,[41] the Nigerian Supreme Court had to consider the effect of a sub-lease which did not comply with the provisions of the Crown Land Ordinance[42] with regard to the prior consent of the Governor to the alienation. The facts were that the appellant was a lessee of Crown land and had built a shop on the land which he later sublet to the respondent. This sub-lease was without the consent of the which did not comply with the provisions of the Crown Land Ordinance. There was no evidence, however, to show that the respondent knew that the land was Crown land. The landlord (i.e. the Crown lessee) later re-entered the land and the respondent sued for inter alia, damages for unlawful ejectment. He was successful in his claim at the lower court. On appeal it was argued on behalf of the appellant that the sub-lease was illegal and could not found an action in favour of the respondent. In rejecting this submission Bairamian, J., who heard the case on appeal, reviewed the authorities and continued:

> " The inference that the sub-letting without consent is a prohibited act is already contained in the opinion that it is against public policy, and the view that the sub-lessee is in unlawful occupation likewise hangs upon that opinion. Public policy is, as the judgment states, a very unruly horse and ' judges are more to be trusted as interpreters of the law than expounders of what is called public policy '. I distrust that unruly horse and prefer to act on the accepted principle that a contract freely entered into should be enforced unless it is clearly shown to be illegal under some authoritative decision in the common law or to be illegal under a statute, and in dubious cases to give it the benefit of the

doubt and to enforce it. If the sub-lease without consent is not illegal, it will follow that the sub-lessee's occupation is not unlawful. The question can be best resolved by considering the aim and object of the crown lands ordinance and the nature of its provisions on leases. I have not seen any authority for saying that a sub-lessee whose contract was made in breach of a covenant not to let without consent is in unlawful occupation in the case of private land, and I have no reason for saying that he is in unlawful occupation in the case of Crown land. It is an accepted rule that a person is not guilty of an offence unless he clearly comes within the wording of the enactment creating the offence. I think that in the absence of some clear provision in the ordinance that such a sub-lessee is in unlawful occupation or at least that the subletting is an illegal act, it cannot be said that the sub-lessee is guilty of an offence under section 35. . . . From whatever angle the question is looked at the conclusion is that the sub-lease, though in breach of a covenant, is not an illegal contract. The doctrine of estoppel makes it binding as between the lessee and the sub-lessee, and the lessee is not entitled to eject the sub-lessee except in conformity with the law for the recovery of possession."[43]

His Lordship did not consider the provision of a penalty under Section 35 of the Ordinance for unlawful occupation of Crown land, conclusive in determining the illegality of the transaction. The earlier case of *Esi* v. *Moruku*[44] in which it was held that such a transaction was illegal, was said to have been wrongly decided. We are respectfully in agreement with the learned judge that the object of the enactment was not to prohibit the granting of sub-leases but to regulate them. The imposition of a penalty for non-compliance does not alter the position at all. It is easily distinguishable from the Moneylenders Ordinance the object of which is to protect the public from the odd indiscreet lender. This distinction was in issue in the Nigerian Supreme Court appeal of *Solanke* v. *Abed & anor.*[45] in which Section 11 of the Nigerian Land and Native Rights Ordinance,[46] was under consideration. This was concerned with the nature of the title of a lessee of a right of occupancy granted without the consent of the Resident (Northern Nigeria). It was held that the alienation was not illegal. On the effect of the absence of any provision for a penalty in the event of non-compliance with the provisions of the section, the court had this to say:

"The Statute at present under consideration says that it shall be unlawful for the occupier to alienate his right of occupancy, but does not provide any penalty . . . nor would it appear necessary in the interests of public policy for an agreement of alienation to be treated as illegal. Public policy can be adequately safeguarded by the Government's power of revocation. In these circumstances I hold that the contract was not illegal."[47]

In other words their Lordships came to this conclusion partly because no penalty was provided for any non-compliance with the provisions of the section.

Three observations must be made on the above passage. Firstly, it is not clear if the *Solanke* case can be said to be authority for the view that the provision of a penalty is conclusive in determining the illegality of any transaction that did not comply with the terms of a statute stipulating for the penalty. Such a conclusion would of course be *obiter* since the provision of a penalty was not in issue in the *Solanke* case. In fact their Lordships stressed the fact that it was necessary in the interests of public policy that agreements for alienation should not be made illegal if an alternative course could reasonably be adopted. It would also be a startling proposition in view of the fact that different enactments have the attainment of different objects in view. Where an enactment did not intend the prohibition as a particular act, the stipulation of any penalty for non-compliance with any of its provisions will not *ipso facto* render any transaction under it illegal. A transaction under the *Crown Lands Ordinance* is a case in point.[48]

Secondly, and following from the first point, it cannot be said that the Supreme Court has by implication overruled the statement of the law in the previous case of *Harry* v. *Martins*.[48] It will be recalled that it was held in that case that the provision of a penalty was not conclusive. It can further be argued, however, that the object of the enactment of the Crown Lands Ordinance was the regulation of dealings in Crown lands, while the main object of the Land and Native Rights Ordinance was the management and control of Crown lands. In the latter it appears to have been the provision of safeguards against natives disposing of their land rights without adequate supervision. On this principle the provision of a penalty in the former enactment would not be very significant for the purpose of determining the illegality of a transaction in breach of its provisions. The case might well be different if a penalty was stipulated in the latter enactment.

Finally, it is not clear to what extent the basis of the *Solanke* decision has been altered by the *Northern Nigeria Land Tenure Law*[49] which has repealed the Land and Native Rights Ordinance (i.e. to the extent the latter statute is in force in Northern Nigeria). Section 26 of the Land Tenure Law provides for the imposition of inter alia, penal rent for any alienation without the necessary consent. The penal provision is equally applicable to natives and non-natives of the Northern Region who have not complied with the provisions with regard to consent before any alienation, and continues for each day the default is continued. One view of the effect of the new enactment is that the provision for the imposition of penal rent to be levied on any owner of a right of occupancy who alienates without consent, has operated to render any such alienation illegal. In other words such an alienation will come within the prohibition of the enactment and will be treated by the courts as any other breach of an absolute statutory prohibition. Accordingly the Land Tenure Law will come under the same category of enactments as the Moneylenders Ordinance or the Auctioneers Legislation. Another view of the new Northern Nigeria enactment is that it will be absurd to read into it an absolute prohibition of land alienation. If the legislature intended this as the effect of the Law, they could have said so in clear terms. It is not enough to infer such a radical change of legislative intention from the provisions for penal rent.

The Land Tenure Law has not therefore altered the basic assumption of the former Land and Native Rights Ordinance which is that alienations of land without consent are not illegal per se.

A second exception to the *in pari delicto* rule is that where the object of a statute is the protection of a particular class to which the plaintiff belongs, he will be allowed by the courts to recover any money or property that had passed as a result of the illegal transaction, his own guilt notwithstanding. Thus if a moneylender had received any security on a transaction which has been declared illegal under the Moneylenders Ordinance, the borrower can recover the security without being ordered to pay the loan. This was the decision of the Privy Council in the Nigerian appeal of *Kasumu* v. *Baba Egbe*[50] where the administrator of a moneylender's estate was ordered to reconvey real property which had been obtained on a transaction that contravened section 19 of the Nigerian Moneylenders Ordinance, to the borrower without the latter being put on terms.[51]

This principle has been applied in transactions declared illegal under the Ghana Hire Purchase Act, 1958;[52] the Nigerian Illiterates Protection Ordinance and under the Restriction of Rents legislation in both Ghana and Nigeria.[53] With regard to alienations of land without statutory consents, this exception to the *in pari delicto* rule was fully discussed in the recent Uganda appeal to the Privy Council of *Singh* v. *Kulubya*.[54] The case raised the question whether, as a consequence of granting an illegal lease, the lessor was debarred from recovering possession from his lessee during its currency. The plaintiff was an African and the registered proprietor of certain land known as " mailo " land, situate in Buganda. The land was divided into three plots, and during 1946 and 1947, the plaintiff leased each of the plots upon yearly tenancies to the defendant, who was an Indian. The defendant continued in occupation until he was given seven weeks' notice to quit at the end of 1959, i.e. after being twelve years in occupation. The plaintiff thereafter brought an action reclaiming possession. The leases were unlawful since they contravened the *Possession of Land Law*[55] and the *Land Transfer* Ordinance.[56] These provisions required the consents of the Governor and the Lukiko for a lease to a non-African, and both parties committed offences in not securing that approval. The plaintiff had argued that the necessary consents had not been obtained but the defendant had replied that as the plaintiff was also a party to the illegality he could not rely on it for purposes of regaining possession of the land. The trial judge dismissed the plaintiff's claim on the ground that the parties were equally guilty in the breach of the law as to consents and could not rely on the courts to enforce any rights under the transaction. On appeal to the Court of Appeal for Eastern Africa the decision was reversed. A further appeal to the Judicial Committee of the Privy Council confirmed the judgment of the East African appeal court. The court gave two reasons for their decision only the second of which is relevant here. This was that the purpose of the prohibitory legislation was to protect African landowners, a class to which the plaintiff belonged. He was therefore entitled to succeed, following a well recognised rule that a member of a class protected by such a statute is not *in pari delicto* with the party with whom he contracted for purposes of recovery of possession. Thus as a member of the specially protected class the plaintiff (Kulubya) even if *particeps criminis* " may recover from the other notwithstanding that both have been parties to the illegal contract."[57]

Now, the Uganda legislation with regard to " mailo " land is in similar terms to the Northern Nigerian Land Tenure Law. It is likely, therefore, that if the defendant in the earlier Nigerian case of *Solanke* v. *Abed & anor.*[58] had instituted an action for possession instead of forcibly evicting the tenant who had taken possession under an unlawful sub-lease, he might well have been successful, on the *Kulubya* principle. The latter decision is, however, not binding on the Nigerian courts but will be accorded high persuasive force.[59] A third exception to the *in pari delicto* rule is that where an agreement which is legal as formed can be performed either legally or illegally, the law presumes, in the absence of any evidence to the contrary, that the parties intended not to break the law and will enforce the rights and duties of the parties under it.[60]

This exception was in issue in the Nigerian case of *Agbakobar v. Meka*[61] which was concerned with the alleged infringement of the *Pharmacy Ordinance.*[62] The facts of the case were that the respondent, a licensed chemist and druggist, supplied the appellant with drugs on credit over a period. Some of the drugs were poisons as defined by Part III of the First Schedule to the Pharmacy Ordinance.[63] It is an offence under the Ordinance for a licensed chemist and druggist to sell or deliver any poison as so defined except upon an order signed by one of certain specified persons or upon a prescription. At the trial of a counterclaim by the respondent for the amount due for the supply of the drugs, the appellant contended that the supply of the poisons was illegal. There was no evidence as to whether or not the poisons were supplied on prescription. Appealing against a judgment in favour of the respondent for the amount claimed, the appellant contended that the onus lay on the respondent to prove that the supply of the poisons was legal. The High Court sitting in its appellate jurisdiction held that the contract between the appellant and the respondent for the supply of the poisons was not on its face illegal, and the onus lay on the appellant to prove illegality.[64]

Gaming and Wagering agreements

Three types of transactions have often been discussed under this heading namely betting, gaming and lotteries, and five facets of the discussion ought to be recognised and clearly distinguished. The first is their nature, i.e. what constitutes a bet, a gaming agreement or a lottery, and the extent to which they are lawful. The second is concerned with the rights and duties of the parties to the transaction *inter se*. This is of course the whole question of the right of the plaintiff to recover any monies won on a bet or other wager. The third facet is the relationship between the parties to a wager and a third party, in particular an agent of both parties or any one of them.

The fourth is concerned with the recovery of securities deposited as a result of gaming or other wager. Finally there is the question whether loans made for bets or other wagers are recoverable.[65]

NOTES

1. See *Halsbury's Laws*, (3rd ed.) vol. 8 pp. 125-152; *Pollock on Contracts* (13th ed. 1950) pp. 260 et seq. On Isalmic law, see J. Schacht, *An Introduction to Islamic Law* (Oxford, 1964) pp. 144-160. On some

Nigerian cases on this head, see J. L. McNeil & R. Rains, *Nigerian cases and Statutes on Contract and Tort* (London, 1965) pp. 58-79. On illegality at the customary law, see R. S. Rattray, *Ashanti Law and Constitution*, (London O.U.P. 1956) pp. 287 et seq. M. Green. *Ibo Village Affairs*, (London, 1947) Chapter 9.

2. Several modes of classification have been adopted by various writers and judges. Pollock's chapter on "unlawful agreements" consists of three categories namely (a) those contrary to positive law, (b) those contrary to positive morality, and (c) those contrary to the common weal. Cheshire & Fifoot have classified illegal agreements under statutory and common law illegality; sub-dividing the latter into illegal contracts so called, and illegal contracts traditionally so called. Corbin has however, based his own classification on the degrees of illegality in any particular type of agreement, the breach of a dog licensing law ranking lower than an agreement to rob a bank; in the two cases of *Bennett* v. *Bennett* (1952) 1 KB. 249 at pp. 260-1 and *Goodinson* v. *Goodinson* (1954) 2 QB. 118, a new system of classification has emerged, based on (i) agreements which are illegal because they are against criminal law, and (ii) agreements that have no such taint. It is submitted that the merit of any system of classification should be assessed on the basis of harmony in the remedies available to the parties.

3. For example in agreements that are absolutely illegal any collateral transactions are also affected by the original illegality. In void transactions i.e. those merely void, collateral rights are enforceable.

4. Act 31. This Act has repealed all statutes of general application on gaming or wagering agreements that were in force in Ghana before its enactment. See Section 26 and second schedule.

5. Cf. S. 18 of the Gaming Act, 1845 (England) which has similar provisions. This section has been applied in the Nigerian case of *Chemor* v. *Sahyoun* (1946) 18 N.L.R. 113 in which case the 1845 Act was said to be in force in Nigeria. But see S. 236 of the Nigerian Criminal Code which prohibits certain games.

6. Cf. Part 1 of the Restrictive Trade Practices Act, 1956 (England) and the Re-sale Prices Act, 1964 (England).

7. Cf. *Dunlope* v. *Selfridge* (1915) A.C. 847.

8. Cap. 176, Laws of the Gold Coast, (1951).

9. (1956) A.C. 539.

10. For a fuller discussion of this case, see post pp. 312 et seq. Also for a fuller investigation of the implications of a penalty provision in enactments, see pp. 226 et seq. infra.

11. S. 38 (3), Pawnbrokers Ordinance, cap. 189 (1951, Laws).

12. Other enactments with similar provisions in Ghana and Nigeria include, (i) For Ghana: Sale of Goods Act, 1962 (Act 137); Rent (Stabilization) Act 1962 (Act 109); Rent (Stabilization) (Amendment) Act, 1963 (Act 168); Control of Prices Act, 1962 (Act 113); Manufacture of Spirits Act, 1962 (Act 154);
(ii) For Nigeria: The Moneylenders Act and Laws of the Federal Territory and the Regions respectively; The Auctioneers legislation of all the five jurisdictions; The Pawnbrokers laws; The Rent Act and the Control of Rents Laws of the Eastern, Western and Mid-Western Regions. For other legislation which renders the agreement void but not illegal, see the Ghana Concessions Act, 1962; the Illiterates Protection legislation in Ghana and Nigeria; transactions under the Sunday

Observance Act; and the Northern Nigeria Land Tenure law, cap. 59, Laws of Northern Nigeria (1963).

13. Legal Practitioners Act, 1962 (Nigeria), No. 33 of 1962; for Ghana see Legal Profession Act, 1960 (Act 32).

14. Medical Practitioners and Dentists Act, Cap. 116 Laws of Nigeria (1958 Revision); for Ghana, see Medical Practitioners and Dentists Ordinance, cap. 69, Laws of the Gold Coast (1951 consolidation).

15. Pharmacy Act, cap. 152, Laws of Nigeria (1958 Revision); see for Ghana Pharmacy and Poisons Ordinance, cap. 70, Laws of the Gold Coast (1951).

16. Pawnbrokers Act (Lagos) and the Pawnbrokers Laws of all the four Regions, cap. 146, Laws of Nigeria (1958). For Ghana, see Pawnbrokers Ordinance, cap. 189, Laws of the Gold Coast (1951).

17. The Moneylenders legislation in all the jurisdiction in Nigeria and Ghana.

18. The Auctioneers Ordinances in Ghana and Nigeria.

19 See the Western Nigeria Mercantile Agents Law, cap. 77 of Laws (1959).

20. Cf. *Kasumu* v. *Baba Egbe* (1956) A.C. 539 where illegality precluded the appellants from being put on terms, and *Harry* v. *Martins* (1949) 19 N.L.R. 42 where the Nigerian Supreme Court refused a plea of illegality by a defaulting defendant in a trespass action under the Crown lands Ordinance (Nigeria).

21. See the *Kasumu* case, supra.

22. *Everet* v. *Williams* cited by *Pollock on Contracts* (13th ed. 1950) p. 262 n. 6.

23. This position is equally true of any agreement that contravenes any of the provisions of the criminal codes in Ghana and Nigeria. Knowledge of the parties at the time of making the transaction that it constituted an offence, is not relevant. Ignorance of the law is not an acceptable plea.

24. (1933) 1 KB. 822 see also *Brown Jenkins & Co. Ltd.* v. *Percy Dalton (London) Ltd.* (1957) 2 QB. 621. Cf. *Hardy* v. *Motor Insurance Bureau* (1964) The Times, Tuesday May 12, where recovery was allowed.

25. (1921) 3 K.B. 327 see also *James* v. *British & General Insurance Co.* (1927) 2 K.B. 311. Cf. the Canadian case of *O'Hearn* v. *Yorkshire Insurance Co. Ltd.* (1921) 50, Ontario L.R. 377, where the Ontario appeal Court held that the plaintiff could not recover on facts similar to those in the *Tinline* case. Negligence is, however, an offence under the Ontario Road Traffic legislation while in English law as well as in Ghana and Nigeria, negligence is only an offence in so far as it can be inferred from the offences of dangerous driving, driving without due care and attention or reckless driving.

26. S. 11 of the Legal Practitioners Act, 1962 (Nigeria, Federation and Regions), No. 33 of 1962.

27. Cap. 184, Laws of Nigeria (1958 Revision).

28. Cap. 184, Laws of Nigeria (1958 Revision).

29. The allowing of claims against insurance companies under these heads can thus be said to be an exception to the maxim *ex turpi causa non oritur actio*.

30. The most obvious doubt has arisen in the field of the passing of property under illegal transactions. The Privy Council has held in a recent appeal from Malaya that there is such passing of property in illegal transactions. This was in the case of *Singh* v. *Ali* (1960) 2 W.L.R. 180. In that case, the plaintiff and the defendant were said to be " con-

spirators engaged in practising a deceit on the public administration of the country." In spite of this, Lord Denning had had this to say about the effect of the transaction: "In order to succeed in detinue, it was essential for A to show that he had the right to immediate possession of the lorry at the time of commencing the action, arising out of an absolute or special property in it. . . . And their Lordships think he succeeded. Although the transaction between A and S was illegal, nevertheless it was fully executed and carried out and in that account it was effective to pass the property in the lorry to A. The reason is because the transferor, having fully achieved his unworthy end, cannot be allowed to turn round and repudiate the means by which he did it— he cannot throw over the transfer. And the transferee having got the property, can assert his title to it against all the world, not because he has any merit of his own, but because there is no one who can assert a better title to it." It is likely that this view of the position will be adopted by the courts in Ghana and Nigeria.

31. It has already been mentioned that knowledge of the breach of the law is not relevant in cases of absolute prohibition.
32. (1957) W.R.N.L.R. 45. See also *Eke* v. *Odolofin* (1961) W.N.L.R. 151, where a breach of S. 13 was also in issue.
33. Cap. 83, Laws of Nigeria (1958). This is in similar terms to the corresponding provisions in the other Nigerian jurisdictions and in Ghana. The enactment does not apply to legal practitioners in either Ghana or Nigeria.
34. (1958) N.R.N.L.R. 33.
35. (1960) N.R.N.L.R. 34.
36. (1961) N.R.L.R.I. See also the Ghana case of *Fulani Mamidu* v. *Aban & Anor.* (1964) High Court Accra 20/11/64. Unreported.
37. It seems that an agreement that does not comply with the section is still admissible in evidence: *Amao* v. *Ajibike & Ors* (1955-56) W.R.N.L.R. 121, and *Akohwere of Okan* v. *Emayobor & Anor.* (1959) W.R.N.L.R. 83. But cf. *Eke* v. *Odolofin* (1961) W.N.L.R. 151 where Madarikan, J. cast doubts on the authority of the *Emayobor* decision. See also on the Illiterates Protection Ordinance, *Ntiashagwo* v. *Amadu* (1959) W.R.N.L.R. 273; *Lagos Timber Co.* v. *Titcombe* (1943) 17 N.L.R. 14; *Lodder* v. *Alowey* (1904) A.C. 442. On illiterates and printed conditions, see *Otegbeye* v. *Little* (1906) I N.L.R. 70.
38. *Muffat* v. *Trading Association of Nigeria Ltd. & ors.* (1926-29) Div. ct. 7.
39. *U.T.C.* v. *Okoro* (1965) High Court Sekondi 22/2/65. Unreported.
40. *Ofosu* v. *Bernie* (1964) High Court, Accra 22/12/64. Unreported; *Agberyedzoe* v. *Atta* (1964) High Ct. Ho. 4/12/64. Unreported.
41. (1949) 19 N.L.R. 42. Cf. *Esi* v. *Moruku* (1940) 15 N.L.R. 116 which was said to have been wrongly decided.
42. Cap. 29, Laws of Nigeria (1958 Revision) S. 7.
43. Op. cit. pp. 43 et seq. Text cited from J. L. McNeil & R. Rains. *Cases and Statutes on Contract and Tort* (London, 1964) pp. 70-71.
44. (1940) 15 N.L.R. 116.
45. (1962) N.R.N.L.R. 92.
46. S. 11 provided as follows: "Except as may be otherwise provided by the regulations in relation to native occupiers, it shall not be lawful for any occupier to alienate his right of occupancy, or any part thereof by sale, mortgage, transfer of possession, sub-lease or bequest or otherwise howsoever without the consent of the Governor first had and obtained,

and any such sale, mortgage sub-lease transfer or bequest effected without the consent of the Governor shall be null and void."
47. Op. cit. p. 95.
48. See *Harry* v. *Martins* (1949) 19 N.L.R. 42.
49. Cap. 59, Laws of Northern Nigeria (1963).
50. (1956) A.C. 539.
51. For a fuller discussion of the implications of this decision, see infra p. 312.
52. *U.T.C.* v. *Johnson Okoro* (1965) High Court Sekondi 19/1/65. Unreported. This Act has now been repealed and re-enacted under the Ghana Sale of Goods Act, 1962, Act 137.
53. Under the Ghana Rent Control Ordinance any rent paid in excess of the Ordinance stipulation is refundable to the tenant. Cf. *Moubarak* v. *Duke Banson* (1965) High Court, Sekondi, 8/2/65. Unreported. See also the decisions under the Rent (Stabilization) Act, 1962 (Act 109); the Rent (Cocoa Farms) Regulations, 1962 (L.I. 186) and the Rent (Cocoa Farms) (Amendment) Regulations, 1965 (L.I. 382); *Ofosu* v. *Bernie & ors* (1964) High Court, Accra, 22/12/64. Unreported. On Nigeria, see the cases discussed by M. O. Onwuamaegbu, *Nigerian Law of Landlord and Tenant*, (London, 1965) pp. 243 et seq.
54. (1963) 3 All E.R. 499.
55. (Buganda) S. 2.
56. Uganda, ss. 2, 3 and 4 are in similar terms to the Northern Nigeria Land Tenure Law, cap. 59, Laws of Northern Nigeria (1963).
57. Per Lord Morris of Borth-Y-Gest, who read the advice of the Privy Council. See also *Kiriri Cotton Co.* v. *Dewani* (1960) A.C. 192, a Kenya appeal.
58. (1962) N.R.N.L.R. 92.
59. Considering the earlier Malaya appeal in which their Lordships of the Privy Council decided that property passes under an illegal agreement: *Singh* v. *Ali* (1960) A.C. 167; see also *Palaniappa* v. *Cheffier* (1962) A.C. 294, it can be argued that the Kulubya principle has application only in land matters. This view is reinforced by the fact that the Kasumu decision (a Nigerian appeal) was also concerned with the reconveyance of land. Cf. the Kenya case of *Denning* v. *Edwards* (1961) A.C. 245 (P.C.).
60. *Chitty on Contracts* (21st ed. vol. 1, para. 894), p. 467.
61. (1962) N.R.N.L.R. 1.
62. Cap. 152, Laws of Nigeria (1958 Revision).
63. S. 32 (i) of the Ordinance provides as follows: " No selling dispenser or chemist and druggist shall sell or deliver any poison in Part III of the first Schedule except on an order signed by a registered or licensed medical practitioner, registered or licensed dentist, qualified veterinary surgeon, or selling dispenser or chemist and druggist; or on and in accordance with a prescription given by a registered or licensed medical practitioner, registered or licensed dentist or qualified veterinary surgeon."
64. It has not been considered necessary to discuss the other exceptions to the *in pari delicto* rule since these involve a repetition of the existing English judicial authority on the subject.
65. For the detailed position in English law, see *Halsbury's Laws* (3rd ed.) Vol. 18 pp. 167-245. The position in Ghana is now governed by the Lotteries and Betting Act, 1960 (Act 31) which has repealed and re-enacted all imperial legislation on the subject which hitherto was in force

in Ghana. The Ghana enactment is in more comprehensive terms than the Betting Gaming and Lotteries Act, 1963 (England), (the latter does not deal with the effect of gaming and wagering agreements). What the Ghana enactment achieved was a simplification of the language generally and the inclusion of the terms of the Gaming Act, 1892 (in respect of agents in gaming and wagering agreements). This latter imperial statute was of course, not a statute of general application in Ghana. It was necessary to include this bit in view of the effect of the House of Lords decision in *Read* v. *Anderson* (1882) 10 Q.B.D. 100 which judgment had brought about the Gaming Act, 1892.

CHAPTER 15

AGREEMENTS THAT INFRINGE PUBLIC POLICY[1]

Assessing Roscoe Pound's contribution to sociological jurisprudence Julius Stone has had the following to say:

> " The due appreciation of the relationship between law and social
> facts involves four main inquiries:
>
> (i) ascertainment of what are the *de facto* interests which in
> the particular civilisation men are pressing;
>
> (ii) definition of the limits within which these will be given legal
> support;
>
> (iii) what legal precepts and concepts and machinery for their
> enforcement are available to secure these interests; this third in-
> quiry involves a fourth, namely
>
> (iv) what are the limitations upon effective legal action which
> may prevent or limit the legal support which can be given even
> to interests which it is designed to secure?
>
> It is in the field of these four inquiries that Professor Pound's
> important contribution to sociological jurisprudence as distinct
> from the theory of justice has been made."[2]

The first and second of these inquiries will be discussed in the
next following part; and the third will be investigated under the
part on Remedies. It is with the fourth that we are concerned here.[3]
    This is the whole question of the extent to which the parties'
freedom of contract is limited by considerations of public policy.
The concept of public policy has of course, got its broad and
narrow signification. Broadly it is another name for the fundamental ethical, political and social principles which guide legal
evolution, whether in legislation or legal administration, at any
given time.[4] In this sense public policy is enabling and creative,
helping to shape the ethos of any given society. The utilitarians
for instance, believed in and advocated a legislative and legal
policy based on the " hedonic calculus." The narrower view of
public policy, and the one with which we are here concerned, was
recognised by the House of Lords in the old case of *Egerton* v.
Brownlow.[5] In this case Lord Alford had been given an enormous

property under a will. But there was a proviso that if he should die without having acquired the title of Duke or Marquis of Bridgewater, the gift should be void. By a majority of 11-2 the Lords were advised that the condition was valid. The House, however, accepted the minority opinion and held the condition void. Pollock, C.B. one of the judges in the House, recognised a distinct principle of public policy as

> " a principle of law which holds that no subject can lawfully do that which has a tendency to be injurious to the public, or against the public good."

In this latter and more specific sense, public policy is disabling.[6] It has been said that in English law it fulfils the limited function of supervising the validity of certain transactions in the light of principles of interpretation adapted, from time to time, to the changing needs of the community. This summary of the position by Sir Percy Winfield[7] emphasises the varying nature of public policy from one age to the other. Thus while people were very touchy on religious issues in medieval Europe and any unconventional view was treated as heresy, the principle of religious tolerance was however, recognised in the light of altered public policy in *Bowman* v. *Secular Society*[8] (in regard to secular movements) and in *Bourne* v. *Keane*[9] (in regard to catholic masses). Again, in the days of James I of England, titles and honours could be bought and sold and public policy saw nothing reprehensible in this. But the integrity of political life was recognised in the light of changed public policy in the cases of *Egerton* v. *Brownlow*,[10] and *Parkinson* v. *College of Ambulance*.[11] In each of these cases, the courts declared agreements for the sale of honours or titles to be contrary to public policy. In *Beresford* v. *Royal Insurance*,[12] however, Lord Wright brought out the limits set to judicial law-making by the recognition of changing moral ideas when he said:

> " Opinions may differ whether the suicide of a man while sane should be deemed to be a crime, but it is so regarded by our law. . . . While the law remains unchanged the court must, we think, apply the general principle that it will not allow a criminal or his representative to reap by the judgment of the court the fruits of his crime."[13]

Since the enactment of the Suicide Act, 1961, the taking of one's own life is no longer an offence in England. It is likely, therefore, that the decision of Swift, J., who heard the Beresford case at first instance, reflects the current English law position on the subject. He had held that the reprehensibility of suicide had changed sufficiently to allow the representatives of a person who had committed suicide to recover the sum for which his life was insured.[14]

Agreements and public policy in Ghana and Nigeria[15]

(A) THE IMPORTED LAW

At the date of reception of English law in Ghana (and *a fortiori* in Nigeria) the following heads of public policy had been recognised, namely

   (a) Contracts to oust the jurisdiction of the courts;[16]

   (b) Agreements that are prejudicial to the status of marriage;[17]

   (c) Agreements in unreasonable restraint of trade;[18]

   (d) Agreements contrary to morals or good manners.[19]

All these agreements were declared void by the courts on the grounds of the infringement of public policy.[20] What we propose to do here is to examine the suitability of the rules governing each of the four heads above to the local conditions existing in Ghana and Nigeria.

(a) *Contracts to oust the jurisdiction of the courts*

This has to be distinguished from transactions in which the parties do not intend to create any binding legal relations. The general rule is that contracting parties may not exclude the supervision of the courts over any agreement that they may make. Any term excluding the court's jurisdiction is void and cannot be enforced.[21] A provision for arbitration in an agreement does not come within the prohibition of this rule, provided an appeal lies to the courts at the instance of any of the parties to the agreement.[22] The court will enforce the award of the arbitration if properly made, any provisions as to the finality of the said arbitration notwithstanding. The enforcement of such an award was in issue in the Ghana case of *Angoe* v. *Nketsia*.[23] The facts were that the parties by consent agreed to refer an issue in dispute to arbitration and further undertook to treat any order of the arbitrators as final and that neither party had power under the agreement to appeal to any court. The plaintiff brought this action to enforce the award but it was argued for the defendant that the agreement was void since it tended to exclude the jurisdiction of the courts. This argument was rejected by the trial judge who held that the plaintiff was entitled to succeed in his claim. An appeal to the Full Court was dismissed. Smyly, C.J., one of the judges of the Full Court who heard the appeal, had this to say about this type of provision:

" In my opinion the agreement to submit to arbitration did not become illegal by reason of the clause in dispute, although by reason of that clause the agreement could not be made a rule of court. But I see nothing in the agreement to preclude the courts from granting specific performance of the award once it was made, and am of the opinion that any appeal from such judgment would only have reference to the judgment, and that there would be no appeal on it as to the terms of the award."[24]

In other words, if instead of the appellant raising the issue as an objection i.e. the finality of the award, he had appealed against the award on its merits, the court would not have accepted a defence based on the provision to exclude the agreement from their jurisdiction. It is submitted that there is nothing peculiarly English in this aspect of the common law. The parties are free to enter into a transaction which will not affect their legal relationships. This will be called a gentleman's agreement and the courts will not interfere. But where they have elected to alter their legal relationship, they cannot at the same time validly exclude the supervisory role of the courts.

(b) *Agreements that are prejudicial to the status of marriage*

Although marriage in the imported law sense is the union for life of one man and one woman to the exclusion of all others, the state preserves its sacrosanctity by regulating its formation and dissolution. Any agreement between two or more parties to impugn this sanctity will be void as contrary to public policy. Thus where A pays B to introduce her to prospective husbands such an agreement is void and any amount paid is recoverable.[25] Also where X promises to marry Y on the death of the latter's husband, the courts cannot sustain an action for breach of promise of marriage founded on such circumstance.[26]

This aspect of the subject is of special importance in Ghana and Nigeria where three categories of marriage are recognised, namely, the monogamous imported law variety and the potentially polygamous customary and Islamic laws varieties. If for instance a man who is married under customary law rules promises to marry another woman under the marriage Ordinance, is such a promise void as being contrary to public policy? Will it make any difference in the validity of the promise if it was made to the same woman who was already married under customary law? To attempt the answer to the former question first, such a promise if fulfilled will constitute an offence under Section 47 of the Nigerian Marriage Ordinance,[27] which provides as follows:

"Whoever contracts a marriage under the provisions of this Ordinance, or any modification or re-enactment thereof, being at the time married in accordance with native law or custom to any person other than the person with whom such marriage is contracted, shall be liable to imprisonment for five years."

It is doubtful therefore, that the courts will award any damages for the breach of a promise which, if it was fulfilled would constitute an offence. It is equally doubtful if the knowledge of the promisee as to the married status of the promisor will affect the principle. The English authorities on the effect of such knowledge do not appear to be of any guide since customary marriage is not covered by any of the Matrimonial Causes Acts (England). Again, ignorance of the law will not be acceptable as a plea by a plaintiff who is seeking to recover damages for the breach of promise.[28] The answer to the second question may well be different, since the promise if fulfilled, will not come within the prohibition of section 47 of the Ordinance. The plaintiff will not be "any person other than the person with whom such (customary) marriage is contracted." It is unlikely, however, that the promisee will get more than nominal damages.[29] Again, in Ghana and Nigeria, as in the other African countries, the practice of giving marriage consideration is still very much part of the customary law variety of marriage. There has developed a prevalent practice of carrying out these formalities even in marriages conducted under the provisions of the Marriage Ordinance.[30] This may take the form, inter alia, of giving customary drinks to the prospective bride's uncles or cousins who might help to persuade an otherwise reluctant spouse or parent. It will be a startling proposition to suggest that such gifts are void as being contrary to public policy under the rule in *Hermann* v. *Charlesworth*.[31] The fact that the Ghana Court admitted evidence of such gifts in proving the existence of an Ordinance marriage in the case of *Savage* v. *Macfoy*,[32] would tend to support the theory that such transactions will not be held by the courts to be an infringement of any head of public policy.

(c) *Agreements in restraint of trade*[33]

The modern English law position in agreements in restraint of trade has been summarised by the learned authors of *The Law of Contract*[34] as follows:

"First, the fundamental principle is that every restraint, partial as well as general, is contrary to public policy and is prima facie void. Secondly, this presumption of invalidity is rebutted by proof that the restraint is reasonable. Thirdly, the restraint must be reasonable in the interests of both contracting parties and also in the interests of the public. The onus of proving reasonableness between the parties lies upon the covenantee, but the onus of proving that the contract tends to injure the public rests with the covenantor. Fourthly, a restraint, to be reasonable between the parties, must be no wider than is reasonably necessary to protect the covenantee's interest. The existence of some proprietary interest calling for protection must first be proved, and it must then be shown to the satisfaction of the court that the restraint, as regards its area and time of operation and the trades against which it is directed, is not excessive. Finally, whether a restraint is reasonable is a question for the court, not for the jury."

In Ghana and Nigeria, however, only cases of restraint involving employers and employees have exercised the minds of the courts and in this, there has been a total reliance on the current English law position. Thus in *C.F.A.O.* v. *Leuba*,[35] Pennington Ag. C.J. in the Nigerian Full Court held void a covenant in which an assistant employed by the plaintiff in Lagos had bound himself " not to take part under any title (patron, partner, party interested or clerk) in any commercial or industrial enterprise in West Africa during a period of twelve months from the moment, when, for any reason whatsoever, he ceases to be a member of the staff of the company."

The West African Court of Appeal came to a similar conclusion on similar facts in the later case of *U.T.C.* v. *Hauri*.[36] One takes leave to doubt the wisdom of the heavy reliance on English judicial authority. Surely, restraints which have been held reasonable in England, are not necessarily so in Ghana and Nigeria. The social and economic conditions are different. Thus while a restraint excluding the appellant from competing in the trade purchased by the respondents in the whole of Europe, was found reasonable in *Nordenfelt* v. *Maxim Nordenfelt*,[37] such a holding in Ghana and Nigeria will be wholly unnecessary in view of the communications difficulties in the latter territories.

On combination for the regulation of trade relations, Part II of the Western Nigeria Co-operative Societies Law[38] provides as follows:

> " 14 (i) A registered society which has as one of its objects the disposal of any article produced or obtained by the work or industry of its members whether the produce of agriculture, animal husbandry, forestry, fisheries, hand crafts or otherwise may provide in its bye-laws or may otherwise contract with its members:
>
> (a) that every such member who produces any such article shall dispose of the whole or any specified amount, proportion or description thereof to or through the society; and

(b) that any member who is proved or adjudged in such manner as may be prescribed by the regulations to have committed a breach of the bye-laws or contract shall pay to the Society as liquidated damages a sum ascertained or assessed in such manner as may be prescribed by the aforesaid regulations.

(2) No contract entered into under the provision of this section shall be contested in any court on the ground only that it constitutes a contract in restraint of trade."

This provision reverses the common law position with regard to agreements between members of the society. At common law any such restriction is void and cannot be enforced unless it is reasonable between the parties and consistent with the interests of the public.[39] Under the Co-operative Societies laws, however, reasonableness and consistency with public interest are presumed. The object of the enactment is, of course, to improve credit and marketing facilities for the members. Any restraint on their freedom of action is the sacrifice they make in the attainment of better economic security.[40]

(d) *Agreements that are contrary to morals or good manners*

Most of the agreements under this sub-head also come under contracts that are prejudicial to the status of marriage. There is, however, a residual group which belong to no other head of public policy and are therefore lumped together under agreements that are contrary to morals or good manners. Agreements that derogate from the dignity of national honours[41] come under this category.

(B) CUSTOMARY AND ISLAMIC LAW

(i) *Customary law*

Customary law also recognises and imposes limits to the freedom of the parties to make any agreement they please. These limits do not and need not coincide with the existing heads of public policy under the imported law, but like the latter, they vary in form and content from one society to the other. The example of sales of family property without the necessary consents has already been discussed. It is enough to mention here that such sales are merely void and not illegal, and that they are void on the generally recognised principle that only an authorised body can make a valid alienation of family property.

Other limits on contractual freedom have been imposed by the Akans (Ghana). Concubinage agreements are frowned on by the society and the parties are not allowed to recover what has passed between them as a result of the relationship. Sarbah has set out the limits of the application of this custom in the chapter on Marriage in his *Fanti Customary Laws*.[42] Thus, the validity of any collateral transaction during the currency of the relationship is not affected by the principle. This was the decision in the case of *Hughes* v. *Davies*,[43] where the Full Court allowed the plaintiff to recover a loan made to the defendant for trading purposes. Transactions between the parties after the termination of the relationship are also not affected by the Sarwie custom. This exception to the rule, was in issue in the Full Court decision of *Ansa* v. *Sackey*.[44] In this case one Prince Albert Ansa had, 19 years earlier, had a child with his mistress Emma Akua Sackey. The plaintiff had left the then Gold Coast for England, while the defendant was in a petty trading business. The plaintiff sent certain empty bags to the defendant on the expressed intention that the latter should dispose of the bags and forward the proceeds to the plaintiff. The bags were sold but the defendant kept the proceeds and when sued by the plaintiff's attorney, pleaded the Sarwie custom. The trial judge rejected the defendant's plea and held in favour of the plaintiff. This was upheld by the Full Court on appeal.[45]

(ii) *Islamic law*

It has aptly been pointed out by a learned author that Islamic law does not recognise the liberty of contract, but it provides an appreciable measure of freedom within certain fixed types. Freedom of contract would, of course, be incompatible with the ethical control of legal transactions.[46] As a result, those transactions which are forbidden by the principle of the *sharia* cannot be enforced as valid agreements. They are void, or as they are more often described in Islamic law, fásid.[47] We shall be looking at some of these transactions.

Firstly, any agreement which contravenes the rules prohibiting *ribā* is *fásid*. Ribā has been defined as "a monetary advantage without a countervalue which has been stipulated in favour of one of the two contracting parties in an exchange of two monetary values."[48] This rule is, of course, part of the general policy of the sharia which frowns at any cases of unjust enrichment. Under this rule the sharia prohibits the reletting of a hired object for a greater sum, the re-selling at a higher price of a bought object before payment has been made for it; and the taking of interest generally. The rules prohibiting ribā are only applicable, however, to objects which can be valued and weighed and in addition, belong to the same species. Where these conditions are satisfied, any excess in quality or delay in performance are forbidden. Any agreement concluded in contravention of these rules is fásid. Where, however, the objects are different, e.g. dates and rice, or the object cannot be measured or weighed, e.g. cloth made of one material with another made from another material, the rules against ribā do not apply but under no circumstances will delay in performance be permitted.

Another category of agreement that is forbidden by the shariā is the undertaking of risk (gharar). This prohibition has been traced back to the Koranic attitude towards a certain game of hazard called *maysir*. Thus the shariā insists that there must be no doubt concerning the obligations undertaken by the parties to an agreement. An example of this type of agreement is the selling of unripened dates to be delivered when ripened. Such a transaction is fásid. Following from the prohibition against the undertaking of risk, gambling and other aleatory transactions are fásid under the shariā. Two exceptions have, however, been recognised, namely agreements making provisions for prizes for the winner or winners of horseraces. This is because of the importance horsemanship played during the holy war. Another predictable exception is an agreement for prizes for the winner or winners of competitions concerning knowledge of Islamic law.

A third instance of the limits placed on the contractual freedom of a moslem by the shariā is the prohibition against a stipulation in a contract of sale (bay') which provision is collateral to the main purpose of an agreement. Such a stipulation is fásid, and any sale that takes place conveys an invalid title and can be set aside. The right of rescission is, however, lost when the article has been resold by the purchaser.[49]

Other prohibitions connected with sale include the rule against the sale of a carcase. Any such sale is void since a carcase is not a proper subject matter of ownership in Islamic jurisprudence.[50] Another one is the conclusion of an agreement at the time of the call to the Friday prayer. Such an agreement has been said to be reprehensible but not void, by Schacht,[51] but Ruxton[52] is of the view that such a contract is fásid. Here, one is, of course, up against the profound problem of translating arabic terms into their precise English law equivalents. In view, however, of the importance of the Friday prayer in the life of a moslem, Ruxton's view appears to be the more logical one. Such a conclusion also compares favourably with the effect of certain agreements that are concluded on a Sunday in contravention of the Sunday Observance Act.[53]

The problems posed

Two problems would seem to be posed by the above limits on

the contractual freedom of a moslem. The first is how a rigid application of the prohibitions would be reconciled to any theory of economic development generally and the advancement of commerce in particular. How could the rules prohibiting ribā be reconciled to hire-purchase and moneylending transactions or to the idea of economic co-operatives? How could the law of insurance be developed if the shariā is so rigid in its prohibition against the assumption of risk? Could these two facets of the shariā be harmonised with the general welfare of the state, the guide-light in most instances of public policy? The answers to these lie partially in the degree to which the ideal theory of the shariā succeeded in imposing itself on the practice of commercial life. There is little doubt that the grip of theory over practice was very firm in the field of family law and the law of wakf (i.e. pious foundations), and weakest or even non-existent on penal law, taxation, constitutional law and the law of war.

The law of contractual obligations appears to occupy an intermediate position between the two extremes. Here, although the shariā had to resign an ever increasing sphere of its influence and rules to practice and custom, its main principles and institutions were respected. This was achieved with the aid of legal fictions or hiyal,[54] as it is called in Islamic law parlance. An example of this is the circumvention of the prohibition against the taking of interest in moneylending or hire-purchase transactions. A prospective debtor could purport to sell some valuable security[55] to a prospective lender at a price of say £40 and would immediately re-purchase the security for £60. While the original £40 was paid in cash, the latter £60 was not. It was a loan on the security of an object but with £20 interest. Since the Kadis in Islamic law were encouraged to look at the form and not the substance of any transaction for purposes of the prohibition of the shariā, there was nothing reprehensible in this sort of arrangement, and it has been widely used in other types of transactions.[56] Also, the prohibition against the undertaking of risk, was reconciled to the needs of commerce by a resort to a type of credit co-operative (Sharikat alwujuh) and the sleeping partnership (Mudaraba). In the former the partners pool their credit for buying goods, resell them and share the profit, while in the latter the active partner occupied a fiduciary relationship in respect of the interest of the sleeping partner and any profits are shared by the parties.

In this way, the strict requirements of the shariā are tempered by the needs of commerce. The resulting conflict is not as serious as the theory would tend to indicate.

The second problem is the one posed by the involvement of a

T

non-moslem in a particular transaction. This raises the issue of internal conflict of laws which will be more fully discussed in the next following part. It is enough to point out at this stage that this aspect of the issue has not agitated the courts in either Ghana or Nigeria in the field of obligations. This is understandable in view of the fact that the bulk of commercial activity is in the hands of non-religious bodies. These bodies employ labour, award contracts, appoint local buying agents, and do other types of business. It will be unlikely that they would voluntarily opt for the application of the principles of the sharia to govern their transactions with a moslem. Short of legislative imposition (a rather remote contingency), the problem of internal conflicts in transactions between moslems and non-moslems in Ghana and Nigeria is unlikely to assume any importance in the law of obligations in the two countries.[57]

NOTES

1. We are not here concerned with the origin, history and development of the concept of public policy in English law. For these, see: Knight, " Public Policy in English Law " (1922) 38 L.Q.R. 207; P. Winfield, " Public Policy in the English Common Law " (1928) 42 Harry. L.R. 78 (reprinted in *Select Legal Essays* (1952), p. 241); also " Ethics in English Case Law " (1931) 45 Harv. L.R. 112 (reprinted in *Essays*, p. 266); Gelhorn, " Contracts and Public Policy " (1935) 35 Col. L.R. 679; Lord Mansfield, C.J. in *Holman* v. *Johnson* (1775) 98 E.R. 1120; Julius Stone, *The Province and Function of Law* (1950), pp. 494-504; D. Lloyd, *Public Policy* (Athlone Press, 1953); W. Friedmann, *Legal Theory* (4th ed.), pp. 444-453. For public policy in Islamic law, see J. Schacht, *Introduction to Islamic law* (Oxford, 1964) Chaps. 20 and 21; L. Milliot, *Introduction a l'etude du droit musulman* (Paris), S. 792. On customary laws see R. S. Rattray, *Ashanti law and Constitution* (London, 1956), pp. 294 et seq.; M. Green, *Ibo Village Affairs* (London, 1947); C. K. Meek, *Law and Authority in a Nigerian Tribe* (Oxford, 1937); P. Bohannan, *Justice and Judgment among the Tiv* (Oxford, 1957) passim.
2. Stone, op. cit., chap. 20.
3. For other aspects of this fourth inquiry, see the discussion on incapacity, informality and illegality.
4. Friedmann, op. cit., p. 444.
5. (1853) 4 H.L. Cas. 1.
6. It could be said that illegal contracts come under this head as well. In a general way this is true, but contracts void on the ground of infringement of public policy in the specific sense mentioned above form a separate category of agreements from those that are illegal.
7. " Ethics in English Case Law ", supra.
8. (1917) A.C. 406.
9. (1919) A.C. 815.
10. (1853) 4 H.L. Cas. 1.
11. (1924) All E.R. 325.

12. (1937) 2 K.B. 197. Cf. *Cleaver* v. *Mutual Reserve Fund Life Association* (1892) 1 Q.B. 147, where a third party beneficiary was allowed to recover.
13. At p. 219.
14. Other instances of variation in public policy have also been recognised by the courts. In *Rodriguez* v. *Speyer* (1919) A.C. 116, the majority of the House of Lords held that the degree to which intercourse with enemies is prohibited in war was a matter not of strict law but of public policy. The extent to which the sanctity of the marriage tie prevented freedom of action where the spouses had obtained a decree nisi was decided in *Fender* v. *Mildmay* (1938) A.C. 1; when a bare majority decided that a spouse, after decree nisi, could make a valid promise of marriage. The rules about restraint of trade cases, and the concept of natural justice in trade union and other group expulsion cases, are other facets of the varying nature of public policy from one age to the other.
15. The controversy between those who argue that no new head of public policy can now be invented (often called the restrictionists) and those who assert that the courts are free to explore new ground, need not detain us here. For this see Julius Stone, op. cit., pp. 494-501, and W. Friedmann, op. cit., pp. 445 et seq.
16. *Thompson* v. *Charnock* (1799) 8 Term Rep. 139.
17. *Lowe* v. *Peers* (1768) 4 Burr. 2225.
18. *Mitchel* v. *Reynolds* (1711) 1 P. Wms. 181.
19. *Egerton* v. *Brownlow* (1853) 4 H.L. Cas. 1.
20. Public policy has also been used in Nigeria and Ghana to disallow any rules of customary law which the courts consider to be contrary to natural justice, equity and good conscience.
21. *Goodinson* v. *Goodinson* (1954) 2 Q.B. 118.
22. *Scott* v. *Avery* (1856) 5 H.L. Cas. 811.
23. (1920-21) F. Ct. 75.
24. Op. cit. at p. 76.
25. *Hermann* v. *Charlesworth* (1905) 2 K.B. 123.
26. *Wilson* v. *Carnley* (1908) 1 K.B. 729.
27. Cap. 115, *Laws of Nigeria* (1958 Revision).
28. The reverse position i.e. where a person married under the Ordinance promises to marry another under the customary law will be covered by section 48 of the Ordinance. But customary breach of promise actions are uncommon.
29. See *Ugboma* v. *Morah* (1940) 15 N.L.R. 78. See also the Ghana case of *Ayeh* v. *Kumordzie* (1965) C. Cases, 45.
30. See *Savage* v. *Macfoy* (1909) Ren. 504. See also the Eastern Nigeria Limitation of Dowry Law, No. 23 of 1956, which tacitly recognised the concept of incidental expenses.
31. (1905) 2 K.B. 123.
32. Supra. (N. 10).
33. There are of course three facets of this category of contracts, namely those between employees and employers; those between vendors and purchasers of businesses; and those between manufacturers or merchants. It has not been considered necessary to discuss these in any detail because of heavy reliance on English judicial authority.
34. Cheshire and Fifoot (6th ed.), p. 328.
35. (1918) 3 N.L.R. 60.

36. (1940) 6 W.A.C.A. 148. See also *John Holt & Co. Ltd.* v. *Chalmers* (1918) 3 N.L.R. 69.

37. (1894) A.C. 535.

38. Cap. 26 of 1959, Laws of Western Nigeria. See also S. 16 of the Eastern Nigeria Co-operative Societies law, Cap. 28, Laws of Eastern Nigeria (163 consolidation); and S. 14 of the Northern Nigeria Co-operative Societies law, Cap. 26, Laws of Northern Nigeria (1963).

39. *McEllistrim* v. *Ballymacelligott Co-operative Agricultural and Dairy Society* (1919) A.C. 548.

40. See the dictum of Scrutton, L.J. in the English case of *English Hop Growers* v. *Dering* (1928) 2 K.B. 174 at p. 181: " There was nothing unreasonable in hop growers combining to secure a steady and profitable price, by eliminating competition amongst themselves, and putting the marketing in the hands of one agent, with full power to fix prices and hold up supplies, the benefit and loss being divided amongst the members."

41. *Parkinson* v. *College of Ambulance* (1924) All E.R. 325.

42. At p. 42, " A woman living in concubinage cannot sue the man with whom she is so living for any maintenance, nor can her family or parents sue the man for any satisfaction or maintenance. Whatever is given or entrusted by a man or woman, to the person with whom he or she is living in concubinage cannot be reclaimed on any consideration whatsoever. This custom is called ' Sarwie '."

43. (1909) Ren. 550.

44. (1923-25) F. Ct. 113.

45. Other agreements that will be held void on grounds of the infringement of public policy include marriage within the prohibited degrees of relationship; among the Ibos and the Yorubas (Nigeria) any agreement for service to be performed on any of the days on which local bye-law prohibits people going to farm; and any agreement for the cutting of palm fruits on a communal land when the cutting season has not been officially opened. On these, see R. S. Rattray, *Ashanti law and constitution* (London, 1947), pp. 292 et seq.; C. K. Meek, *Law and Authority in a Nigerian Tribe* (London, O.U.P., 1937), pp. 17 et seq.; and pp. 207 et seq.; M. Green, *Ibo Village Affairs* (London, 1947), pp. 32-48, 149 et seq. On the Tiv, see P. Bohannan, *Justice and Judgment Among the Tiv* (London, O.U.P., 1957), pp. 70 et seq.

46. J. Schacht, *Introduction to Islamic Law* (Oxford, 1964), p. 144.

47. We are only concerned with the concept of *fásid* in obligations created by agreement.

48. J. Schacht, op. cit., p. 145.

49. If, for instance, one buys leather on condition that the seller should make it into shoes, the contract would be *fásid* under the above rule, but this prohibition has not been strictly observed. It has in fact been suggested that the contract is valid, e.g. by *istihsan*.

50. Abdur Rahim, *Muhammedan Jurisprudence*, p. 200.

51. Op. cit., p. 152.

52. F. H. Buxton, *Maliki Law* (London, 1916). The learned author may of course be stating the position in the Maliki School. Schacht was describing the general position.

53. See the Ghana case of *Testa & Co.* v. *Duncan* (1926-29) Div. Ct. 191, where the Act was said to be in force in Ghana. It is doubtful, however, that this decision will be widely followed today.

54. This has been defined as the use of legal means for extra-legal ends,

ends that could not, whether they themselves were legal or illegal, be achieved directly with the means provided by the sharia.

55. Before the abolition of slave trade and slavery, this type of security used to be a slave.

56. e.g. to overcome the rule about the irrevocability of a sale of land, borrowers have devised a means whereby money is obtained from a lender on the security of land; the lender making use of the land in the meantime and reconveying to the borrower when the loan is repaid. This device also circumvents the prohibition against the taking of interest. The use of the land by the lender constituted the interest paid on the loan.

57. S. 5 of the Civil Justice Ordinance of the Sudan excludes the application of Islamic law in commercial transactions. There is no such provision in the Northern Nigeria High Court law but most of the reported decisions in the Superior Courts of the Region in this branch of the law, have been based on imported law rules. Cf. *Alhaji Amadu "John Holt"* v. *Idah* (1956) N.R.N.L.R. 81 (on defect discovered after sale); and *Dan Juma* v. *Standard Co. of Nigeria, Ltd.* (1922) 4 N.L.R. 52, on acceptance of groundnuts.

CHAPTER 16

DEFECTS DUE TO IMPOSSIBILITY OF PERFORMANCE

We have so far been examining defective agreements in the light of

(a) defects in reaching an agreement; and

(b) defects in the validity of an agreement.

In this section we shall be investigating agreements which have become defective because of an impossibility of performance. In this respect it is important to state and discuss the distinction between initial impossibility and supervening impossibility. While the former properly belongs to the creation of agreements (thus preventing such creation, e.g. defective consent), the latter concerns the question of frustration. The former was fully discussed under (a) above, and it is with the latter that we are here concerned.

The doctrine of frustration

It can be said that the judicial supervision of the creation and performance of agreements reached its apogee in the invention of the doctrine of frustration. It is unquestionably illogical that the courts whose primary duty is and should be the enforcement of contracts that are valid for all purposes, should refuse this enforcement on the ground that the parties have undertaken what in the court's opinion, is an impossibility. This doctrinal ambivalence led to a very restricted definition[1] of the concept of frustration and has become an inherent source of weakness in its growth and development. Yet it is in the overall interest of the society that when the basis on which the parties contracted has altered, or the performance of an agreement, has become illegal after the making of such an agreement, or performance will make the contract radically different from the one in the contemplation of the parties at the time of the making, the law should intervene to put them on terms. This is what the doctrine of frustration is about, and although judicial and legislative caution have so far prevailed, there is little doubt that the doctrine is being used as a check on the freedom of the parties to insist on the performance of certain agreements or certain terms thereof.

The origin and development of the doctrine in the common law need not detain us here. It must, however, be mentioned that the old case of *Taylor* v. *Caldwell*[2] has often been cited as the beginning of its recognition by the courts. In that case the plaintiffs entered into an agreement with the defendants for the hire of a certain music hall for the purpose of giving a series of concerts. Before the series was due to begin, the hall was destroyed by accidental fire. In an action for damages for breach of contract, it was held that the destruction of the hall excused both parties from the performance of their promises. In English law there is considerable doubt as to whether or not the doctrine of frustration applies to leases.[3]

Extent to which doctrine applies

There is no doubt that *Taylor* v. *Caldwell*,[4] on which case the common law doctrine is based, is part of the imported laws of Ghana and Nigeria, being decided in 1863. What is not so obvious is whether the *Schlesinger* and *Cricklewood Properties* line of cases, which excluded executed leases from the operation of the doctrine, will be followed by the courts of Ghana and Nigeria. Both cases are post-1900 decisions of English courts, and it has already been convincingly argued in another place that such decisions are not binding on Ghana and Nigerian courts. It is suggested that the doctrine of frustration should apply to leases whether executory or executed, as much as it applies to any other category of contracts. The reasons given by Lush, J. in the *Schlesinger* case for excluding leases, and his basis of distinguishing leases from other categories of contracts are, it is submitted with respect, tenuous and unpersuasive. His Lordship had this to say:

> " It is not correct to speak of this tenancy agreement as a contract and nothing more. A term of years was created by it and vested in the appellant, and I can see no reason for saying that, because this order disqualified him from personally residing in the flat, it affected the chattel interest which was vested in him by virtue of the agreement."[5]

In view of the fact that what the doctrine of frustration sets out to achieve is the disengagement of the parties when the basis on which they contracted has radically changed, it is not easy to evaluate the importance of the distinction which his Lordship tried to draw between leases and other types of contract. This distinction becomes more farcical when executory leases are held to come within the operation of the doctrine.[6] The conflicting opinions of their Lordships of the House of Lords in the *Crickle-wood* decision as to whether or not the doctrine applies to executed leases, emphasised the sterile nature of the argument for their exclusion.[7] It is difficult to distinguish between a contract for the delivery of machinery which was held to have become frustrated as a result of the outbreak of war, and a lease of a flat in which the lessee can no longer reside, also because of the outbreak of war. It is not enough to argue that such an alien enemy could sub-let to a national who could then pay the reserved rent to the superior landlord, since even the sub-lease will be held illegal as an agreement with an alien enemy.[8] It is therefore submitted that the exclusion of executed leases from the operation of the doctrine of frustration in English law, is unnecessary, and should not be followed in either Ghana or Nigeria.

Legal consequences of holding an agreement frustrated

What are the rights and duties of the parties to an agreement when the doctrine of frustration has operated to bring their contract or any terms thereof, to an end? This is the question that we have to investigate in this sub-section. Lord Wright attempted to summarise the position at common law in the *Fibrosa*[9] case, when he said that " The contract is automatically terminated as to the future, because at that date its further performance becomes impossible in fact, in circumstances which involve no liability for damages for the failure on either side." The vital question is whether, after the occurrence of the frustrating event, any rights which had accrued earlier could be enforced and any sums paid in pursuance of the agreement before the frustration, are refundable. In this respect two streams of authority developed at common law. The first was the one relating to entire contracts which had its origin in the case of *Cutter* v. *Powell*.[10] In that case it was held that " if a sailor hired for a voyage, takes a promissory note from his employer for a certain sum, provided he proceed, continue, and do his duty on board for the voyage, but before the arrival of the ship he dies, no wages can be claimed either on the contract or on a *quantum meruit*. This principle operated to bar a plaintiff's claim for the value of work done on a premises which agreement provided for payment at the completion of the work but the premises was burnt down before the said completion.[11] In such cases the plaintiff recovers nothing since no right accrued before the completion of the assignment. There are, however, some exceptions to the rule in *Cutter* v. *Powell*.[12] The other stream of authority was that based on the curious case of *Chandler* v. *Webster*[13] to the effect that after the frustrating event, the loss lies where it falls. Thus in such a case, accrued rights are enforceable and any money paid in pursuance of the agreement is not recoverable. This rule was the target of severe judicial criticism in the House of Lords in the *Fibrosa* case. Lord Shaw described it as a maxim that worked well enough among tricksters, gamblers and thieves. In the earlier case of *Russkoe Obschestvotvo d'lia Izgstovlenia* v. *John Stirk & Sons Ltd*,[14] Atkin, L.J. had doubted whether any two business people in the world would ever make a contract which embodied such a doctrine as *Chandler* v. *Webster* laid down. It is not surprising, therefore, that the rule was rejected by the House of Lords in the *Fibrosa* case. The current English law position in this second facet of frustrated contracts, is that contained in the Law Reform (Frustrated Contracts) Act, 1943, which recognises the problem posed by *Chandler* v. *Webster* and empowered the courts to order the refund of any sums that had passed having regard to the rights of the parties and the circumstances of the case.

The position in Ghana and Nigeria

The position in Ghana and the various jurisdictions in Nigeria is a bit confused. Part I of the Ghana Contracts Act, 1960[15] has adopted the English law position on the rights and duties of the parties after a contract has been held frustrated. In Nigeria, the English legislation on the subject has been copied in the Law Reform (Contracts) Act, 1961[16] (Federation), and the Western Nigeria Contracts Law[17] which is also in force in the Mid-Western Region. It is not clear if the courts of Eastern and Northern Nigeria will still prefer to follow *Chandler* v. *Webster* or the later House of Lords decision in the *Fibrosa* case. A case for prompt legislative action in this aspect of the law in the two latter regions can hardly be overemphasised.

Critique of the position

Having said this, one has to advert to the confusion in this branch of the law in Ghana and Nigeria, and the limited scope of the enactments on the subject to date. Surely, the legislature ought to do something to clear the doubts there are as to the application of the doctrine. In English law it is still not clear if it applies to leases. The Act of 1943 did not tackle the problem of the limits of the doctrine in any serious way. By copying the English enactment without comment, the legislatures in Ghana and Nigeria perpetuated the uncertainty and did nothing to remove the existing confusion.

Secondly, neither the Nigerian nor the Ghana enactments made any attempt to get round the anomalous situation created by the rule in *Cutter* v. *Powell*. Consequently, it is still possible to argue that the Acts do not apply to entire contracts. In fact Section 9 of the Western Nigeria enactment which is in similar terms to the Ghana and Nigerian (Lagos) provisions, lends greater weight to the argument that *Cutter* v. *Powell* is still very much in force. This section provides as follows:

> "Where any contract to which this part applies contains any provision which, upon the true construction of the contract, is intended to have effect in the event of circumstances arising which operate, or would but for the said provision operate, to frustrate the contract, or is intended to have effect whether such circumstances arise or not, the court shall give effect to the said provision and shall only give effect to the provisions of this part to such extent (if any) as appears to the court to be consistent with the said provision."[18]

In other words, if as happened in the *Powell* case, A agrees to pay B a specified sum on the completion of a voyage, the fact that B dies just before the said completion of the voyage will not be considered as frustrating the further performance of the agreement for purposes of the Act. It is submitted that the better position would be to allow recovery on a quantum meruit, having regard to all the circumstances. In this connection Section 40 of the Apportionment Act, 1870 (England) appears to be more happily worded for purposes of doing justice between the parties to a partnership.

NOTES

1. For instance, if the parties knowingly contract to do what is physically impossible, the court will not apply the doctrine to discharge them from their obligations. There is also the serious doubt as to the application of the doctrine to leases in English law. See the Ghana case of *Teming Amoako* v. *Bartholomew & Co.* (1955) 1. W.A.L.R. 4.
2. (1863) 3 B & S. 826. It was in this case that the old rule as to absolute contracts as enunciated in the case of *Paradine* v. *Jane* (1647) Aleyn, 26, was limited by the acceptance of the doctrine of frustration. Cf. *London and Northern Estates Co.* v. *Schlesinger* (1916) 1 K.B. 20, where it was held that the rule did not apply to leases.
3. See *Cricklewood Property and Investment Trust Ltd.* v. *Leighton's Investment Trust Ltd.* (1945) A.C. 221.
4. (1863) 3 B & S. 826.
5. At p. 24. The facts of the case were that the defendant, an Austrian, was a lessee of a flat at Westcliff-on-Sea. On the outbreak of war the defendant became an alien enemy and as such was prohibited from living in certain places, including the place where the flat was situate.

Refusing to pay his rent, the plaintiffs brought this action to recover it. The plea of frustration was rejected by the court and judgment was entered for the plaintiffs.

6. *Cricklewood Property & Investment Trust Ltd.* v. *Leighton's Investment Trust Ltd* (1945) A.C. 221.

7. Compare the opinions of Lords Simon and Wright who held that the doctrine equally applies to leases, and those of Lords Russel of Killowen and Goddard, L.C.J.; who argued in favour of the exclusion, in the *Cricklewood* decision.

8. See *Furtado* v. *Rogers* (1802) 3 Bos. & P. 191.

9. (1943) A.C. 32, at p. 70.

10. (1795) 6 T.R. 320.

11. *Appleby* v. *Myers* (1867) L.R. 2 C.P. 651. See also *Whincup* v. *Hughes* 1871) L.R. 6 C.P. 78.

12. The rule does not apply (1) where the parties agreed to rescind and substitute a new contract; (2) where the completion of the assignment was prevented by the other party to the agreement; (3) where the contract has been substantially performed; and (4) where the impossibility arose from factors unconnected with the contract. See *Dakin* v. *Lee* (1916) 1 K.B. 566. C.A.

13. (1904) 1 K.B. 493 (C.A.).

14. (1942) 1 K.B. 12 at p. 28. See also Cmnd. 6009 of 1939, where the Law Revision Commission (England) criticised the rule.

15. Act. 25.

16. No. 64 of 1961.

17. Cap. 25, Laws of Western Nigeria (1959 Revision).

18. See also S. 3 (2) of the Law Reform (Contracts) Act, 1961 (Nigeria, Federation) and S. 3 of the Ghana Contracts Act, 1960 (Act 25).

PART V

OBLIGATIONS CREATED BY
AGREEMENTS: A FUNCTIONAL
ANALYSIS[1]

INTRODUCTORY NOTE

In this part we propose firstly to examine the role of the courts[2] in Ghana and Nigeria in the construction of obligations created by agreement, and secondly the place of agreements as an integral part of the legal systems of the two countries. The importance of a functional reappraisal of agreements can hardly be over-emphasised. Several factors account for this importance of which the following are but a few:

Firstly, an agreement, it has been said, is a set of promises which the law will enforce.[3] The primary role of the courts, therefore, has been to delimit the scope and interpret the sense of the promises exchanged by the parties. If, in the opinion of the court, no agreement has been created, then that is the end of the matter, at any rate as far as enforcing the obligations created by the alleged agreement goes. The way the courts have construed the terms of an agreement, therefore, assumes a new importance in an analysis of the law of obligations.

Secondly, Professor Kahn Freund has recently described " the implied intention of the parties " to an agreement as a " protective cover behind which the judges legislate in many countries."[4] How far is this statement representative of the positions in Ghana and Nigeria?

Thirdly, there is the vital phenomenon of the changing nature of the concept of agreement brought about by modern economic trends. Multiple firms and large monopolistic combines are in fact replacing the small trader and the family company. Equality of bargaining power which was an essential attribute of agreements has yielded place to standard-form contracts in which strange things are done in the name of equality. The menace of exception clauses has posed many unanswered questions about the suitability of the existing rules of contract in the solution of modern economic and social problems. What are the Ghana and Nigerian courts doing and what is yet to be done in this sphere of the law?

Finally, one of the primary functions of the state is to balance the realisation of reasonable individual expectations with the overall interest of the Society. To what extent have the legislatures in Ghana and Nigeria adverted to this postulate and what measure of success has there been so far? The answer to these and to many ancillary questions will be attempted in this chapter.

NOTES

1. See W. Friedman, *Law in a Changing Society* (London, 1959), Chapter 4; B. N. Cardozo, *The Nature of the Judicial Process* (New Haven, Yale Univ. Press, 1925); F. P. Walton, *The Egyptian Law of Obligations* (London, 1920), Vol. 11, pp. 261-285; M. S. Amos, " Common law and Civil law in the British Commonwealth " (1937) 50 Harv. L.R. 1249; C. K. Allen, " The Judge as a man of the world " (1930) 46 L.Q.R. 151; L. Duguit, " Collective acts as distinguished from Contracts " (1930) 27, Yale L.J. 753; SS. 2-302, *United States Uniform Commercial Code*; Hale, " Bargaining, Duress and Economic Liberty " (1930) 43 Col. L.R. 603.
2. Courts here are used to mean both the Superior and Customary Courts so far as the decisions of the latter are ascertainable.
3. *Anson's Law of Contract* (22nd ed., 1964), Intr. Chap.
4. An Inaugural lecture delivered to the University of Oxford on 12th May, 1965—" Comparative law as an academic subject."

CHAPTER 17

AGREEMENTS AND THE COURTS

" The function of the court is not to carry out a psychological investigation, but to interpret the sense of the reciprocal declarations in a manner which was commonly accepted by the parties, or, in the absence of a commonly accepted particular sense, in such a way as a reasonable man would understand them in the circumstances."[1]

The above statement by Dean Roscoe Pound summarises the basic attitude of Anglo-American jurisprudence with regard to the construction of agreements by the courts. Their concern is not what the parties willed, but a reasonable construction of the external manifestations of their dealing. This is what has often been called the objective theory of contracts. The exceptions to its general application in English law have been recognised in cases of misrepresentation, fraud, duress, undue influence, and defective consent (i.e. mistake). This approach has often been contrasted with the " will " or subjective theory of contracts in the continental systems. Here the courts set out to discover what the parties willed and will enforce such a " will " as the contract between them. It must be stressed, however, that the gap between the subjective and objective theories is not as wide as it has often been made to appear. The basic similarities between the English and the continental approaches to the interpretation of agreements need not detain us here. Our concern is to examine the role of the courts in Ghana and Nigeria in the enforcement of agreements. For this purpose we shall be looking at the roles of both the customary and superior courts.

(i) Customary[2] Courts

Here mention must again be made of the civil jurisdiction of these courts. In Ghana before their abolition by the Courts Decree, 1966,[3] the Local Courts had jurisdiction to hear personal şuits where the debt, damage or demand does not exceed £100.[4] Thus the courts administered both the customary and imported laws according to the nature of the transaction or the intentions of the parties. In Northern Nigeria Sections 23 and 24 (4) of the Native

265

Courts Law[5] empower the native courts to apply both English and native law with similar qualifications to those in the Ghana enactment. These provisions have been repeated in the Area Courts Edict, 1967. Corresponding provisions are also found in the Eastern, Western and Mid-Western Regions of Nigeria. The question that arises here is, what factors guide the courts in determining and enforcing the terms of an agreement? In other words, on what ethical assumptions are their decisions based? This question must be distinguished from the issue of the intentions of the parties as to the law applicable (i.e. whether it is native or the imported law that applies to the transaction). To go back to the former question, a close study of the decisions of several customary courts in Ghana[6] and Nigeria has not revealed any sound basis for extracting some general principles on the factors that guide them in coming to their decisions. What one finds is a more or less general pattern of a given set of facts and a decision on the facts by the court. There is a remarkable dearth of reasoned judgments. The following ten cases taken from two local court areas in Ghana for the year 1963-64 will illustrate our point here.

A. AMENGI LOCAL COURT—AKROPONG

1. *Johnson Ikoro* v. *Samuel Omoware*
   Suit No. 13/64.

Plaintiff claims from the defendant the sum of £70 amount defendant received from the plaintiff as dowry in respect of a marriage between plaintiff and Rosaline, a daughter of the plaintiff; but defendant having received the said sum despatched the said Rosaline to Nigeria without the knowledge and consent of the plaintiff and the defendant has refused to refund the money to the plaintiff.

Judgment—in favour of plaintiff for £70 with £4.11.6d. costs.

It is not clear here whether the plaintiff sued for breach of promise of marriage or on a total failure of consideration. The decision appears to be based on the latter head.

2. *Ama Ediyaah* v. *Offori*
   Suit No. 232/62.

Plaintiff claims £1.5s. from defendant being the cost of fufu bought from plaintiff's chop bar and defendant has failed payment upon several demands.

Judgment—for plaintiff for £1.5s. plus costs at £1.10s

making a total of £2.15s. I order that defendant pays the amount in full at the end of current month (i.e. the month of November, 1962).

Perhaps the court was influenced here by the importance of the plaintiff's service to the community through his chop bar business. The amount of £1.10s. costs on a claim for £1.5s. is obviously very excessive.

3. *Kwame Enin* v. *Eyewfi*
Suit No. 16/63.

Plaintiff claims £11.13s. from the defendant. £10 being money defendant obtained from the plaintiff for clearing a rice farm and £1.13s. being expenses incurred by plaintiff during the demands which the defendant has failed payment since 12 years ago.

Court—I enter judgment for plaintiff for £10 plus costs at £1.17s.6d. I order that the defendant pays the costs.

In this case nothing appears to have been said about the debt being statute-barred. All the parties appear to have presumed the application of native law. The fact that the plaintiff has got more than he claimed tends to indicate that the court places great importance on the performance of promises. In this case, it is of course in the general interest of agriculture that such promises be kept.

4. *Kojo Addae* v. *Kwabina Ansah*
Suit No. 269/63.

Plaintiff sues for judicial relief for defendant to show cause why he should refuse to give ⅓ share of corn from farm to plaintiff's niece Gyanea, whom the defendant has stayed with as concubine since three years and the defendant could not perform marriageable contingencies until defendant separated her—contrary to Wasa Amengi marriage Bye laws.

Judgment—in favour of plaintiff with costs assessed at £6.8s.6d. Plaintiff's niece is entitled to ⅓ share of the corn which is reaped at present and also ⅓ share of the farm itself.

Quite apart from this case being evidence of specific performance in the customary courts (not to say anything about illegal contracts, i.e. immoral), one finds here an instance of the courts enforcing what the parties willed at the inception of their obligations.

5. *Kofie Ampong* v. *Amoaful*
   Suit No. 14/64.

Plaintiff claims judicial relief for the defendant to show cause why the defendant should sell the cocoa proceeds and fail to give the plaintiff's share of ⅓ as already scheduled by both parties.

Judgment—for plaintiff with costs assessed at £9.15s.6d. Plaintiff is entitled to ⅓ share of all proceeds realised from the cocoa by the defendant.

Here is another instance of the court enforcing the will of the parties.

B. KADE AKWATIA LOCAL COURT, EASTERN REGION

1. *Kwasi Odame* v. *Kwadjo Danso & ors*
   Suit No. 291/63.

Plaintiff claims from the defendants the sum of £8 being amount received from plaintiff by E. K. Boadi with intent to give plaintiff a land to build a house as per receipt on hand dated 19th November, 1957, and defendant has refused plaintiff the land, as defendant has refused payment of the money after incessant demands.

Here it is doubtful if the plaintiff could have obtained specific performance of the sale of land. Ollennu seems to suggest he would.[7]

2. *Suit No. 407/63.*

Plaintiff claims from the defendant the sum of £30 being cost of cover cloths plaintiff gave to defendant for washing; which said cover cloths defendant alleged to have been missing; that defendant agreed to pay for the cost of the said cover cloths, but failed to fulfil his promise after incessant demands.

Judgment for plaintiff for £30 and 33s. costs. It is not clear whether the court's decision would have been any different if there had been an exception clause in the washing agreement.

3. *F.B. Gyasi* v. *Sowonu*
   Suit No. 467/63.

Plaintiff claims from defendant the sum of £2 being an advance received from plaintiff against one cupboard to be made for the plaintiff but defendant failed to make the said cupboard and also to refund the said £2.

Ex parte judgment for plaintiff for £2 with 16s.6d. as costs. A similar decision was reached in *Ayisi* v. *Ahyia Suit No.* 465/63, a claim for refund of £6 for the weaving of Kente cloth which defendant had failed to do.

4. *Kwame Asare* v. *Kwaku Sono*
Suit No. 462/63.

Defendant employed the plaintiff as his farm labourer at Tweapease, a place known and called "Aprokumaso" under the Abunu system. The plaintiff had worked for the defendant for three years by cultivating all the defendant's farmstead, forest land for farm, replanted cocoa tree where necessary; but the defendant refused to give "agreement paper" on the abunu system, nor to give part share of the cocoa plantation to the plaintiff. Defendant had stopped plaintiff from further cultivation. Plaintiff therefore claims from the defendant the sum of £99—being £75 for three years' labour and £14 being expenses incurred by the plaintiff in building a hut of 2 rooms and a kitchen at the defendant's request.

Judgment—for plaintiff for £99 with costs assessed at £8.13s.

Although this decision appears to be based on a quantum meruit it is doubtful if the absence of an "agreement paper" affected the validity of the abunu system. This system does not depend on writing to be valid.

5. *J. B. Baidoo* v. *Abene Korkor & anor.*

Suit No. 469/63.

Plaintiff claims from defendants £50 damages jointly and severally for breach of marriage contract in that the second defendant as mother of first defendant after receiving £1 introductory drink from plaintiff and further accompanying plaintiff to her relatives at Kwae for additional drink of £1.2s. which was paid by plaintiff, have both agreed to disappoint plaintiff in the said marriage contract and that the second defendant has given the first defendant in marriage to one Addai at Akim Oda.

Judgment—no cause to sue. Claim dismissed. £20 costs allowed to the defendant.

Perhaps the decision might have been different if the plaintiff's claim had been for the refund of the amount he had spent instead of a claim for damages for breach of promise of marriage.

Rationale of the cases

Three principles emerge from a study of the cases. Firstly, the courts tend to operate on the basis that whoever seeks the aid of the court first, must be the aggrieved party and therefore has a better case. Apart from case No. B (5) on an action for breach of promise of marriage (which in any case is not recognised in customary law),[8] all the other plaintiffs in the cases were successful in their claims, and each of them in fact got more than he claimed since costs form a regular feature of the awards.

The second principle follows from the first, which is that the courts are anxious to preserve the sanctity of agreements. Broken promises are punished with heavy legal costs. Only in this way can business be encouraged (as in the fufu case), and agricultural progress enhanced (the farm cases). These examples are, of course, a strong case in support of the existence of agreements in customary law.

The third principle that emerges is the presumption that native law applies in transactions between natives. In none of the cases was it ever argued that the parties intended the application of any other law. It is doubtful if the conflict between the imported and customary laws is of any great significance in the customary courts.

(ii) THE SUPERIOR COURTS

Here the position is a bit more complex. The courts are face to face with the problem of finding out the intentions of the parties not only as to the terms of the agreement but also as to the applicable law. The latter task is made more difficult by the fact that there are statutory provisions in Ghana[9] and in all the jurisdictions in Nigeria[10] for the freedom of the parties to choose either the imported or customary/Islamic laws to govern their transactions. In practice they hardly ever do so. The courts have therefore been up against the difficult exercise of finding out what law the parties intended to govern their obligations. This aspect of the subject has often been discussed under the heading of internal conflict of laws. We feel, however, that in a study on the law of agreements it appropriately belongs to the interpretation of agreements by the courts. In this sub-section, therefore, we shall be examining the factors that guide the courts in getting at the intentions of the contracting parties (A) as to the law applicable to the transaction, and (B) as to the meaning of the terms used in the agreement.

(A) Intention as to the law applicable:

" Daily the European buys from the native, daily he makes use of his services and labour both inside and outside the home, in the office, on the estate and in connection with his transport; and yet in these matters judgments are scarce as long as land and houses are not involved. On the one hand, this is due to the fact that the amounts concerned are so small that they would not warrant the expense of a law suit, and on the other because when larger suits are involved, use is made of a means that is encountered in many colonies where the European law of contract is not applicable, i.e. the right of the native party to choose the European civil law in respect of a certain transaction. The European often makes this voluntary submission one of the conditions of the contract if it is at all important, so that inter-racial conflict is nipped in the bud."[11]

If the above passage is representative of the position in the former Dutch Colonies of the Malaya Archipelago, it is only partially true of the state of the law in Ghana and Nigeria. There are, of course, many instances of transactions that are unknown to traditional native law. Examples of these are company shares, bankruptcy and banking laws. Here the nature of the transaction indicates the application of rules other than those of customary law. We shall be discussing some of these cases presently. The importance of determining what law the parties intended to apply arises from the fact that a difference in the law applicable to a transaction might well spell the difference between losing a claim and obtaining a judgment in one's favour. This is most true in cases where a claim is statute-barred if the imported law governed the transaction.[12] Other instances are cases where certain formalities prescribed by the imported law are not observed. Non-compliance with the Statute of Frauds as to writing in certain contracts and absence of consideration in conveyances[13] are some other examples of the difference in the effect of the transactions.

The case-law on the subject can be discussed under two sub-headings, namely (1) where either or both of the contracting parties are non-natives; and (2) where both the contracting parties are natives.

(1) Where either or both of the contracting parties are non-natives

Before 1960 there were very similar provisions in both Ghana and Nigeria for the freedom of the parties to choose the law governing their transaction. The normal pattern was often a general provision for the application of the imported law to all persons, similar to the jurisdiction of the High Court of Justice in England. Then there would be a more limited provision for the application of customary law under certain circumstances. Section 27 of the High Court of Lagos Act [14] is characteristic of the provisions of the latter category, this states :

> " 27 (1) The High Court shall observe and enforce the observance of every native law and custom which is applicable and is not repugnant to natural justice, equity and good conscience, nor incompatible either directly or by implication with any law for the time being in force, and nothing in this ordinance shall deprive any person of the benefit of any such native law and custom.
>
> 27 (2) Any such native law and custom shall be deemed applicable in causes and matters where the parties thereto are natives and also in causes and matters between natives and non-natives where it may appear to the court that substantial injustice would be done to either party by a strict adherence to any rules of law which would otherwise be applicable.
>
> 27 (3) No party shall be entitled to claim the benefit of any native law or custom, if it shall appear either from express contract or from the nature of the transactions out of which any suit or question may have arisen, that such party agreed that his obligations in connection with such transactions should be exclusively regulated otherwise than by native law and custom or that such transactions are transactions unknown to native law and custom."

One obvious effect of this section is that it empowers the courts to enforce either the imported or customary laws according to the choice of the parties or the nature of the transaction. Another effect is that it does not appear to cover situations where neither of the parties is a native. The latter instance will be governed by the general provisions for the application of the imported law.[15] Thus it is doubtful if two parties none of whom is a native would have the freedom to choose, say, Ashanti customary law to govern their transaction. It is contended, however, that if contracting parties have the freedom to choose, e.g. German or Soviet law to govern the terms of their obligations, the same freedom will be accorded to them if they prefer any particular rule of customary law, barring any considerations of public policy. The courts will come to such a conclusion only on the express words of the agreement between the parties. Thus, where both the parties are non-natives, there is a presumption that the imported or general law applies, but this presumption is rebuttable by the express choice of law by the parties.

Where either of the parties is a non-native, barring any express choice of law governing the transaction, the courts have paid lip-service to the " substantial injustice " rule in determining the intention of the parties. Here the presumption is that the parties intended their obligations to be governed by the rules of the imported law, but this presumption is rebutted by evidence to the effect that substantial injustice would be done to either party by a strict adherence to the imported law rules. It is remarkable that while this rule operated to bar the plaintiff's claim in *Koney* v. *U.T.C.*,[16] it was one of the reasons for the plaintiff's success in the later case of *Nelson* v. *Nelson*.[17] The facts of the *Koney* case were as follows:

> The defendants, a European company, supplied the plaintiff, an educated African carpenter, with a portable sewing machine. The order was obtained from Switzerland in October 1924. By the terms of a written agreement between the parties dated 3rd November, 1924, the defendants agreed to sell the machine to the plaintiff, but there was express provision for the title in the machine remaining in the defendants till the full purchase price had been paid. In fact, the machine turned out to be unfit for the purpose for which it was bought, all attempts at repairs notwithstanding. On 7th November, 1927, the plaintiff demanded his deposit from the defendants adding that they should take back the machine. The machine was, in fact, returned to the defendants, but no refund of deposit was made to the plaintiff. In his claim for damages of £500 for breach of contract, which claim he made on 26th September, 1933, the defendants contended that English law applied and that the claim was statute-barred.

Dean, C.J., who decided the case at first instance in Accra Divisional Court held that native law applied and awarded the plaintiff £329 with costs. On appeal to the West African Court of Appeal the vital issue before the court was whether this was a case in which substantial injustice would be done to either of the parties by a strict adherence to the rules of English law. On this, Kingdon, C.J. (Nigeria) had this to say:

> "Now in one sense there must always be an injustice when a plea under the statutes is set up and succeeds. The plaintiff may or may not have a good case, but good or bad it is refused a hearing on its merits. If I understand the reasoning of the statute aright it is that a greater injustice is likely to be done by allowing stale claims than by refusing them a hearing on the merits. Any plaintiff against whom the statute is successfully pleaded must feel a sense of grievance and that he has suffered a hardship. But I think the words of Section 19 of the Ordinance 'substantial injustice' impute something more than this, something more than the ordinary hardship which always occurs when the

statute is enforced. I cannot find that this 'something more' is present in the case now under appeal. The case appears to me to be typical of the cases at which the statute is expressly aimed, viz: cases in which the plaintiff cannot be expected to have kept available the evidence necessary to answer the plaintiff's case. The plaintiff is a native of the literate class, the members of which are, in my experience, well able to take care of themselves and their legal rights. There is very strong suspicion in this case that the delay has been deliberate and I think it would be a dangerous precedent to offer encouragement to such conduct. Moreover, are the equities really all on the plaintiff's side? It was he who had the idea of experimenting with this machine and it was he who stood to make a profit if the experiment were successful. Is it not fair that he should bear the loss and why should it all fall on the defendants? They are suffering some anyway."[18]

Reversing the decision of the Court of first instance, it was held that the claim was statute-barred. The decision of Hutchinson C.J. in *Fischer & Co.* v. *Swaniker*,[19] as to the circumstances under which the Statute of Limitations will be applicable to transactions between natives and Europeans, was followed. These circumstances were similar to those in the *Koney* case. On the other hand, in *Nelson* v. *Nelson*[20] Ga customary law was held applicable in a transaction between the plaintiff's agent and the second and third defendants who were non-natives. The West African Court of Appeal reversed the decision of Smith, C. J. (Gold Coast) and held that substantial injustice would be done to the plaintiff by a strict adherence to the principles of English law. Verity, C.J. who read the Court's judgment felt that such an adherence to English law would defeat the intentions of the plaintiff's father, the testator. His obvious intention from the facts of the case was that all transactions concerning the land should be as much as possible regulated by the principles of customary law. Also in *Asante* v. *Gold Coast Drivers' Union*,[21] one of the issues before the court was the law that the parties intended to apply to their transaction, in this case the hiring of rooms. The defendants, an unincorporated association of drivers, had agreed to rent the plaintiff's rooms but had in fact broken the contract. In a claim for damages for the breach, the court had to decide (1) whether an unincorporated association of natives was a native for the purposes of the jurisdiction of the native courts, and (2) if the answer to (1) is negative, whether the parties intended the application of English law, having regard to the nature of the transaction. Adumua-Bossman, J. determined the first question in the negative, holding that such an association was necessarily a non-native. On the second question he held that native law had no notion of the renting of rooms and that the parties intended the application of English law. The defendants' appeal based on a plea to the jurisdiction of the Native Court was therefore allowed.[22]

Quite apart from the contested finality of the assertion that the hiring of rooms was unknown to traditional native law, it is curious that the learned judge did not advert to the " substantive injustice " principle in adjudicating on the rights of the parties. The court quoted with approval several passages from Sarbah's works to support the view that land could be rented out in customary law, but did not see any connection between a house (or the rooms therein) and land. It is submitted with respect that any definition of land that excludes a house or part thereof is a very narrow one indeed. In fact, land is defined in the Ghana Interpretation Act, 1960, to include " land covered by water, any house, building or structure whatsoever, and any estate, interest in or right in, to or over land and water ".[23]

On the question of the nationality of the Drivers' Union, there is evidence that it was not incorporated under the then Companies Ordinance. It was not, therefore, a legal person for purposes of that Ordinance. In order to determine its nationality, one has got to look at the nationality of its members. On this test, there is no evidence that any of the members was a non-native. In the light of these facts, it is not easy to see the basis on which the learned judge came to the conclusion that it was a non-native. It is submitted with respect that the *Asante Case* is a poor guide to the courts in determining the implied intentions of the parties to any given transaction.

(2) *Where both parties are natives*

Here the presumption is that natives intend their obligations to be governed by native law, and whoever asserts the contrary has the onus of adducing evidence to prove it. This is as far as theory goes. In fact, the superior courts have often proceeded on the assumption that the parties intended the application of the general law and that anyone who asserts that native law applies should adduce evidence to prove it. The cases here will be discussed under two sub-headings, namely, where the parties made use of documents, and where the nature of the transaction is alien to customary law notions.

(a) *Where the parties made use of documents.*[24]

It has often been stated that traditional customary law knew of no writing. It is also true that since the later decades of the 19th century documents have been in ever increasing use by natives.

Allott[25] has set out some of the pertinent legal questions that arise from the use of writing by natives. These are:

(i) Does the writing serve only as a memorandum of the agreement or transaction; or does it bind like an English deed, excluding (subject to equity) all evidence of the transaction between the parties?

(ii) Does the use of writing or of any particular form of writing indicate a desire on the part of the parties to be bound exclusively, or substantially, by the rules of English law?

(iii) Does the use of conveyances mean that thenceforth land is held not under "native tenure," but under English real property law?

(iv) Does the use of writing in the transfer of land mean that thenceforth subsidiary interests created over the land are subject to English law?

(v) Does the use of writing take consideration of any matter concerning the transaction out of the jurisdiction of the native courts, and into the original and exclusive jurisdiction of the Supreme Court?

These questions are, of course, interconnected and a discussion of one might well involve the discussion of the case law on many others. An attempt to answer the first question will be made in the next section. Here we are primarily concerned with the answer to the second question, i.e. the intention of the parties as to the law applicable to a given transaction.

Rotibi v. *Savage*[26] was an action between two Nigerians at the town of Owerri (in Eastern Nigeria). The plaintiff had lent the defendant £336 free of interest in 1933, and received from the defendant a "paper" which the court found to be an I.O.U. or an acknowledgement of the debt, but not a promissory note within the meaning of that term in the *Bills of Exchange Ordinance (Nigeria)*. Further loans totalling £97 were also made in 1941. The defendant pleaded the Statute of Limitations as regards the original loan made in 1933. The defendant had written a letter to the plaintiff on the 22nd November, 1942, which the court would have held to be a sufficient acknowledgement to revive the debt, had it been found that the Statute of Limitations was applicable to the transaction.

The issue that arose was whether the use of the I.O.U. was sufficient to take the transaction out of the domain of customary law. The court found as a fact that both parties were natives and that under their native law there was no period of limitation in an action of recovery of debt. It was also found that the plaintiff had done nothing more than lend the money free of interest, and had not entered into any obligation towards the defendant which he had agreed should be regulated exclusively by English law. The obligations were all on the defendant's side. In a review of the authorities, Waddington, J. referred to the cases of *Egebor* v. *Agberegbe*,[27] *Bakare* v. *Coker*[28] and *Pearse* v. *Aderoku*.[29] In each of these cases (transactions between natives), promissory notes were used and the Statute of Limitations was held to apply. He, however, distinguished the *Rotibi* case from the other cases holding that the transaction was governed by the rules of customary law. On the use of the documents the learned judge had this to say:

> " While after prolonged consideration I have formed the opinion that plaintiff must succeed in this action on grounds upon which no argument was addressed to me, and therefore no need to discuss the above arguments arises, I think I might usefully make an observation on this document (i.e. the I.O.U.) and its effect. In *Bakare*'s case the court expressed the view that the giving and taking of a promissory note is very strong evidence that the parties intended their transaction to be governed exclusively by English law. With this view, with respect, I agree. But I think care should be taken against applying that principle where the document amounts to no more than the kind of ' paper ' which most natives nowadays like to have as evidence of a money transaction, and which at this day is, I suppose, quite a familiar object in most native courts, and frequently bearing an impressive array of stamps."[30]

With this view of the learned judge we are, respectfully, in agreement. It would be anomalous in the extreme if the mere use of documents should be sufficient to exclude the application of customary law. The distinction between a document intended only as evidence of a money transaction and the instrument on which any claims on a transaction must be based, ought to be maintained. Unfortunately the decisions of the courts in Ghana and Nigeria are not neatly divisible along these lines.

In *Ajike* v. *Souza*[31] the Court presumed that the parties intended the application of English law since promissory notes were used. Also where the plaintiff had given the defendant's predecessor £780 loan and the deceased gave a note called " promissory note " in which he undertook to sell his land to the plaintiff in default of payment of the loan, the Privy Council held the note to be a promissory note within the terms of the Bills of Exchange Ordinance (Nigeria) and applied English law to the transaction.[32] But in *Green* v. *Owo*[33] native law was excluded on the ground that there was no native law or custom as regards the effects of purely documentary titles in English conveyancing form.

Unfortunately also, the distinction between a document as evidence of the transaction and an instrument of the said transaction, was not observed in the important Ghana case of *Hughes* v. *Davies & Co.*[34] In this case the plaintiff sought to recover from the defendants, the executors of one late R.A. Harrison, the sum of £250.1s.7d. said to have been lent at different times to the deceased by the plaintiff. The defendants had contended among other things that the debt was statute barred. Both parties were natives, but it was argued for the defendants that the use of I.O.U.s by the deceased and the keeping of a sales book in the plaintiff's store in which entries of goods sold were made, excluded the application of customary law. As regards the I.O.U. the trial court disposed of the defendants' argument by asking itself two questions. Firstly, " Would Mr. Harrison have liked the public to know that he was borrowing money from the plaintiff, or would he have preferred to have the matter known only to the two?" In answer to this the court stated that Mr. Harrison would rather that the matter rested between them. Secondly, " Can it therefore be contended that the plaintiff in merely accepting the I.O.U.s had such knowledge of the difference of the effect of native law or custom and English law bearing on the transaction? i.e. in the one case time can be no bar to her remedy, and in the other it would deprive her of that remedy, and agreed to be bound that time should be a bar to her remedy." The court considered all the surrounding circumstances and answered the latter question in the negative. Having also found that the sales book was kept by the deceased and not by the plaintiff, it was held that the parties intended their obligations should be regulated by customary law rules and since this law did not admit of limitation periods to debt claims, the plaintiff's action succeeded. This decision was lightly set aside by the Full Court[35] in a very brief judgment. Thus unlike the decision in the Nigerian case of *Rotibi* v. *Savage*[36] discussed above, the use of an I.O.U. was deemed by the court to mean that the parties had opted for the application of English law. It is curious, however, that the Full Court did not deem it wise to give reasons for upsetting the rather sounder judgment of the trial court. It might be naive to suggest that they were swayed by the personality of Sarbah who argued the case for the defendants. Equally curious is the difficult case of *Aradzie* v. *Yaandor & Anor*,[37] a loan transaction between two native chiefs. Here English law was deemed to be the law the parties intended to govern their obligations. The reason for this was that the parties made use of a document which was construed by Treacy Ag.J., by no means one of the leading judges in the territory, to be a promissory note. In his judgment the learned Judge referred to Sarbah with approval on the traditional methods of making a loan.[38] He continued:

> " With increasing commerce, however, a quicker and more private mode of effecting a loan was found desirable and under the English law the promissory note system met this need. From the lender's point of view this method had the disadvantage that after the lapse of a certain time the debt became irrecoverable, but often the lender, who sees large interest and what appears sound security, is as anxious to lend as the borrower is to borrow. Be that as it may, the promissory note has become a popular institution in the Gold Coast. I can conceive an ignorant native making a loan on a promissory note believing that he would still have the right to recover after any lapse of time, and if the court were convinced that he really believes so, probably it would hold that the statute did not apply, but in the present case the substantial sum of £250 was lent by one African chief to another, so we may take it that both parties knew the native custom with regard to loans, and I think one may not unfairly surmise that they also knew the English law especially as the loan was made in a timber district long after the timber trade had been well established, yet they deliberately selected the English method. There is nothing before me to show why they did so, but both parties must have found it convenient. This being so, it is impossible for me to decide in favour of one party and to the detriment of the other that having realised the advantages of this method he failed to realise the disadvantages. The whole nature of the transaction shows that both parties intended to be bound by English law at the time when the note was made, and that such intention must be taken to form part of the agreement."

Three objections immediately leap to one's mind after reading the above judgment. The first is the learned judge's suggestion that the charging of interest is a peculiar feature of the imported law. This is obviously not borne out by the authorities. In fact, the case of *Fynn* v. *Quassie*[39] is a direct authority for the contrary view. Here it was held that interest is chargeable on customary loans. Secondly, the learned judge tended to be influenced by the amount of money involved in the transaction to hold that the parties must have intended the application of English law. He did not, however, indicate the financial limits of customary law transactions nor did he rely on any authority for suggesting that there was. It is submitted with respect that there is no authority for the view that £250 is outside the ambit of customary law transactions except, perhaps, his lordship's decision. Thirdly, the learned judge emphasised the decisive nature of the use of a promissory note in excluding the application of customary law. It has already been shown above that there is a distinction between a document as evidence of a transaction and an instrument of the said transaction. It could still be argued, however, that the decision was right but for the wrong reason. If the plaintiff decided to sue on the document he should be held bound by its limitations in the imported law sense.[40]

(b) *Where the nature of the transaction is alien to customary law notions*

Mention has already been made of transactions such as company shares, bankruptcy law and banking as matters that are alien to customary law concepts. Other transactions in which the courts have excluded the application of native law are where the parties make use of technical terminology. This is most common in land matters. Thus in the Ghana case of *Kwesi-Johnson* v. *Effie*,[41] a land transaction between two natives, it was held that as a conveyance forms no part of a sale by native law and custom, the parties intended the application of English law. In that case the defendant first got a receipt for the purchase price of a house from the vendor. The receipt wound up with the words " . . . . and in pursuance of the terms of the conveyance to be prepared in this behalf." Later the defendant also received another receipt from the same vendor for £3 " tirama." This latter sum represented earnest money in customary law transactions. The plaintiff claimed the house from the defendant on the strength of a conveyance in English form which he had obtained from the vendor. This conveyance was found to be valid under the imported law. The question that the court was to decide was whether the original transaction between the defendant and the vendor was a valid customary law sale. If this issue was determined in favour of the application of native law, then the defendant's title which was prior in time would be a better one. The court, however, considered the fact that the parties were educated natives and their use of technical conveyancing terms was deemed to import the application of English law. The trial court held, therefore, that the parties intended English law to govern their transaction. This decision was affirmed by the West African Court of Appeal. Referring to the use of the " tirama " in this transaction, Foster-Sutton, P., who read the judgment of the court, observed, approving of the dictum of the trial judge, " old customs die hard, and deeds drawn by lawyers according to English law frequently specify ' tirama '."

This decision has been criticised[42] on three grounds. Firstly, that although traditional customary law knew no writing, the modern tendency has been for natives to make use of the device resorted to by the defendant in this case, i.e. following a customary law transaction with an English conveyance. But this decision tends to overlook this fact. Secondly, in customary law transactions, the payment of *ntrama* completes a customary sale of land. Danquah[43] was cited as the authority for this view. Thirdly, that there was no evidence from the facts of the case to indicate that the parties opted for the exclusive application of English law to their transaction. We may add that it is sad that not sufficient evidence was adduced to establish the effect of delay in completing the payment of ntrama. It is anomalous that customary law which does not recognise any periods of limitation should construe two days' delay as fatal to the validity of a customary sale.[44]

The position in Ghana since 1960

Paragraph 64 (1) of the *Courts Decree,* 1966 has given the courts a clearer guide in determining the intention of the contracting parties as to the law applicable to their transaction. The paragraph provides:

> " 64 (1). Subject to the provisions of any enactment other than this sub-section, in deciding whether an issue arising in civil proceedings is to be determined according to the common law or customary law, and, if the issue is to be determined according to customary law, in deciding which system of customary law is applicable, the court shall be guided by the following rules, in which references to the personal law of a person are references to the system of customary law to which he is subject or, if he is not shown to be subject to customary law, are references to the common law.
>
> Rule 1:
>
> Where two persons have the same personal law one of them cannot, by dealing in a manner regulated by some other law with property in which the other has a present or expectant interest, alter or affect that interest to an extent which would not in the circumstances be open to him under his personal law."

Thus, if A and B have interests (vested or contingent) on a piece of land and this interest is regulated by, say, customary law, A cannot by dealing with the land or part thereof under any other law exclude B's interest under customary law which binds both of them. This provision, of course, is the ratio of the *Nelson* v. *Nelson*[45] decision discussed above. It is not clear, however, if B's delay in objecting to any dealings in the common property by A will not be

w

a vital issue in determining whether he can get relief. Presumably such a delay would defeat his claim since section 66 (3) of the Courts Act provides for savings for the doctrines of equity.

> " Rule 2:
>
> Subject to Rule 1, where an issue arises out of a transaction the parties to which have agreed, or may from the form or the nature of the transaction be taken to have agreed, that such an issue should be determined according to the common law or any system of customary law, effect should be given to the agreement."[46]

" Transaction " was defined to include marriage. Here the position is not very clear. If an issue arises from a transaction between A and B, in the absence of any express statement as to the law applicable, the courts are to infer the intention of the parties from the form and nature of the transaction. The two vital words are " form " and " nature." It has already been shown above that neither form (as seen in cases where the parties used documents) nor nature (as in cases where technical terms were used) is a safe guide in determining the intention of the parties as to the law applicable. What the above rule has done is to enact in statutory form the confusion existing in the case law on the subject without indicating sufficiently or at all the circumstances under which a particular type of law is presumed to apply to a transaction. Perhaps definitions of " form " and " nature " in the interpretation part of the Courts Act, 1960, would have gone a long way to clarifying the position. It is respectfully submitted that the above rule has not done anything to improve the law on the subject.

> " Rule 6:
>
> " Subject to the foregoing rules, an issue should be determined according to the common law unless the plaintiff is subject to any system of customary law and claims to have the issue determined according to that system, when it should be so determined."[47]

This is, of course, a vital rule in the law of agreements. The effect appears to be that any issue before the courts (superior or local) will prima facie be determined according to the common law, but if the plaintiff reasonably claims the application of customary law he will be entitled to the benefit of such a claim. This rule, of course, presumes the existence of the other rules, particularly the rule on the power of the Court to refuse to apply the law chosen by the plaintiff, if it will unduly prejudice the rights of the defendant, where they both have an interest in the same subject matter.

It is also an enactment of the practice of the superior courts who have hitherto operated on the theory that the parties intended the application of the general law, until a contrary intention is shown either by express words or by inference from the nature of the transaction.[48]

(B) Intention as to the meaning and effect of terms used in the agreement[49]

So far we have been considering the principles that guide the superior courts in determining the law that the parties intended to govern their transactions. In this section we are concerned with the examination of the ways in which the courts have construed the terms and determined the effect of stipulations in agreements. Three issues must be clearly distinguished here, namely, the distinction between mere representations which are not intended to be terms of the agreement and the other statements which are; secondly, the relative importance of the terms used in the agreement; and finally the total effect of the terms used on the rights and duties of the parties. These will be examined seriatim.

(i) *Representations and terms*

During the course of negotiations leading to the conclusion of a binding agreement, one or other of the contracting parties may make a statement or give an assurance calculated to produce in the mind of the other party a belief that facts exist which render the proposed bargain advantageous to his interests. When, later, there is disagreement, a court will have to decide whether this statement or assurance formed part of the contract, or whether it was merely a representation which the party making it did not intend to be binding on him. If the agreement is an oral one as many are, the determination of the parties' intention as to what is binding and what is not is one of considerable difficulty.[50] Here the courts will rely solely on the deportment of the parties and the credit and credibility of their witnesses. Where, however, the agreement is in writing, the courts in Nigeria are guided by the Evidence Ordinance.[51] Sections 131-133 of this Ordinance lay down the conditions under which parole evidence is admissible in construing the terms of an agreement. Section 131 is as follows:

" 131 (1). When any judgment of any court or any other judicial or official proceedings, or any contract, or any grant or other disposition of property has been reduced to the form of a document or series of documents, no evidence may be given of such judgment or proceedings, or of the terms of such contract, grant or disposition of property except the document itself, or secondary evidence of its contents in cases in which secondary evidence is admissible under the provisions hereinbefore contained; nor may the contents of any such document be contradicted, altered, added to or varied by oral evidence: [52]

Provided that any of the following matters may be proved: —

(a) fraud, intimidation, illegality; want of due execution; the fact that it is wrongly dated; existence or want or failure, of consideration, mistake in fact or law; want of capacity in which a contracting party acted when it is not inconsistent with the terms of the contract; or any other matter which, if proved, would produce any effect upon the validity of any document, or of any part of it, or which would entitle any person to any judgment, decree or order relating thereto;

(b) the existence of any separate oral agreement as to any matter on which a document is silent, and which is not inconsistent with its terms, if from the circumstances of the case the court infers that the parties did not intend the document to be a complete and final statement of the whole transaction between them."

Other exceptions to the parole evidence rule include the proof of the existence of any separate oral agreement constituting a condition precedent to the attaching of any obligation under any contract, grant or disposition of property.[53] There are also instances of conditions subsequent, usage or custom (where these are not repugnant or inconsistent with the express terms of the written agreement).[54]

There have, of course, been some decided cases in Ghana and Nigeria on the admissibility or otherwise of parole evidence in determining the parties' intention as contained in a written agreement. Thus in the Ghana case of *African & Colonial Co. Ltd.* v. *Blemir Syndicate*[55] the defendants sought to adduce oral evidence as to the family ownership of a piece of land. This evidence conflicted with the unambiguous terms of a lease which was in the name of an individual member of the family. The trial court held that such oral evidence was inadmissible, and this decision was affirmed on appeal by the Full Court. Also in *Thomas Hutton-Mills* v. *Nkansah II & ors*[56] the question before the court was whether or not oral representations made to the plaintiff (respondent) but which were not contained in the commission deed, formed part of their agreement. The West African Court of Appeal resolved the question against the plaintiff, i.e. in the negative. The Ghana Court of Appeal (as it then was) came to a similar conclusion in the recent case of *Gold Coast Industrial Development Corporation* v. *Duncan*.[57] Here the plaintiffs sued the defendant for the recovery of £4,590-14-2d. under a written agreement. The facts were that the defendant planned to establish a cassava factory on a commercial scale. To this end he borrowed various sums of money from the plaintiff corporation. Between the 18th July, 1949 and the 3rd May, 1952 these amounts totalled £4,300. By agreement dated the 25th August, 1952 the defendant agreed to repay this sum (with interest) by quarterly instalments over a period of three years, the first repayment to be made on the 15th April, 1953. No such payments being made, on the 29th October, 1954 the plaintiffs sued for the debt and interest outstanding. The defendant denied liability alleging that the plaintiffs were in fact in breach of an oral agreement reached with him in July, 1949. The terms of this agreement included a promise to give the defendant adequate assistance to enable him to establish his cassava factory on a commercial scale. Also in March 1952, another oral promise was made to the defendant, this time of £3,000 but the plaintiffs refused him the loan on his application for it. The defendant had proceeded with the factory in reliance on the promises and had suffered damage. One of the issues before the court was the significance of the oral promises made by the plaintiffs to the defendant. On this it was held that the oral agreement merged in the written agreement of August, 1952, which superseded the oral agreement without incorporating it. It was not, therefore, admissible to vary the terms of the written agreement. It appears, however, that the court left considerable emphasis on the ultra-vires nature of the oral agreement, which was therefore void. In the absence of this vital factor, it would be curious that the court did not consider the collateral oral agreement as binding as the subsequent written contract.

On the other hand, in *Pickard* v. *Innes*[58] the defendants agreed in writing to engage the services of the plaintiff as mining surveyor at a salary of £150 a month and some other allowances. The plaintiff brought an action for damages for the breach of the contract but the defendants pleaded the existence of an oral agreement which operated as a condition precedent to the contract in writing. The oral agreement was to the effect that the plaintiff was to get what was described as " an amicable clearance " from his former employers with whom the defendants were in cordial business relationships. It was held by the Full Court that this oral agreement was admissible to prove the intention of the parties and to defeat the plaintiff's claim since he did not get the " amicable clearance." Also in the Nigerian case of *I. T. Palmer of Nigeria*

Ltd. v. *Julia Fonseca*,[59] Jibown J. considered oral evidence in varying the terms of an agreement between a principal and his agent. Citing the old English authority of *Goss* v. *Nugent*,[60] the learned judge drew attention to Section 131 (1) (d) of the Nigerian Evidence Ordinance which deals with the admission of oral evidence to vary a written document under certain circumstances. He held that the conditions for the admission of such parole evidence were present in the case. A fair assessment of the rationale of the cases is that whether or not preliminary negotiations form part of the agreement (whether oral or written) depends on the circumstances of each particular case. Where the agreement is in writing the onus of proving that oral negotiations formed part of the contractual terms is a heavy one and it is on him who alleges it to prove same. Prima facie the courts operate on the basis that the written agreement is all the contract between the parties until the contrary is proved.[61]

Certainty, of course, demands that the court should rely on what is before them in the form of a document until any additional or other terms are established by evidence. But a rigid application of this rule in a jurisdiction where the vast majority of the people are illiterate is bound to inflict hardship on some of the parties.[62] Although the Illiterates Protection Ordinances in Ghana and Nigeria have gone some way in safeguarding the rights of illiterates, it is contended that the Ordinances have no answer to situations where the illiterate is himself relying on the document. In such cases the courts have always stuck to the principles of the imported law.

(ii) *The relative importance of the terms used*

There are three main facets of any discussion on the terms of an agreement. The first is the distinction between express and implied terms. Express terms are apparent on the face of the agreement, while the implied terms are those that are read into it as a result of custom, statute or by the court. The second is the effect of a purported exclusion from liability by the parties in the event of any breach of the terms (express or implied). The third is the relative importance of the terms used in the agreement. The first two aspects will be considered in the next following section. Here we are concerned with the third facet, i.e. the relative importance of the terms used.

It has aptly been pointed out by Cheshire and Fifoot[63] that " common sense suggests and the law has long recognised that the obligations created by a contract are not all of equal importance.

It is primarily for the parties to set their own value on the terms that they impose upon each other." But explicit hierarchical ordering of contractual stipulations is a rare phenomenon. The courts are therefore up against the task of construing the meaning and assessing the importance of the terms used.

English law has adopted the terms " conditions "[64] and " warranties " in discussing the various provisions of an agreement. The former is defined as a stipulation in an agreement the breach of which may give rise to a right to treat the contract as repudiated, while the latter is also a stipulation but its breach gives rise to an action in damages.[65]

Objection to the division of contractual terms into conditions and warranties has been based mainly on the fact that a breach of condition need not only entitle the plaintiff to repudiate the agreement. In many cases, where the plaintiff has affirmed the contract or done any act that is not consistent with the owner's continued title, his only remedy is in damages and in such a case there is no distinction between a condition and a warranty.[66] It was with a view to avoiding this confusion that the *Indian Contract Act*, 1872, preferred the phrase " reciprocal promises."

It must be observed, however, that the vital consideration is not whether or not contractual terms are neatly divisible into conditions and warranties. It is rather that the importance of a term in an agreement should be reflected in the type of remedy available for its breach. In deciding on the available remedy the courts will consider each term in relation to the agreement as a whole. This approach will render unnecessary the controversy about the wisdom of the division of terms into conditions and warranties.[67]

(iii) Effect of terms on obligations of the parties:

In the two preceding sub-sections we have examined the distinction between mere representations and terms of an agreement, and the relative importance of the stipulations. An attempt will be made here to analyse the legal effect of the terms used by the parties as seen by the courts. An examination of the law on the subject has revealed a more or less neat bifurcation of approach by the courts. We shall call these the *purist individualistic approach* and the *paternalistic approach*. The first approach, which roughly coincides in time with the period 1874-1958[68] except in money-lending transactions, is concerned among other things with contracts of employment, guarantees, sale of goods (including standard-form contracts and exception clauses) and commission contracts. The latter approach, which is a more dynamic view of the function of agreements, is concerned mainly with money-lending and hire-purchase transactions.[69] A critique of each of the approaches will be attempted as we go along.

(a) THE PURIST INDIVIDUALISTIC APPROACH

Wealth in a commercial age has been said to be made up largely of promises. An important part of everyone's substance consists of advantages which others have promised to provide for or to render to him; of demands to have the advantages promised, which he may assert not against the world at large, but against particular individuals.[70] In this process of enforcing promises and demands, the role of the courts assumes a unique feature in shaping the economic basis of the society. Here we are concerned with the underlying principles that have served as a guide-light to the courts in construing the effect of contractual terms in Ghana and Nigeria between the years 1874-1958.

The reception of English law into Ghana and Nigeria has already been referred to in another place.[71] It is enough to mention here that the date of reception (i.e. 24th July, 1874, in the case of Ghana, and 1st January, 1900, in the case of Nigeria) coincided with an era in the English law of contract when the emphasis of the courts was on the freedom of the individual to enter into any type of agreement he liked (barring public policy considerations). In legal theory this was the age of the mechanical positivists who viewed law negatively as " a system of hands off while men do things "[72] rather than as a system of ordering to prevent friction and waste so that they may do things. Freedom of economic motion and locomotion was its logical extension into the arena of agreements. Equality of the parties was presumed and any interference by either the state or the courts with contracts, was viewed with undisguised disapproval. This then was the state of contractual theory when it was imported into Ghana and Nigeria.

Now, in the two territories (i.e. Ghana and Nigeria) the personnel of the superior courts during the period under review were substantially British. Their legal training and background was English (here we include Scots and Irish laws). Also the circumstances in the two countries favoured a *laissez faire* attitude towards agreements freely entered into by the parties. The slave trade had been abolished and several European companies extended their other commercial operations to the West African territories. These companies enlisted the services of natives as agents in collecting raw materials from the farmers; employed them as workers in their local branches; exported raw materials to the home market (i.e. to Europe) and imported the finished goods back to West Africa to sell to the natives. This explains the fact that most of the local cases during this period and long afterwards dealt with agency agreements, contracts of employment, sale of goods, guarantees and trade marks.[73] The basic attitude of the courts was to interfere as little as possible with these agreements. This attitude of non-interference with contracts freely entered into by the individuals is what we prefer to discuss under the name of a purist individualistic approach to the construction of agreements.

Contracts of Employment[74]

This approach has been most evident in contracts of employment. Section 5 of the Conspiracy and Protection of Property Act, 1875, which makes the breach of an agreement of service an offence, and Section 3 (3) of the Employees and Workmen Act, 1875 (both are English Statutes) which gave the Courts power to order specific performance of certain service contracts,[75] indicate quite clearly the sanctity of this category of agreements during this period. In Ghana and Nigeria two streams of authority in this aspect of the law have been recognised. The first relates to the obligations of the parties while the employment lasts, and the second relates to their rights and duties at the termination of the relationship, especially when the termination was wrongful. In both groups of cases the courts have tended to treat the provisions by the parties as sacrosanct. In the latter group of cases, however, there is a noticeable tendency on the part of the courts to imply terms into the agreement made by the parties. We shall be looking at these presently, but first we shall examine the former group of decisions.

In *John Holt & Co. Ltd.* v. *Lafe*[76] the plaintiff employed Stephen Lafe, the defendant, as a salesman and produce buyer. A clause of their written agreement was that the defendant gave credit to customers at his own risk and any balance due must be paid off by him before stock-taking. Another clause of the agreement made the defendant responsible for any loss or shortage whether caused by himself or any person to whom he might delegate any of his duties. Subsequently, and perhaps as a result of trade competition and in order to attract more customers, the plaintiff's local agent orally agreed to waive the "no credit" clause during the cocoa season. The present action was a claim for the losses sustained by the plaintiffs partly as a result of goods sold by the defendant on credit. The defendant pleaded the oral agreement to waive the "no credit" clause, but the plaintiffs replied by pleading the Statute of Frauds which required such variations to be in writing. Jackson Ag. J. held that the oral waiver was only a "forbearance for a limited period or variation of the manner of fulfilling the original agreement " which need not be in writing to be pleaded. Accordingly, judgment was given in favour of the defendant on this head of claim.[77]

G. B. Ollivant Ltd. v. *Adetutu*[78] was a claim for £387-0-7d. by the plaintiffs against the defendant, their employee, being shortages in the plaintiffs' store manned by the defendant. The defendant had had the written permission of the company to give goods on credit to certain specified persons and the shortage occurred partly as a result of the credit given within the relevant period. The issue before the court was whether the plaintiffs could be allowed to retain any profits made by the defendant's credit system while debiting him with any losses. On this Carey, J. remarked:

> " In my experience of claims such as this it is invariably asserted and not disproved that unless the salesman gives credit to customers he will practically do no business and yet the large firms also engage such salesmen, tie them down not to give credit but know they will and must do so, and they turn their blind eye on the breach of such a provision until such time as a default is made by a credit customer and then they hold the salesman liable. To my mind this is an iniquitous practice. There should be a definite provision one way or the other which should be strictly adhered to."[79]

The learned judge held that the defendant was not liable for the shortages since these arose as a result of the plaintiff's written consent to give goods on credit. Also in another case where the plaintiffs acquiesced in the giving of goods on credit by the defendant contrary to the written terms of their employment agreement, the court held the defendant was not liable for shortages in the stock which arose as a result of the credits given.[80]

On the other hand the Ghana Court of Appeal (as it then was) found against the defendant in the recent decision of *Korsah-Brown* v. *John Holt & Co. Ltd.*[81] The facts were that the appellant was a servant of the respondent company responsible for the purchase of cocoa with cash supplied by the company. A clause in the service agreement made him liable to them for any loss which they might sustain by reason of such produce not conforming with the standards of purity and quality required by their instructions or by current legislation. The appellant was to be paid commission on his purchases but such payment was to be made after the verification of his accounts following a stock-taking.

The plaintiffs claimed £3,538-10-10d. being the cost of 383 bags of cocoa which the defendant claimed to have purchased but which were not found in their stores. The defendant counter-claimed for the same amount being the price he paid for the bags of cocoa, and also for £83-15-8d., his commission for the purchases based on the terms of the agreement. He denied liability for the loss of the bags of cocoa, adding that it was due to thieves who broke into the store. In fact, police investigation revealed that the burglary was " staged " by the defendant.

The court found as a fact that the defendant was the servant of the plaintiffs and that the property in the cocoa purchased had passed to the plaintiffs. But it was held that the onus of proving that the loss was due to burglary lay on the defendant and since he had not discharged that onus he was liable under the terms of the agreement. It was held further that the defendant had not faithfully discharged his obligations as a servant and therefore was not entitled to the commission.

The remarkable fact about this decision is that it in effect places the defendant in the position of an insurer for the plaintiffs' goods. By attaching responsibility for the loss of the goods to the defendant in default of a strict proof of a burglary the court raised the onus of proof in the civil claim to that of a criminal prosecution. One should have thought that the onus on the defendant as a bailee, was to prove that he exercised due care (which would rebut any allegation of negligence).

Secondly, by depriving the defendant of his commission on the ground of bad faith, the court was in effect convicting him of the larceny of the goods. As the facts of the case did not establish this beyond reasonable doubt, it is submitted with respect that the decision was rather hard on him. In deciding where the loss of the amount claimed should lie the court ought to have considered who stood to gain if the goods were sold in the normal course of business. If that test were applied, there is no doubt that the plaintiff's claim would have been lost.

The other line of authority to which reference has already been made is concerned with cases of wrongful termination of employment.[82] The issue in most of them is the importance the courts attach to the remedies to which the plaintiff is entitled under the agreement if the dismissal was found to be wrongful.

In *Bisset* v. *Prestea Block A. Ltd.*,[83] however, the issue was whether or not the plaintiff had been wrongfully dismissed (i.e. dismissed contrary to the terms of the employment agreement). Bisset was engaged as a miner by the defendant company and one of the terms of the agreement was as follows: " I agree to do the work I am engaged for, or any other work that the management may reasonably require me to do." The plaintiff, however, refused to work underground since he claimed that the work was the sort

that was done by the " natives." He would not, however, have
minded doing the work alone but he objected to sharing the same
tank with a " native." The defendant company dismissed him on
grounds of refusal to carry out the terms of the employment
agreement. His action for damages for wrongful dismissal (among
other things) was dismissed by the trial judge and this decision
was affirmed on appeal by the Full Court (Gold Coast).

In *Bonney* v. *Findlay*[84] the Divisional Court at Accra was to
decide whether the plaintiff's damages for wrongful dismissal were
to be assessed on the basis of the unexpired term of his contract
of service for a fixed period (in this case 5 years), or on the basis
of the period within which the plaintiff ought to have found himself another employment. After a review of the English authorities
on the matter, Michelin J. ruled that the plaintiff was entitled to
one year's salary and commission for the breach of the contract
of employment. The court purported to follow the leading English
case of *Addis* v. *Gramophone Co. Ltd.*[85] But in the Addis case the
House of Lords in fact held that where a servant is wrongfully
dismissed from his employment, the damages for the dismissal
cannot include compensation for the manner of the dismissal, for
his injured feelings, or for the loss he may sustain from the fact
that the dismissal in itself makes it more difficult for him to obtain
employment.[86] It is curious in the extreme that the court awarded
a whole year's salary and commission as damages to the plaintiff
in purported reliance on the authority of the *Addis* decision. Perhaps the court in implying into the service agreement a term that
the defendants will pay the plaintiff a year's salary and commission for any breach of the said agreement, was influenced by the
difficulty of obtaining alternative employment in the territory.
This view is re-inforced by the later decision in *Tay* v. *Walken*,[87]
a claim for damages for refusal to employ the plaintiff after he had
paid some security in favour of the plaintiff's claim. The Divisional
Court cited with approval the statement of the law on the subject
by Erle, J. in the English case of *Beckham* v. *Drake*[88] as follows:

> " The measure of damages for the breach of promise now in
> question is obtained by considering what is the usual rate of
> wages for the employment here contracted for, and what time
> would be lost before a similar employment could be obtained.
> The law considers that employment in any ordinary branch of
> industry can be obtained by a person competent for the place,
> and that the usual rate of wages for such employment can be
> proved, and that when a promise for continuing employment is
> broken by the master, it is the duty of the servant to use diligence
> to find other employment."

Although the *Tay* decision can be distinguished from the *Bonney* case on the basis that in the latter case the plaintiff had had employment with the defendants for some time before the dismissal while in the *Tay* case there never was any employment at all, it is submitted that this distinction does not affect the substance of the claims. In both cases the plaintiffs' claims were for the breach of the contract of employment. It is contended that the *Tay* decision has a sounder and more rational basis than its predecessor.[89]

In the interesting case of *Sackey* v. *Sick-Hagemeyer* (*Ghana*) *Ltd.*,[90] Bannerman J. was faced with construing the meaning of a term in an agreement of service giving the employee certain benefits if his employment was terminated under specified circumstances. The relevant provision in the agreement was as follows:

> " Article 24—Payment of indemnity (Gratuity). Employees who are covered by this agreement on leaving the employment at the request of the employer, on grounds of redundancy, ill-health supported by medical evidence or old age shall qualify under this article."

The plaintiff had worked for the defendants for 39 years, and was being retired by the company when he was 60 years of age. The issue was whether or not he was entitled to any benefits under the agreement. The defendants claimed that the plaintiff would only be so entitled if his termination of appointment was premature. The letter that retired the plaintiff was in these terms :

7th February, 1963.

" Dear Sir,

Much to our regret we have to inform you that the time of your retirement has come. According to information received, the maximum age of retirement is 60 years and since you have reached that age on December, 1962, we are obliged to ask you to take your retirement.

It may be that you don't feel yet that you need to leave the work, but unfortunately we must stick to what is customary and we cannot establish a precedent by allowing an employee to exceed the age of retirement. Therefore we suggest that you leave the service of this company at the end of next month, or earlier if you wish to do so.

Yours faithfully,
C. Van Aken, Manager,
Sick-Hagemeyer (Ghana) Ltd."

The plaintiff contended among other things that he was still young in heart, that he did not see the provision in issue at the time of his employment, but as he was being retired on account of old age when he was still willing to work, he was entitled to the benefit. In a judgment that depended more on logic than on the provisions of the law,[91] the learned judge held in favour of the plaintiff's claim.

In Nigeria the position as derived from the authorities is that in cases of wrongful dismissal the courts are guided by the period of notice as specified in the contract of employment.[92] In the absence of any specific provision for notice in the agreement damages are assessed on what the court considers to be a reasonable notice. Reasonable notice in cases of employment for a fixed period has been held to be the unexpired term of the employment agreement.[93]

Thus in *Cattareo* v. *Da Rocha & anor*[93] the plaintiff was engaged as manager of the defendants' hotel, and being later dismissed by the said defendants, brought an action for wrongful dismissal claiming £440 damages. This amount represented the full amount of the plaintiff's salary, allowances and passage money, to which the plaintiff was entitled if the contract had run its full and normal course. The trial court found as a fact that the dismissal was wrongful and that the employment was for a fixed period which had not expired at the time of the dismissal. The plaintiff's claim was allowed in full. On appeal to the Full Court, the principle of allowing damages for the expired term was affirmed by the court, although certain deductions were made from the claim for what the court described as " these amounts being payable *de praesenti* instead of their due dates."

On the other hand in *Madrides* v. *Tangalakis & Co.*,[94] the plaintiff was in the employment of the defendants in Nigeria under an 18-months' contract which expired in January, 1929. At the request of an authorised agent of the defendants his stay was extended and he was promised continued employment after his leave. In fact the defendants refused to re-engage him after his leave and in an action for the breach he claimed the full amount of his salary and other allowances for the unexpired term of the agreement. The contract, however, contained a clause under which the company could terminate the employment at any time by giving the plaintiff one month's notice or paying him one month's salary in lieu of notice. A judgment by the trial court giving the full amount claimed to the plaintiff was upset by the Full Court on appeal. It was held that the plaintiff's damages were limited to the period specified in the agreement.[95]

Ahuronye v. *The University College, Ibadan*[96] dealt with the peculiar situation of an employment for an indefinite period with no provision for notice in the agreement. Here the plaintiff had worked for the defendants for seven years as a printer and had been dismissed. His annual salary at the time of his dismissal was £144 paid at the monthly rate of £12. In an action for damages for wrongful dismissal it was argued for the plaintiff that an employment at a salary per annum represented a general or indefinite hiring, meaning a hiring for a year certain and then from year to year and determinable only by a period of notice expiring at the end of the year. In rejecting this submission Hedges, Ag., C.J. held that the plaintiff belonged to a category of employees whose contracts were terminated at one month's notice by the University, and that the plaintiff was entitled to a similar period of notice. The important point about the case is that the court was ready to imply a period of notice similar to those of other employees comparable in status with the plaintiff.

Two recent decisions of the Nigerian Supreme Court have raised afresh the vital issue of the role of the courts in the security of employment in Nigeria. The first is *David Nwaokoro* v. *Sapele Urban District Council*.[97] In this case the plaintiff was a labourer in the service of the plaintiff council. Although he was rated on a daily basis he was in fact paid on a monthly basis. A letter purporting to terminate his appointment was in these terms:

> " Termination of Appointment:
> I regret to inform you that in view of the heavy rains, and the fact that you are lazy and idle, you have been found redundant, and the council has decided that you be terminated. This serves as a week's notice to you, and your services will not be required as from the 29th August, 1960. You should report to collect your money after this date."

In an action for damages for wrongful dismissal, it was argued for the plaintiff that the letter of termination did not comply with a regulation of the Local Government (Staff) Regulations, 1960 of Western Nigeria,[98] and that on the English authority of *Vine* v. *National Dock Labour Board*[99] the plaintiff's damages were his wages from the time of dismissal to the date of judgment. Regulation 91 of the Local Government (Staff) Regulations provided as follows:

> " 91. The appointment of a daily paid employee may not be terminated on the grounds of inefficiency unless he has within the immediately preceding six months been warned in writing that his work or conduct has been unsatisfactory."

In fact, no such written warning had been given to the plaintiff. The trial magistrate therefore allowed the plaintiff's claim, but on appeal to the High Court this judgment was set aside on two grounds, namely, that the plaintiff did not belong to the category of workers covered by the regulations, but that even if he did, the Council acted within their powers under Section 32 of the Labour Code Ordinance, which provides for seven days' notice to terminate the employment of daily paid labourers.[100]

Secondly, that the English decision was no guide since it was based on English legislation not in *pari materia* with the local enactments on the same subject. The Federal Supreme Court affirmed the decision of the High Court.

Several issues are raised by the above decision, but the one that concerns us here is the argument put forward by the Supreme Court in support of the defendants' case. Referring to the reasons for the dismissal, his Lordship had this to say:

> " If a master gives his servant a week's notice orally and tells him it is because he is lazy, he may feel that he did not deserve the epithet and ought not to be discharged, but cannot complain that he was wrongly dismissed; so, too, if the master gives notice in writing and adds that the servant is lazy and idle: the servant need not show the letter to anyone. We are concerned with a claim based on breach of contract, and with the power to discharge and the sufficiency of notice given by the Council in this case, in the light of the law of Nigeria."[101]

It is submitted with respect that this view of the role of the courts in safeguarding the interests of the parties in employment cases is a very narrow one. There is no reason why the law in Nigeria should not provide a remedy, not only for cases of wrongful dismissal (i.e. breach of contract as at present defined), but also instances of arbitrary dismissal. If employers are allowed to terminate the appointment of any employee even without good cause shown, there is a strong case for a re-examination of the legal rules governing the security of employments.[102]

The second case in *Anene* v. *J. Allen & Co. Ltd.*[103] This was another claim for among other things damages for wrongful termination of employment. The plaintiff had been in the service of the defendants for 25 years. On 5th July, 1960, he took part in a strike called by Joe Allen African Workers' Union (a registered trade union) of which he was a member. The strike lasted two weeks. In a settlement of the trade dispute between his Union and the defendant company (to which settlement the Government Industrial Relations Commissioner represented the Federal Ministry of Labour) the following terms were agreed on inter alia:

" (2) both the Management of the Company and the Union agreed that all employees of the Company who do not elect t return to work should be given their full normal benefits.

(3) the Union recognises a process of gradual recovery to normal production at all establishments of the Company, which will entail taking on those who elect to work by stages. The Company undertakes to re-employ as many staff as work can be found for.

(4) with a view to facilitating these arrangements, the management offers to restrict overtime for the time being.

(5) the Company will review all staff re-employed within a period of three months with a view to making a special recommendation to the Board for reinstatement of back service and all benefits attached to it."

The plaintiff had applied for reinstatement but the defendants replied informing him that they regarded the withdrawal of his services as his resignation and that they were entitled to this view on the basis of the agreement reached with his Union to which the Industrial Relations Commissioner was a party. Both the trial court and the Supreme Court accepted the defendants' contention. Accordingly the plaintiff lost both his claim for damages for wrongful dismissal and for other benefits. Again this is another hard case on the employee. It is not easy to see how a union whose primary function is to safeguard the interests of its members, could have intended the meaning read into the clauses of the agreement by his Lordship. It is submitted with respect that this is another sad instance of the purist individualistic approach to the construction of agreements.[104]

Sale of goods

This is another aspect of the law in which the judges have adopted the purist individualistic approach to the interpretation of agreements. Contracts relating to the sale of goods are regulated in England by the Sale of Goods Act, 1893. This Act is also in force in Nigeria (except in the Western Region)[105] since it is a pre-1900 English Statute of general application.[106] It is not, however, in force in Ghana, and before July, 1962, the Ghana Courts had to rely on common law rules when any dispute arose between the parties to an agreement for the sale of goods.[107] The present position in Ghana is regulated by the Sale of Goods Act, 1962 (Act 137). Thus in the two territories with which we are here concerned the subject is governed by three separate though substantially similar enactments, namely, the Sale of Goods Act, 1893 (England) which is substantially in force in Nigeria (Federal Territory), Eastern and Northern Nigeria; the Sale of Goods Law, 1959,[108] which is in force in the Western and Mid-Western Regions of Nigeria; and finally the Sale of Goods Act (Ghana), 1962, which regulates the subject in Ghana.

It must be observed that the position is not as complicated as it at first sight appears to be. In Eastern and Northern Nigeria the Sale of Goods Act, 1893, is in force. The position is different from the current English law on the subject, since the Law Reform (Enforcement of Contracts) Act, 1954, which in England repeals Section 4 of the Sale of Goods Act, 1893, does not apply to the two regions. Thus in both the Eastern and the Northern regions contracts for the sale of goods of up to and above £10 are only enforceable if they are evidenced in writing.[109]

The Nigerian Law Reform (Contracts) Act, 1961 (Federation),[110] by its Section 7 adopts the current English law position with regard to contracts made after the commencement of the enactment (i.e. 28th December, 1961). The effect of this is that for those contracts made before 28th December, 1961, the Sale of Goods Act, 1893, is still in full application.

The Western Nigeria Sale of Goods law also adopts the current English law position on the sale of goods. It is arguable, however, if pre-1959 contracts are affected by the new enactment in view of Section 4 (c) of the Law of England (Application) Law, which makes savings for existing " rights, privileges, obligations or liability which accrued " or were incurred under any hitherto applicable imperial statute. Although one would stipulate for a more uniform law on the sale of goods in all the Nigerian jurisdictions, it must be emphasised that there has not been any noticeable divergence from the position in England.

The Ghana legislation, however, quite apart from its being more comprehensive and wider in scope[111] than its English and Nigerian counterparts, also makes slight departures from the English model.

Firstly, Section 1 (i) defines a contract of sale of goods as a " contract whereby the seller agrees to transfer the property in goods to the buyer for a consideration called the price, consisting wholly or partly of money." Thus in Ghana unlike in England and Nigeria, the price of goods need not be wholly in money form. Although there have been no local judicial decisions on the meaning of this section, it is contended that it includes in the category of sale of goods such situations as trade by barter where the differences in value are made up by one of the parties in the form of money.

Secondly, Section 8 of the Ghana Act, provides for what is

described as the " fundamental obligation " of the seller of goods. There is an express prohibition against his excluding any liability on himself for a breach of this obligation. This is an obvious step forward in this aspect of the law. It is an improvement on the English position.[112]

Thirdly, Section 16 (2) provides that unless a contrary intention appears, stipulations as to the time of delivery are conditions of a contract of sale. This is of course an enactment of the common law position where time is of the essence of the contract unless the parties expressly make it not so.[113]

Finally, the Ghana legislation provides against the forfeiture by the buyer of any sums paid by him in furtherance of the sale. The provision is as follows:

" 57 (1) Where under a contract of sale the buyer has paid a part or all the price to the seller and the seller refuses or neglects to deliver the goods to the buyer, having the right so to do, or, after delivering the goods, recovers the possession thereof having the right to do so, the buyer is entitled (without prejudice to any other rights, but subject to any counterclaim for damages by the seller) to recover from the seller the amounts which he has paid.

(2) This section applies whether the amounts paid by the buyer were expressed to be by way of part payment or deposit or otherwise, and notwithstanding any agreement to the contrary.

(3) Nothing in this section affects any case where the seller's refusal or neglect to deliver the goods, or his recovery of the possession thereof is wrongful."

There is no corresponding provision in the English or Western Nigeria enactment on the subject. The meaning of the section was in issue in the recent Ghana case of *Obeng* v. *Gyamfi*[114] decided by Charles, J. at Sunyani (Brong Ahafo Region). This was a claim by the plaintiff for £500 or, in the alternative, a car on which he had paid a deposit but which the defendant had sold to a third party. The facts were that the plaintiff had entered into a credit sale agreement with the defendant one of the terms of which was " that according to the tenor of this agreement if the second party shall fail the terms herein stated the first party shall have to seize the vehicle and give him one month notice in writing and if he shall still fail, the vehicle must be sold by the first party for money to cover or liquidate the then balance of its actual cost." The plaintiff had paid an initial deposit of £150 and had paid only £20 in instalments after three months. In fact he was to pay £40 monthly. The defendant therefore seized the car but without the requisite notice, sold it. Charles, J. held that the sale was wrongful and applied Section 57 (1) of the Sale of Goods Act, 1962 in awarding the plaintiff £170 damages based on his £150 initial deposit and £20 subsequent payment.

It is, of course, too early to comment on the impact of Section 57 of the Ghana Act, but if the *Obeng* case is anything to go by, then it is submitted with respect that the Ghana experiment can hardly recommend itself to any other jurisdiction. Perhaps the courts may yet adopt a more liberal interpretation of the provision.[115]

Standard form Contracts and Exception Clauses[116]

The practice of one party preparing the terms of an agreement in advance and offering them on a take-it-or-leave-it basis to a mass of consumers has become a characteristic feature of modern contracts.[117] This ready-made contract, usually called the " standard form " contract, but sometimes called the rather uncommunicative name of " contracts of adhesion,"[118] seems to have first appeared in the courts in England in the so-called " ticket-cases." In these cases terms were printed on the receipt that the traveller got when he deposited his bag with the station attendant. Common-sense would dictate that such a document is but an acknowledgement of the fact that a passenger has paid his fare or left his luggage at a particular store, but the courts did not adopt this course even as a working principle.[119]

There has, however, been a phenomenal use of standard forms in all kinds of commercial transactions in recent years. In themselves these forms are of vital service to modern commerce. It is a timely answer to the problems posed by the large volume of modern economic activity in the age of automation. If the Electricity Board or the Gas Board had to enter into separate and different negotiated contracts with their consumers the resultant delay would be frustrating in the extreme. Having said this, one has to advert to the more fundamental issues raised by standard forms. We shall be examining two of these issues here, namely, the reasonableness of the terms embodied in the agreement, and secondly, the freedom of the parties to exclude themselves from liability for a breach of the terms. The subsidiary issue of the impact of illiteracy on this aspect of the law in Ghana and Nigeria will also be investigated.

Reasonableness of the terms

A remarkable feature of standard form agreements is the basic inequality of the parties. With the increasing concentration of business in the hands of a few large monopolies and multiple firms, and more threats of take-over bids, equality of bargaining power has become a transparent farce. Sir Henry Maine's statement in 1851 that "the movement of progressive societies has hitherto been a movement from status to contract,"[120] is now in obvious reverse. The position now appears to be from contract to status. The question that arises is, how far are the courts prepared to go in protecting the victim of patently unreasonable terms? Two hypothetical examples of such terms have been put forward. Professor Milner in his Cases and Materials on Contracts, has the following:

> "I am wholly responsible for the return of the said article or articles and upon failure to return it or them on the due date, it shall be lawful for the lessors, their servants, or agents and with such other assistant or assistants, as they may require, at any time during the day or night to enter in or upon my lands, tenements, houses and premises wheresoever and whatsoever, where the said articles or any part thereof may be and for such persons to break and force open doors, locks, bolts, fastenings, hinges, gates, fences, houses, buildings, enclosures and places for the purpose of taking possession of and removing the said articles for the purpose of regaining possession of them."[121]

Bramwell, L.J. in the *Parker* case has also the following:

> "It is asked: What if there was some unreasonable condition, as for instance to forfeit £1,000 if the goods were not removed in forty-eight hours? Would the depositors be bound?"[122]

The answer to the questions posed by similar terms has agitated the English Courts for nearly a century. Their basic attitude to these terms is exemplified in the statement of Erle, J. in the Exchequer Chamber decision of *McManus* v. *Lancashire and Yorkshire Railway*,[123] that "the notion that customers of railways require protection on account of incapacity to resist oppression, is not more true than the notion that, against a large proportion of customers, railway companies stand in need of every aid the law can afford." Even if this approach was consistent with 19th century economic theory in England, there has been a large volume of protest against its continued application in the present century.[124] It is obviously unsuitable for present-day conditions in both Ghana and Nigeria often described as welfare states. Yet the local judicial opinion in the two countries has had very little to offer in any attempt to make the claim real.

Their approach to the construction of terms in contracts of employment has already been discussed. This attitude has been followed up in contracts of guarantee where the courts have persistently refused to exonerate the surety from his obligations even in clear instances of variation.[125] Fire and accident insurance policies have also been construed in this light. Thus in a recent case before the Ghana Supreme Court the plaintiff was injured in a motor accident and sued the defendants who were the insurers. The facts were that the plaintiff was picked up as a passenger for a fare from Accra to Aburi. The car, a private car, belonged to X (the insured) and was driven by Y. On the way the car ran into a ditch and the plaintiff sustained injuries. He did not in fact pay the fare because of the accident. The plaintiff obtained judgment against Y in the High Court for £1,473.10s. and since the car was covered by the defendant under Section 10 of the Ghana Motor Vehicle (Third Party Insurance) Act, 1958, he sued the defendants for the amount. The defendants argued that the car was covered for social, domestic and pleasure purposes, and for the insured's business only and did not cover use for hire and reward, or for racing, pace-making, reliability and speed tests, etc. The trial court held that the terms of the policy were wide enough to cover the plaintiff but this decision was upset on appeal by the Supreme Court.[126] The Nigerian Supreme Court arrived at a similar conclusion in the case of *Malik Matter* v. *Norwich Union Fire Insurance & Anor.*[127] But there was a counterblast in the Enugu High Court decision of *Oduah* v. *The Lion of Africa Insurance Co. Ltd*[128] where Palmer, J. found for the plaintiff.

In cases involving the carriage of goods both by sea and on land the courts have also adopted the attitude of presuming that the terms used by the parties are fair and therefore should not be interfered with. It need hardly be pointed out that such a presumption in jurisdictions where the mass of the population are illiterate reflects a very poor image of the law. As has been aptly pointed out by Sir Frederick Pollock in another connection " no law has ever been able to ignore the economic stratification of society."[129] We would add that the law should equally reflect the social stratification of society. Thus the position as set out in Section 70 of the *American Restatement of Contract* that " One who makes a written offer which is accepted or who manifests acceptance of the terms of a writing which he should reasonably understand to be an offer or proposed contract, is bound by the contract though ignorant of the terms of the writing or of its proper interpretation,"[130] is hardly applicable in its entirety to Ghana and Nigeria. It is no defence to rely on the Illiterates Protection Ordinances, which provide that any terms should be interpreted to the illiterates by licensed letter-writers. Quite apart from the difficulties of translating technical terms into vernaculars (which the letter-writers are rather ill-equipped to undertake), it is submitted the unconscionable terms do not become less so by reason only of their being rendered in vernaculars. If the aim of contract is to regulate the economic life of the society there is no reason why the doctrine of repugnancy should not be imported by the courts into this aspect of the law to strike down any terms which are repugnant to the general principles of fair dealing. In this way the courts will regain the confidence both of business and the common man in the judicial process and arrest the increasing tendency of resorting to extra-judicial measures to redress breaches of agreements.[131]

Exception clauses[132]

The other problem posed by the prevalence of standard forms is the regular practice of one of the parties inserting terms in the agreement to the effect that he will not be liable in the event of any breach of some of or all the obligations created by the contract. These clauses are most common in cases of carriage, bailment and sale of goods. Consistent with their theory of the equality of the parties to an agreement, the English courts (with a few dissenting voices) have often been ready to enforce the agreement freely entered into by the said parties. But as has already been noted, not all the stipulations of an agreement go to its root. Also some of the terms are implied into the contract either by trade usage or by statute. Examples of such implied terms are found in cases of carriage by sea and sale of goods.[133] The vital question that arises is the extent to which (if at all) the parties will be permitted to exempt themselves from liability for breach of the terms, express or implied, of their agreement. This problem has been accentuated by the prolixity of modern business, the comprehensive nature of the documents used, with the clauses almost always in very fine print, in nearly all cases hardly read by the other party.[134]

The orthodox treatment of this subject has been befogged by the use of such words and phrases as conditions, warranties, fundamental terms and fundamental obligations. A case study of the meaning of each of these words and phrases leaves an enquirer more confused than he began.[135] The recent House of Lords decision of *Suisse Atlant* v. *N. V. Rotterdam* etc.[136] in which Viscount Dilhorne and Lord Upjohn tried obiter to distinguish between a fundamental term and a fundamental breach, stresses the urgency of a clear statement of policy in this branch of the law. The Northern Nigerian High Court was up against the same problem in *Ogwu* v. *Leventis Motors Ltd.*[137]

Three questions appear to us pertinent in any discussion of the subject of exception clauses. Firstly, have the parties or any of them the freedom to exclude themselves from liability for the breach of any of his obligations under the agreement? Secondly, if the answer to the first question is positive, are there any, and if so, what exceptions to the general rule? In other words, are there any terms which the parties cannot exclude liability for under the agreement? Finally, what is yet to be done in this aspect of the law?

(a) *Freedom to exclude terms*

The presumption that the equality of the parties to a contract is the basis of the English law of agreements, has been sufficiently discussed. The basic inequality of these parties in modern contractual situations has also been mentioned. In spite of the latter tendency, there is still statutory and judicial support for the view that the parties are free to exclude any liability for the breach of certain terms. In respect of sale of goods and hire-purchase contracts, the Ghana Sale of Goods Act, 1962,[188] provides as follows:

> " S.76: Subject to the provisions of this Act, the rights, duties and liabilities of the parties to a contract of sale, as laid down in this Act may, as between the parties themselves, be varied by express agreement, or by the course of dealing between parties, or by trade usage, or by custom (whether a rule of customary law or not) which the parties may be taken to have agreed to be applicable to the contract."

A peculiar feature of the Ghana enactment is that the freedom of the parties to exclude terms is subject to the provisions of the Act. Thus under Section 8 of the Act, which deals with the fundamental obligations of the seller, it is provided that any provision in a contract of sale which is inconsistent with, or repugnant to, the fundamental obligation of the seller, is void to the extent of the inconsistency or repugnance.[189] In the *Suisse Atlant*[140] case where the House of Lords had to determine the effect of an exception clause in a charter party, it was held among other things that:

> " There is no rule of law that an exception clause is nullified by a fundamental breach of contract or breach of a fundamental term, but in each case the question is one of the construction of the contract whether the exceptions clause was intended to give exemption from the consequences of fundamental breach; if a breach occurs, entitling the other party to repudiate the contract, but he elects to affirm it, the exception clause continues unless

on the true construction of the contract the exceptions clause is not intended to apply to and to continue after such a breach, in which case the party in breach is unable to rely on the exceptions clause."

Without at this stage going into the distinctions between a fundamental breach and the breach of a fundamental term, it must be observed that this decision of high authority summarises the position in English law. The parties are free to exclude any terms from their agreement; all the courts do is to construe the effect of the exclusion clauses having regard to the dealings between the parties. The Nigerian courts, on the other hand, have adopted the position that, although the parties are free to exclude themselves from liability for the breach of certain terms of the agreement, there are some obligations which are vital to the very existence of the agreement where no such exclusion will be recognised.[141] This is, of course, the position in Ghana in view of Section 76 of the Sale of Goods Act, 1962, to which reference has already been made.

(b) *Limits on the parties' freedom to exclude terms*

Two recent decisions of the Nigerian courts have attempted to delimit the scope of the freedom of the parties to exclude any liability for their breach. In the first case, the defendant had agreed by correspondence to buy a specified quality of foreign cloth from the plaintiffs. A sample had been supplied the defendant and it was a term of the contract that the consignment should correspond to the sample and description. The agreement also contained an exemption clause to the effect that the plaintiffs did not undertake any guarantees or admit any claims for foreign goods beyond such as were admitted by the manufacturers. In fact the first consignment did not conform to the description and the defendant rejected the goods. The plaintiffs sued for the price of the consignment and the defendant counterclaimed for the breach of contract. The plaintiffs relied on the exemption clause. The trial court found for the defendant but this was upset by the Federal Supreme Court on appeal. The defendant appealed to the Judicial Committee of the Privy Council where it was held, inter alia, that an exemption[142] clause in a contract will avail a party only if he is carrying out the contract in its essential respects; and a breach which goes to the root of a contract disentitles the party from relying on such clause. In this case, the exemption would apply only if the goods were in accordance with the contract: as they were substantially different, the exemption cannot avail the respondent (plaintiffs).[143] In the second case where the defendant delivered a car four years older than the one contracted for and in many respects radically different (except the number plate), Smith, S.P.J. in the Northern Nigeria High Court, held that there had been a breach of a fundamental term of the contract and that the exception clause did not avail the respondents.[144] The latter decision has been criticised on the ground that the exclusion clause in the agreement exempted the defendants from liability only for breach of warranties and not for breach of conditions. In fact, what occurred was a breach of condition and so the exception clause did not apply. But the court decided the case on the basis of a breach of a fundamental obligation, which would introduce some confusion into this aspect of the law.[145] We are in agreement with the learned author that the introduction of such phrases as fundamental breach of agreement or the breach of a fundamental term would further confuse rather than explain the law. This is borne out by two dicta from the House of Lords. The first in *Smeaton Hanscomb and Co. Ltd.* v. *Sassoon and Sethy Son & Co.* is as follows:

> " It is, no doubt, a principle of construction that exceptions are construed as not being applicable for the protection of those for whose benefit they are inserted if the beneficiary has committed a breach of a fundamental term in the contract. . . . I do not think that what is a fundamental term has ever been clearly defined. It must be something, I think, narrower than a condition of a contract, for it would be limiting the exceptions too much to say that they applied only to breaches of warranty. It is, I think, something which underlies the whole contract so that, if it is not complied with, the performance becomes something totally different from that which the contract contemplates."[146]

And the second by Viscount Dilhorne and Lord Upjohn and to which reference has already been made is an attempt to distinguish a fundamental breach from the breach of a fundamental term.[147]

On the other hand, we must with respect differ from the author's substitute of conditions and warranties as a safer test in assessing the importance of the stipulation in a contract. This is because there is no magic in the words. In fact, the courts are still up against the task of determining the remedies due to a plaintiff who has affirmed an agreement in which there has been a breach of condition.[148] It is submitted that what the courts require is the acceptance of a theory of agreements based on fair play and good faith. Any stipulation in a contract that is repugnant to this theory will be void to the extent of the inconsistency. If after removing the void stipulations of an agreement the contract can no longer exist as such, then the rights and duties of the parties will as much as possible be restored to *status quo ante*. This approach will conveniently avoid the hair splitting distinctions of conditions, warranties, etc. with their attendant dead weight of judicial and academic literature.

This approach is also consistent with the Islamic law view of exception clauses. It is against the general theory of Islamic law for a party to insert a clause that will exclude him from liability for the breach of his obligation under any transaction. We would commend this view for quick importation into the general law of agreements.[149] So the answer to the second question is that any exclusion of liability for the breach of any stipulation in an agreement should be consistent with a general theory of fair dealing and good faith in contracts.

(c) *What is yet to be done in this aspect of the law?*

The experience of English law in respect of standard forms and exception clauses has belied the suggestion of the French philosopher, Voltaire, that even the worst of evils become respectable with age. In fact, the menace of exclusion provisions is still very real. The attempts so far made, or which ought to be made, by the legislatures of Ghana and Nigeria to curb the worst excesses of this development will be discussed later.[150] Mr. Sales in the article,[151] to which reference has already been made, has advocated a more liberal approach by the courts to the construction of these terms. He has also proposed a supervisory body in the form of a Consumers' Board to oversee the terms of agreements. Allott, in a proposal called " *Fair Contracts* (*Consumers Protection*) *Act* "[152] has proposed a Consumers' Court to protect the interest of the parties to certain agreements. The remarkable feature of the latter proposal (which will be discussed in some detail in a subsequent section) is the sweeping powers that the Consumers' Court will possess. These powers will mainly be exercised in favour of the consumer. It need hardly be said that no weapon is too lethal in the defence of the otherwise helpless consumer, in the face of the fast moving avalanche of monopolies and multiple firms. Such powers will also be a necessary corrective to the so many weaknesses of the purist individualistic approach to the construction of agreements.

(b) THE PATERNALIST APPROACH[153]

Under this subheading we shall be examining two categories of agreements—hire purchase and moneylending transactions. Although the former has often been subjoined to a discussion of the sale of goods, and the latter under illegal agreements, we feel, however, that the courts in Ghana and Nigeria adopt a basic similarity of approach in dealing with cases arising under these heads. The similarity in the end results of these cases justifies the joint treatment and it is the approach that the courts have adopted that we are here to explore. The principle that runs through most of the cases is that of a court posing as a father-figure to protect the hirer and the borrower against the owner and the moneylender respectively.

(i) *Hire-purchase transactions*

The increasing variety of the amenities of modern life, the limits imposed by limited incomes, and the economic theory of choice all combine to welcome the timely arrival into the commercial scene of payment by instalments either in the form of credit sales or of hire-purchase transactions. This practice which has reached a high degree of sophistication in the more highly industrialised countries,[154] is fast becoming an important factor in the commercial life of the people of Ghana and Nigeria. In Ghana a hire-purchase contract is defined as a contract of sale of goods in which the price is paid in five or more instalments.[155] It is distinguished from credit-sale agreements in this respect that in the latter the property in the goods passes to the purchaser on delivery, while in the former the title does not pass until after the payment of the last instalment. An attempt to evolve a third category called "work and pay" contracts in the case of *Dodoo* v. *Ashitey*[156] was disallowed by Archer, J. at the High Court, Accra. Distinguishing it from a credit sale agreement, he added:

> "I regret I have not been able to classify it and as I do not wish to take judicial notice now of the concept of 'work and pay', it is my hope that another judge well-versed in the niceties of ascertaining and taking judicial notice of such amphibious commercial concepts will be bold enough to do so with confidence."

Before 1958, hire-purchase in Ghana was regulated under the common law which in this case meant the agreement of the parties. Thus even if 99 per cent of the purchase price had been paid the owner could seize the goods from the hirer who would have no remedies under the agreement in the event of a default. In such a case the owner would often get more than his due share of profit on a particular transaction. It must be added that some hirers exploited hire-purchase facilities to acquire goods that they had no means of paying for. The Hire-Purchase Act, 1958[157] (Ghana) was enacted on the model of the 1938 English Act to regulate these transactions. Among other things the Act provided for a resort to the courts by the owner in order to recover possession of the goods if three-quarters of the price had been paid by the hirer. The Sale of Goods Act, 1962 (Ghana), which now regulates hire-purchase contracts in Ghana, substitutes 50 per cent of the price for 75 per cent.[158]

The remarkable fact is that the courts, perhaps as a result of the general feeling that hirers of goods are a class which the Act was intended to protect, have resorted to a strict construction of the provisions of the enactments. The general attitude has been that of allowing the hirer to recover all his instalments and any initial deposit, if there was a slight deviation from the terms laid down in the Acts. Thus in *U.T.C.* v. *Johnson Okoro*,[159] the High Court at Sekondi (Ghana) was faced with the effect of Section 17 of the 1958 Act. This was the section that dealt with the restrictions on the owner's right to recover possession when three-quarters of the purchase price had been paid. In the present case the defendant had in fact paid more than the statutory provision on the first agreement, but the plaintiffs had purported to substitute a second hire-purchase agreement. This second agreement did not, however, comply with the schedule of the Act in respect of the owner not being allowed to retake possession if three-quarters of the purchase price had been paid. The court therefore held that the second agreement was void. Since the plaintiffs had taken possession of the vehicle, the subject-matter of the agreement, and were suing for the balance of instalments due, the court was to decide whether the defendant was liable. The defendant had counterclaimed for his initial deposit and the instalments already paid. It was held that the defendant was entitled to recover. Also in *Yeboah* v. *C.F.A.O.* (Technical),[160] Section 12 of the Hire-purchase Act, 1958, was in issue. The facts were that:

In 1960, the plaintiff, a timber contractor, bought a tractor on hire-purchase from the defendants at a cost of £9,810. When £5,360 had been paid, the tractor developed some trouble and was taken in by the defendants for repairs. In 1961 the account was transferred to a new tractor and a new agreement was made between the parties. The cost of the new tractor was £9,950, and since £5,360 had been paid the defendants could not take the tractor without the consent of the plaintiff or a court order. In fact, the defendants had repaired the said tractor and had sold it because the plaintiff had not continued with his instalments nor paid for the repairs. In an action for the refund of his deposit and instalments, it was held that he was entitled to succeed.

In addition to the sums so refunded the court also awarded the plaintiff £5,360 damages for what it called wrongful seizure of the vehicle. This was the amount paid on the first transaction which, as has been noted, was transferred to the new agreement. The court further awarded £2,000 damages against the defendants for their selling the vehicle while proceedings were already instituted. Costs totalling 200 guineas were added on to the pile. In effect, the defendants, in addition to losing £7,985 4s.7d. which was paid back to the plaintiff, were also ordered to pay £7,570 in the form of damages. Perhaps the court was influenced by the fact that the defendants made some good profit from the sale of the tractor and the fact that the sale took place while the proceedings were before their lordships. If this can be said for the £2,000 damages, it is difficult to find any support for the additional £5,360 based on an agreement that was neither before the court nor in issue. It is respectfully submitted that with this approach to the interpretation of this category of agreements no hire-purchase company can stay in business very long. The whole purpose of this type of agreement will be sadly defeated.[161]

This attitude of the courts since the enactment of the Hire-purchase Acts is in vast contrast to the position before the Acts. Thus in *Swanzy Ltd.* v. *Djarnie*[162] an action by the plaintiff company to recover arrears of instalments after taking possession of the lorry (the subject-matter of the agreement), it was held that the defendant would forfeit his £100 deposit and was also liable for the arrears of instalments. A plea of illiteracy did not avail the defendant. Also in *Sani* v. *U.T.C.*,[163] the plaintiff bought a lorry from the defendants on hire-purchase, and in January, 1928, was in arrears to the extent of £34 2s.6d. Then he bought a second lorry, paying a deposit of £102. Subsequently he paid £26 and £28, but nothing was said as to which lorry the payments were for. The defendants seized the first lorry on account of the arrears and the plaintiff sued for its return. It was held by the Divisional Court (Accra) that the defendants were entitled to appropriate the payments to the second lorry.[164]

There was no enactment regulating hire-purchase in Nigeria before the Hire-purchase Act, 1965, and this Act applied only to the Federal territory. Under Section 9 of the Act, the owner cannot retake possession of the goods hired without obtaining a court order, if the hirer had paid three-fifths of the purchase price in the case of motor-vehicles, and half the price in other cases.[165] This Act has now been extended by decree to the other regions of Nigeria by the National Military Government as it was then called. No reported decisions have, however, been made in any of its provisions.[166]

(ii) *Moneylending transactions*

In both Ghana and Nigeria moneylending transactions caught the attention of the legislatures at an earlier period than did hire-purchase agreements. This may be due to the high rates of interest charged by these lenders. Thus as early as 1918 the Ghana Loans Recovery Ordinance was enacted, Section 3 of which empowered the courts to reopen transactions between moneylenders and borrowers with a view to disallowing cases of excessive interest.[167] A similar provision against excessive interest is found in the Nigerian Moneylenders Ordinance,[168] Section 14 of which imposes a penalty on any moneylender who charges interests higher than those provided in the enactment. The whole tenor of the Nigerian and Ghana legislation, as is the English Moneylenders Acts of 1900 and 1927, is on the protection of the public against the excessive charges of some moneylenders. Thus in each of them the money-lender must be properly licensed,[169] must keep correct and consistent records[170] and must furnish certain information on demand.[171] While the English legislation makes any agreement that does not comply with the enactment unenforceable, both the Ghana and the Nigerian Ordinances impose penalties on the defaulting lender, thus making the agreement illegal and void.[172] There is, however, in the latter enactments, protection of the rights of third parties who have acted in good faith and without notice.

We shall now look at the way the courts have construed the provisions of these Ordinances. In *Nwosu* v. *Ekezies*,[173] Section 6 of the Lagos Moneylenders Act[174] was in issue. The facts were that a moneylender obtained a licence on a certificate which was defective as it did not specify the name and address of the bank at which the moneylender maintained a current account as required by Section 6 (3A) of the Moneylenders Act. In an action to recover the loan from the defendant it was argued that the omission did invalidate the certificate and that the transaction was unenforceable. It was, however, held by De Lestang, C.J., that the plaintiff should succeed. The reason for the holding was that the omission was not the fault of the plaintiff but that of the magistrate who issued the certificate without adverting to the new provision regulating the giving of certificates.

In *Abesin & anor.* v. *Iyaegbe*[175] the respondent was a moneylender who had succeeded in the lower court in an action for a claim of £100 from the appellants. In fact, the memorandum relied on by the respondent was not shown to have been signed by the moneylender or her agent in compliance with Section 12 (1) of the Ordinance, and the interest charged on the loan was said to be excessive[176] (in contravention of Section 13 (1) of the same Ordinance). The High Court at Abeokuta (W. Nigeria) held that the agreement was unenforceable, thereby allowing the appeal. The respondent's plea of illiteracy and that the document was signed by a deceased agent, was lightly dismissed by the Court.[177] But where the loan was secured with a mortgage and the moneylender had exercised his power of sale under the mortgage, it was held that the title of the innocent purchaser for value without notice of the defect in title was not defeated by the said defect.[178] This decision is, of course, in accordance with Section 23 of the Ordinance which makes saving for the title of innocent assignees. Also in *Sanusi* v. *Daniel & anor.*[179] an innocent purchaser at an auction sale validly conducted by the agent of a moneylender who had contravened Section 12 (1) of the Ordinance, was held to have acquired a good title. A remarkable feature of these decisions is that although the innocent assignees acquire good title, the overriding consideration is not that of the moneylender's interest but that of the third party. This view is reinforced by the provision for a penalty against the moneylender under Section 14 of the Ordinance.[180]

It is Section 19 of the Ordinance that has agitated the courts most. In the leading case of *Kasumu* v. *Baba-Egbe*[181] the respondent had mortgaged some leasehold land to a licensed moneylender as security for a loan. The appellants were the administrators of the moneylender's estate. The moneylender had admittedly kept no book recording the transactions as required by Section 19 of the Moneylenders Ordinance. The respondent therefore instituted proceedings claiming the redemption of the property and the recovery of possession. The relevant provision of the Ordinance is as follows:

" 19 (1) Every moneylender shall give a receipt for every payment made to him on account of a loan or of interest thereon. Every such receipt shall be given immediately the payment is made.

(2) Every moneylender shall keep a book (which shall be securely bound and paged so that leaves cannot be removed or inserted without apparent damage) in which he shall enter in connection with every loan made by him—

(a) the date on which the loan was made;

(b) the amount of the principal;

(c) the rate of interest;

(d) all sums received in respect of the loan or the interest thereon, with the dates of payment thereof, and shall produce such book when required to do so by any court.[182]

(4) Any moneylender who fails to comply with any of the

requirements of this section shall not be entitled to enforce any
claim in respect of any transaction in relation to which the default
shall have been made. He shall also be guilty of an offence under
this Ordinance and shall be liable on conviction to a fine of ten
pounds or in the case of a continuing offence to a fine of five
pounds for each day or part of a day during which such offence
continues."

The issue before the court was whether the respondents would
be allowed to regain possession of the mortgaged land without
making good the loan from the deceased moneylender. The
appellants had relied on the leading English authority of *Lodge* v.
National Union Investment Co. Ltd.[183] where it was held by
Parker, J. that in an equitable action by a borrower to recover
securities mortgaged to an unregistered moneylender the mortgagee
will not be ordered to give up to the mortgagor the securities the
subject of the mortgage except upon the terms that the mortgagor
shall repay the money which has been advanced to him. The
respondents on the other hand had relied on the judgment of
Eve, J. in the equally important case of *Chapman* v. *Michaelson*[184]
where it was held that in an action by the trustee of a debtor
under a scheme of arrangement with his creditors against an
unregistered moneylender who had taken a mortgage from the
debtor to secure a loan, the court will make a mere declaratory
order that the mortgage is illegal and void under Section 2[185] of
the Moneylenders Act, 1900, although no ancillary relief is asked.
In such a case the court will not impose upon the plaintiff
equitable terms as to repayment of the actual money advanced as
a condition of making the declaratory order. The Supreme Court
of Nigeria ruled that an account be taken by the parties and
that the appellants be paid any outstanding balance as a condition for the delivery of the premises. On appeal to the West
African Court of Appeal[186] this ruling was set aside and it was
held that the loan and mortgage transaction was void as being
contrary to the provisions of the Moneylenders Ordinance. This
decision was affirmed on appeal by the Judicial Committee of the
Privy Council.

Lord Radcliffe, who read the judgment of the Committee,
stressed the impact of the penal provision in Section 19 of the
Nigerian Ordinance to which there is no corresponding provision
in the English enactment. To ask the respondents to refund the
amount borrowed as a condition for regaining possession, was, in
his Lordship's view, tantamount to enforcing what the legislature
had expressly prohibited. Secondly, the respondents were not asking
for an equitable relief but a declaration that the transaction was

Y

void. Thus the *Lodge* case was distinguishable while the *Chapman* decision was more applicable. The result was that the respondents kept both the £1,541.2.6. being the balance found by the Supreme Court of the loan of £2,000, and in addition had reconveyed to them the premises which the deceased moneylender had occupied for five years before the proceedings were instituted.

Two aspects of the *Kasumu* decision deserve some comment. Firstly, it is not helpful to distinguish between a legal and an equitable remedy in a court where both law and equity are to be administered concurrently. To continue to draw this distinction is to allow the decision in a case to depend on the form of the plaintiff's claim and not the substance of the action. The distinction between a declaration that the mortgage transaction is void and an order for the cancellation of the mortgage (legal and equitable remedies respectively) is, it is submitted, a question of the use of words. The legal effect of the two should not be as vastly different as the *Kasumu* case tends to suggest.

Secondly, their Lordships argued that the Moneylenders Ordinance was intended to protect a class of people to which the respondents belonged. The effect of this is that they are not themselves guilty of breaking the provisions of the Ordinance and are therefore entitled to relief. The *Kasumu* decision, however, goes much farther than protecting borrowers. It provides them with a safe avenue for financial advancement at the expense of an unfortunate moneylender who happened to omit an entry into his books. He loses both his money and any security he may have received. Surely the court ought to be given some discretion in the matter so that they can adjust the equities of the parties. It is submitted that the present rigid application of the provisions of the Moneylenders Ordinance underestimates the service that these licensed lenders give to the society. A discretion similar to that given to the courts in cases of frustrated contracts[187] ought to be imported into moneylending transactions. This will be a better way of adjusting the rights of the parties. It is obviously a worthwhile boost to the moneylending business.[188] The latter suggestion is equally true of all the other decisions on the various sections of the Ordinances both in Ghana and Nigeria.[189]

Critical assessment of the role of the courts in the construction of agreements:

We have so far been concerned with a case-study of the role of the courts in the construction of agreements. It has been shown that in one group of cases the courts treat the terms used by the parties as more or less sacrosanct, while in another group of decisions they assume the role of protecting the less privileged party to the agreement. The question that must be answered here is whether the courts have done all that they should do in reconciling the conflict between individual liberty and the general welfare of the community through the construction of agreements.

It must be pointed out that none of the two approaches described above is adequate on its own. The dissenting opinion of Frankfurter, J. in the leading United States case of *Bethlehem Steel* v. *United States Steel Corporation*,[190] demonstrates very clearly the absurdity of the purist individualistic approach to the interpretation of agreements. In that case the United States Government sought to recover from the Bethlehem Steel Corporation vast profits claimed under wartime contracts made in 1918 between Bethlehem Steel and the U.S. Steel Corporation. Bethlehem Steel undertook to build a number of ships to meet the emergency caused by German submarine warfare during the second world war. The Government claimed that the agreed profits averaging over 22 per cent of the computed cost were excessive and, due to the exploitation by Steel Corporation of a wartime emergency, the Government, it was contended, was compelled to accept the terms of the country's leading shipbuilder. The majority of the U.S. Supreme Court rejected this attempt to apply what it described as "corrective justice," on the principle of "social solidarity" in wartime to a commercial contract. One reason for this decision was the rejection of the suggestion that the U.S. Government was in a position of bargaining inferiority; and the other was that the court felt that it was for Congress to determine the proper method of obtaining war supplies from the citizens and not for the court to do so. Frankfurther, J., on the other hand, held that "the court should not permit Bethlehem Steel to recover these unconscionable profits and thereby make the court the instrument of injustice." With this dissenting opinion of the learned judge we are respectfully in agreement. The judicial process should not shy away from the vital task of social and economic redistribution. Wholesale enforcement of the terms set down by the parties is hardly consistent with the attainment of this cherished goal.

On the other hand, the extreme attitude of construing the statutory provisions in hire-purchase and moneylending transactions strictly against commerce[191] cannot be justified. What is required is an element of discretion in the courts which will be exercised in a manner consistent both with the advancement of modern business and the freedom of the individual.

NOTES

1. R. Pound, *An Introduction to the Philosophy of Law* (Los Angeles, 1953).
2. In Ghana these were called Local Courts, in Northern Nigeria they are called Native Courts. Here we use "Customary Courts" to refer to all of them since it appears to be the more common form. In Eastern, Western and Mid-Western Regions of Nigeria, they are referred to as Customary Courts.
3. Decree No. 84, (C.A.) 1966.
4. S. 98 (f) Ghana Courts Act, 1960 (C.A. 9). The Courts Act, 1960, has been repealed by the Courts Decree, 1966, which has abolished the Local Courts and transferred their jurisdiction to the District Courts.
5. Cap. 78, Laws of Northern Nigeria (1963).
6. Cases on Contract and allied matters decided in the Ghana Local Courts for the year 1963 were as follows: Central Region 8090; Western Region 11407; Ashanti Region 4884; Volta Region 2593; Northern Region 870; Upper Region 163. Figures extracted from Ministry of Justice File—Accra, Ghana.
7. See the Ghana case of *Lartei* v. *Fio* (1960) G.L.R. 119.
8. See, for instance, the judgment of the court in the Nigerian case of *Ugboma* v. *Morah* (1940) 15. N.L.R. 78—where it was stated that the action for breach of marriage promise is not recognised in customary law.
9. S. 66 (1) Rule (2) of the Ghana Courts Act, 1960 (C.A. 9).
10. SS. 12 and 13 of the Western Nigeria High Courts Law Cap. 44, Laws of Western Nigeria; and SS. 15 and 20 of the Eastern Nigeria High Court Law, Cap. 61, Laws of Eastern Nigeria; see also SS. 13 and 27 of the High Court of Lagos Act, Cap. 80, Laws of the Federation (1958).
11. R. D. Kollewijn, "Inter-Racial Private Law" in the *Effect of Western Influence on Native Civilization in the Malaya Archipelago* (ed. B Schrieke, 1929).
12. Compare the results of the Nigerian cases of *Rotibi* v. *Savage* (1944) 17 N.L.R. 77, where the Statute of Limitations was held not applicable, and *Bakare* v. *Coker* (1935) 12. N.L.R. 31, where it was held to apply to the transaction. See also the Ghana cases of *Ferguson* v. *Duncan* (1953) 14 W.A.C.A. 316 and *Kwesi-Johnson* v. *Effie* (1953) 14 W.A.C.A. 254. The latter decision was criticised by Allott in *Essays*, p. 252. The Statute of Limitations was also in issue in *Amarquaye* v. *Broener* (1889) Ren. 145 and *Hughes* v. *Davies* (1909) Ren. 556.
13. *Mue* v. *Nyumutei* (1926-29) Div. Ct. 93; *Muffatt* v. *Trading Association* (1926-29) Div. Ct. 59. See also the Nigerian case of *Savage* v. *Uwechia* (1961) 1 All E.R. 830. P.C.
14. Cap. 80, Laws of the Federation and Lagos (1958).
15. See S. 13 of the Lagos High Court Act; S. 30 of the Northern Nigeria High Court Law and S. 12 of the Western Nigeria High Court Law.
16. (1934) 2 W.A.C.A. 188.
17. (1951) 13 W.A.C.A. 248.
18. Op. cit. at p. 191.
19. Redwar's *Comments on Gold Coast Ordinances*, p. 137.
20. (1951) 13 W.A.C.A. 248.
21. (1957) 3 W.A.L.R. 5. See also *Hamilton* v. *Mensah* (1937) 3 W.A.C.A. 224.
22. The question of the jurisdiction of the native or local courts as to the

law and persons is now purely an academic one in Ghana in view of SS. 96 and 98 of the Courts Act, 1960 (C.A. 9). Also the Court Decree, 1966, has abolished the Local Courts. See N.L.C. Decree No. 84 of 23rd September, 1966.

23. S. 32 (1) of the Interpretation Act, 1960.

24. For a comprehensive study of this aspect of the law, see Allott, *Essays*, Chapter 10.

25. *Essays*, p. 242. It may be added that question (v) is no longer important in Ghana since the Courts Act, 1960, has no formal limits on the jurisdiction of the local courts.

26. (1944) 17 N.L.R. 77.

27. Supreme Court Suit 194/1933—Unreported.

28. (1935) 12 N.L.R. 31, concerning the sale of goat skins to the defendant who gave a promissory note in return.

29. (1936) 13 N.L.R. 9—claim on account stated.

30. pp. 79 et. seq.

31. (1938) 14 N.L.R. 103; affirmed (1939) 5 W.A.C.A. 134.

32. *Savage* v. *Uwechia* (1961) 1 All E.R. 830.

33. (1936) 13 N.L.R. 43.

34. (1909) Ren. 550.

35. (1909) Ren., at p. 556.

36. (1944) 17, N.L.R. 77.

37. (1922) F. Ct. 91.

38. Sarbah's *Fanti Customary Law*, pp. 74-77 on Suretyship.

39. (1873) Ren. 1. See also Polly Hill, *Migrant cocoa-farmers of Southern Ghana* (1961); *Report of the Commission on the marketing of West African cocoa*—1938 Cmnd. 5845; Sir Casely-Hayford, Gold Coast Native Institutions (1903).

40. See also *Quartey* v. *Akuah, Redwar*, p. 138 and *Adoo* v. *Bannerman Redwar*, p. 139. See also *Ferguson* v. *Duncan* (1953) 14 W.A.C.A. 316.

41. (1953) 14 W.A.C.A. 254.

42. A. N. Allott, *Essays*, p. 252.

43. J. B. Danquah, *Cases in Akan Law*, p. xxxii, cited by Allott, supra.

44. For other cases on this head, see for Ghana: *Asamoah* v. *Mprenguo* (1949) W.A.C.A. Civil Appeal No. 72/48—Unreported; in Nigeria *Green* v. *Owo* (1936) 13 N.L.R. 14; *Griffin* v. *Talabi* (1948) 12 W.A.C.A. 371. See also cases cited by Allott in *Essays*, Chapter 10.

45. (1951) 13 W.A.C.A. 248.

46. *Courts Decree, 1966* (Ghana) Paragraph 64 (1) Rule (2). See also Rule 3 of the same section which makes similar provisions with regard to disposition of property generally.

47. S. 66 (1) Rule (6), *Courts Act, 1960* (C.A. 9).

48. In Nigeria there are no statutory provisions similar to the Ghana choice of law provisions.

49. See L. M. W. Melville, " The core of a contract " (1953) 19 M.L.R. 26; Prof. Unger, " The doctrine of the Fundamental Term " (1957) Business Law Rev. 30; K. W. Wedderburn, " Collateral Contracts " (1959) C.L.J., pp. 66-7; R. Berger, " Usury in instalment sales " (1943) 2 Law & Contemp. Prob. 148; Hale, " Bargaining, Duress and Economic Liberty " (1930) 43 Col. L. Rev. 603; W. Friedmann, *Law in a Changing Society*, Chapter 4; B. Coote, *Exception Clauses* (London, 1964).

50. See for instance the difficulty that confronted the court in the Ghana

case of *Ankrah* v. *African Trading Company* (1905) Ren. 400; and also in *G. B. Ollivant* v. *J. Allen & Co.* Sup. Ct. 88/1964, unreported.

51. Cap. 62, Laws of Nigeria (Federation, 1958).

52. See also *Halsbury's Laws* (2nd ed.), Vol. VIII, p. 321:

> " But when a contract has in fact been completed and reduced to writing the court is not entitled to consider antecedent acts or correspondence, or to look at words deleted before the conclusion of the contract, in order to ascertain the meaning of the contract in writing finally agreed upon."

cf. *Chief Okoro Orukumakpor* v. *Itebu & ors.*, Privy Council Appeal No. 42 of 1959, reported in (1961) 5 J.A.L. 159, in which the Privy Council considered the effect of S. 12 of the Evidence Ordinance on the construction of the written agreement between the parties.

53. S. 131 (1) (c) of the Evidence Ordinance.

54. S. 131 (1) (d) and (e).

55. (1923-25) F. Ct. 40. See also *Russell* v. *Martin* (1900), Ren. 193, where a strong Full Ct. composed of Sir William Brandford Griffith and Mr. Justice Nicoll held that in every case in which a member of a family holds himself out as owner, and is allowed by the family to so hold himself out, very satisfactory evidence is required to prove that the land or house is not his sole property.

56. (1940) 6 W.A.C.A. 32.

57. (1959) G.L.R. 444.

58. (1919) F. Ct. 12.

59. (1946) 18 N.L.R. 49.

60. (1833) 2 L.J. K.B. 127.

61. Cf. Lord Russell of Killowen, C.J. in *Gillespie Bros.* v. *Chenex Eggar & Co.* (1896) 2 Q.B. 59 at p. 62; and also K. N. Wedderburn, "Collateral Contracts" (1959) C.L.J. 58 at pp. 59-64. The learned author stated in this article "that a document which looks like a contract is to be treated as the whole contract."

62. Cf. *Graves* v. *Ampimah* (1905) Ren. 318 where the court considered the defendant's inability to read and write and amended the written contract on that ground. On writing and illiterates generally, see Nwogugu (1968) J.A.L. 27.

63. *The Law of Contract* (6th ed., 1964), p. 122.

64. This use of the term is easily distinguishable from conditions precedent and conditions subsequent. See the analysis of James L. J. in *Re Lees* (1875) L.R. 10. Ch. App. at p. 372, where the learned judge used condition in three different ways: precedent, subsequent, inherent.

65. See SS. 11 (1) and 62 of the *Sale of Goods Act*, 1893 (England).

66. See Cheshire & Fifoot, op. cit., pp. 123-129. See also Williston, *Contracts*, S. 665.

67. The Sale of Goods Act, 1893 (England) is still in force in the Eastern and Northern Regions of Nigeria as well as the Federal Territory, there is a Sale of Goods Law in the Western and Mid-Western Regions, but the division into conditions and warranties has been followed in all the jurisdictions. The Ghana Sale of Goods Act, 1962, (Act 137) has adopted the phrase "fundamental obligation," although warranties and conditions still remain in her Merchant Shipping Act.

68. There is no special significance in the choice of the dates except that the cases could be conveniently analysed on this basis.

69. Hire-purchase has often been treated as an aspect of the sale of goods. The separate treatment here is brought about by the different attitude

of the courts to this category of transactions from those in other facets of sale of goods.

70. Anson's Law of Contract (22nd ed., Guest, 1964).

71. See pp. 31 et. seq.

72. Roscoe Pound, *Introduction to the Philosophy of Law* (Yale, 1961), p. 143.

73. Land agreements also loomed large during this period because of the rise in the economic value of land particularly in the urban areas.

74. See G. de N. Clark, " How wrong is wrongful dismissal?" (1966) 63 Law Society Gazette, p. 255.

75. cf. Fry, L.J. in *De Francesco* v. *Barnum* (1890) 45 Ch.D. 430 at p. 438: " I should be very unwilling to extend decisions to compel persons who are not desirous of maintaining continuous personal relations with one another, to continue those personal relations lest they should turn contracts of service into contracts of slavery."

76. (1939) 15, N.L.R. 14. In *Peters of Oron* v. *Symmons* (1924) 5, N.L.R. 79 the court implied into the oral agreement between the plaintiff and the defendants the term that the plaintiff was to be paid according to the rate prevalent at Oron instead of a higher rate which he was paid while at their Calabar Stores.

77. In *Morris* v. *Baron* (1918) A.C. 1. the House of Lords drew a distinction between cases of variation (where writing was required for contracts that must be in writing) and cases where one party at the request of and for the convenience of the other forbears to perform the contract in some particular respect according to its letter, e.g. *Ogle* v. *Vane* (1868) L. R. 3 Q.B. 272.

78. (1940) 15, N.L.R. 99.

79. Op. cit., at p. 101.

80. *U.A.C. & Co. Ltd.* v. *Argo* (1935) 14, N.L.R. 105.

81. (1959) G.L.R. 75.

82. It is felt that this class ot cases will assume less and less importance as trade unionism and its membership becomes better organised and more widespread. Industrial rather than legal action will then be the sanction for most wrongful dismissal cases. See the Nigerian Labour Code Ordinance, Cap. 91, Laws (1958); and the Ghana Industrial Relations Acts 1958, 1962 and 1965. See also *Anene* v. *J. Allen* Sup. Ct. suit 88/1964 (Nigeria) unreported.

83. (1913) Ren. 761.

84. (1921-25) Div. Ct. 98. See also *Lawson* v. *Walkden* (1926-29) Div. Ct. 77.

85. (1909) App. Cas. 488.

86. cf. *Nagle* v. *Fielden* (1966) 2 W.L.R. 1027 at 1034 per Lord Denning, M.R.: " I have said before, and I repeat it now, that a man's right to work at his trade or profession is just as important to him as, perhaps more important than his rights of property. Just as the courts will intervene to protect his rights of property, they will also intervene to protect his rights to work."

87. (1921-25) Div. Ct. 176. See also *Belfield* v. *Gold Coast Amalg.* (1910) Ren. 583.

88. (1894) 2 H.L. Cas. 579.

89. See also *Shaul* v. *African & Eastern Trade Corpn.* (1923-25) F. Ct. 66 and *Onogen* v. *Leventis* (1959) G.L.R. 105; *Dixon & ors.* v. *Gold Coast Amalgamated* (1911) Ren. 615.

90. High Ct. Accra, 15th August, 1966. Unreported.

91. The issue revolved on the meaning of " old age " in the agreement.

In this respect the Ghana Industrial Relations Act (Act 299) would have been a safe guide to the judge. In fact, no reference was made to the Act in the judgment.

92. *Madrides* v. *Tangalakis & Co.* (1932) 11, N.L.R. 62. See also *Walters* v. *Harrison* (1922) 4, N.L.R. 71.

93. (1932) 11, N.L.R. 57.

94. *Madrides* v. *Tangalakis & Co.* (1932) 11, N.L.R. 62. See also *Walters* v. *Harrison* (1922) 4, N.L.R. 71.

95. See also the old English cases of *Hartley* v. *Harman* 113 E.R. 617 and *French* v. *Brookes* 130 E.R. 141 on which the Nigerian Court relied heavily for the decision of the *Madrides* case.

96. (1959) W.R.N.L.R. 232.

97. Supreme Court Suit No. 180/1963, 25th June, 1965—unreported.

98. *Regulation 91, Part IX.*

99. (1956) 3 All E.R. 946.

100. Cap. 91, Laws of Nigeria (1958). Labour being a Federal Subject under the *Nigerian Constitution* (1963), the Federal provision is equally valid in the Western Region.

101. *Op. cit.*, p. 4. See also to the same effect *Choizie* v. *U.A.C. Ltd.* (1956) 1 E.R. N.L.R. 28.

102. In the *Nwaokoro* case the Magistrate found that in fact the plaintiff was dismissed because he refused to offer £5 as bribe to the councillors which all the other labourers had done to retain their jobs.

103. Supreme Court Suit No. 88/1964, 15th Feb. 1965—unreported.

104. See also *Moeller* v. *Monier Construction Co. (Nigeria) Ltd.* (1961) 1 All N.L.R. 67; *Carabedian* v. *Jamakani* (1961) 1 All N.L.R. 177.

105. See the *Western Nigeria Sale of Goods Law,* Cap. 115 of 1959. This enactment has been part of the law of the Mid-Western Region since the creation of the latter in 1963.

106. *Nigerian Sweet Confectionery Co. Ltd.* v. *Tate & Lyle (Nig.) Ltd.* Supreme Ct. Suit No. 380/1964—unreported; *S.C.O.A.* v. *Ndaeyo*, High Ct. Portharcourt (E. Nigeria) 45/A/60 (1960)—unreported.

107. See *Simmons* v. *B.B.W.A.* (1905) Ren. 344; *Akotey* v. *Commonwealth Trust*; (1923-25) F. Ct. 78.

108. Cap. 115.

109. The value of writing has been discussed under defective agreements, supra—p. 212.

110. No. 64 of 1961 (Federation).

111. The Ghana enactment also deals with C.I.F. and F.O.B. contracts under its Part VII, and Hire Purchase contracts under Part VIII, both of which subjects are treated under different Acts in England and in Nigeria.

112. More will be said about this provision in the discussion on exception clauses, infra—p. 303.

113. *Parkin* v. *Thorold* (1852) 16 Beav. 59; *Bowes* v. *Shand* (1877) 2 App. Cas. 455 which was a case on the time for the performance of a sale of rice. This presumption as to time is saved under the Common Law provisions of the *Sale of Goods Act, 1893*—See *S.* 62.

114. High Court, Sunyani—29/1/65.—unreported.

115. It has not been considered necessary in view of the heavy reliance on English judicial authority, to undertake a detailed discussion of the case law on the subject. For these see—(1) Ghana: *Simmons* v. *B.B.W.A.* (1905) Ren. 344; *Mercer* v. *Anglo-Guinea Produce Co.* (1922) F. Ct. 114; *Akotey* v. *Commonwealth Trust* (1923-25) F. Ct. 78;

Nanka-Bruce v. *Laing & Anor.* (1923-25) F. Ct. 89 (P.C.); *Ampofo* v. *Quartey* (1926-29) Div. Ct. 151; *Atchiapong* v. *Miller* (1926-29) Div. Ct. 207; *Dodoo* v. *Ashitey* (1965) Current Cases, No. 6 (2) Nigeria; *Halliday* v. *Alapatira* (1881) 1, N.L.R. 1; *Dan Juma* v. *Standard Co. of Nigeria Ltd.* (1922) 4, N.L.R. 50; *Western African Import & Export Co.* v. *Jasser* (1939) 15, N.L.R. 21.

116. See particularly H.B. Sales, "Standard form Contracts" (1953) 16 M.L.R. 318; Richard O'Sullivan, "A scale of values in the common law" (1937) M.L.R. 27; American Law Institute *Uniform Commercial Code* SS. 2-302; J. B. Milner, *Cases and Materials on Contracts* (Toronto, 1963) pp. 497-540.

117. Standard forms were more regularly used in shipping and insurance transactions, e.g. charter parties, bills of lading and marine policies.

118. From the French *Contrat d'adhesion*, apparently because one party expects the other to adhere to his terms or not to deal at all.

119. See the English Court of Appeal decision of *Parker* v. *South Eastern Railway Co.* (1877) 2 C.P.D. 416.

120. Sir Henry Maine, *Ancient Law* (Ed. Firth, 1963). See also *Henson* v. *London & North Eastern Railway* (1946) 1 All E.R. 653—per Scott, L.J. "It is such misuse of contract which makes the legislature tend to substitute status."

121. Op. cit., p. 498.

122. Cf. *Watkins* v. *Rymill* (1883) 10 Q.B.D. 178 where such impossible conditions were disallowed by the court.

123. (1859) 157 E.R. 865.

124. See Sales, supra; W. Friedmann, *Law in a changing society*, (London, 1959) Chapter 4; Hale, "Bargaining, duress and economic liberty" (1930) 43 Col. L.R. 603.

125. *Ode* v. *J. F. Sick & Co. and Anor.* (1939) 15, N.L.R. 4, where the 2nd deft. was held liable for debts incurred before he undertook the guarantee; *Molade* v. *John Holt & Co.* (1937) 13, N.L.R. 150, where the plaintiff was held liable for shortages due to burglary (see W.A.C.A. 3rd Nov. 1937); *Bucknor & Anor.* v. *Barclays Bank* (1924) 7, N.L.R. 1, where the court allowed the defendant bank to take additional security without giving further credit; *Miller Bros. Ltd.* v. *Oyegunde & ors.* (1924) 5, N.L.R. 97, where the court held that additional responsibilities on the employee did not absolve the surety from liability; cf. *Pettiford* v. *May* (1937) 13, N.L.R. 138 where surety was absolved because the full amount stated was not paid by the plaintiff. See also *Bamiro* v. *John Holt & Co.* (1938) 14, N.L.R. 63.

126. Supreme Court Suit 21/6/65.—unreported (Ghana).

127. Supreme Court Suit No. 217/1963 (Nigeria) unreported. See also *Okenla* v. *Royal Exchange Assurance Co. Ltd.* (1958) W.R.N.L.R. 185; *Jia Enterprises* v. *British Comm. Insurance Co. Ltd.* (1965) N.M.L.R. 147.

128. High Court Suit No. E/72/62 (Enugu, E. Nigeria) unreported. Here the defendants sought to enforce a provision in the policy to the effect that the plaintiff would lose his rights to any sums if he failed to inform the company of any claims promptly.

129. Cited by Holdsworth in *H.E.L. Vol. VIII*, p. 479.

130. Cf. *Halliday* v. *Alapatira* (1881) N.L.R. 1, where it was held that the delivery of a printed circular to an illiterate person without an explanation of its contents does not convey notice of an act of bankrupcty

available for adjudication under English law, and that any payment by the illiterate to the bankrupt after the receipt was a valid payment.

131. Legislative efforts in curbing unreasonableness of contractual terms will be discussed intra—p. 327.

132. See B. Coote, *Exception Clauses*, (London, 1964); E. M. Harrington, " A case study of conditions and warranties " (1965) Nigerian Law Journal, p. 289.

133. e.g. S. 35 (3) of the *Nigerian Marine Insurance Act (Federation)*, No. 54 of 1961; and S. 11 of the *Sale of Goods Act*, 1893.

134. The position is much worse where the other party has to rely on an interpreter to tell him the meaning of the terms used. This is the problem of illiteracy and exclusion clauses.

135. Compare *Wallis* v. *Pratt* (1910) 2 K.B. 1003; *Karsales (Harrow) Ltd.* v. *Wallis* (1953) 1 W.L.R. 1468; and *Smeaton Hanscomb and Co. Ltd.* v. *Sassoon & Sethy Son & Co.* (1911) A.C. 394; *Andrews* v. *Singer* (1934) 1 K.B. 17.

136. (1966) 2 All E.R. 61.

137. (1963) N.N.L.R. 115. See also *Boshali* v. *Allied Commercial Exporters Ltd.* (1961) 1 All N.L.R. 917.

138. Act 137 (Ghana). See also S. 55 of the *Western Nigeria Sale of Goods Law*, Cap. 115, laws (1959); and S. 55 of the *Sale of Goods Act*, 1893, all of which are in similar terms to the Ghana provision. In this connection it must be observed that Islamic law regards as invalid (fasid) any provision in an agreement purporting to exclude any of the parties from liability for a breach of any term. See Schacht, *Introduction to Islamic Law*, (Oxford, 1964).

139. S. 8 (3) of the Act, (Act 137, Ghana).

140. (1966) 2 All E.R. 61.

141. *Boshali* v. *Allied Commercial Exporters Ltd.* (1961) 1 All N.L.R. 917; and *Ogwu* v. *Leventis Motors Ltd.* (1963) N.N.L.R. 115. The facts of these cases will be discussed below. No local cases in either Ghana or Nigeria have been decided on the question of sufficient notice, but the dicta of Carey J. in *Bamiro* v. *John Holt & Co. Ltd.* (1938) 14 N.L.R. 63, that " in dealing with a semi-educated African, one would expect a reputable English firm, in spite of the unwisdom of the surety in not acquainting himself with the precise terms to be inserted in the service agreement, to bring the latter to his notice especially where, in effect, the property of the surety was being jeopardised every month," tends to indicate that the standard of notice is higher for illiterates than for literate parties.

142. The clause has been variously called exception clause, exemption clause and exclusion clause.

143. The *Boshali* case—supra.

144. (1963) N.N.L.R. 115, His Lordship purported to follow the English decision of *Andrews* v. *Hopkinson* (1957) 1 Q.B. 229.

145. E. M. Harrington, " A case study of conditions and warranties " (1965) Nig. Law Journal, 289.

146. (1911) A.C. 394.

147. At p. 304 supra.

148. See *Ruben* v. *Faire* (1949) 1 All E.R. 215.

149. See F. H. Ruxton, *Maliki law* (London, 1916); A. Rahim, *Muhammedan jurisprudence*.

150. See p. 327 infra.

151. (1953) 16 M.L.R. 318.

152. Proposal made in April, 1966, School of Oriental and African Studies, African Law Section.
153. See R. Berger, "Usury in instalments sales" (1935) 2 Law and Contp. Prob. 148; J. B. Birkhead, "Collection tactics of illegal lenders" (1941) 8 Law and Contp. Prob. 78; A. L. Diamond, "The hire purchase dealers' liability" (1958) 21 M.L.R. 177; A.D.M. Oulton, "Loans in Kenya on the security of chattels" (1960) 4 J.A.L. pp. 17; 79.
154. S. 21 of the *Hire-purchase Act*, 1964 (England), specifies three kinds of agreement under which goods are acquired by payment of instalments. These are hire purchase, conditional sales and credit sales agreements. In England these are regulated by the *Hire-purchase Acts*, 1938, 1954 and 1964, and to some extent, the *Sale of Goods Act*, 1893.
155. S. 81 of the *Ghana Sale of Goods Act*, 1962 (*Act* 137).
156. (1965) Current Cases, No. 6. These agreements which are in regular use by taxi drivers are in the following form: the driver accepts delivery of the vehicle on payment of a deposit and pays the remaining amount by instalments. It has most of the elements of a credit sale agreement. It is curious that the learned judge distinguished it from the latter. See also *Kofi* v. *Mensah* (1930) 1 W.A.C.A. 76.
157. No. 55 of 1958 (repealed by Act 137, 1962). But while under the Hire Purchase Act, 1938, financial limits were placed on transactions to which the English Act applied, the Ghana Act had no such provision. It is strange that the Ghana Parliament thought it wise to provide for the parties opting out of the 1962 Act in transactions where the amount involved exceeds £1,000. The Law Commission in England has recommended that there should be no such financial limits. These limits still exist in the 1964 English enactment on the subject.
158. Act 137. More will be said below about its provisions, see p. 327.
159. (1965) Current Cases, No. 54.
160. (1965) Current Cases No. 166. Cf. *Awortwi* v. *Hendersons (Manchester) Ltd.* (1925) F. Ct. 139, i.e. before the 1958 Act. But see *Akuffo* v. *Asante* (1953) 14 W.A.C.A. 275.
161. See also *Dodoo* v. *Ashitey* (1965) Current Cases No. 6, to which reference has already been made, supra p. 308 S. 57 of the Ghana Sale of Goods, Act, 1962 (Act 137) was then in issue; and *Obeng* v. *Gyamfi* (1965) Current Cases No. 64.
162. (1926-29) Div. Ct. (Ghana), 178. Here the defendant relied on Lord Kinnear's statement in the Privy Council decision of *Kwamin* v. *Kufuor* (1874-1928) P.C. at p. 36 as follows: "When a person of full age signs a contract in his own language, his own signature raises a presumption of liability so strong that it requires very distinct and explicit averments indeed in order to subvert it. But there is no presumption that a native of Ashanti who does not understand English and cannot read or write, has appreciated the meaning and effect of an English instrument, because he is alleged to have set his mark to it by way of signature. That raises a question of fact to be decided like other such questions upon evidence." But the court found that he understood the nature of the document.
163. (1926-29) Div. Ct. See also *Sengena* v. *Poku* (1943) 9 W.A.C.A. 143.
164. See also *Atchiapong* v. *Miller* (1926-29) Div. Ct. 207.
165. One important effect of this enactment is that agreements made in Lagos but which are performed outside the Federal territory will be governed by their proper law, in this case, the Hire-purchase Act,

1965. In 1965 the Northern Regional Government published proposals for a hire purchase law. These were in many respects similar to the Lagos enactment on the subject. In their analysis of the proposals David Carroll and Zaccheus Aje have pointed out some of the more obvious defects and made suggestions about changes in accordance with the Hire Purchase Act, 1964 (England). See Law in Society (1966) pp. 1-63.

166. The Nigerian cases on this head follow the pre-1958 pattern of the Ghana decisions. Thus *Amao* v. *Ajibike & ors.* (1955-56) W.R.N.L.R. 121 dealt with the distinction between outright sale and payment by instalments; *G. B. Ollivant & Co.* v. *Akinsanya & Anor,* (1930) 10 N.L.R. 73 on the test as to whether it is hire-purchase or credit sale; *Joe Allen* v. *Adewale* (1929) 9 N.L.R. 111; *Williams* v. *U.A.C. Ltd.* (1937) 13 N.L.R. 134; *M. & K.* v. *Economides* (1957) W.R.N.L.R. 94; *Atere* v. *Dada & anor* (1957) W.R.N.L. 176.

167. See also the Ghana Moneylenders Ordinance, cap. 176, Laws of the Gold Coast (1951 Revision).

168. Cap. 124, Laws of Nigeria (Federation, 1958).

169. S. 4 of the Ghana Ordinance; S. 4. of the Nigerian Ordinance and S. 4. of the Eastern Nigeria Moneylenders Law, Cap. 84, Laws (1963).

170. SS. 19, 20 and 24 of the Ghana Ordinance, and the corresponding sections in the Nigerian enactment.

171. S. 20 of the Ghana Ordinance and S. 20 of the Nigerian Ordinance.

172. S. 5 of the Ghana Ordinance and S. 5 of the Nigerian Ordinance.

173. (1963) L.L.R. 53.

174. The Lagos Act is in the same terms as the Moneylenders Ordinance which is in force in all the jurisdictions in Nigeria except such Regions as have enacted a local statute to replace it (e.g. the Eastern Region, Cap. 84). S. 6 (1) provides as follows: " A moneylender's licence shall not be granted except to a person who holds a certificate granted in accordance with the provisions of this section authorising the granting of licence to that person, and a separate certificate shall be required in respect of every separate licence. Any moneylender's licence granted in contravention of this section shall be void." See also the Money-lenders (Amendment) Act, 1960, which applies only to Lagos and on which the Nwosu case was argued.

175. (1958) W.R.N.L.R. 67.

176. The respondent had charged 48 per cent interest on a loan secured by a third party as guarantor. The statutory maximum for this class of transaction is 17 per cent. See *Section* 13 of the Ordinance.

177. See also *Kadiri* v. *Olusoga* (1956) F.S.C. 59; *Oguachuba* v. *Minimeh* H. Ct. Enugu 10/59, unreported; *Fashina* v. *Odedina* (1957) W.R.N.L.R. 45 where an interest of 9d. in the £ was charged in spite of the security of a car; *Molake* v. *Tinibu* (1959) L.L.R. 128 on S. 12 (3) of the Ordinance.

178. *Baloguu* v. *Obisanya & anor* (1956) F.S.C. 22; see also the Ghana case of *Offi & ors* v. *Appiah & ors* (1965) Current Cases 193.

179. (1956) F.S.C. 93. See also *Ajetunmobi* v. *Omowunmi* (1961) All N.L.R. 120.

180. See *Kadiri* v. *Olusoga* (1956) F.S.C. 59 and *Fashina* v. *Odedina* (1957) W.R.N.L.R. 45.

181. (1956) A.C. 539.

182. It was this sub-section that was in issue.

183. (1907) 1 Ch. 300.

184. (1908) 2 Ch. 612. See also Cohen v. Lester (1939) 1.K.B. 504.
185. This section provides for registration of all moneylenders.
186. Under the name *Gbadamosi Baba-Egbe* v. *Patience Kasumu & ors.* (1954) 14 W.A.C.A. 444.
187. See Section 3 (4) of the Law Reform (Contracts) Act, 1961 (Nigeria), No. 64 of 1961.
188. For other moneylending cases, see *Ukhueduan* v. *Okoye* (1958) E.R. N.L.R. 32 on limitation—*S.* 30 of the Ordinance; *Efuwape* v. *Ologbosere & anor.* (1960) L.L.R. 328—on *SS.* 12, 19, 23 of the Ordinance; *Nwankwo* v. *Orji* H. Ct. Enugu 94/60—unreported; *Okworo* v. *Onwussilike*, H. Ct. E/23/60—*S.* 26.
189. See the Ghana case of *Offi & ors* v. *Appiah & ors* (1965) C.C. 193 where S. 4 (1) (moneylenders must take out licences); S. 9 (transfer of business premises); S. 12 (form of a moneylending contract), and S. 26 (1) (penalty for taking promissory notes with blanks) of the Money-lenders Ordinance (Cap. 176, Laws of the Gold Coast, 1951) were in issue.
190. 315 U.S. 289 (1942).
191. These were discussed in the cases, supra pp. 308 et seq.

CHAPTER 18

AGREEMENTS AND THE STATE

In this chapter we are concerned with the role of the State in the regulation of obligations created by agreement. An attempt will be made to find answers to the questions: (1) Ought the State to interfere with the freedom of the parties to make whatever pacts they please? and (2) To what extent have the legislatures in Ghana and Nigeria interfered with this freedom?

(1) *Ought the State to interfere?*

Political theorists admit with varying degrees of persistence that the overall interest of the State takes priority over that of any single individual or a group.[1] Whether we accept the thesis that the State is nothing but the protector of individual rights and liberties,[2] or that it is a great public utility company,[3] we still have to contend with the task of adjusting any conflicts between the individual and the society of which he is part. This conflict is most apparent in the law of agreements.

Mention has already been made of the presumption of the equality of bargaining power of the parties to an agreement, as the basis of the English law of contract. The extent to which this assumption is out of touch with the realities of the modern law has also been discussed. When a labourer on weekly wages and notice is equated in bargaining strength to a giant concern such as the Imperial Chemical Industries, even a transparent fiction is strained. Should the State sit back while the parties made any agreements they like without any guidance to the courts on what agreements should be enforced? Our answer to this question is a categorical no, and for the following reasons. If the State undertakes to direct the economy as is in fact the case in both Ghana and Nigeria, run most of the social services and determine the foreign policy of the country, it cannot at the same time admit the maintenance of contract relations contrary to those it envisages. If the Constitution prohibits forced labour and human slavery, nobody will be permitted to enslave himself by contract or otherwise. The weaker sector of the community ought to be protected against the stronger arm and purse of the more privileged. Thus the State ought to intervene on behalf of minors, illiterates.

lunatics and other victims of harsh bargains. On the other hand, the State ought also to protect business against indiscreet dealers and habitual debtors. The administration of credit facilities[4] and the improvement of bankruptcy laws ought to be instances of State regulation of commercial transactions.[5] The answer to the question posed above, i.e. whether the State ought to intervene is positive, but that such interference should only be in the overall interest of the society as in the instances of the administration of credit, or in cases of individual hardship.[6]

(2) *To what extent have the legislatures in Ghana and Nigeria interfered with this freedom?*

We shall here be examining the extent of legislative interference in the making and regulation of agreements. This interference has taken many forms. Firstly, there is the group of enactments in Ghana and Nigeria which lay down the basis on which the parties can contract. The Ghana Industrial Relations Acts,[7] the Eastern Nigeria Co-operative Societies law[8] and the Nigerian Labour Code Ordinance[9] are instances of this category of statutes.

Other enactments prescribe the only permissible form to which a particular type of contract must conform. The Nigerian Marine Insurance Act,[10] the Bills of Exchange Acts[11] of Ghana and Nigeria; and the Ghana Merchant Shipping Act, 1963[12] are examples of this type of legislation.

There has also been interference in the form of the imposition of terms which must be incorporated in specified types of agreements. These are duties which are imposed on one of the parties to an agreement and which he cannot exclude by agreement. Thus the duty imposed on the seller of goods in Section 8 of the Ghana Sale of Goods Act, 1962,[13] cannot be excluded by agreement.[14] Also the terms to be implied under Section 13 (1) (a) of the same Act as to quality and fitness of the goods cannot be excluded by agreement.[15] In hire-purchase transactions, Section 66 of the Ghana Sale of Goods Act lays down the duties of the owner. Failure to perform them or any of them will render the agreement void.[16] Similar provisions in respect of the duties of money-lenders are found in the Moneylenders Ordinances of Ghana and Nigeria.[17] Auctioneers,[18] pawnbrokers[19] and mercantile agents[20] are regulated in similar terms.

Another method of interference is the prohibition of the inclusion of certain terms. Section 62 of the Ghana Sale of Goods Act provides as follows:

" Any provision in a hire-purchase contract whereby the seller or any person acting on his behalf is authorised to enter upon any premises for the purpose of taking possession of the goods, or is relieved from liability for any such entry, is void."

Thus in construing any agreement in which the above terms have been inserted the courts will operate on the basis that the insertion would not affect the rights and duties of the parties.[21] Section 1 (1) of the Rents (Stabilisation) Act, 1962 (Act 109) prohibits the charging of rents higher than those laid down in the Act. Similar prohibitions are found in the Loans Recovery Ordinance,[22] Moneylenders Ordinances[23] and the Auctioneers Laws.[24]

Other instances of State interference with the parties' agreement include the development of the concept of frustration of contract to adjust the rights of the parties when enforced performance would be radically different from what the parties originally intended. To this effect enactments in both Ghana and some jurisdictions in Nigeria regulate frustrated contracts.[25] Protection of minors and illiterates, and limitation statutes are some more examples of this interference.[26]

Critique of the role of the legislation in Ghana and Nigeria:

From the above analysis, it is clear that apart from the isolated instances of rules regulating frustration of contracts and the Ghana provision about the seller's fundamental obligation, the legislatures have not adverted sufficiently or at all to the problems posed by the inequality of the parties in the modern law of contract. The problem of standard form contracts and exception clauses has already been discussed. It is enough to repeat here the menace of harsh and unreasonable terms to which the courts have no effective answer under the present law. Mr Sales in his article to which reference has already been made recommended a consumers board to oversee into the reasonableness of terms included in standard forms.[27] The *United States Uniform Commercial Code* has the following provision about the unconscionable terms:

" (1) If the Court as a matter of law finds the contract or any clause of the contract to have been unconscionable at the time it was made the Court may refuse to enforce the contract, or it may enforce the remainder of the contract without the unconscionable clause, or it may so limit the application of any unconscionable clause as to avoid any unconscionable result.

(2) When it is claimed or appears to the Court that the contract or any clause thereof may be unconscionable the parties shall be afforded a reasonable opportunity to present evidence as to its commercial setting, purpose and effect to aid the Court in making the determination."[28]

It is interesting to note that *Article 1* of this code preserves the parties' freedom of contract. Such freedom must, however, be consistent with the obligation of good faith, diligence and reasonableness. A similar note is struck by Allott's recent proposal referred to above.[29] The proposal which tends to cover all the situations we are concerned with here is in the form of a model enactment in the following terms:

"*Fair Contracts (Consumers Protection) Act,* 1966.

1. This Act shall apply to all contracts for the supply of goods or services, and its provisions shall take effect in addition to any other restrictions or requirements imposed by law. It shall not apply to contracts for the sale of land.

2 (1) A consumers' court shall have power to vary the terms of or revoke, any contract which shall appear to the court to be unfair in any substantial respect, so as to render the contract fair as between the parties thereto.

(2) A contract is unfair in which it appears that a supplier of goods or services is able, by reason of the disparity between his own economic position and that of the consumer to whom he supplies goods or services, to impose conditions on the consumer which the consumer would not otherwise be prepared to accept.[30]

(3) In particular, but without derogating from the generality of other provisions of this Act, the following classes of contract shall be deemed to be unfair until the contrary is proved to the satisfaction of a consumers' court:

(a) a contract to which one of the parties is a monopoly supplier of the goods or services affected by the contract;

(b) a contract which is in standard written form habitually employed by a supplier for the purpose of regulating the supply of the particular goods or services concerned.[31]

(c) a contract which contains conditions derogating from the common law or statutory rights of the consumer or obligations of the supplier.

For the purposes of this section 'monopoly supplier' includes any supplier who enjoys 50 per cent or more by value of the market, locally or nationally, in the particular goods or services concerned.

3 (1) Any consumer who objects to the terms of any contract to which he is a party affected by this Act on the ground that it is unfair, may apply to a consumers' court for an order to vary or revoke such contract in accordance with the powers provided under S. 2.

(2) Where any such application has been made under S. 3 (1), or when a contract has been deemed unfair under S. 2 (3), the

supplier shall not have power to enforce any term or condition of the contract until the consumers' court has so ordered.

4 (1) The Consumers' Council may in respect of any contract affected by this Act, and a supplier may in respect of any contract or class of contracts affected by S. 2 (3) of this Act, apply to a consumers' court for an advisory opinion on the fairness of such contract or contracts.

(2) The consumers' court, by its advisory opinion,

(a) shall declare the said contract to be fair or unfair in whole or in part; and

(b) may recommend such variance of the contract or contracts as would in its opinion render the contract fair.

(3) If the consumers' court has, by its advisory opinion, declared a contract or class of contracts to be fair, or has recommended its or their variance so as to render it or them fair, a supplier may enforce any contract having the same terms and effects as the contract declared fair, notwithstanding the provisions of SS. 2 and 3.[32]

5 (1) Every consumers' court shall consist of: —

(i) a president, being a person who holds or has held judicial office in a superior court of record in Britain or in any other common law jurisdiction, or is qualified to hold such office;

(ii) two assessors, being persons designated by the president of the court from a panel of assessors for that court.

(2) The Lord Chancellor shall have power to designate persons as presidents of consumers' courts; to assign areas of jurisdiction, whether geographically or by subject-matter, to such courts; and to appoint fit and proper persons to the panels of assessors for such courts. In the appointment of assessors, the Lord Chancellor shall have proper regard to the necessity for the representation of consumers' interests.

(3) The Consumers' Council shall have the right to be represented by counsel and to be heard as *amicus curiae* before the consumers' court in any case falling within this Act.

6. This Act shall be liberally interpreted. In case of doubt or inconsistency affecting the proper interpretation of this Act, such doubt or inconsistency shall be resolved in favour of the consumer where it is possible so to do."[33]

Mention has already been made of the fact that the proposal is weighted heavily in favour of the consumer. Thus apart from Section 4 (3) of the proposal, all the other provisions of the model Act are designed to protect the consumers' interests.[34]

Another unique feature of the model is the vast powers of the proposed consumers' court. It can give advisory opinions on the fairness or otherwise of terms to be included in an agreement and any terms so included will be binding on the parties (S. 4 (1) and (2)). It can also vary the terms of an agreement already concluded between the parties and can declare void any particular provision or series of stipulations that it considers unconscionable in an agreement (S. 3 (1) and (2)). Any doubts in the meaning of the provision in any agreement will be resolved in favour of the consumer.[35]

Apart from the omission from the panel of assessors to assist the consumers' court,[36] of somebody representing the interests of suppliers, one would recommend the model Act for a wholesale adoption in Ghana and Nigeria.[37]

NOTES

1. In countries often described as part of the free world, this is most true in times of national emergency.
2. See Jeremy Bentham, *A fragment on Government and the principles of morals and legislation.* (Oxford, 1948).
3. L. Duguit, *The Law and the State* (1917); see also *Law in the Modern State* (1921) trans. by H. Laski.
4. E.g. hire-purchase and moneylending transactions. See also the Bills of Exchange Acts in Ghana and Nigeria. See also the Eastern Nigeria Co-operative Societies Law, Cap. 28.
5. See the Ghana Insolvency Act, 1962 (Act. 153). See also Allott, "Legal development and economic growth in Africa" [in] *Changing law in developing countries* (ed. Anderson, 1963) p. 194.
6. See A. S. Miller "Government Contracts and social control: A preliminary enquiry" (1955) 41 Va.L.R. pp. 56-7; W. Friedmann, *Law and Social Change in Contemporary Britain* (1951) pp. 71 et seq.; F. Cohen, *Law and Social Order* (1933) pp. 102 et seq.
7. Acts 7, 119 and 299 (Ghana).
8. Cap. 28, Laws of Eastern Nigeria (1963).
9. Cap. 91, Laws of Nigeria (Federation, 1958).
10. No. 54 of 1961 (Nigeria).
11. Act 55 (Ghana) and Cap. 21, Laws of Nigeria (1958).
12. Act 183 (Ghana). See also the Ghana Bills of Lading Act (Act 42) 1961; State Property and Contracts Act, 1960 (C.A. 6).
13. Act 137 (Ghana).
14. S. 8 (3) of Act 137 (Ghana).
15. S. 13 (3) of Act 137 (Ghana).
16. S. 66.
17. Cap. 176 (Laws of the Gold Coast, 1951); Cap. 124 (Laws of Nigeria, Federation, 1958).
18. See S. 22 (j) of the Western Nigeria Auctioneers Law, Cap. 9 of 1959 Laws; and also a corresponding provision in the E. Nigeria Auctioneers Law, Cap. 12 of 1963.
19. Western Nigeria Pawnbrokers Law, Cap. 87 (Laws 1959).
20. W. Nigeria, Mercantile Agents Law, Cap. 77 (Laws, 1959).

21. Cf. S. 43 (7) of the Transport Act, 1962 (England). " The Boards shall not carry passengers by rail on terms or conditions which (a) purport, whether directly or indirectly to exclude or limit their liability in respect of the death, or bodily injury to, any passenger other than a passenger travelling on a free pass, or (b) purport, whether directly or indirectly, to prescribe the time within which, or the manner in which, any such liability may be enforced."
22. Cap. 175 (Laws of the Gold Coast, 1951) S. 2 (3).
23. Supra.
24. Supra. See particularly S. 25 (iii) of the Western Nigeria enactment.
25. S.1 of the Ghana Contracts Act, 1960 (Act 25). See also S. 2 of the Law Reform (Contracts) Act, 1961 (Nigeria, Lagos).
26. Illiterates Protection Ordinance, Cap. 83, Laws (Nigeria, Fed. 1958), Ghana Administration of Estates Act, 1965.
27. (1953) 16 M.L.R. 318.
28. See the comments in the *American Uniform Commercial Code Handbook* (New York, 1964).
29. See p. 307 supra.
30. These sub-sections are in similar terms to the *American Law Institute Uniform Commercial Code,* to which reference has been made.
31. This deals with the problem of standard form contracts.
32. The question of advisory opinion is in line with Mr. Sales' proposals about the powers of a Consumers' Board.
33. It has been found necessary to reproduce the whole of Allott's proposal because of its concise covering of all the situations where consumers' interests clash with those of the suppliers.
34. Also while the interests of the consumers are represented in the panel of assessors in the courts, the same favour is not extended to suppliers.
35. S. 6. of the model Act.
36. See S. 5 (2) of the proposal.
37. Since the constitution of the Consumers' Council is not given it is likely that the suppliers' interests would be represented on such a council.

CHAPTER 19

ULTIMATE REMEDIES FOR THE BREACH OR OTHER AVOIDANCE OF OBLIGATIONS [1]

The enforcement of obligations created by agreement has been fully discussed in Section I of this part. What we propose to do here is a critical examination of the effectiveness of remedies available to the plaintiff in the law of agreements. Conventional treatment of " remedies " in the law of contract has often been on the basis of what the plaintiff can sue for.[2] Having obtained judgment, writers on the law of agreements are no longer interested in what happens next. The general attitude has been that of leaving such matters to civil procedure, which treats them under the head of " execution of judgment." Whether or not the judgment was satisfied is of no interest to the traditional writer on contracts, or indeed, any other facet of the law of obligations. It is submitted, however, that in so far as what happens to the parties to a case after judgment, will affect the formation or performance of future obligations between the same parties, and to some extent, others, the satisfaction or otherwise of a judgment in a contract case, is of great significance in any functional study of the law of obligations. It need hardly be argued that the way the law treats a debtor will to a very large extent determine the future conduct of the creditor towards credit generally. The importance of this approach to the subject for our purpose here, is accentuated by the divergent modes of enforcement in customary laws on the one hand, and the imported law on the other. We shall examine each of these modes of enforcement and their effectiveness.

(i) THE POSITION IN THE IMPORTED LAW

> " I think we would be deceiving ourselves if we were to believe that the respect of the ordinary citizen for his formal contractual obligations is as great today as it was, say, a hundred years ago."[3]

The above statement on the general attitude towards contractual obligations, by Sir David Hughes Parry, echoes an earlier statement of the position by J. H. Gebhardt in his article in the Modern Law Review, entitled, " *Pacta servanda sunt*," where the learned author had said,

> "In the area of English law there exists neither a legal nor a moral duty to carry out a contractual promise for damage; this, subject to the discretion of a judge in certain narrowly circumscribed cases."[4]

These two passages above represent what has often been called the "compensation theory" of agreements. In opposition to the "compensation theory" is the "enforcement theory" exemplified in the statement of Thomas Erskine Holland in his book on Jurisprudence in 1916, as follows:

> "When the law enforces contracts it does so to prevent disappointment of well-founded expectations, which, though they usually arise from expressions truly representing intention, yet may occasionally arise otherwise."[5]

In support of Holland's contention, A. L. Goodhart has also stated that

> "the normal basis of contract is that the promisor has by his promise created a reasonable expectation that it will be kept."[6]

In spite of the obvious merits[7] of the latter theory, the common law has come to accept the position that the primary obligation of the promisor is to buy off his promise rather than perform it. In many cases the promisor gets away without doing either. Thus in any action on a contract, the courts are more readily disposed to award damages for breach, than to order specific performance. Further there is even no certainty with regard to the award of damages. The action may have become statute-barred, or frustrated, or illegal, informal, or either of the parties may have been devoid of contractual capacity.[8] In each of these cases the plaintiff is denied both specific performance and the right to any damages. Even when all these factors are not present, and the plaintiff has been awarded damages by the court, there is still no certainty that he will recover all or any of it. The defendant may be a "man of straw," or may have become insolvent or is just unwilling to pay. The position is much more acute in Ghana and Nigeria where insurance has not been sufficiently developed.

There are of course at least three modes of obtaining satisfaction for a judgment debt in both Ghana and Nigeria. The first is that laid down in the Rules of the Supreme Court of the two countries, under execution of judgments.[9] The second, in the case of Ghana (and for companies in the case of Nigeria) is that laid down in the Ghana Insolvency Act,[10] and the Nigeria Companies

Ordinance respectively. The third is available in the case of a guaranteed liability. Here the creditor can look to the guarantor for the satisfaction of his claim.[11]

(a) *Execution of judgment*

Part III of the Sheriffs and Civil Process law of Eastern Nigeria[12] which is in similar terms to the corresponding provisions in the Supreme Court Rules of the other jurisdictions with which we are here concerned, makes provisions for the execution of the judgments of the superior courts and the committal of debtors. The judgment creditor can proceed against any ascertainable assets of the judgment debtor for the satisfaction of the debt.[13] He can seize a specified category of his goods,[14] can attach his debts,[15] levy execution against his immovable property,[16] or proceed by way of judgment summons.[17] On the face of it, the above arrangement is adequate to secure satisfaction for the judgment debt. In practice, however, this is only so if the judgment debtor is able and willing to pay. If he is able to pay (and the test of this is his ascertainable means of income), but unwilling to do so, in both Ghana and all the jurisdictions in Nigeria, there is provision for his being sent to prison to remain so imprisoned until he can pay the debt.[18] But in many cases, the means of income is difficult to ascertain. In such cases, sending the debtor to prison would not avail the creditor since he still has to pay the subsistence allowance of the debtor for as long as he is in prison.[19] At this point the law is powerless to help the judgment creditor and any satisfaction of the debt may well depend on the benevolence of his debtor or other extra-legal factors such as ridicule. We shall be looking at the merits or otherwise of this system presently.

(b) *Under the Insolvency Act, 1962*[20]

One of the terms of reference of the Insolvency Commission in Ghana in 1960, was to consider the better protection by law of creditors and debtors in case of insolvency. This, the Commissioners claimed, involved wide considerations of human behaviour, property relationships, economic advancement, and ultimately, the sort of society that the people of Ghana intended to establish. The Commissioners found in course of their investigations that difficulties in granting credit arose from lack of security, attitudes towards repaying, and lack of remedies for non-payment. Their answer to the demand for reform was the Insolvency Bill, which later became law (with minor amendments) in November,

1962. The Act sets up under Section 1 the office of the Official trustee to whom creditors are empowered, under Section 8, to apply for a protection order against the assets of an insolvent debtor. An insolvent debtor is defined to mean any debtor who is unable to meet up his debts within three months;[21] such debts not being less than the sum of five hundred pounds (£500). Provision is made for the public examination of the insolvent at which examination he has to declare any assets that he may have. These will be applied to a satisfaction of the debts if sufficient to meet all the liabilities, or on *pro rata* basis. The Official Trustee is empowered to allow assets up to £50 to be kept by the insolvent. If however, the insolvent has been guilty of misconduct, he might, after the public examination, be adjudged a bankrupt which carries more far-reaching disabilities than just being an insolvent.[22]

It must be repeated that the provisions of the Insolvency Act will only apply where the liquidated debt is not less than £500.[23]

(ii) POSITION IN THE CUSTOMARY LAWS

The relationship between a debtor and a creditor is so universal that all organised societies have their laws and customs for its regulation. This is particularly true of the traditional societies in Ghana and Nigeria. In Ghana, Sarbah[24] has described three modes of enforcing payments. The first is the one he called *dharna*. This method involved the creditor in an uninterrupted fasting until the debt was paid by the debtor. It frequently happened that the creditor starved himself to death in an attempt to get his debt paid! No doubt this is a very curious way of enforcing one's obligation.

The second mode described by the learned author is that of *panyarring* or the kidnapping of the debtor or persons connected with him, or in some cases, even strangers. The seized person was detained until the debt was paid, and if payment was not effected within a reasonable time, he was sold into slavery. It was also possible to *panyarr* the debtor's goods and other moveable property, retaining such goods until the debt was paid.

The third mode of enforcement was more prevalent in the more centrally organised systems. This involved detention of the debtor in the chief's prison or village lock-up until payment was made.

Of the three modes of enforcement, *dharna* appeared to have been the least used. In fact a learned author has stated that it was unknown among the Ashanti.[25] *Panyarring* later became unpopular and was in fact abolished by the Bond of 1844.[26]

Writing on the Ashanti, Rattray included the effect of ridicule as one of the debt enforcement factors.[27]

In Nigeria C. K. Meek has had this to say about the Ibos:

> " Again, if a member of one local group had been seized by a member of another on account of a debt, the *ikoro-oha* of the debtor's group would go to the *ikoro-oha* of the creditor's group and ask for him to be released, in return for an undertaking that, if the debt were proved, it would be paid. The *ikoro-ohas* acting in conjunction, were collectors of debt, receiving for their trouble fees proportionate to the amount of the debt. If a debtor refused to pay, the *ikoro-oha* would seize one or two of his goats."[28]

The function of the *ikoro-oha* in the Owerri society about which Meek was writing, is to cater for the general well-being of the village group. Like other age-group systems it looks after the interests of the village as a whole during its period of office.

It must be observed that the traditional systems of debt-enforcement were greatly modified by the introduction of extraneous concepts of justice and judicial practice. The seizure of the goods or other property of the debtor became a more regular feature of enforcing the payment of a debt.[29]

In Maliki law, however, imprisonment for debt after investigating a debtor's ability to pay, was widely recognised. It was stated by the Northern Nigeria High Court in the recent case of *Atayi* v. *Maohnagoru*,[30] that " according to our understanding of Maliki law, before committing a judgment debtor to prison, investigation of his ability to pay is necessary; the Order XXV of the Native Court Rules, makes such an investigation an essential preliminary before committal."

The Northern Nigerian Native Court Rules, based on the Native Courts law, is therefore a statutory recognition of the Maliki law mode of executing judgments.

Critique of machinery for enforcement of obligations in Ghana and Nigeria:

We shall now examine the merits or otherwise of the current modes of enforcing obligations in Ghana and Nigeria. The first step in the recovery of a debt is, of course, for the creditor to satisfy the Court of the amount of the debt and that the debt is owing, and to obtain the leave of the Court to enter judgment, to this effect. The creditor applies to the Court by writ of summons, a copy of which must be served on the debtor by personal service. The Court, if satisfied that the debt is owing, gives the creditor leave to enter judgment for the amount of the debt. After obtaining judgment, the creditor may then proceed to execution.

The initial problem that arises here is that of the difficulty of effecting personal service on the defendant. He may be a man of no fixed address, or a difficult debtor who would do anything to avoid being served on by the bailiff. The position is made much more acute by the paucity of bailiffs who, in both Ghana and Nigeria, are the only persons authorised to serve processes on the parties.[31] Although substituted service has been allowed in certain cases, this has not in fact made any noticeable impact on the actual recovery of the amounts involved. A man of straw is not any the less so by reason only that he has been served by substituted service.[32] In any case, the Courts in Ghana and Nigeria are reluctant to allow substituted service because of its obvious proneness to abuse by plaintiffs.

Secondly, even after the defendant has been duly served, except in the case of the summons procedure under Order 14 of the Supreme Court (Civil Procedure) Rules, Ghana,[33] there might well be considerable delay before the case is listed for hearing. A clear evidence to this effect was seen by the present writer during his field studies in the Superior Courts of Ghana and Nigeria in 1965. Many of the appeals which were heard in the Supreme Courts of both countries in 1965, were on cases that arose three to four years earlier. Surely, it will be very frustrating to a lender if he has to wait this long to realise his loan. The consequent adverse effect this trend will have on economic development generally, is obvious. It is submitted that an improvement of the existing position is called for, and this should take the form of extending the scope of the Order 14 procedure to include cases of unliquidated damages where the defendant has not entered an appearance. Secondly, an increase in the number of Courts, and of the magistrates and judges, would go a long way to relieve the current congestion.

Thirdly, even after judgment has been obtained the existing mode of execution has been found to be most ineffective in compelling the debtor to pay. This is because of the ineffectiveness of the system of judgment summons in Nigeria or summons to show cause in Ghana. These modes of enforcement were introduced in each of the two countries to allow the courts a discretion in the matter of sending a debtor to prison for the debt.[34]

The courts now have to consider the conduct of the debtor having regard to his ascertainable means of income. It is over the question of the requisite evidence in the ascertainment of the debtor's income, that the machinery breaks down. The onus is on the judgment creditor to show that the debtor can pay but is unwilling to do so. Further, the Court is more easily disposed to accept the evidence of the debtor as to his means of income, and has not infrequently ordered him to pay nominal instalments to clear the debt. As was noted by the Commissioners:

> "The principle underlying the 1935 changes (i.e. the abolition of the writ of Ca.Sa)[35] was that while the courts were no longer compelled to send a defaulting debtor to prison irrespective of his conduct, these debtors who were guilty of misconduct could still be gaoled if they refused or neglected to pay. In practice things have not worked out this way. To those using this procedure (i.e. summons to show cause), it often seems that the courts will accept any proposal by the debtor, however inadequate, rather than send him to prison. Thus although imprisonment continues to exist as a potential threat, recalcitrant debtors are nowadays seldom gaoled as a result of a summons to show cause, although they are not infrequently put inside for failure to obey a court order arising from such summons."[36]

In respect of the evidence necessary for the ascertainment of the debtor's means of income, it is clear that the *ikoro-oha* system described by Meek, if modified to suit modern conditions, will prove to be more effective in getting the debtor to pay. This involves any member of the community who has any knowledge about the debtor's means of income, coming forward to give such evidence. This can be achieved by putting up a public notice to this effect. If the members of the family of the debtor desire to avoid such adverse publicity, they will act quickly to pay the debt. This method of enforcement may not change the position very much where the debtor is totally unable to pay but it will achieve the very desirable effect of checking the debtor who is able but unwilling to pay. In such latter instance, imprisonment may not have any deterrent effect. It may in fact be a safe resort for the debtor after the planting season, since he will be well-fed while in prison.

Another method of improving the system of evidence is that suggested by the Evershed Committee[37] in England, where the same problem arose under the English Rules of the Supreme Court. The Committee made two recommendations. The first was that of giving more inquisitorial powers to the examiner who questions the debtor on his means of income. Hitherto, the examiner, although an officer of the Court, had always been satisfied with whatever statements as to his income were made by the debtor. The committee recommended that the examiner should satisfy himself as to the veracity of the debtor. Secondly, that when a judgment debt had been unpaid for 14 days, the judgment creditor should be entitled to call upon the judgment debtor to make within 14 days a sworn affidavit of his assets. In Appendix XI to the Report the committee suggested a form of notice and affidavit which could be used for this purpose. It required the debtor to give details of his marital status, dependants, employment, trade or profession, income after paying income tax, outgoings on house owned or rented, banking accounts, stocks and shares and other securities, insurance policies, house and other property, and debts owing to the debtor. In the views of the committee, an examination as to the debtor's means after such an affidavit had been filed, will prove more effective than the existing system. We are respectfully in agreement with the learned members of the Evershed committee in this respect.[38] It is submitted that the adoption of these recommendations will (in the case of Ghana) improve the system of enforcing obligations, particularly where the amount involved is less than £500, as in such cases, the Insolvency Act, 1962, is inapplicable. In the case of Nigeria, the recommendations will, no doubt, stimulate economic growth which results from credit mobility.[39]

NOTES

1. See J. S. Pawate, *Contract and the freedom of the debtor in the common law*, (Tripathi Ltd; Bombay, 1953); O. W. Holmes, *The Common Law* (42nd Imp.) pp. 298-302; Sir David Hughes Parry, *The Sanctity of Contracts in English Law*, (London, Stevens & Sons, 1959). For the position in customary laws, see R. S. Rattray, *Ashanti law and constitution*, 1956, pp. 285 et seq; C. K. Meek, *Law and authority in a Nigerian Tribe* (1937) pp. 207 et seq. especially p. 231. See also *Odgers* on pleading and practice, (London, Stevens & Sons, 1966) pp. 379 et seq.
2. These have usually been damages, injunction and specific performance, rescission or restitution of property or money.
3. Cited by K. W. Wedderburn, in (1959-63) 5-7 Journal of the Society of Public Teachers of law, at p. 145.
4. (1947) 10, M.L.R. 159 at p. 167-168
5. T. E. Holland, *Jurisprudence*, (12th ed. 1916) p. 262.
6. A. L. Goodhart, *English law and the moral law*, (London, Stevens & Sons, 1953), p. 101. See also to the same effect, *Corbin on Contracts*, (1950) vol. 1 p. 2.
7. Historically, failure to perform one's obligation was regarded as a sin, since contracts were enforced by the Ecclesiastical Courts. Also, commercially, the whole basis of any economic structure is based on the security of credit. People should be able to rely on the performance of promises made to them by others. It is equally inequitable not to perform one's obligations to one's neighbour.
8. These have all been treated under " defective agreements." Supra.

9. For Ghana, see the Courts Decree, 1966. Paragraph 89 which by implication makes saving for the existing Rules of the Supreme Court. For Nigeria, see the *Handbook of the Federal Supreme Court* (1954), and the Sheriff and Civil Process Laws of the four regions.

10. 1962. Act 153.

11. It can be argued however, that this is preliminary to a resort to any one of the two other modes of satisfaction.

12. Cap. 118, Laws of Eastern Nigeria (1963 consolidation).

13. This is of course, done through the agency of the Sheriff.

14. SS. 24-28 of the Eastern Nigeria Sheriffs and Civil Process Law.

15. S. 82 of the Eastern Nigeria enactment.

16. SS. 43-45 of the Eastern Nigeria enactment.

17. S. 54 of the Eastern Nigeria law.

18. S. 64 of the Eastern Nigeria law.

19. S. 77 of the Eastern Nigeria law. For Ghana, see the Supreme Court (Civil Procedure) Rules, 1954, appended to the former Courts Ordinance.

20. See Polly Hill, *The Gold Coast cocoa farmer* (London, O.U.P., 1956); also *the pledging of cocoa farms, terms and conditions* (University College of Ghana, 1959); P. T. Bauer, *West African Trade* (London, O.U.P., 1954); P. C. Garlick, *African Traders in Kumasi* (U.C.G., 1959); A. N. Allot, " Legal development and economic growth in Africa " [in] *Changing law in developing countries* (ed. J. N. D. Anderson, 1962), p. 194; B. A. Kwaw-Swanzy, *Constitutional development in the Gold Coast*—(1901-1925), an unpublished work submitted to the University of Cambridge in 1955; *Report of the Commissioners appointed to enquire into the insolvency law of Ghana* (Govt. Printer, Accra, 1961). For the legislative history of Insolvency law in Ghana, see pp. 7-17 of the Report. It may be observed that no date has yet been specified for the coming into force of the Insolvency Act, 1962.

21. S. 9 of the Act defines an insolvent to include anybody against whose property a sheriff has proceeded against in respect of a judgment debt of not less than £500. Such execution being either pending, or levied within the preceding three months.

22. See SS. 23 and 24 of the Act.

23. The third mode of enforcing debt is of course by proceeding against the guarantor if the liability was guaranteed. Suretyships and guarantees were discussed under defective agreements, and in the first Section of this Part.

24. J. M. Sarbah, *Fanti customary laws*, pp. 114 et seq.

25. R. S. Rattray, *Ashanti law and constitution* (1956), p. 370.

26. See also Native jurisdiction Ordinance, 1883, No. 5 of 1883, which made panyarring an offence under native law.

27. Op. cit., pp. 372-373.

28. C. K. Meek, *Law and authority in a Nigerian Tribe* (London, O.U.P., 1937), p. 207. See particularly pp. 231 et seq.

29. See *Handbook of Native Courts in Ashanti* (Govt. Printer, Accra, 1954).

30. (1959) N.R.N.L.R. 36.

31. See pp. 25-29 of the *Ghana Insolvency Commission's Report* (1961).

32. i.e. delivery to an inmate living in the same house, or to an agent, by advertisement, by notice or by registered letter.

33. (1954). There is also the question of flimsy counter-claims and sets-off, which also help to delay the final judgment.

34. After the abolition of the writ of Ca. Sa.
35. Capius ad satisfaciendum.
36. Ghana Insolvency Commission Report, pp. 31-32.
37. Evershed Committee on Supreme Court Procedure and Practice, Cmnd. 8878 (England). See paras. 450-454.
38. The Ghana Insolvency Commission was of the same opinion. See p. 34 of their Report.
39. It has not been considered necessary to subjoin an examination of the various kinds of remedies available to the plaintiff, i.e. damages, specific performance, injunction, rescission, cancellation and rectification, and other equitable remedies. Fascinating as this facet of the subject is, all the existing judicial authority points very clearly to a total adoption of the current English law position. For the local cases, see: *S.C.O.A.* v. *Ogana* (1958) N.R.N.L.R. 141—self-help; *Okenla* v. *Royal Exchange Assurance Co. Ltd* (1958) W.R.N.L.R. 185, damages in insurance cases; *Solomon* v. *Pickering & Co. Ltd.* (1926) 6 N.L.R. 39—nominal and special damages; *Taiwo* v. *Princewill* (1961) 1 All N.L.R. 240—adoption of the rule in *Hadley* v. *Baxendale* (1854) 9 Ex. 341; also *Poole & Co. Ltd.* v. *Salami Agbaje* (1922) 4 N.L.R. 8; *Economic Exports Ltd.* v. *Odutola* (1959) W.R.N.L.R. 239—measure of damages according to Section 50 (2) or (3) of the Sale of Goods Act, 1893 (England); *Garabedian* v. *Jamakani* (1961) 1 All N.L.R. 177—measure of damages in wrongful dismissal cases; *Ilso* v. *Iketubosin* (1957) W.R.N.L.R. 187—measure of damages in breach of marriage promise actions; *Williams* v. *Smith & ors* (1948) 19 N.L.R. 21—specific performance; *Zard* v. *Saliba* (1955-56) W.R.N.L.R. 63—injunction to restrain use of land in breach of covenant. On the question of specific performance in customary laws, it is submitted that Ollennu's contention that it exists for executory transactions, as contained in the recent case of *Lartei* v. *Fio* (1960) G.L.R. 119, tends to stand alone.

SELECT BIBLIOGRAPHY

Allen, C. K., *Law in the Making* (7th ed. 1965).

Allott, A. N. (ed.). *The Future of law in Africa* (1960).

——. *Judicial and Legal Systems in Africa* (London, Butterworths, 2nd ed. 1969)

——. *Essay in African Law* (1960).

——. *New Essays in African Law* (Butterworths, 1970).

Anderson, J. N. D. (ed.). *Changing Law in developing Countries* (London, Allen & Unwin, 1963).

——. *Islamic law in Africa* (London, H.M.S.O. 1954).

——. *Islamic Law in the Modern World* (London, Stevens, 1959).

Atiyah, P. S. *Introduction to the Law of Contract* (1962).

——. *Sale of Goods* (1961).

Anson, Sir W. *Law of Contract* (22nd ed. 1964).

Austin, J. *Lectures* (1863).

Barnes, C. H. (ed.). *Kent's Commentaries on American Law* (Boston, 1884).

Bauer, P. T. *West African Trade* (London O.U.P. 1954).

Bennion, F. A. R. *Constitutional Law of Ghana* (London, 1962).

Bentham, J. *A fragment on Government and the principles of morals and legislation* (Oxford, 1948 impression).

Bentsi-Enchil, K. *Ghana Land Law, An exposition analysis and critique* (London, 1964).

Blackstone, Sir W. *Commentaries on the Laws of England.*

Bohannan, P. *Justice and judgment among the Tiv;* (London, O.U.P. Int.-Afr Inst. 1957).

Bryce, Lord. *Studies in History and Jurisprudence* (1901, Vol. II).

Brown, C. V. *The Nigerian Banking System* (Glasgow, 1966).

Buckland, W. W. *Roman Law and Common Law* (2nd ed. 1952).

Burns, Sir Alan. *A History of Nigeria* (London, 1956).

Cardozo, B. N. *The Nature of the judicial process* (New Haven, Yale Un. Press, 1925).

Casely-Hayford. *Gold Coast Native Institutions* (1905).

Cheshire G. C. *The Law of Contract* (6th ed. 1964).

Chubb, L. T. *Ibo Land Tenure* (2nd ed. 1961) Ibadan.

Cohen, F. *Law and Social Order* (1933) New York, Baker.

Coker, G. B. A. *Family Property among the Yorubas* (2nd ed. London, Sweet & Max. 1966).

Coote, B. *Exception Clauses* (London, Butterworths, 1964).

Danquah, J. B. *Akan Laws and Customs* (1928).

——. *Cases in Akan Law* (1928).

Daniels, W. C. E. *The Common Law in West Africa* (London, Butterworths, 1964).

Dawson, J. P. *Unjust enrichment; a comparative analysis* (1951).

Dicey, A. V. *Conflict of Laws* (6th ed. 1960).

Dike, K. O. *Trade and Politics in the Niger Delta* (Oxford, 1956).

Duguit, L. *Law in the modern State* (Trans. H. Laski, 1921).

——. *The Law and the State* (1917).

Elias, T. O. *Nigerian Land Law and Custom* (2nd. ed. 1953).

——. *The Nature of African Customary Law* (Manchest, 1956).

Elias, T. O. *The Nigerian Legal System* (2nd ed. 1961).
——. *British Colonial Law* (1962)
Fage, J. D. *An Introduction to the History of West Africa* (3rd ed. Camb. 1962).
Fifoot, C. H. S. *History and Sources of the Common Law (Contract and Tort)*.
Friedmann, W. G. *Law in a Changing Society* (London, 1959).
——. *Law and Social change in Contemporary Britain* (London, Stevens, 1951).
——. *Legal Theory* (4th ed. 1960).
Fridman, G. H. L. *The Law of Agency* (1960).
Gardner Lord ed. *Law Reform Now* (London, 1963).
Garlick, P. C. *African Traders in Kumasi* (U.C.G. 1959).
Gluckman, M. *The Judicial process among the Barotse* Manchester Uni. Press, 1955.
——. *African Jurisprudence* (1961).
Goff, R. *The Law of Restitution* (London, Stevens, 1966).
Goodhart, A. L. *The migration of the Common Law* (1960).
Gower, L. C. B. *The Principles of Company Law* (2nd ed. 1957).
Green, M. *Ibo Village Affairs* (London, 1947).
Griew, E. J. (ed.) *Bowstead on Agency* (12th ed. 1959).
Griffith, Sir W. B. *A note on the History of the British Courts in Gold Coast Colony* (1930).
Hailey, Lord. *African Survey* (1956).
Hall, P. *A Treatise on the Foreign Jurisdiction of the British Crown* (1894).
Harvey, W. B. *Law and Social change in Ghana* (Princeton Uni. Press, 1966).
Hill, P. *The Gold Coast Cocoa Farmer* (London O.U.P. 1956).
——. *The pledging of Cocoa Farms, terms and conditions* (U.C.G., 1959).
——. *Migrant Cocoa Farmers of Southern Ghana* (London, 1961).
Hobhouse, L. T. *Morals in Evolution* (7th ed.).
Holdsworth, Sir W. *History of English Law*, Vol. 8.
Holland, T. E. *Jurisprudence* (12th ed. 1916).
Holmes, O. W. *The Common Law* (42nd Imp.).
Hughes-Parry, Sir D. *The Sanctity of Contracts in English Law* (London, Stevens, 1959).
Jackson, R. M. *History of quasi-contract in English Law* (1936).
Jennings, Sir W. Ivor. *The Law and the Constitution* (3rd ed.) London, 1959.
Jethro-Brown, Ed. *The Austinian Theory of Law* (1926).
Jowitt, Earl. *Dictionary of English Law* (1959).
Kahn-Freund, O. *Comparative Law as an academic subject* (Oxford, Clarendon P. 1965).
Keener, W. A. *Quasi-Contracts* (1893).
Kollewijyn, R. D. *Inter-racial Private Law* (1929).
Kwaw-Swanzy. *Constitutional developments of the Gold Coast 1910–1925* (Camb. Un. 1955).
Lawson, F. H. *A Common Lawyer Looks at the Civil Law* (1953).
Lawson, F. H. (ed.). *Amos and Walton's Introduction to French Law* (2nd ed. 1963)
——. *Negligence in the Civil Law* (Oxford, 1950).
Lloyd, D. *Public Policy* (Athlone Press, 1953).
Lloyd, P. C. *Yoruba Land Law* (Oxford, 1962).
McNeil and Rains. *Nigerian Cases and Statutes on Contract & Tort* (London, Sweet and Max. 1965).
MacGillivray, E. J. *On Insurance* (5th ed. Vol. 1).
Marshall, O. R. *The Assignment of choses in Action* (1960).
Maxwell, Sir P. B. *Interpretation of Statutes* (11th ed.).
Meek, C. K. *Land Law and Custom in the Colonies* (Oxford, 1946).
——. *Law and Authority in a Nigeria Tribe* (Oxford, 1936).

Milliot, L. *Introduction a l'etude du droit (Musulman)* (Paris, 1953).

Milner, J. B. *Cases and materials on Contracts* (Toronto, 1963).

Morris, J. (ed.) *Chitty on Contracts* (22nd ed. Sweet and Maxwell, 1961).

Nwabueze, B. O. *The Machinery of Justice in Nigeria* (London, Butterworths, 1963).

Obi, S. N. C. *Ibo Law of Property* (London, Butterworths, 1963).

——. *Modern family law in Southern Nigeria* (London, Butterworths, 1966).

Odgers, C. E. *The Construction of deeds and Statutes* (4th ed. London, Sweet & Maxwell, 1956).

——. *On Pleading and Practice* (London, Stevens, 1966).

Ollennu, N. A. *Customary Land Law in Ghana* (London, Sweet & Maxwell, 1962).

——. *The Law of testate and intestate succession in Ghana* (London, Sweet and Maxwell, 1966).

Onwuemegbu, M. O. *Nigerian Law of Landlord and Tenant* (London, Butterworths, 1965).

Park, A. E. W. *Sources of Nigerian Law* (London, Butterworths, 1963).

Paton, G. *A Textbook of jurisprudence* (1st ed. 1946).

Pawate, I. S. *Contract and the freedom of the debtor in the common law* (Tripathi Ltd. Bombay, 1953).

Pollock Sir F. *First Book of jurisprudence* (6th ed. 1929).

——. *Principles of the law of torts* (15th ed. 1950).

Pollock & Maitland. *History of English Law,* Vol. II.

——. *Principles of Contracts* (25th ed. 1959).

Pound, R. *An Introduction to the Philosophy of Law* (Los Angeles, 1953).

Rahim, A. *Muhammedan Jurisprudence* (1906).

Rattray, R. S. *Ashanti Law and Constitution* (London O.U.P. 1929).

Read, J. S. & Morris H. F. *Uganda, the development of its Laws and Constitution* (London, 1966 Stevens and Sons.).

Redwar, A. *Comments on Gold Coast Ordinance* (1909).

Roberts-Wray, Sir K. *Commonwealth and Colonial Law* (London Stevens, 1966).

Rubin, L. *Unauthorised administration in South African law* (Cape Town, 1958).

Rubin & Murray *Constitution and Government of Ghana* (2nd ed. 1964).

Ruxton, F. H. *Maliki Law* (London, 1916).

Ryan, K. M. *An Introduction to the Civil Law* (Australia, 1962).

Salmond, J. *Jurisprudence* (10th ed. 1947).

Sarbah, J. M. *Fanti Customary Law,* 1903.

St. Germain, C. *Doctor and Student* (1523).

Schacht, J. *Introduction to Islamic Law* (Oxford, Clarendon Press, 1964).

Schapera, I. *A Handbook of Tswana Law and Custom* (London, O.U.P. 1955).

Schulz, P. *Classical Roman Law* (Oxford, 1951).

Seagle, M. *The quest for law* (New York, Knopf 1941).

Stoljar S. J. *The law of agency* (1961).

——. *The law of quasi-contracts* (1964).

Stone, J. *Province and function of law* (1950).

Wade, J. W. *Cases and Materials on Restitution* (1958).

Walton, F. P. *Egyptian Law of Obligations* Vol. 1 (London, 1920).

Waters, D. M. W. *The Constructive Trust* (London, Stevens, 1964).

Williams, G. L. *Joint Obligations* (1949).

Williston, S. *Contracts* (1957).

Winfield, Sir P. *Quasi-contracts* (1952).

——. *Province of the Law of Tort* (1931).

——. *Select Legal Essays* (1952).

Woodward, F. C. *The law of quasi-contracts* (1903).

Wright, Lord. *Legal Essays and addresses* (1939).

A 1

ARTICLES

Abrahams, Sir Sidney. "The Colonial legal service and the administration of justice in the colonial dependencies" (1948) *J. of Comp. Leg.* 8.

Ajayi, F. A. "English law and Customary law in Western Nigeria" (1960) 4 *J.A.L.* 98

Allen, C. K. "The judge as a man of the world" (1930) 46 *L.Q.R.* 151.

Allen, D. E. "An equity to perfect a gift" (1963) 69 *L.Q.R.* 238.

Allott, A. N. "Restatement of laws in Africa" (1963).

——. "The Common law of Nigeria" (1965) 1 *C.L.Q.* Supplementary Publication No. 10 p. 32.

——. "The extent of the operation of native customary law" (1950) 2 *J.A.A.* 4.

——. "The authority of English decisions in Colonial courts" (1957) 1, *J.A.L.* 23.

——. "Family property in West Africa: its jurisdic basis, control and enjoyment" (1965).

——. "Legal development and economic growth" in *Changing law in developing countries* (ed.) *J.N.D.* Anderson, 1963, p. 194.

——. "Ashanti Law of Property" (1966) 68 *Z.F. Vergl. Rechtswis.* 129–215.

Amos, M. S. "Common Law and the Civil Law in the British Commonwealth" (1937) 50, *Harv. L.R.* 1249.

Anderson, J. N. D. "The Moslem ruler and contractual obligations" (1958) New *York Un. L.R.* 917.

——. "The future of Islamic Law in British Commonwealth Territories" (1962) *Law and Contemp. Prob.* 617.

——. "Waqfs in East Africa" (1959) 3 *J.A.L.* 152.

Asante, S. K. B. "Interests in land in the customary law of Ghana; a new appraisal" (1965) *Yale L.J.* 848.

——. "Fiduciary principles in Anglo-American and Ghanian customary law; a comparative study" (1965) 14 *I.C.L.Q.* 1144.

——. "Stare decisis in the Supreme Court of Ghana" (1964) *Un. of Gh. L.R.* 52.

Atiyah, P. S. "Mistake in the construction of Contracts" (1961) 24 *M.L.R.* 421.

——. "The liability of infants in fraud and restitution" (1959) 22 *M.L.R.* 270.

Bailey, S. J. "Assignment of debts in England" (1931) 47 *L.Q.R.* 516.

Berger, R. "Usury in Instalmental Sales" (1953) Law & Contempt. Prob. 148.

Birkhead, J. B. "Collection tactics of illegal lenders" (1941) Law and Contemp. Prob. 78.

Brett, Sir L. "Stare decisis in Nigeria—some random thoughts" (1965) 6 *N.B.J.* 74.

Chaffee, S. J. "Equitable servitudes on chattels" (1928) 41 *Harv. L.R.* 945.

Clark G. de N. "How wrong is wrongful dismissal?" (1966) 63 *Law Society Gazette*, 255.

Corbin, A. L. "Contracts for the benefit of third parties" (1930) 46 *L.Q.R.* 12.

Cotran, E. "The law of civil wrongs and obligations in Commonwealth countries" (1966).

Diamond, A. L. "The Hire-purchase dealer's liability" (1958) 21 *M.L.R.* 177.

Denning, A. T. "The way of an iconoclast" (1959–63) *Journal of Soc. of Public Teach. of Law*, 77.

Dowrick, F. E. "The relationship of principal and agent" (1954) *M.L.R.* 24.

——. "A jus quaesitum tertio by way of contract in English law" (1956) 19 *M.L.R.* 374.

Driberg, J. H. "The African conception of law" (1934) *Journal of Comp. Leg.* 230.

Duguit, L. "Collective acts as distinguished from contracts" (1930) 27 *Yale L.J.* 753.

Elias, T. O. "Colonial courts and the doctrine of judicial precedent" (1955) 18 *M.L.R.* 356.

Evans, D. M. "The Anglo-American mailing rule" (1966) 15, *I.C.L.Q.* 553.

Farnsworth, E. A. "Law reform in a developing country: a new code of obligations for Senegal" (1964) 8 *J.A.L.* 6.

Field, J. O. "Sales of land in an Ibo community" (1945) *Man.* Vol. XLV No. 47.

Fitzpatrick, Sir D. "Non-Christian marriage" (1900) 2 *Journal of Comp. Leg.* 379.

Fridman, G. H. L. "Quasi-contractual aspect of unjust enrichment" (195) 34 *Cam. D.R.* 393.

Furmston, M. P. "Return to Dunlop *v.* Selfridge?" (1960) 23 *M.L.R.* 373.

Gelhorn, T. "Contracts and public policy" (1935) 35 *Col. L.R.* 679.

Goodhart, A. L. "Blackmail and consideration "(1928) 44 *L.Q.R.* 436.

———. "The importance of a definition of law" (1951) *J.A.A.* 106.

Gutteridge, C. "Unjustified Enrichment" (1934) 5 *Camb. L.J.* 304.

Hale, L. "Bargaining, Duress and economic liberty" (1930) *Col. L. R.*603.

Hannigan, A. St. J. J. "The present system of succession amongst the Akan people of the Gold Coast" (1954) *J.A.P.* 166.

Harrington, E. M. "A case study of conditions and warranties" (1965) *M.B.J.* 289.

Harrison, M. E. "The first half-century of the California Civil Code" (1921–22) 10 *Cal. L.R.* 185.

Holleman, F. D. "The recognition of Bantu customary law in South Africa" in *The Future of Customary Law in Africa* (Africa Institute London, 1955).

Jegede, M. I. "The position of head of family in relation to family property. Is he a trustee in the English sense?" (1966) *N.B.J.* 21.

Kerr, A. J. "The reception and codification of systems of law in Southern Africa" (1958) 2 *J.A.L.* 82.

Knight, P. "Public policy in English law" (1922) 38 *L.Q.R.* 207.

Kollewyjn, R. D. "Inter-Racial private law" in *Effects of Western Influence on Native Civilization in the Malaya Archipelago;* (ed. B. Shrieke, 1929).

Lewin, J. "Some problems involved in the recognition of African Native law" (1941–43) 24 *J. of Comp. Leg.* 108.

Lloyd, Sir W. J. "Consideration and the seal in New York" (1948) *Col. L.R.* 1.

Maitland, Sir F. W. "The History of the register of original writs" 1879 in *Select Essays in Anglo-American legal history* (1908).

Melville, L. M. W. "The core of a contract" (1953) 19 *M.L.R.* 26.

Miller, A. S. "Government contracts and social control: a preliminary enquiry" (1955) 41 *Va. L.R.* 56.

Muller, F. W. "The undisclosed principal" (1953) 16 *M.L.R.* 299.

Newman, N. "Doctrine of Cause" (1952) 30 *Can. B.R.* 662.

Nwabueze, B. O. "Integration of the law of Contracts" (1964).

Nussbaum, A. "Comparative aspects of Anglo-American offer and acceptance doctrine" (1936) 38 *Colum. L.R.* 290.

Ollennu, N. A. "The influence of English law in West Africa" (1961) 5, *J.A.L.* 21.

Oulton, A. D. M. "Loans in Kenya on the security of chattels" (1960) 4 *J.A.L.* 17, 79.

Pound, R. "Common law" (1931) 4 *Enc. Soc. Sci.* 70.

Radcliffe-Brown. "Primitive law" in *Structure and function in Society*, London, Cohen & West, 1952; also in (1933) *Enc. of Soc. Sci.* 202.

Rene-David. "A civil Code for Ethiopia" (1962–3) 37, Tul. *L.R.* 187.

Roberts-Wray, Sir K. "The adaptation of imported law in Africa" (1960) 4 *J.A.L.* 66.

Schapera. I. "Contracts in Tswana law" (1966).

———. "Contracts in Tswana law" (1966) 19 *J.A.L.* 142.

Shatwell, K. O. "The supposed doctrine of mistake in contract; a comedy of errors" (1953) 33 *Can. B. Rev.* 164.

Slade, C. J. "Auction sales of goods without reserve" (1952) 68 *L.Q.R.* 238.

——. "The myth of mistake in the law of contract" (1954) 70 *L.Q.R.* 385.

Stern, W. "Consideration and gift" (1965) 14 *I.C.L.Q.* 675.

Stimson, R. "Effective time of offer and acceptance" (1939) Minn. *L.R.* 776.

Treitel, G. H. "The Infants Relief Act, 1874" (1957) 20 *M.L.R.* 37.

Tuck, R. "Intent to contract and mutuality of assent" (1943) 21 *Cam. B. Rev.* 123.

Unger, J. "The doctrine of the fundamental term" (1957) *Business Law Review* 30.

——. "Identity in contract and Mr. Wilson's fallacy" (1955) 18 *M.L.R.* 259.

Wade, E. C. S. "Restrictions on user" (1928) 44 *L.Q.R.* 51.

Waler, Prof. "Some characteristics of Scots law" (1955) 18 *M.L.R.* 321.

Wedderburn, K. W. "Collateral Contracts" (1959) *C.L.J.* 66.

Williams, G. L. "Mistake as to party in the law of contract" (1945) 23 *Cam. B. Rev.* 271.

——. "Mistake and rectification in contract" (1954) 17 *M.L.R.* 154.

——. "Contracts for the benefit of third parties" (1944) 7 *M.L.R.* 123.

——. "International law and the controversy concerning the word 'law'" (1945) *B.Y.B.I.L.* 146.

Wilson, J. F. "Identity in contract and the Pothier policy" (1954) 17 *M.L.R.* 515.

——. "The problem of the enforcement of promises in Anglo-American law" (1958) 32 *Tul. L.R.* 371.

Winfield, Sir P. "Some aspects of offer and acceptance" (1939) 55 *L.Q.R.* 499.

——. "Ethics in English Case Law" (1931) 45 *Harv. L.R.* 112.

——. "Necessaries under the Sale of goods Act, 1893" (1942) 58 *L.Q.R.* 82.

Woodman, G. R. "The alienation of family land in Ghana" (1964) *Un. of. Gh. L.J.* 23.

GENERAL INDEX

349

B 1

For Product Safety Concerns and Information please contact our EU
representative GPSR@taylorandfrancis.com
Taylor & Francis Verlag GmbH, Kaufingerstraße 24, 80331 München, Germany